Creating Your Windc
Emergency Repair Kit

1. Find the 25-digit software key on the Windows 2000 CD jewel box and write it down on the back of this sheet.

2. Open a Command Prompt window, type the command `ipconfig /all`, and press **Enter**. Record the network details where indicated on the back of this sheet.

3. Get five high-density 1.44MB floppy disks. Label the first four disks as **Windows 2000 Setup Disk #1** through **#4**. Label the fifth disk **Windows 2000 Emergency Repair Disk** and add today's date.

4. Insert the Windows 2000 Professional CD into the CD-ROM drive.

5. Click **Start**, choose **Run**, and enter the following command:

```
<d:>\bootdisk\makeboot a:c1
```

FOLD HERE, THIS SIDE IN

---

6. Follow the onscreen instructions, supplying disks when prompted, to create the four boot disks.

7. Insert the Emergency Repair Disk into the floppy drive. Click **Start**, choose **Run**, type the command `ntbackup`, and press **Enter**.

8. After the Backup Wizard appears, click the **Emergency Repair Disk** option and follow the prompts to create the ERD. (*Remember to update this disk every time you add to or change your hardware.*)

9. Fold this sheet where indicated, *with this side facing in;* staple or tape to create an envelope, and insert the five disks you just created.

10. Store this emergency kit and the Windows 2000 CD in a safe place where you can easily find them in the event your system fails to start properly.

System Configuration Details

Software Key

[ ] [ ] [ ] [ ] [ ]

Network Settings

IP address: _____ . _____ . _____ . _____

Subnet mask: _____

Default gateway: _____

DHCP enabled: ❏ Yes ❏ No

DHCP server: _____

DNS servers: _____ . _____ . _____ . _____

Ed Bott's Windows 2000
Emergency Repair Kit

To repair your system, insert the floppy disk labeled **Windows 2000 Setup Disk #1** and restart your system. Insert additional disks when prompted. Follow the onscreen instructions to use Windows 2000's repair options.

PRACTICAL

Microsoft© Windows© 2000 Professional

Ed Bott

Contents
at a Glance

A Division of Macmillan USA
201 West 103rd Street
Indianapolis, Indiana 46290

Practical Microsoft© Windows© 2000 Professional

International Standard Book Number: 0-7897-2124-4

Library of Congress Catalog Card Number: 99-65439

Printed in the United States of America

First Printing: February 2000

02 01 00   4   3   2   1

Trademarks

Warning and Disclaimer

Associate Publisher
Jim Minatel

Acquisitions Editor
Jill Byus

Development Editor
Lorna Gentry

Managing Editor
Matt Purcell

Senior Editor
Susan Ross Moore

Copy Editor
Barbara Hacha

Indexer
Heather McNeill

Proofreader
Rachel Lopez Bell

Technical Editor
Kyle Bryant

Team Coordinator
Vicki Harding

Interior Design
Nathan Clements

Cover Design
Rader Design

Copy Writer
Eric Borgert

Production
Dan Harris
Tim Osborn
George Poole
Gloria Schurick
Mark Walchle

Contents

About the Author

Ed Bott is a best-selling author and award-winning computer journalist who has specialized in technology topics for more than two decades. As senior contributing editor of *PC Computing* magazine, he is responsible for the magazine's extensive coverage of Microsoft Windows, Microsoft Office, and Internet issues. From 1991 until 1993, Ed was editor of *PC Computing*, and for three years before that he was managing editor of *PC World* magazine. He currently writes a weekly Web-based column for TechRepublic.com, a leading resource for information technology professionals. He has written a dozen books on Microsoft Windows and Microsoft Office, all for Que.

Ed is a three-time winner of the Computer Press Award, most recently for *PC Computing*'s annual Windows SuperGuide, a collection of tips, tricks, and advice for users of all versions of Windows. For his work on the 1997 edition of the Windows SuperGuide, Ed and co-author Woody Leonhard earned the prestigious Jesse H. Neal Award, sometimes referred to as "the Pulitzer Prize of the business press." He lives in the sunny Southwest with his wife Judy and two amazingly smart and affectionate cats, Katy and Bianca. In his spare time, you'll find him at the racetrack with other members of the Cyberspace Racing Team.

Dedication

To Judy, who keeps me happy and healthy.

Acknowledgments

Over the past five years I've written more than a dozen books for Macmillan USA. This one was particularly enjoyable because I had the privilege of working with some old friends and making a few new ones.

A big tip of the hat and a hearty *mahalo* to Acquisitions Editor Jill Byus and Associate Publisher Jim Minatel, who understood that Microsoft takes its own sweet time with operating system upgrades.

It was a particular pleasure to work again with Lorna Gentry, who helped to develop my very first Windows book in the dark ages before Windows 95. Thanks, Lorna!

Project editor Susan Moore would make a great traffic cop—she handled this entire project with professionalism and aplomb. Barbara Hacha is a skilled and sensitive copy editor who helped smooth over the rough edges in my prose. And thanks to technical editor Kyle Bryant for asking tough questions and forcing me to get every step just exactly right.

My heartfelt appreciation goes to Claudette Moore and Debbie McKenna of Moore Literary Agency, who do a masterful job with all the behind-the-scenes business details that go into a book like this one.

And finally, a special thank you to all my fellow beta testers and the Microsoft development team, who worked with Windows 2000 for years to make this the best Windows version yet.

Tell Us What You Think!

As the reader of this book, you are our most important critic and commentator. We value your opinion and want to know what we're doing right, what we could do better, what areas you'd like to see us publish in, and any other words of wisdom you're willing to pass our way.

As a publisher for Que Corporation, I welcome your comments. You can fax, email, or write me directly to let me know what you did or didn't like about this book—as well as what we can do to make our books stronger.

Please note that I cannot help you with technical problems related to the topic of this book, and that due to the high volume of mail I receive, I might not be able to reply to every message.

When you write, please be sure to include this book's title and author as well as your name and phone or fax number. I will carefully review your comments and share them with the author and editors who worked on the book.

Fax: 317.581.4666

Email: opsys@mcp.com

Mail: Publisher
Que Corporation
201 West 103rd Street
Indianapolis, IN 46290 USA

introduction

I t seems mind-boggling to contemplate that Windows is entering its third decade, especially when you realize that some of the most famous names in computing—Yahoo!, for instance—didn't even exist five years ago.

Of course, if you look back on that very first version of Windows, from the mid 1980s, it seems positively prehistoric. Really, it wasn't much more than a layer of not-so-pretty pictures sitting on top of MS-DOS. The entire operating system fit on two floppy disks, and hardly anyone outside of Microsoft used it.

Fast forward to the 21st century and Windows 2000, and you can see how far Windows has evolved in a very short time:

- Windows 2000 demands a ton of hardware. If you don't have a gigabyte of free disk space and at least 64MB of RAM (preferably more), you shouldn't even think of installing Windows 2000. (By the way, those upgrades would have cost you close to $20,000 ten years ago; today, you can buy a 10GB hard disk or 64MB of RAM for well under $200.)

- Windows 2000 speaks fluent Internet. When Windows 95 first appeared, most ordinary mortals needed a Microsoft Certified System Engineer and a witch doctor to make an Internet connection. With Windows 2000, Internet connectivity is practically automatic. Seriously.

- For everyday tasks, Windows 2000 is easier to use overall than any previous Windows version. The utilities for finding files and installing programs, for example, are admirably simple and straightforward.

- Windows 2000 rarely crashes. If you've cursed at Windows 95 or 98 because it regularly and mysteriously refuses to respond to any input, you'll be amazed at the capability Windows 2000 has to emulate the Energizer bunny—it just keeps going, and going, and going…Buggy programs may crash—the operating system can't do anything about that—but they won't take the rest of your running programs with them.

And now for the reality check: You will continue to curse at Windows. I guarantee it. Whatever choice words you've hurled at previous versions of Windows will remain in your vocabulary indefinitely. Unfortunately, despite the many, many improvements in Windows 2000, it's still Windows. The security features that make Windows 2000 a great choice for corporate computing professionals can make it a nightmare for even an experienced Windows user trying to get work done.

In fact, much of your previous Windows experience is irrelevant with Windows 2000. If you mastered all the ins and outs of Windows 95, you may be baffled when you first encounter the mandatory logon dialog box in Windows 2000, when you attempt to format a new hard disk, or when you attempt to change the settings for a piece of hardware. Unlike Windows 95 and 98, Windows 2000 doesn't contain a speck of MS-DOS code, and it's built from the ground up with security in mind, even if the unfortunate side effect is to lock you out of your own computer and files.

Of course, struggling with a PC is probably not part of your job description. No one pays you to install software, to learn how to use it, or to poke through dialog boxes and pull-down menus and troubleshooting wizards so that you can print a report that was due yesterday. Before you call for help from your favorite network administrator or witch doctor, I suggest you look for the answers in this book.

About This Book

The first word in this book's title is *Practical*—and that's the concept I kept in mind as I organized and wrote this book. I also made some assumptions about you. I'm guessing that you're not afraid of computers; in fact, you probably use a PC at work every day and have another computer at home for work and play. I'm reasonably certain that you've used previous versions of Windows, and you may even consider yourself an expert on Windows 95 or Windows 98. I know you're busy, so you want answers and no-nonsense explanations about how you can make this software do what it's supposed to do.

I'm sure you don't want to read long-winded explanations of the inner workings of technology; instead, you want step-by-step instructions with as little jargon as possible.

And I'm absolutely certain you're no dummy, so I won't insult your intelligence with half-baked humor and condescending instructions on how to use a mouse.

With the help of some skilled editors and designers at Macmillan USA, I've organized this book so that you can quickly find the answers you're looking for. Each section covers an essential Windows topic, and every chapter stands on its own—if there's important information in another chapter, you'll find a cross-reference to that part of the book so that you can quickly jump there.

Before you can do anything with Windows 2000, you have to install it on your PC and configure its components to do your bidding. Part I, "Getting Started," explains the essential differences between Windows 2000 and previous Windows versions. In fact, I called Chapter 1 "Read Me First!" because it includes information that will help you make sense of every succeeding chapter. This section also details all your Setup options; compared to its corporate personality, Windows 2000 is a dramatically different beast at home and in a small office. If you need to keep your computer and its data secure, be sure to read Chapter 4, "Controlling Access to Your Computer."

The point of an operating system is to let you work with programs and data. Part II, "Working with Windows 2000," explains how to install new programs and get to work with a minimum of fuss, how to manage files and folders using the improved Windows 2000 Explorer, and how to set up any printer, whether it's connected to your machine or on your corporate network. If you don't like the basic look and feel of the Windows 2000 colors and backgrounds, check out Chapter 8, "Customizing Windows 2000," for advice on how to change things. I've also packed this chapter with productivity-enhancing tips and tricks that help you avoid some of the most annoying new features of Windows, such as its insistence on hiding choices on the Start menu.

If you're even thinking of adding a new hard disk, printer, scanner, or other peripheral, you'll find valuable advice in Part III, "Windows 2000 and Hardware." Your DOS and Windows 95 experience won't help you set up a new hard disk using Windows 2000's complex Local Disk Management Tools, but Chapter 10, "Managing Disks and Drives," has the answers you're looking for. If you find yourself facing startup troubles, especially after installing a new piece of hardware, take a deep breath and turn to Chapter 12, "System Maintenance and Troubleshooting," where I explain the step-by-step procedures to help you get your system back in order.

Part IV, "In the Office," covers the essentials of setting up a small network, connecting to large network, and using shared files, folders, and printers. If your computer is connected to one or more Windows 2000 servers in a domain, be sure to read the sections in Chapter 14, "Working with a Network," where I explain how the Active Directory lets you find people and computers.

Of course, Windows 2000 includes a full complement of tools for finding and managing information on the Internet. Part V, "Exploring the Internet," includes details on how to set up any Internet connection quickly and securely. If you want time-saving tips on how to avoid wasting time on the Internet, especially when searching for information, be sure to read Chapter 17, "Using Internet Explorer." And if you've struggled with previous incarnations of Microsoft's free email client, Outlook Express, look in Chapter 19, "Managing Email with Outlook Express," where I explain how to solve common email setup problems. In fact, for many users the best solution may be to choose another email program completely—a topic I cover at the beginning of that chapter.

Expert users should find valuable information in two appendixes. Appendix A, "Managing a Windows 2000 Computer," introduces the sometimes-buried utilities you need to use when setting up a shared computer in a home or a small office. And if you've mastered the DOS command line, discover Windows 2000's far more capable c:> prompt in Appendix B, "Using the Command Line." In fact, a number of Windows 2000 tasks can be accomplished only by typing commands into this somewhat old-fashioned window.

Conventions Used in This Book

Commands, directions, and explanations in this book are presented in the clearest format possible. The following items are some of the features that will make this book easier for you to use:

- **Menu and dialog box commands and options.** You can easily find the onscreen menu and dialog box commands by looking for bold text like you see in this direction: Open the **File** menu and click **Save**.

- **Hotkeys for commands.** The underlined keys onscreen that activate commands and options are also underlined in the book, as shown in the previous example.

- **Combination and shortcut keystrokes.** Text that directs you to hold down several keys simultaneously is connected with a plus sign (+), such as **Ctrl+P**.

- **Cross-references.** If the book contains information that's specifically related to the topic that you're reading, you'll find the cross-reference to that information following the current steps or section. The cross reference looks like this:

SEE ALSO
➤ *To learn more about managing disks and drives with Windows 2000, see Chapter 10, page 231.*

- **Glossary terms.** For all the terms that appear in the glossary, you'll find the first appearance of that term in the text in *italic*, along with its definition.

- **Sidebars.** Information related to the task at hand or "inside" information from the author is offset in sidebars. Each sidebar has a short title to help you quickly identify the information you'll find there.

Finally, please remember that depending on the options you choose during installation and your system's unique hardware setup, your screen may look slightly different from some of the examples in this book.

part

1

GETTING STARTED

1

2

3

4

Read Me First!

What's New in Windows 2000?

Linux and Windows 2000

Of all the competitors to Windows, the one that has received the most publicity is Linux, a free version of UNIX. Linux and Windows 2000 may be archrivals in the marketplace, but they cooperate nicely on a network. With the proper technical support, you can connect a PC running Linux to one running Windows 2000 and freely exchange files and share other resources.

If you use a personal computer, you know Windows. Despite the presence of alternative operating systems, the overwhelming majority of desktop and notebook computers sold today use one form of Windows or another. Windows 2000 is the most recent in a long line that stretches back to the mid-1980s.

Tracing the ancestry of Windows 2000 may seem like a dry academic exercise, but it's not. Despite some surface similarities, Windows 2000 is not a direct descendant of Windows 98, Windows 95, or Windows 3.1. Instead, its roots go back through earlier versions of Windows NT. In fact, Windows 2000 is technically version 5.0 of Windows NT.

For anyone familiar with Windows 95 or Windows 98, many features in Windows 2000 will be new and potentially unsettling. Unlike those earlier consumer-oriented operating systems, Windows 2000 tightly integrates security features (such as the requirement to log on). In a corporate setting, you may discover that some features, such as the capability to install programs or customize your desktop, simply aren't available because your system administrator has disabled those features for network users.

If, on the other hand, you're upgrading to Windows 2000 from a previous version of Windows NT, the security features will be familiar, but the techniques you use to run programs, work with files, and browse the Web will be noticeably different.

The Windows 2000 Family

Windows 2000 actually consists of four separate products. This book covers Windows 2000 Professional, which is intended for use on desktop and notebook PCs. The Server, Advanced Server, and Datacenter Server editions of Windows 2000 are all designed to serve the needs of business networks of varying sizes and levels of complexity.

Something Old, Something New: The Windows 2000 Interface

If you've used any previous version of Windows, you'll recognize the basic elements of the graphical user interface for Windows 2000. But the Windows interface wasn't all designed at once; instead, it's grown over time like a sprawling city in which different neighborhoods developed over many years. Think of the Windows 2000 interface as a collection of multiple layers, each dating back to a different era. Some icons, dialog boxes, and other interface features are brand new in Windows 2000, whereas others are updates of those introduced in previous versions of Windows and Internet Explorer.

Figure 1.1 illustrates the basic building blocks of the Windows 2000 interface.

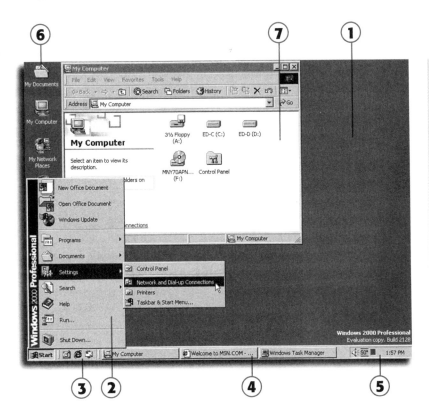

FIGURE 1.1
With a few exceptions, the basic elements of the Windows 2000 interface have been around since Windows 95.

1. Desktop
2. Start menu
3. Quick Launch bar
4. Taskbar
5. Notification area (tray)
6. My Documents folder for storing data files
7. My Computer— contains icons for all local drives, mapped network drives, and Control Panel

How much of the interface will seem familiar to you? Most of the basic elements, including the Start menu, the taskbar, and the Windows desktop, have been present in every version of Windows since Windows 95. Other interface pieces, such as the Quick Launch bar and the drag-and-drop Programs menu, are of more recent vintage, introduced as part of the Windows Desktop Update in Internet Explorer 4 and Windows 98.

Add the security features of Windows NT, such as the requirement to log on using Ctrl+Alt+Del, and this Windows version is certain to require some getting used to, regardless of your previous experience.

Some parts of the Windows interface are brand new to Windows 2000, and most (but not all) should make computing at least a little

Upgrading from Windows 3.1?

If you're upgrading directly from Windows 3.1 to Windows 2000, expect a particularly steep upgrade path. You'll need to adjust to the basic Windows interface, all the security features of Windows 2000, and Internet Explorer 5.0. For a complete overview, read this chapter carefully.

easier than with previous Windows versions. Many of these changes are subtle but significant enhancements to the Windows interface, designed to make it more usable. Here's a partial list of what you can expect.

No more Channels bar!

Windows 98 and Internet Explorer 4 insisted on cluttering up the desktop with a Channels bar containing icons to some decidedly non–business-oriented Web sites. With Internet Explorer 5 and Windows 2000, the Channels bar is officially retired. If you upgrade and this folder is still on your desktop, feel free to close it for good.

- **Personalized Menus.** This is the most controversial of the new features. Windows hides any item on commonly used menus (Programs and Favorites, for instance) when you haven't used that item for a while. If you install a software package that adds several items to your Programs menu, for example, but you only use one of them, Windows will eventually show you only the shortcuts you've used recently.

SEE ALSO

➤ *For a full explanation of how to control Personalized Menus, see "Changing the Appearance of the Start Menu," p. 187.*

- **Explorer bars.** These panes appear along the left side of an Explorer window and allow you to search for Web pages or files and folders; to see the History folder, which contains Web pages you've previously viewed; or to browse the contents of your Favorites folder. You can also show or hide the Folders pane, which lets you see a tree-style view of all files on your PC and your corporate network.

SEE ALSO

➤ *For details on how to use Explorer panes with Web pages, see "Time-Saving Navigation Shortcuts," p. 371.*

Show the entire menu?

You say you already know that you want to turn the Personalized Menus feature off, *right now*, and you would rather not skip to another chapter for the details? I understand completely. Click the **Start** button, choose **Settings**, and click **Taskbar & Start Menu**. On the **General** tab of the Taskbar and Start Menu Properties dialog box, click to remove the check mark from the **Use Personalized Menus** box. Click **OK** to save the change.

- **New common dialog boxes.** When you choose **Open** or **Save As** from the **File** menu of any program, Windows displays a dialog box that's actually a stripped-down version of an Explorer window. From one of these dialog boxes, you can browse for files and folders and do basic file-management tasks. In Windows 2000, these dialog boxes are noticeably different from their predecessors and are much easier to use, thanks to the column of five icons along the left side (see Figure 1.2). Click any of these shortcuts to immediately display the contents of these commonly used locations.

FIGURE 1.2
The Places Bar along the left side of this dialog box makes it easier to get to commonly used files and folders. Click any icon to browse for files and folders starting at that location.

- **Search Assistant.** This Web-style interface replaces the three-tabbed Find Files dialog box from previous versions of Windows.

SEE ALSO

➤ *For help finding information on your computer or in a shared network location, see "Searching for Files and Folders," p. 115.*

➤ *To learn more about searching for information on the Internet, see "Secrets of Successful Web Searches," p. 384.*

- **My Documents and My Pictures.** The My Documents folder has been around in one form or another since shortly after the introduction of Windows 95. In Windows 2000, it serves as the common location for you to save personal files. New to this Windows version is the My Pictures folder (see Figure 1.3), which is intended for use with scanners, digital cameras, and image-editing software. A special viewing pane makes it easier to manage pictures because you can see the image itself instead of having to guess what picture a sometimes cryptic filename describes.

SEE ALSO

➤ *For instructions on how to work with graphics files in Windows, see "Previewing Pictures in an Explorer Window," p. 126.*

As you work with Windows 2000, you'll discover many more small changes in the arrangement of menus, icons, and dialog boxes, generally making work easier. Windows 2000 has more wizards than its predecessors, usually offering a simple path through complex tasks. Many dialog boxes have been completely reorganized and error messages rewritten for clarity. Compared to previous Windows versions, there are fewer icons in the My Computer window and more in Control Panel.

A single Explorer

In earlier versions of Windows, you had to deal with three separate versions of Explorer—Internet Explorer for Web sites, the two-pane Windows Explorer, and the My Computer window, which shows the contents of one folder or drive at a time. Windows 2000 has only one Explorer, and you can shift from the Web to Windows and show or hide the Folders bar with just a click or two.

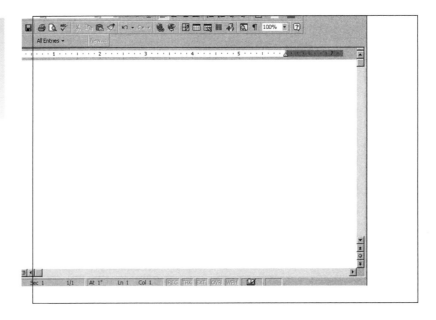

FIGURE 1.3
The My Pictures folder is the preferred location for scanned images and other graphics files.

Try Control Panel first

If you previously used Windows 95 or Windows NT 4.0, you're used to looking for configuration options in all kinds of locations—Dial-Up Networking in the My Computer window, Folder Options in an Explorer window, and various hardware options scattered throughout Control Panel. In Windows 2000, the organization is much more logical (although not perfectly consistent). If you're looking for data, start in the My Computer window or in My Network Places. To configure any part of Windows or your computer, start with Control Panel.

Power users will find even more surprises, including useful changes in file properties and the capability to create associations between files and programs. You can select multiple buttons on the taskbar to close or rearrange a group of windows all at once, and the Start menu is far more customizable than ever before.

Some changes are strictly cosmetic. Visual enhancements change the look of pull-down and right-click menus, for example, which appear to slide or fade into place in Windows 2000. If your display adapter supports high-color resolutions, title bars use a slick-looking, two-color gradient instead of a solid blue.

Streamlined Setup

With every new version of Windows, Microsoft changes the tools and techniques you use to install the operating system. Windows 2000 is no exception. The good news is that the new Windows Installer is generally easy to use (especially when compared to the cumbersome and overly technical setup utilities in Windows 95 and Windows NT 4.0). The bad news is that most options require advanced technical skills.

If you buy a new computer that includes Windows 2000, you may never need to deal with the Windows Installer. If, on the other hand, you plan to upgrade over an existing version of Windows on a system at home or in a small office workgroup, the installation process should be relatively straightforward. However, if you have special requirements—if you want to switch between two or more Windows versions on the same computer, for example, or you are part of a corporate network—you should expect some challenges.

SEE ALSO

➤ *For thorough instructions on how to set up Windows 2000, either as an upgrade or on a new PC, see "Setting Up Windows 2000, Step by Step," p. 33.*

Support for New Hardware

In theory, at least, Windows 2000 supports every imaginable type of device. Unlike the original release of Windows 95 and Windows NT 4.0, it allows you to plug peripherals into *Universal Serial Bus* connectors. Like Windows 95 and 98, it fully supports the *Plug and Play* standard, which automatically detects and configures most add-on hardware. And like Windows 98, Windows 2000 allows you to connect two or more display cards and monitors to your system so you can expand the size of the Windows desktop and work with multiple screens at once.

SEE ALSO

➤ *For instructions on how to add multimonitor support, see "Display Adapters and Monitors," p. 264.*

Some notebook users will see dramatic differences in the way Windows 2000 manages battery power. For systems that support the *Advanced Configuration and Power Interface (ACPI)*, you can control all aspects of power management, including the function of the power button and lid on a portable computer; select the **Power** option in Control Panel, as shown in Figure 1.4.

In theory, ACPI systems can pay off on the desktop as well. For example, a well-behaved system can learn to shift into low-power mode when you haven't used it for a while, but come back to life quickly when you tap a key or click a mouse button.

SEE ALSO

➤ *For a full description of Windows 2000's power-management features, see "Making Batteries Last Longer," p. 297.*

Don't take Windows for granted

Windows 2000 can be deceptively simple to set up—so simple, in fact, that it's possible to make a mess without even realizing it. If you run into problems during Setup—especially those that involve network or hard disk settings—stop and make sure you know the consequences of any choice you make. In extreme cases, the wrong settings can make it impossible for you to start your computer or connect to the Internet. Don't take chances; read this book carefully, and use the online Help to get any additional information you need. If you still can't find the answer, ask a support expert for help instead of guessing.

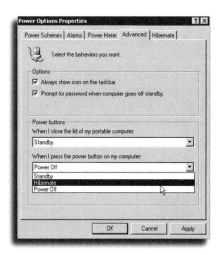

FIGURE 1.4
On systems that support the ACPI standard, Windows can handle virtually all power-management features.

期待 奇蹟

Don't expect miracles

ACPI sounds wonderful, but it requires precision hardware engineering, and the task is much more difficult than many computer makers originally anticipated. Most systems manufactured in 1999 or earlier will have problems with power management, and even some new models won't work properly. You may be able to fix problems by updating the software in the computer's BIOS chip—if you run into power problems, check with the PC maker to see whether a Windows 2000–compatible BIOS is available.

Management Tools

You don't have to be a network administrator for a Fortune 500 corporation to need good computer-management tools. The following management tools are new or improved in Windows 2000:

- **Add/Remove Hardware.** Located in Control Panel, this wizard lets you install, configure, and uninstall hardware devices from one central location.

SEE ALSO

➤ *For full instructions on how to use the Add/Remove Hardware Wizard, see "Using the Wizard to Add or Remove Hardware," p. 258.*

- **Add/Remove Programs.** Also located in Control Panel, this is a convenient place to install, change, and remove programs on your system. Although Windows 95 and 98 have similar capabilities, options in Windows 2000 are far more extensive and flexible. (Figure 1.5, for example, shows the extra details you see here, such as the total disk space that a program uses.)

可能性
易操縱從

- **Device Manager.** Although it's superficially similar to its Windows 95/98 counterpart, the Windows 2000 version offers more control over hardware settings, including the capability to enable or disable devices. It also provides links to troubleshooters that help resolve common hardware problems.

SEE ALSO

➤ *To learn more about using Device Manager, see "Before You Add New Hardware...," p. 252.*

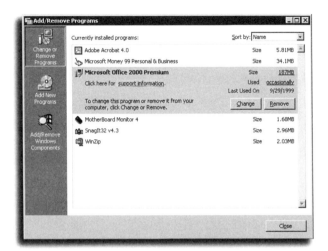

FIGURE 1.5
Open this dialog box to install, change, or remove programs. This utility offers much more information than its Windows 95/98 counter-part. 极相似

- **Microsoft Management Console.** This utility is the Swiss Army knife of Windows management tools. Its two-pane view (similar to an Explorer window) lets you gather administrative tools (known as *snap-ins*) into collections (called *consoles*) that are convenient for you to work with. Windows 2000 Professional includes approximately 20 ready-made consoles. The Computer Management console, shown in Figure 1.6, includes many of the most common administrative tools in a single window.

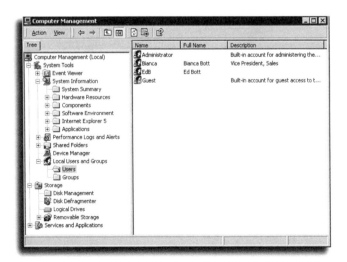

FIGURE 1.6
Each of the items in the left tree pane of this Microsoft Management Console is called a snap-in. Settings you can adjust appear in the right pane.

SEE ALSO

➤ *For details on how you can create a custom management console, see "Creating Custom Management Consoles," p. 446.*

Hardware Requirements

Does your PC have what it takes to run Windows 2000 Professional? If the system was built in 1999 or later, it probably does. Older hardware, however, may require upgrades to reach the following minimum recommended standards for acceptable performance:

- **CPU.** Windows 2000 will install on any Pentium-class or better PC. As a general rule, consider 200MHz the absolute minimum speed for acceptable performance with a single business application. Double that minimum speed to 400MHz if you intend to run more than two or three full applications at once or use demanding software such as desktop publishing or image-editing programs.

- **Memory.** Don't even think of starting with less than 64MB of RAM, and remember that more is better. If you use a demanding business suite such as Office 2000, you'll notice dramatic performance improvements by increasing system memory to 128MB or more.

- **Disk space.** You need 500MB or more of free disk space just to set up Windows 2000. I strongly recommend that you start with at least a 6GB disk drive and keep at least 500MB of disk space free at all times so that Windows 2000 can swap data in and out of memory without having to search for free space.

Of course, you need a keyboard and a mouse to run Windows properly, and the quality of your display adapter will determine the number of colors and pixels you can see on the screen at any one time, as well as how fast those images appear. If images seem to take a long time drawing on the screen, consider upgrading your older display adapter with a newer model.

Finally, don't overlook the hardware that's attached to your PC. Windows 2000 requires *device drivers* for every peripheral, whether they are installed in an internal slot or plugged into an external port. If your work depends on a particular piece of hardware, be sure to

Microsoft's mythical minimums

Pay no attention to the minimum requirements listed on the box for Windows 2000 Professional. Yes, you can install and run Windows 2000 on some relatively old and slow systems, but do you really want to? If productivity matters to you, follow the guidelines I list here instead.

Disk maintenance pays off

Windows 2000 includes several tools you can use to keep your hard disk running at peak performance. Check each drive regularly in the My Computer window to see how much free space is available, and use the Disk Cleanup Wizard if necessary to free up space. Also, use the Disk Defragmenter at least once a month to consolidate free space into large blocks that Windows can use more effectively.

verify that a Windows 2000–compatible driver is available before upgrading your operating system.

SEE ALSO

➤ *For instructions on how to determine whether your hardware will work with Windows 2000, see "Checking Compatibility," p. 254.*

Security Considerations

Security is at the heart of Windows 2000. Before you can begin using your computer, you have to log on with a username and password. By assigning *permissions* to files and folders, you can control exactly who has access to which files. By setting security options carefully, an administrator can configure a computer so that two or more people can use programs, browse the Internet, and save files— all without fear that other users will be able to poke around in their private files.

Every Windows 2000 computer includes a range of security features. Some are mandatory, others are optional, and still others are available only in certain configurations.

Windows 2000 includes the following basic security features, which you can use to lock down data and programs so that only authorized users can access them:

- **User accounts and passwords.** These are the basic building blocks of Windows 2000's security system. When you set up Windows 2000 for the first time, the operating system automatically creates an Administrator account; it also lets you create a default user account. If you log on with the Administrator account, you can add more accounts.

- **Secure logon.** Unlike Windows 95 and 98, Windows 2000 requires that you press Ctrl+Alt+Del and enter a valid username and matching password at startup. If the username you enter is not in the current list of accounts, or if the password you enter doesn't match the one defined for that account, you will see an error message and you won't be able to start Windows 2000. This step prevents unauthorized users from tampering with confidential files.

A big step up from Windows 95/98

If you've upgraded to Windows 2000 from Windows 95 or 98, these security features are dramatically different from anything you're used to. In those Windows versions, security is literally nonexistent, and the only way to keep your private files safe is to use third-party encryption utilities.

Special treatment for Guests

One built-in account gets special treatment. When you enable the Guest account, users can log on to the computer using any username and password. That's handy if you want to put a computer in a central location in your office so that any employee or visitor can use it, but you also run the risk of potentially allowing a stranger to access confidential information. Normally, the Guest account is disabled. Do not enable it unless you're certain you understand the consequences.

19

- **File access permissions.** On drives formatted with the NTFS file system, you can choose which users and groups have access to files, folders, and entire drives. By carefully managing permissions, you can guarantee that sensitive information is only available to the right users.

- **Group accounts.** By defining groups of users, you can control access to information based on group membership. For instance, you might create a group called `Art_Dept`, giving members of that group the right to open graphical files and publications in a shared location and print them on an expensive color laser printer. When a new employee joins the department, all you have to do is add the newcomer's username to the Art_Dept group to give the person the same access as other department members.

- **Group policies.** A system administrator can set up policies that apply to all users of a given computer or all members of a group. Using policies, for example, you can require users to change their passwords every 30 days, prevent them from installing new hardware drivers, and control which users can log on to a machine locally.

SEE ALSO

➤ *For details on how to set up a security policy for your computer, see "Managing Security Settings," p. 441.*

Who's Managing Your Computer?

When you press the power switch to turn on a computer, Windows 2000 goes through a fairly lengthy boot-up process. During startup, the system configures all attached hardware devices, makes network connections, and loads preferences and policies that apply to all users. At that point, the system stops and displays the Logon dialog box. What happens next depends on the username and password you enter. By default, Windows 2000 restricts most system management features to specially privileged users called *administrators*; unlike Windows 95 or 98, you cannot perform most management tasks unless you log on using an administrator's account.

Using the Administrator's Account

As part of the setup process, Windows 2000 creates a built-in account called Administrator and requires you to enter a password for that account. It also creates a built-in group account called Administrators—any user who is a member of this group can perform management tasks as well. This structure has two common effects:

- You can add users to the Administrators group if you want to delegate management of a PC. When members of the Administrators group log on to that computer, they may perform any action, the same as if they had used the account named Administrator.

- If you join a Windows NT or Windows 2000 *domain*, all domain administrators are automatically added to the Administrators group on the local PC. That means anyone who has administrator's rights on your network can also manage your computer.

As a member of the Users group, you can install programs, add printer drivers, log on locally, and shut down the PC—unless, of course, your network administrator has changed the settings for this group. But when you try to access administrative utilities such as the Local Disk Manager or Device Manager from an ordinary user account, you see an error message, as shown in Figure 1.7.

Be cautious with Administrator rights

Although it's tempting to make your everyday user account a member of the Administrators group, I strongly recommend that you avoid doing so—and Microsoft echoes this advice. You should avoid accessing the Internet when logged on as an administrator, for example, because if you encounter a virus or other dangerous program on the Web, it can use your administrative privileges to do extensive damage to your system and data. As I explain later in this section, you should always run under an ordinary user account and switch to an account in the Administrators group only when you have to.

FIGURE 1.7
If you're not an administrator, Windows 2000 denies you the right to perform many system management tasks.

Do you have to shut down your computer and log in again to perform administrative tasks? Usually, the answer is no. Instead, just start up the appropriate administrative utility using a different account. For some options, this step is easy: if you double-click the **Users and Passwords** option in Control Panel, for instance, Windows 2000 demands that you enter a username and password with administrative privileges, or it refuses to let you continue. In the case of other tools, such as those in the Administrative Tools group in Control Panel, you can right-click to choose a **Run as** menu option that lets you enter a different username and password in the dialog box shown in Figure 1.8. To make this option available for any program, hold down the **Shift** key as you right-click the program icon.

Users or power users?

Windows 2000 refers to common groups by several names. When you add a local user account, you can add that account as a Standard User or a Restricted User. The Standard User is a member of the built-in Power Users group, whereas the Restricted User belongs to the Users group, which has fewer rights and privileges.

FIGURE 1.8
To perform quick administrative tasks, don't log off—hold down the **Shift** key, right-click any program icon, and choose **Run as** to display this dialog box.

Defining Local Users and Groups

If you're administrator of a machine that is not part of a network or that is connected to other machines in a simple workgroup environment, you can add, change, and remove local user accounts and set up local groups whenever you like.

When you first set up Windows 2000, you create an Administrator account for the local machine, and you have the option to create a local user account. Later, you can open the Users and Passwords dialog box (see Figure 1.9) to create additional user accounts and assign them to existing groups.

One notable exception

You can perform almost any task by running a utility using an administrator's account. However, it's next to impossible to change network settings as an ordinary user. If you need to change settings for your network, you must log off and log back on using an administrator's account.

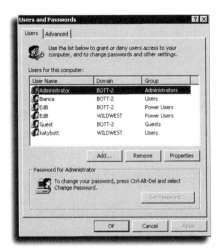

FIGURE 1.9
The Users and
Passwords dialog box
lists users for the local
machine and (optionally)
your domain. By placing
each user account in a
group, you define its permissions globally.

SEE ALSO
➤ *For a detailed explanation of how group accounts and user accounts work together, see
"Assigning Users to Groups," p. 73.*

Although you can create your own groups for special purposes, most
of the time you'll use one of the following built-in group accounts,
which include a standard set of user rights and permissions:

- **Power Users.** This group can install new hardware drivers and
  programs but cannot change network settings or access other
  users' files.

- **Users.** Assign a new user account to this restricted group when
  you want that person to be able to run programs you've installed
  but you don't want them to install new programs or change
  system settings.

- **Administrators.** By default, this group includes the local Administrator account and any accounts in the Domain Administrators
  group. Accounts in this group can install new devices and programs, change passwords, and access other users' files.

Domains are different

Confusingly, the Users and
Passwords option works
differently if you're part of
a Windows NT or a
Windows 2000 domain.
Although the dialog box
looks almost identical, the
procedures for adding a
local user in these circumstances are slightly different. See "Managing Users
and Groups," Chapter 4
(p. 70) for full details.

- **Backup Operators.** As the name implies, accounts in this group have access to all files on the computer, but only when they're using backup software.
- **Guests.** This is the least privileged of all groups. Assign user accounts to this group when you want someone to be able to log on to a local machine and run programs installed there without accessing network resources or changing any system settings.

Managing Your User Profile

When you log on to a system for the first time, Windows creates a collection of files and folders exclusively for your personal use. Collectively, these make up your *user profile*, the location where Windows saves all your personal data files and preferences, such as desktop colors, printer and network connections, and your Internet Favorites folder.

In a tightly managed corporate environment, you may not be able to control your user profile. In a workgroup or home setting, however, or in a relaxed corporate network, you can manage this profile directly. By default, Windows 2000 stores all local profiles in a folder called (logically enough) Documents and Settings, on the same drive as the Windows 2000 folder. Each user has a top-level folder that matches his or her username. Figure 1.10 shows the hierarchy of folders for the username Bianca.

Normally, you don't see many of the folders and files that make up your user profile, because Windows hides them from your view. Using the default Explorer settings, which hide system files and folders, you should see only the following five folders: Cookies, Desktop, Favorites, My Documents, and Start Menu. If you customize Explorer to show files and folders that are normally hidden, you can expect to see several other folders.

Windows 2000 lets you work with three types of user profiles:

- A *local user profile* is automatically created the first time you log on to a computer. As the name implies, it is stored on your local hard disk under the Documents and Settings folder. Any changes you make to your local user profile will be visible only when you log on to that computer. If you log on to another computer using the same account name and password, the documents and settings will be different.

Make yourself a Power User

Although you can assign your everyday user account to the Administrators group, don't do it. Instead, make the account you normally log on with a member of the Power Users group, and log on as Administrator only when you need to perform a system maintenance task that requires administrative rights.

Should you worry about your profile?

On most PCs, you should never need to work directly with your profile. If your network administrator adheres to a conscientious backup routine, your data and settings will be safe and sound. On a home or workgroup PC; however, you should make a special point of backing up your profile regularly. When you do your normal system backup, be sure to include at least your own profile; specify the entire Documents and Settings folder if you want to back up files and preferences for all users.

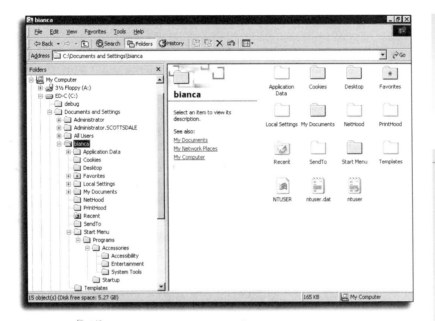

FIGURE 1.10
Whenever you save a document or change a setting, Windows saves it in the local user profile.

Duplicate profiles?

In some cases, you may discover that you have two user profiles on a single machine. This commonly occurs when you have a local user account and a domain account with the same name. In that case, Windows creates different user profiles for each account. Thus, if your username is Bianca and your Windows 2000 domain name is MARKETING, the Documents and Settings folder will contain two sets of folders: the first, called Bianca, contains the profile for your local account, and the second, Bianca.MARKETING (with the domain name in capital letters), holds the profile that was created when you logged in with your domain account.

- A *roaming user profile* is created by your network administrator and is stored on a Windows NT or Windows 2000 server. Any settings you change or documents you save will be stored on the server. If you log on to any computer on the network, you will see the same settings and documents.

- A *mandatory user profile* is a special type of roaming profile. As the name implies, this type of profile defines settings that the user cannot change or override. Mandatory profiles are commonly used in tightly managed corporate environments where administrators expect users to perform only authorized tasks or functions.

Windows 2000 and Your Corporate Network

Is your office network a workgroup or a domain? The answer has a profound effect on the way you work with shared network resources. What's the difference?

- A *workgroup* is a collection of computers capable of sharing files, printers, and other resources. Within a workgroup, each

25

machine enforces its own security. If you want to enable or disable access to shared folders on your computer, for instance, you must set up local user accounts and define access permissions for each one. Anyone can join a workgroup without getting permission by entering the workgroup name as part of the PC's network configuration.

- In a *domain*, by contrast, a designated server called a *domain controller* manages security for the entire network. The names of users, groups, computers, printers, and other network components are stored in the Active Directory—a central repository of domain information. Domain administrators can define policies for all machines on the network, and you can use the domain's directory of user and group accounts to manage security. You can join a domain only with the permission of the domain administrator.

The most important part of any Windows 2000 domain is the Active Directory. As a domain user, you will rarely work directly with the Active Directory. However, you may encounter it when you add a new network printer or attempt to add a domain user account to your local computer, as I've done in Figure 1.11.

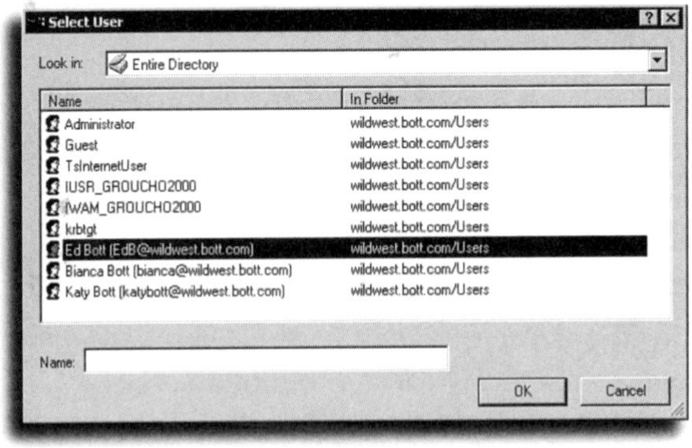

> **Do you need to join a domain?**
>
> You may not need to join a domain to access resources on that domain. In some cases, the network administrator allows outside users to access shared information over the network. If this configuration is permitted on your network, you see a dialog box that asks you to supply the username and password of an authorized domain account the first time you access a shared resource.

FIGURE 1.11
The Active Directory contains records of every user, computer, printer, and other resource in your Windows domain.

Windows 2000 and the Internet

Some of the most profound changes in Windows 2000 involve its Internet capabilities. For starters, most users will find it much easier to connect to the Internet than in previous Windows versions, thanks to a streamlined Internet Connection Wizard. As Figure 1.12 shows, this wizard lets you configure your Net connection in a few steps, regardless of whether you use a modem and a dial-up connection or you have a direct hookup through a network.

FIGURE 1.12
The Internet Connection Wizard runs automatically the first time you try to browse the Web after setting up Windows 2000.

The Internet Connection Wizard icon appears on your desktop when you set up Windows 2000, and if you ignore that icon, the wizard runs automatically the first time you double-click the Internet Explorer icon.

SEE ALSO

➤ *For full instructions on connecting to the Internet, see "Connecting to the Internet," p. 353.*

Windows 2000 includes a full complement of Internet utilities as well, including Internet Explorer 5, Outlook Express, and the Windows Media Player. None of these components are optional. Even if you prefer another browser or email program, they install automatically.

SEE ALSO

➤ *For details on how to configure Internet Explorer, see "Customizing Internet Explorer," p. 391.*
➤ *To set up Outlook Express for the first time, see "Setting Up an Email Account," p. 412.*

It's OK to ignore the wizard

If you already have a working Internet connection, you can safely ignore the Internet Connection Wizard. When it runs, click **Cancel**, and then check the **Do not show the Internet Connection Wizard in the future** box and click **OK**. You can now open the browser directly.

chapter

2

Setting Up Windows 2000

Before You Upgrade...

You may never have to deal with the Windows 2000 Setup program. If your company's computer-support staff handles the details of installing a new operating system, all you have to do is turn on the power and log on with your network username and password. Likewise, if you purchase a new PC that comes preloaded with Windows 2000, you'll be able to unpack the box, connect the components, and get right to work without going through Setup.

But what if you choose to upgrade an existing system to Windows 2000? For most users, most of the time, installing Windows 2000 on a computer in your home or office is a simple, straightforward process—either as an upgrade or as a clean install. Don't take this process lightly, however. If you make a mistake or run into an unforeseen problem, the consequences can be devastating to your productivity—you may be unable to get to the programs and data you need, and in the worst cases, you may even be unable to start your PC.

You can greatly enhance the chances of a successful upgrade by running through this basic checklist before you begin installing Windows 2000:

- **Does your computer meet the minimum standards for Windows 2000?** Most post-1998 models are capable of running Windows 2000, although you may require additional RAM or additional hard disk space to run Setup.

- **Will your existing hardware work properly?** Most standard components work just fine under Windows 2000, but some components will fail to run because they don't have the required driver software. Don't assume that because a particular piece of hardware worked fine under Windows 98 or Windows NT 4.0 that it will work properly with Windows 2000. When in doubt, check Microsoft's Hardware Compatibility List (HCL) and the manufacturer's Web site before starting the upgrade.

SEE ALSO
➤ For more details about hardware compatibility, see "Checking Compatibility," p. 254.

HCL on the Web

The most up-to-date copy of the Windows 2000 Hardware Compatibility List is on the Internet, at `www.microsoft.com/hcl`. Point your Web browser to this location, where you can search by category or by name for a specific product.

Quick fixes available

In some cases, a minor *patch* (also known as an *upgrade package*) is all it takes to fix a program so that it runs properly under Windows 2000. Check the manufacturer's Web site for additional details before starting to set up Windows 2000.

- **Will your existing software work properly?** Many programs originally written for earlier versions of Windows have minor compatibility problems when you try to run them under Windows 2000. Other programs, such as certain disk utilities and communications programs, won't work at all. If your livelihood depends on using a particular program every day, don't upgrade to Windows 2000 until you're certain it will run.

- **Do you have all the information you need to connect to your corporate network?** Windows 2000 does a superb job of connecting to computers running Windows 95, Windows 98, and Windows NT 4.0. However, if your network includes servers running *Novell NetWare* or other network operating systems, you'll need to take special precautions to ensure that everything works properly after setup. On a corporate network, always check with your network administrator before upgrading your operating system.

- **Do you have the time and technical know-how to deal with any problems you might encounter?** If the answer is no, hire a professional to perform the upgrade for you. Particularly in a business environment, the cost of a knowledgeable consultant is trivial compared with the losses you could suffer if your business were unable to access crucial data for even a day or two.

Upgrade or Clean Install?

When you insert the Windows 2000 CD into the CD drive of a computer running any version of Windows, it automatically displays a Startup menu with three choices. Choose the first option, **I**nstall **Windows 2000**, to begin the setup process. After you enter the CD key, the first dialog box you see (shown in Figure 2.1) asks you to make an important decision: should you upgrade or install a fresh copy?

Hey! Don't upgrade yet...

Before you even think of running the Windows 2000 Setup program, make sure you do four things:

1. **Find the CD key.** This 25-character code allows you to install Windows 2000. Without this key (found on the back of the jewel case for the CD), Setup will not proceed.

2. **Back up all your data.** If anything goes wrong and you have to reformat your hard disk, you'll need to restore the data to get back to work.

3. **Make a note of network settings.** Write down your computer name, your username and password (if any), and *TCP/IP* settings, if these are not automatically assigned to you at startup.

4. **Make sure you have a DOS boot disk handy.** You'll need it if you encounter problems accessing your hard disk.

And never start an upgrade late on a Friday afternoon. That's the surest possible way to ruin your weekend.

FIGURE 2.1
There's no turning back if you choose the upgrade option—Windows 2000 completely replaces your previous Windows version.

No CD menu?

Does nothing happen when you insert the Windows 2000 CD? Your system may have AutoPlay turned off. In that case, open an Explorer window, display the contents of the CD, and double-click the **Setup** icon.

Experts only!

Installing new drives and changing partitions is a task best left for experts. If your PC currently has only one drive that uses the letter C and a CD-ROM drive that uses the letter D, it's possible to back up all the data, divide the drive into two partitions (C: and E:), and then install Windows 2000. Or you can add a second hard drive and use it for Windows 2000. Either way, unless you have a ton of experience with setting up, partitioning, and formatting drives, you're better off paying a professional to do the job.

Which option should you choose? Each has pluses and minuses, so think carefully about your requirements before choosing:

- Select **Upgrade to Windows 2000** if you want to completely replace your current operating system. This option requires almost no decisions on your part, and you can continue to use all currently installed programs, provided they're compatible with Windows 2000. If anything goes wrong, however, you can't undo your decision and restore your previous Windows version.

- Choose **Install a new copy of Windows 2000** if you want to keep Windows 95 or 98 on your computer along with Windows 2000 (you'll be able to choose between Windows 2000 and your current version each time you start your computer). When you opt for this configuration, you must reinstall all programs; because you're installing a "clean" copy of Windows 2000, it doesn't pick up any of your settings.

Keeping Your Old Operating System

Do you really want to continue using your previous operating system along with Windows 2000? If so, be aware of two potential gotchas:

- First, although it's technically possible to install Windows 2000 on the same partition as Windows 95 or 98, doing so is a big mistake. Both operating systems use the Program Files folder, and many programs install slightly different files, depending on your Windows version. If Windows 95/98 is on your C: drive, you need to install Windows 2000 on a drive with another letter—D:, for example.

- You must continue to use the FAT or FAT32 disk format for the partition that contains Windows 95 or 98. Under no circumstance should you convert that drive to NTFS format, because only Windows NT and Windows 2000 can read data stored on an NTFS drive.

Setting Up Windows 2000, Step by Step

After you begin running the Windows 2000 Setup program, you must make a series of decisions. The exact options will vary, depending on your system configuration, network availability, and whether you're performing an upgrade or a clean installation.

Regardless of which option you choose, your first step is to read the license agreement for the software and confirm that you agree with it.

Defining Special Setup Options

If you chose the option to install a fresh copy of Windows 2000, you see the dialog box shown in Figure 2.2 immediately after accepting the license agreement. Three options are available to you:

You don't own Windows

Most people blow right past the license agreement for the software they're about to install. If you purchased a legitimate copy of Windows 2000 and you're installing it on a single machine, there's no harm in doing so. But reading the fine print can be instructive. For instance, did you know that you don't actually own the copy of Windows installed on your machine? Instead, when you purchase the shrink-wrapped Windows box from Microsoft, you get a license to use the software on a single computer. If you're a lawyer, the license agreement makes compelling reading; for the rest of us, it might as well be Greek.

FIGURE 2.2
Accept the default settings here unless you plan to use two versions of Windows, or you have special language needs or a visual impairment.

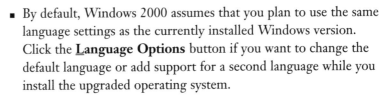

- By default, Windows 2000 assumes that you plan to use the same language settings as the currently installed Windows version. Click the **Language Options** button if you want to change the default language or add support for a second language while you install the upgraded operating system.

- If you intend to keep your current operating system so that you can switch between Windows 95 or 98 and Windows 2000, click the **Advanced Options** button. This displays the dialog box shown in Figure 2.3. Check the box labeled **I want to choose the installation partition during Setup** to make sure Setup doesn't try to install Windows 2000 on the same partition as your existing Windows version. Choose the **Copy all Setup files from the Setup CD to the hard drive** option if you're not certain that the Setup program will be able to read files from the CD-ROM drive after rebooting.

Handle with care!

The advanced options shown here are necessary only if you plan to use two versions of Windows on a single system. Changing the name or location of the folder that contains Windows system files can have unintended side effects. Avoid the temptation to change these settings unless you have a specific need to do so.

FIGURE 2.3
Be sure to check the bottom box shown here if you plan to set up a system that lets you choose different Windows versions at startup.

- Do you have a visual impairment that might affect your ability to see dialog boxes on the screen? Click the **Accessibility Options** button to make the Windows Magnifier and Narrator tools available during Setup.

Checking for Possible Upgrade Problems

If, on the other hand, you chose the upgrade option, Windows 2000 runs through an exhaustive system check before it actually lets you set up the new operating system. The Upgrade Wizard walks you through three steps:

1. First, the wizard prompts you to provide hardware and software upgrade packs. Fixing any known incompatibilities at this stage will save you time and hassle later.

2. Next, it searches for incompatible hardware, software, and system settings. At the end of this search, the wizard displays a dialog box (like the one shown in Figure 2.4) which lists any incompatible devices it found. If you're willing to lose the ability to use the listed devices, it's OK to continue. If the devices are crucial, however, you should cancel Setup at this point.

FIGURE 2.4
As part of its upgrade check, Windows 2000's Setup program identifies devices that need new drivers.

- Finally, the Upgrade Wizard prepares a detailed report listing all the issues it found that might interfere with your ability to install and use Windows 2000 successfully. The report appears in a scrolling box, like the one shown in Figure 2.5.

Don't take the upgrade report lightly. Even if all your hardware and software is compatible with Windows 2000, you may still need to take special precautions to complete the installation. For instance, the upgrade report may recommend that you uninstall a particular program before continuing and reinstall it after setup, or you may be required to reset file permissions on a shared folder.

I strongly recommend that you print out the upgrade report (click the **Print** button) and save a copy to a location other than the hard disk on which you're installing the upgrade (click the **Save As** button).

Patience, patience
In contrast to a clean install, which typically takes less than an hour, the upgrade check can take a long time. Depending on your system's configuration, don't be surprised if this step doubles the setup time.

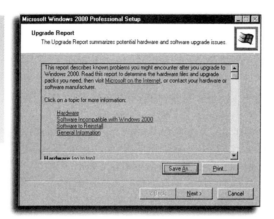

FIGURE 2.5
Read this report carefully before proceeding with a Windows 2000 upgrade—it typically contains important information.

In some cases, the Upgrade Wizard may determine that you cannot successfully upgrade. For instance, if you're short of free disk space, you see the dialog box shown in Figure 2.6. Your only option at this point is to click the **Quit Setup** button, fix the problem, and start over.

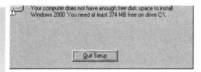

FIGURE 2.6
If you're low on free disk space or memory, the Upgrade Wizard will not allow you to proceed with Setup.

Choosing Disk Options

Regardless of which Setup option you choose, you will see the dialog box shown in Figure 2.7, which offers to upgrade your system drive to NTFS format. Think carefully before proceeding!

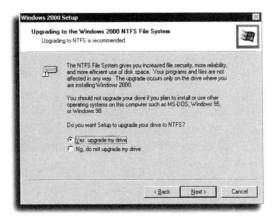

FIGURE 2.7
Upgrade to NTFS only if you're certain you don't want to use your system drive for a previous version of Windows or MS-DOS.

- Choose **Y**es, **upgrade my drive** if you are installing Windows 2000 on its own partition and you are certain you won't want to view the files on that drive when you start up using Windows 95, 98, or MS-DOS. This is the default setting if you've chosen a clean installation.

- Choose **N**o, **do not upgrade my drive** if you need to be able to view files and folders on the Windows 2000 partition using another operating system. For instance, if Windows 98 is installed on drive C:, and drive D: contains data files and a large amount of free space, you should install Windows 2000 on D: and retain the existing disk format so that you can open and edit data files from either operating system. This choice is the default if you're upgrading from Windows 95 or 98.

SEE ALSO

➤ *Not sure whether to upgrade to NTFS? See "Choosing the Right File System," p. 240.*

No turning back

Not certain whether to upgrade to NTFS? Just say no. You can easily convert a FAT or FAT32 drive to NTFS format at any time, but you'll need special utilities and extensive technical knowledge to convert a drive from NTFS format back to one that Windows 95 or 98 can recognize.

After you make your decision, Windows 2000 copies an assortment of files from the CD to the hard drive and gets ready to restart the system. As these activities unfold, you see a succession of dialog boxes that provide details of the progress of the Setup program.

At any time during these initial steps, you can click the **Back** button and change any of the options you selected. After the file copying begins, you can click **Cancel** to stop the Setup Wizard and put things back the way they were. After restarting, however, each succeeding step makes it more difficult to undo the previous one.

If you've chosen to upgrade from a previous Windows version, you can walk away from your computer after the preliminaries are out of the way. Unless something goes wrong, the upgrade process requires no intervention on your part until it's time to log on again.

If you chose a clean install, on the other hand, your system restarts and you see a series of character-based screens, including a menu that gives you the option to set up Windows 2000, repair an existing Windows 2000 installation, or cancel. Press **Enter** to continue.

If you chose the advanced option to select the partition on which to install Windows 2000, Setup lists existing disks, partitions, and free space. At this point, you can choose an existing partition, create a partition from free space, or delete an existing partition. The most likely reason for choosing this option is to avoid disturbing your existing copy of Windows 95 or 98. In that case, be sure not to choose drive C:!

Regional Settings

After finishing all disk options, the Setup program copies files to the hard disk and restarts. During this stage of Setup, you see a series of graphical dialog boxes that let you customize the system or user locale and change the keyboard layout. Users in the United States who don't need to set up support for other languages can continue without clicking the **Customize** button.

Defining a Computer Name and User Accounts

In its final stage, the Windows 2000 Setup program runs the Network Identification Wizard to set your computer's name and create user accounts. In a fresh installation, you'll be asked to enter your **Name** and **Organization**, and then Windows requests that you assign a name to your computer.

Every computer that runs Windows 2000 has a name. If your computer is on a network, other users can locate shared folders on your computer by browsing through the My Network Places folder. If your computer is on a network with a domain, the computer must also have an account on the domain, and the name must be unique. On a computer that isn't connected to a network, the computer

---

Windows 2000×2?

As part of the installation process, Windows 2000's Setup program searches for existing Windows 2000 installations and lists any that it finds. If you're adding a second copy of Windows 2000 to your system, see the section, "Setting Startup Options," in Appendix A for more information on how to proceed.

Format with care

If you're positive you know what you're doing with disks and drives, you can delete an existing partition, create a new one, and format it from scratch at this point. Be extra careful, however: formatting a disk destroys all the data on it! Make sure you have backed up all important files before choosing this option.

Now or later...

Although you may find it convenient to add support for multiple languages at this phase, you can also wait until later. To add support for other keyboards and languages after setting up Windows 2000, open Control Panel's Regional Options dialog box and adjust settings on the **General** and **Input Locales** tabs.

name is irrelevant; feel free to accept the Windows default and go quickly past this step.

In theory, a computer name can be up to 63 characters long and can contain letters, numbers, and all sorts of symbols. In practice, I strongly recommend you keep your computer name to a maximum of 15 characters and use only letters, numbers, and the hyphen character.

SEE ALSO

➤ *For more details on how to share files on a network, see "Sharing Folders and Drives," p. 334.*

➤ *To learn more about user accounts, see "How the Logon Process Works," p. 68.*

What name should you use for your computer? The answer depends on the setup choices you made earlier:

- If you're upgrading over an existing Windows installation and your network does not use a *domain*, Setup automatically picks up your computer's current name. To change the name, enter a new value into the **Computer name** box.

- If you're upgrading over an existing Windows installation on a network with a domain, Setup checks to see if the domain already includes an account for your current computer name. If it cannot find an existing computer account, you see the dialog box shown in Figure 2.8. You cannot change the name shown here, and you must supply a domain administrator's username and password to create the new account.

> **Keep the computer name short**
>
> Choosing a computer name of 15 characters or fewer has two advantages. First, it makes life easier for anyone who has to type in the computer's name. Second, it guarantees that network users running other Windows versions will be able to connect to your computer. Windows 95 and 98, for example, can't deal with long computer names.

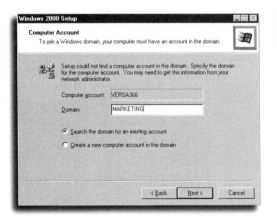

FIGURE 2.8
Only domain administrators can create a new machine account and complete this setup step.

- On a fresh configuration, the Setup program suggests a name for your computer. You can accept the suggested name or change it by replacing the entry in the **Computer name** box.

Next, the Setup program creates a local user account called Administrator. Enter the password you want to use for this account. The next step shows you the Date and Time Settings dialog box. Adjust the date, time, and time zone, if necessary, and follow the wizard's prompts to the next step.

On a fresh Windows 2000 setup, you answer a few basic questions about your networking needs. For starters, a dialog box asks you to choose which networking software to install. If you are on a corporate network that uses *protocols* other than TCP/IP, or if you have to specify settings such as an IP address or DNS servers, choose **Custom Settings** and enter the required information. Most users can safely choose **Typical Settings.**

Choosing a Network Configuration

At the very end of the setup process, the Network Identification Wizard asks whether you want to join an existing network. Decisions you make at this step define some of your computer's most basic settings, particularly what happens each time you start up and shut down your computer. In essence, you can choose any of the following four configurations:

- **Single user with automatic logon.** This configuration is most useful in a home or small business where you're the only person who ever uses the computer and you don't need to protect your files from other people. In this configuration, you don't have to hassle with the logon dialog box each time you turn on your PC—Windows 2000 automatically enters your username and password as part of the startup routine.

- **Single computer, multiple users with secure logon.** Use this configuration if you want several users to share a single computer, or if you want to protect sensitive files. At home, you can set up separate local user accounts for each family member, using file permissions to define who has access to specific areas of the computer. To safeguard confidential company data at the office, be sure to choose a strong, hard-to-guess password for each account.

SEE ALSO

➤ *To learn more about setting up local user accounts, see "Managing Users and Groups," p. 70.*

➤ *For instructions on how to restrict access to files and folders, see "Restricting Access to Shared Folders or Drives," p. 336.*

- **Network user, workgroup only.** This configuration is appropriate when your computer is connected to one or more computers at home or at the office, without a Windows 2000 or Windows NT domain. Computers running Windows 95, Windows 98, Windows NT Workstation, and Windows 2000 Professional can all talk to one another in this configuration. You create only local user accounts, and each computer is responsible for setting its own passwords for sharing folders.

- **Network user on a domain.** In corporations, this configuration is most common. Setting up a *domain controller* gives a network administrator the capability to control the way every computer on the network behaves, including restrictions on the type of software you can install, the appearance of your desktop, and which parts of your system you can change. Computers configured this way have local user accounts but rely most often on a central storehouse of user accounts called the Active Directory. You cannot set up automatic logon in this configuration.

If you upgrade to Windows 2000 on a computer that's currently connected to a domain, your settings migrate automatically. In all other cases, Setup displays the dialog box shown in Figure 2.9, which asks you to specify whether you want to join a workgroup or a domain.

Follow the prompts to enter any required details, including workgroup name, passwords, and other identifying details. After you finish entering information and clicking through dialog boxes, your system restarts one last time.

It's not an option

In Windows 2000, networking isn't an option; the operating system assumes most people will want to connect to the largest network of all—the Internet. The same software that manages the Internet works just fine on corporate networks.

Try a blank password

The automatic logon feature doesn't eliminate the need for a username and password—it just enters the information for you. On a single-user system where you just want to turn on the power and get to work, you can use a blank password if you like. That way, on the rare occasions when you do need to enter a password, you can just press **Enter**. Don't use this tempting shortcut on a machine that's connected to the Internet, however, that blank password makes it too easy for anyone to access shared folders on your computer without permission.

41

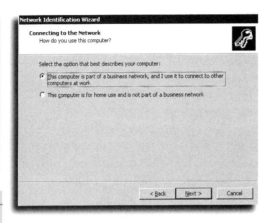

FIGURE 2.9
Choose the top option in this dialog box if you plan to connect to a company network, even if you're not currently connected. Windows lets you enter details later.

Enter the right work-group name

Unlike domains, which require careful planning and configuration, Windows workgroups require almost no advance planning. Enter the name of a workgroup, and Windows looks for other computers connected to your network and using the same work-group name. To change the name of a workgroup, just enter the new name in the System settings for each computer you want in the workgroup.

In a single-user or workgroup configuration, the next dialog box (shown in Figure 2.10) lets you set up automatic logon. Choose **Users must enter a user name and password to use this computer** if you want to set up a secure logon. The second option, **Windows always assumes the following user has logged on to this computer,** lets you bypass the logon box at startup.

Two default accounts are available in the drop-down list shown here: the built-in local Administrator account and the name you entered when you filled in the Name and Organization step earlier. Enter and confirm a password here.

Restart your computer, and you're ready to begin running Windows 2000.

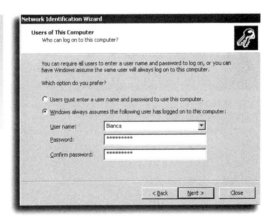

FIGURE 2.10
Choose the bottom option to have Windows automatically enter a username and a password at startup.

Changing System Settings After Setup

After you log on to Windows 2000 for the first time—especially after performing a clean install—you may discover that some basic system settings are incorrect. This section describes the most common areas where you can make changes.

Setting Display Options

Windows offers a world of ways to personalize your desktop, but the most basic settings define the *resolution*, the *color depth*, and the *refresh rate* of your display. Even minor adjustments here can have a major effect on your productivity by allowing you to see more data on the screen and to make the display easier on the eyes.

SEE ALSO

➤ For instructions on how to choose a personalized color scheme and change other visual options, see "Personalizing the Windows Interface," p. 170, and "Taming the Active Desktop," p. 182.

➤ For details about how to change settings for your display adapter or monitor, see "Installing and Configuring Common Upgrades," p. 261.

By default, a clean setup of Windows 2000 sets your display resolution at the absolute minimum resolution of 640 *pixels* across and 480 pixels from top to bottom. (Each pixel is a single color dot on the screen; the higher the resolution, the more data you can see in each window and the more windows you can see side by side.) You should immediately increase your display resolution to the highest setting you can comfortably use (as the resolution setting gets higher, icons and text grow smaller on your display). Many popular Web sites, for example, assume you're using at least 800×600 resolution and are difficult to navigate at lower resolutions.

While you're at it, check your color settings as well. *True color* (24-bit) settings require extra memory on the video hardware and are most appropriate for graphic designers; *high color* (15- or 16-bit) settings will display photographs and graphic images with superb clarity. Avoid 256-color mode, which causes many colors to display as a pattern of dots rather than as well-defined shades. The effect is particularly ugly in gradients, where one color blends into another as part of a background.

Make a mistake? No problem...

If you inadvertently enter incorrect information in any part of the Network Identification Wizard, relax—you can come back and change it later. To rerun the Network Identification Wizard, be sure to log on as an administrator first; then open Control Panel's **System** option and click the **Network Identification** tab. Click the **Network ID** button to rerun the wizard; click the **Properties** button to rename the computer or specify a new domain or workgroup name.

Type carefully

Every time you create or change a password, you have to type the password again to confirm that your fingers didn't slip when you typed it the first name. Don't take this step lightly. If you inadvertently make the same typo in each box when creating the password for an Administrator account, you'll lock yourself out of the computer. After entering the password, be sure to write it down and store it in a secure place; if you lose the password, you risk losing all your data.

Adjusting display settings

1. Click the **Start** button, choose **Settings**, and click **Control Panel**.

2. Double-click the **Display** option. Click the **Settings** tab to see the dialog box shown in Figure 2.11.

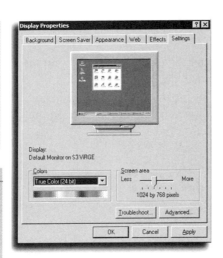

FIGURE 2.11
Use these settings to increase or decrease the amount of data you can see on the screen, as well as the number of colors Windows uses.

Which resolution is right for you?

Choosing a screen resolution is strictly a matter of personal preference in which you have to balance your visual acuity with your display adapter's capability to place pixels on the screen. As a rule of thumb, try a minimum setting of 800×600 for a 14-inch monitor, 1024×768 for a 15- or 17-inch monitor, and 1152×864 for larger monitors. Depending on the capabilities of your hardware, you may have to choose a lower color depth at higher resolutions, and some displays, especially LCD panels on notebooks, are locked into one or two resolutions.

3. Move the sliding **Screen area** control to increase or decrease the display resolution. As you slide the pointer left and right, watch the preview pane change in a relative display of how much data you'll be able to see on the screen. Each notch represents a setting supported by the display adapter in your computer, and the exact resolution in pixels appears below the slider.

4. Use the drop-down **Colors** list to choose a color depth to go with the resolution you've chosen.

5. Click the **Apply** button. Windows displays the confirmation dialog box shown in Figure 2.12. Click **OK** to test the new settings.

FIGURE 2.12
Click OK here to try out a new display resolution. If the changes don't work properly, you can easily restore your previous settings.

6. After making the changes, Windows displays a second dialog box asking you whether you want to make the new settings permanent. If the display looks the way you want it, click **Yes** to save the changes. If anything looks wrong, press **Esc** or click **No** to restore your old settings.

7. Click **OK** to close the Display dialog box and save your changes.

Finally, look for a flickering on the screen, especially when viewing bright white backgrounds. This annoying screen flicker, which can be exhausting on the eyes, is caused when your refresh rate—the number of times Windows "paints" the pixels on the screen—is too low. By default, Windows 2000 sets the refresh rate at 60Hz (one *hertz*, abbreviated Hz, equals one cycle per second). Generally, flicker-free resolution requires a setting of at least 70Hz, and increasing the refresh rate to at least this level can significantly reduce eyestrain and fatigue.

Before you even think about resetting the refresh rate on your display, check the monitor documentation to see which settings it supports. After you discover the correct setting, open Control Panel's **Display** dialog box, click the **Settings** tab, and click the **Advanced** button. On the **Monitor** tab (shown in Figure 2.13), choose the correct setting from the drop-down list. Be careful when setting the refresh rate. On older monitors that don't incorporate safety features, setting a refresh rate that's too high can damage or destroy the hardware; on most modern monitors, however, the worst that happens is you'll have to stare at a blank screen for 15 seconds until Windows restores your old settings.

True color or high color?

The high color setting allows your display hardware (in theory, at least) to choose from a palette of more than 65,000 colors. True color, on the other hand, lets you see more than 16 million colors. Can you really see the difference? For graphics professionals, the answer is yes. For everyday business use, the answer is maybe. Experiment running at both color depths and see if you notice a difference.

Display settings shortcut

If the Windows desktop is visible, you can bypass Control Panel and open the Display dialog box immediately. Right-click any empty space on the desktop and choose **Properties**.

Where did those settings go?

As you increase the display resolution, you may notice that color options disappear. That's normal. The amount of memory on your video adapter is a limiting factor, and at higher resolutions you may not have enough memory to handle all combinations. In that case, Windows doesn't show you the higher color depths. If the lower color depth is OK, choose the higher resolution; otherwise, scale back the resolution until the colors you prefer are available.

Don't panic

If your screen goes black after trying a particular combination of new display settings, keep your hands off the keyboard and mouse for 15 seconds. After that interval has passed, Windows assumes you couldn't see the new settings and restores the display to its previous configuration.

Adjusting the Date and Time

As part of the initial setup of a Windows 2000 system, you may be asked to enter the current date, time, and time zone. Over time, however, computer clocks tend to drift—sometimes a little, sometimes a lot. To adjust the time, open Control Panel's **Date & Time** dialog box (see Figure 2.14). To switch your computer's clock to another time zone or to check settings for Daylight Savings Time, click the **Time Zone** tab.

Currency, Decimal, and Other Regional Options

By default, Windows 2000 sets up your system using settings that make sense in the United States. Dates appear in mm/dd/yy format, the currency symbol is a dollar sign, and a comma is the separator character for numbers of 1,000 or more.

In other countries, these settings are different. For instance, many European countries display dates in dd/mm/yy format and use a period as the thousands separator. In other cases, you may want to change the default options. Start by opening Control Panel's **Regional Options** dialog box (Figure 2.15). Choose the country whose settings most closely match the ones you prefer, and then tweak the settings as necessary.

FIGURE 2.14
Adjust your system's date and time using this dialog box.

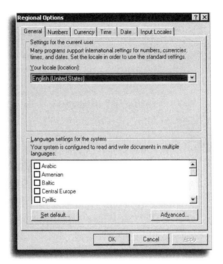

FIGURE 2.15
By choosing a different country from this list, you change a whole host of preferences at once.

The remaining tabs in this dialog box let you fine-tune each option:

- On the **Numbers** tab, use the **Negative number format** setting to change the display of numbers less than zero from a leading minus sign to parentheses; you can also use the **Measurement system** setting if you prefer the metric system over the U.S. system.

- On the **Currency** tab (see Figure 2.16), watch the preview pane at the top of the dialog box as you adjust settings. U.S. users can adjust the number of decimal places that appear by default in currency-based entries and can choose the Euro symbol (€) as the standard symbol if they wish.

Time-saving shortcut

To open the Date & Time dialog box in a hurry, double-click the clock at the far right of the taskbar.

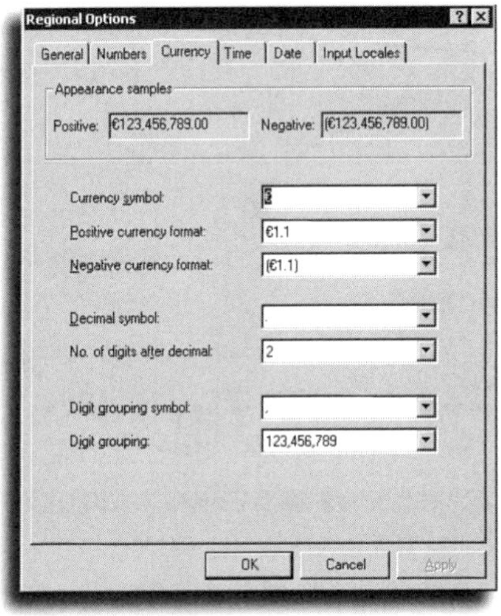

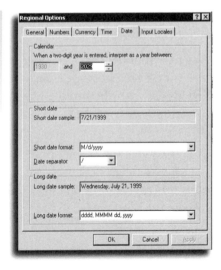

FIGURE 2.16
Watch the preview pane to see the effects of your changes.

Explorer windows use these settings

When you view the contents of a folder using Details view, the date and time stamps on files appear according to the values you set in the Regional Options dialog box.

- Use the **Time** tab to adjust the default display of time values. You can switch to a 24-hour clock, for example, and turn the display of a.m. and p.m. indicators on or off.

- The Date tab (see Figure 2.17) offers one setting that can help you avoid date arithmetic errors caused by two-digit year displays. In the **Short date format** box, make sure the year portion of the date shows as yyyy. This setting causes Windows to display dates using the full four digits for each year rather than only two digits.

FIGURE 2.17
To avoid Y2K-related date errors, be sure your short date format displays four-digit years.

■ Use the **Input Locales** tab to add support for other languages. This dialog box lets you define a keyboard shortcut you can use to switch from one keyboard layout to another—if you want to type German characters on a standard English keyboard, for example.

Setting Sound and Multimedia Options

If your system includes supported multimedia hardware such as a sound card, the Windows 2000 Setup program installs the proper hardware drivers automatically. When you use the default Setup options, Windows 2000 assigns sounds to some *system events*. For example, Windows plays a tune each time you log on or off; it beeps, dings, or chimes when new mail arrives, when you encounter an error message, or when you successfully download a file from the Internet.

SEE ALSO

➤ *For more details on how to install sound cards, see "Multimedia Devices," p. 266.*

Sounds can be annoying or inappropriate under some circumstances. For instance, if your workstation is in a cubicle with several others, you might want to turn sounds down to an extremely low volume. In a home office, you might want to crank up the volume when you play music CDs or games, but keep the volume very soft when you work late into the night. As part of the process of personalizing your PC, maybe you want to replace the default sounds with more entertaining alternatives.

Changing sounds for system events

1. Open Control Panel's Sounds and Multimedia option.

2. Click the Sounds tab and scroll through the Sound Events list (see Figure 2.18) until you find the event sound you want to select or adjust.

3. From the drop-down **Name** list, select the sound file you want to play whenever the selected event occurs. If the sound you want to use is not in the list, click the **Browse** button and locate the file yourself.

Clock stops keeping time?

Is your system clock suddenly losing track of time? If you notice the time or date drifting dramatically or changing to an illogical setting like January 1, 1980, the problem might be a weak battery on your PC's motherboard. Check your computer's documentation to see how to test and replace the battery.

Euro on command

In any application that supports Unicode characters, including WordPad and all Office 2000 programs, you can quickly enter the Euro symbol by pressing **Ctrl+Alt+E**.

FIGURE 2.18
The speaker icon to the left of an entry in the Sound Events list means a sound is associated with that event. Select the item to select a new sound.

Sounds of silence

If the constant beeping from a particular sound annoys you, eliminate just that sound. For instance, select the entry from the Sound Events list and then, from the top of the **Name** list, select **(None)**. To eliminate all sounds for all events, choose **No Sounds** from the **Sc̲heme** list, and then click **Apply**.

No speaker icon?

Normally, Windows installs a volume control icon at the right side of the taskbar. If this speaker icon isn't visible, open Control Panel's **Sounds and Multimedia** option and check the **Show volume control on the t̲askbar** box. If that box is unavailable, check your hardware configuration—most likely you need to install or update a driver for your sound card.

4. If you're not certain what sound a particular file plays, select it from the **Name** list, and then click the **Play** button to its right. This button changes to a Stop icon while the sound is playing.

5. Repeat steps 2–4 for other events you want to adjust.

6. After customizing your sounds, save the settings by clicking **Sa̲ve As**, entering a name for the *sound scheme*, and clicking **OK**. The name you enter appears in the **Sc̲heme** list so you can restore all your sound settings at one time. To reassign the default sounds to system events, choose the **Windows Default** scheme and click **Apply**.

To increase, decrease, or mute the sound volume, take your choice of several volume controls.

- Open Control Panel's **Sounds and Multimedia** option and you'll find a master volume control on the Sounds tab. Drag the slider right or left to increase or decrease the volume of any sounds, including music CDs and sounds associated with system events.

- By default, Windows 2000 adds a volume control in the notification area—the "tray" on the right side of the taskbar. Click that icon to display a slider control that is linked to the master volume control. Drag up to increase the volume or down to decrease it. Check the **Mute** box to temporarily stifle all sounds.

- Double-click the speaker icon at the right of the taskbar to open the full Volume Control window, which includes balance and volume sliders for each type of sound your system is capable of producing.

Figure 2.19 shows the full set of volume controls for the popular SoundBlaster Live! card. In this case, I've set the volume for Wave files (those assigned to system events) to be higher than output from music CDs.

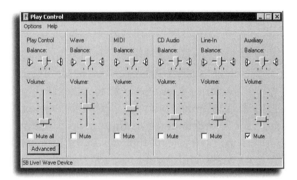

FIGURE 2.19
The full volume control window lets you tweak each type of sound on your system. Use the Mute check boxes to shut down one group of sounds completely.

Changing Power Options

Windows 2000 offers a broad range of power-management settings (although the exact options available depend on the capabilities of your system hardware). Based on your preferences, Windows can temporarily shut down your monitor and hard disks, place your computer in a power-saving state called *standby*, or save the contents of memory to a file on disk and shut down Windows completely (a process called *hibernation*). With the right hardware, you can power your computer down so it uses almost no power but can wake up when the phone rings or another network computer tries to connect.

Although most people think of power management as a feature unique to notebooks and other portable computers, reliable power management can pay handsome dividends on desktop computers as well by reducing your monthly electric bill without decreasing your productivity.

Windows 2000 supports two distinctly different power-saving technologies. The older of the two is called Advanced Power Management (APM); it offers a limited number of power-saving options. The more modern power-management technology, Advanced Configuration and Power Interface (ACPI), offers many more power-management settings.

How can you tell whether your system is using ACPI features? Open Control Panel's **Administrative Tools** group, double-click the **Computer Management** icon, and select **Device Manager**. Expand the Computer branch by clicking on the plus sign to its left; if you see an **Advanced Configuration and Power Interface (ACPI) PC** entry, your system includes ACPI features. If you see **Standard PC** or **MPS Multiprocessor PC**, your system supports only basic power options.

On an ACPI system, double-clicking the **Power Options** icon in Control Panel displays the Power Options properties sheet open to the Power Schemes tab shown in Figure 2.20. (Without ACPI support, only the monitor and hard disk options are available.) Use the drop-down lists to adjust the amount of time for each option here.

SEE ALSO

➤ For details on how to work with power schemes, see "Making Batteries Last Longer," p. 297.

➤ To learn how advanced power options work, see "Controlling How Your PC Uses Power," p. 298.

➤ To set up hibernation on your system, see "Hibernating for Maximum Power Saving," p. 300.

Power debate

Should you turn off your PC every night when you leave work, or should you leave it on all the time? That debate has raged for years, with no conclusive resolution. In general, I recommend that you turn off the monitor but leave the CPU running; that configuration allows you to resume work quickly, without having to wait for a full boot cycle, and it prevents the on/off cycle from stressing your system's components. If you plan to be away for more than a few days, though, consider powering down for the cost savings.

No ACPI? Try a new BIOS

Even if your hardware manufacturer claims that your system is ACPI-compatible, you may discover that Windows 2000 doesn't install the correct hardware. Generally, that means that Microsoft discovered a problem with your system's BIOS that prevents it from using ACPI features properly. In some cases, updating your system BIOS can fix the problem; check with your manufacturer to see if a BIOS update is available, and follow the system manufacturer's instructions to the letter. Then reinstall Windows 2000 to add ACPI support.

FIGURE 2.20
With ACPI support, you can define what happens to each of your systems components after specified intervals.

chapter 3

Finding Answers in Windows Help

Searching for Answers in
Windows Help

How to Read a Help Topic

Finding Detailed Information
on the Internet

Keeping a List of Favorite Help Topics

Copying and Printing Help Topics

Searching for Answers in Windows Help

No Assistant available

If you use Office 97 or Office 2000, you may have used the Office Assistant—a cartoon character that suggests Help topics in response to questions you type into a search box. Although Windows 2000 uses the same format as Office for its Help files, it doesn't have any Assistant characters, nor does it include the "natural language" search feature.

When you're trying to accomplish a task in Windows 2000, detailed explanations and step-by-step instructions are usually just a few clicks away, in the online Help system. The challenge, of course, is finding the right answer. The Help system in Windows 2000 is packed with an enormous amount of detailed information, but it doesn't respond to questions in plain English.

To open the Help system and begin searching for answers, click the **Start** button and choose **Help**. This action opens the two-paned Help window, shown in Figure 3.1.

FIGURE 3.1
Choose a topic from the list in the navigation pane at left; then read the topic in the right pane.

① Help navigation pane

② Topic pane

③ Toolbar

Many roads lead to Help

Although the shortcut on the Start menu is the most convenient way to access Help, it's not the only way. Help is also available when you're working with the contents of a folder, for example. From any Explorer window, pull down the **Help** menu and click **Help Topics** to open the main Windows 2000 Help window.

The Help window's panes vaguely resemble those in an Explorer window. Use lists and trees in the left *navigation pane* to search for information; the *topic pane* on the right displays the current *Help topic*. Note that the navigation pane offers a choice of tabs, each of which organizes Help topics in a different way. (If the navigation pane isn't visible, click the **Show** button.)

From the main Help screen, you can accomplish any of the following tasks:

- **Search for answers to commonly asked questions.** This option is especially useful if you've recently upgraded from

Windows 98 or Windows NT 4.0 and a once-familiar task no longer works the same way. From the opening Help screen, click the text that reads **If you've used Windows before** to display an alphabetical list of terms used in older versions of Windows (see Figure 3.2). Click any item in this list to read an explanation of how that feature works in Windows 2000.

FIGURE 3.2
Have you upgraded from Windows 95, Windows 98, or Windows NT 4.0? This list explains how familiar features work in Windows 2000.

- **Find definitions of terms.** Select the **Contents** tab in the navigation pane and click the **Glossary** link at the bottom. Scroll through the alphabetical list in the topic pane until you find the term that has you stumped.

- **Solve hardware and software problems.** The online Help system includes more than a dozen topics called *Troubleshooters* that help you find and fix common problems. Figure 3.3, for example, shows the opening screen of the Internet Connections (ISP) Troubleshooter. To see the entire list, click the **Contents** tab in the navigation pane, then click the **Troubleshooting and Maintenance** category, and click the **Use the interactive troubleshooters** topic.

Help for special tasks

Many of the utilities in Windows 2000 include their own collections of specialized Help topics, which are not part of the basic Windows 2000 Help system. All the utilities in the Computer Management console, for example, include detailed instructions, as do accessories such as the Imaging and CD Player programs. To access these topics, click the **Help** button (if one is available) or use the **Help** menu.

SEE ALSO

➤ *To troubleshoot disk problems, see "Cleaning Up and Repairing Disks," p. 273.*

➤ *To fix problems that keep you from starting Windows, see "Recovering from Disaster," p. 289.*

- **See a list of topics organized by subject.** To "drill down" through topic areas, going from the general to the specific, start by clicking the **Contents** tab. This display organizes the topics into broad categories, like the chapters in a book. Double-click to expand the list of topics under a category; in some cases, you may need to double-click subcategories as well. Click any of the listed titles to read that topic in the right-hand pane.

FIGURE 3.3
Troubleshooters ask you questions about the problem you're trying to solve and then suggest specific steps you can take.

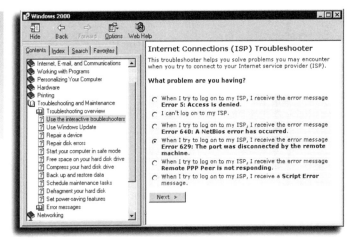

How many clicks?

How do you display a topic after selecting it in the Help window's navigation pane? The answer depends on which tab you're using. Topics listed on the **Contents** tab act like *hyperlinks*; they turn blue when you point to them, and a single click displays the topic. On the other three tabs, however, the topics are simply items on a list. To read the topic, you have to double-click its title, or select the title and click the **Display** button.

- **Find specific topics using an index of keywords.** Click the navigation pane's **Index** tab to display a list of *keywords* in alphabetical order. Unlike the **Contents** tab, this list allows you to find specific topics without having to start with a general category. Scroll through the list of keywords until you find the one you're looking for, or enter the first few letters of the keyword in the box labeled **Type in the keyword to find**; the list of topics scrolls automatically as you type each letter.

- **Search for specific words anywhere in Help.** Click the **Search** tab in the navigation pane and enter one or more words, separated by spaces, in the box labeled **Type in the keyword to find**; then click the **List Topics** button. This option shows topics that contain all the words you entered, in any order. It's especially useful when you want to find detailed information about a baffling dialog box or utility—use a word or phrase from the dialog box as the search text.

Although it's not part of the main Windows Help system, *context-sensitive help* is often available within dialog boxes. For example, if you open a folder window, and then pull down the **Tools** menu and choose **Folder Options**, you'll encounter a dizzying array of choices. If you're not certain what a given option does in this or other dialog boxes, try either of the following techniques to display a pop-up explanation:

- Point to the text that has you baffled and right-click; if a **What's This?** menu choice appears, click it.

- In any dialog box, look at the right edge of the title bar. If you see a question-mark icon, click it. When the mouse pointer turns to a question mark and arrow combination, point to any text, button, or option, and then click.

How to Read a Help Topic

Most Help topics consist of text that explains a feature or a process, often with step-by-step instructions, icons, tables, and other explanatory elements. In addition, some topics contain one or more of the following special elements:

- **Hyperlinks.** These work the same as they do in a Web page—click to jump to another topic or a Web page; or to pop up a Related Topics list.

- **Jump buttons.** These are commonly used when the Help topic explains how to use a utility or a Control Panel option. When you see an arrow icon to the left of a hyperlink, as shown in Figure 3.4, click to open the utility. The Help topic remains open so that you can continue to follow the instructions.

- **Expand/collapse buttons.** These buttons are most common in "overview" topics. Click the plus sign (+) to expand the text below an entry; click the minus sign (−) to collapse the entry.

- **Pop-up definitions.** Underlined words or phrases that look like hyperlinks; instead of opening another topic, however, clicking one of these links displays a definition over the current topic. Click the definition text or press **Esc** to close the pop-up window.

Narrowing down a search

When you enter words into the **Search** tab, use quotation marks to search for phrases and add the keywords AND, OR, NOT, and NEAR to narrow down a search. For example, you might enter **modem Internet** as the search term, hoping to find details of how to set up a dial-up Internet connection. After completing the search, you'll scroll through a lengthy list of topics, all of which contain those two words somewhere in the topic, and most of them barely relevant to what you're trying to accomplish. But enter **modem near Internet** and you'll get back a short list of topics where those two words are within a sentence of each other. The resulting list is much more likely to contain the topic you want.

Retrace your steps

Because the Windows Help system is actually a stripped-down version of Internet Explorer, you can use the **Back** and **Forward** buttons to move between topics. The Back arrow is particularly useful when you follow a hyperlink and want to return to the original topic.

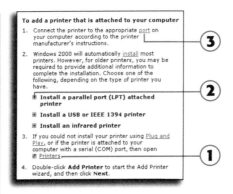

FIGURE 3.4

Want to put Help instructions to work immediately? Click the jump button to open the utility in question—the Printers folder, in this example.

(1) Jump button

(2) Expand/collapse button

(3) Pop-up definition

Know the (color) codes

How do you distinguish between the different types of underlined links? Watch the colors. A hyperlink appears blue until clicked, at which point it turns red. Pop-up definitions are green.

Ctrl+F to search

Because each Help topic is really a Web page, you can use the Windows standard shortcut to search for information within a topic. Click anywhere in the topic pane and then press **Ctrl+F** to open the Find dialog box and search for a word or phrase in the current topic only.

For particularly long and detailed Help topics, it's sometimes useful to hide the navigation tab. Click the **Hide** button on the toolbar at the top of the Help window; then resize the window so you can see more of the Help text.

If you used the **Search** tab to find a topic, the terms you entered are highlighted in blue in the topic window. That can be an extremely useful way to find specific information in a lengthy topic. However, if the search term appears repeatedly in a topic, the blue highlighting can be distracting and make the topic harder to read. To turn this highlighting off, click the **Options** button and choose **Search Highlight Off** from the menu. To turn highlighting on again, click the **Options** button and choose **Search Highlight On**.

Finding Detailed Information on the Internet

What do you do when the problem you're trying to solve isn't listed in the Help files? If you've exhausted all local options, take your question to official and unofficial Windows 2000 sites on the Internet. In general, you'll find more detail on the Web than in the online Help; you'll also find fresher information, particularly when it comes to documenting bugs and program flaws that didn't turn up until after Windows 2000 was officially released.

Two information sources are particularly useful. I'll cover each of them in more detail in the following two sections.

Searching the Microsoft Knowledge Base

You can tap into the same database of information that Microsoft support personnel use when they deal with customer questions. This massive storehouse of information is called the *Microsoft Knowledge Base*, and you can use a fill-in-the-blanks form to search through it.

To access the Knowledge Base, point your Web browser to the following address: http://www.microsoft.com/support/kb.htm. The first time you visit this page, you'll be required to choose the Knowledge Base section that's most appropriate to your system configuration; for most questions that involve how to use Windows 2000 Professional, choose the Personal Online Support option.

When you use the **Advanced** search option (shown in Figure 3.5), you can enter keywords or phrase your request in the form of a question. Your goal is to find a Knowledge Base article (equivalent to a Help topic) that contains a solution to your problem.

A grain of salt

The sheer size and breadth of the World Wide Web practically guarantees that massive amounts of misinformation are available as well. It's easy to find advice from self-styled "experts" that is misleading, outdated, or just plain wrong. Before you rely on information from an unknown Web source, check it out using some of the sources listed here.

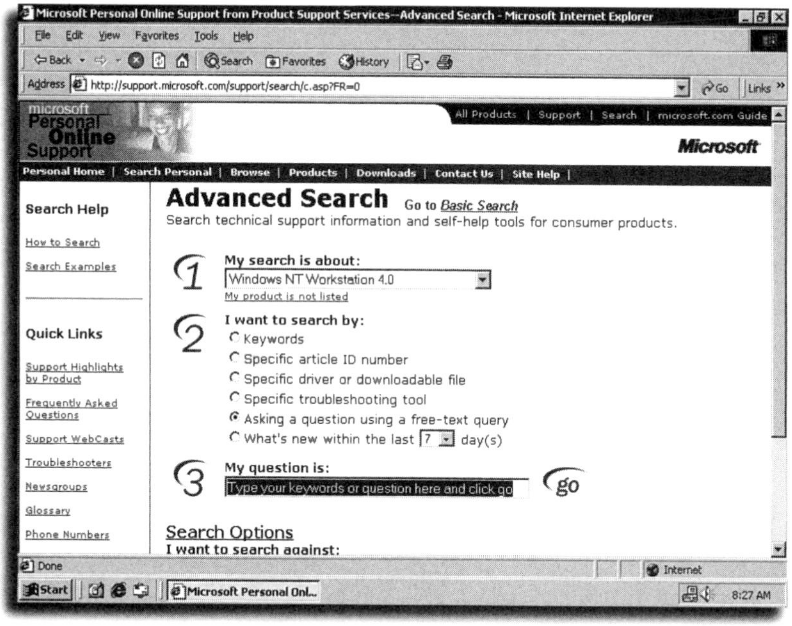

FIGURE 3.5
Choose the **Advanced Search** option to request detailed information from the Microsoft Knowledge Base.

Save that link!

If you use the Microsoft Knowledge Base regularly, select the area you want to search and then save a shortcut to that page. Open the search page in your browser window, pull down the **Favorites** menu, and choose **Add to Favorites**.

Searching the Knowledge Base

1. Open the Knowledge Base search page in your browser.

2. Specify that you want to limit your search to Windows 2000 topics.

3. Choose the type of query you want to use. *Keywords* let you enter terms that appear in the Knowledge Base article (`CD audio`, for example); free-text queries allow you to enter a phrase, such as `CD audio doesn't work`. If you know the ID number of a specific article, you can choose that option as well.

4. Click **Go** to find all the articles that match the search criteria you entered.

5. Scroll through the list of articles and click those that sound as if they might contain the answer you're looking for. If the list contains too many results, click your browser's **Back** button and narrow down your query.

Requesting Help from Newsgroups

Microsoft maintains threaded electronic bulletin boards called *newsgroups*, which cover a variety of support issues for all its products, including Windows 2000. Unlike the Knowledge Base, which contains official information organized by topic, newsgroups consist of free-flowing (and sometimes irrelevant) exchanges of information between users.

If you decide to take a question to a newsgroup, use these guidelines:

- Before you post a question, search through the newsgroup to see if your question has already been asked and answered.

- When posting a question, be as specific as possible and choose a subject line that clearly identifies the issue. One of the most common mistakes made by inexperienced newsgroup users is posting a question with a subject like `I need help!` You'll get better results with a subject like `CD-R drive won't record`.

Support the hard way

Whenever possible, I recommend that you try to find answers in online Help and on the Web before calling for assistance from Microsoft or your corporate Help Desk. With a reasonably fast Internet connection, it takes no more than a minute or two to search through the Knowledge Base. More often than not, other people have had the same problem as you, in which case a detailed solution may be available. Although some Knowledge Base topics are deeply technical, most are written in something fairly close to English.

Articles start with a Q

Every Knowledge Base article has a unique ID that starts with the letter Q, such as Q123456. When you search the Knowledge Base, most entries in the list of results start with the article ID. If you suspect you'll want to consult a Knowledge Base article again, make a note of its ID or save a shortcut to the Web page containing that article.

- Choose the right newsgroup. The `msnews.microsoft.com` server contains hundreds of subgroups, each covering a single topic. To ask questions about installing and configuring new devices, for example, choose `microsoft.public.win2000.hardware`.

- Remember that Microsoft employees do not monitor or run the newsgroups; instead, answers come from volunteers (called MVPs) and other users. The information you read here is not guaranteed to be accurate.

Keeping a List of Favorite Help Topics

How do you save a reference to a Help topic so that you can refer to it again? Add a shortcut to the Favorites tab on the navigation pane. These shortcuts give you quick access to step-by-step instructions for tasks that give you the most trouble—especially those that you use infrequently. For example, if you use the Windows 2000 Fax utility to send a fax every other month, you may need to consult Help each time.

Adding a Help topic to the Favorites tab

1. Open the Help topic you want to save.

2. In the navigation pane, click the **Favorites** tab. You see a dialog box like the one shown in Figure 3.6. Note that the Current Topic box contains the title of the topic you've chosen.

3. If you want to use your own words to identify the entry in the Favorites list, edit the text in the Current Topic box.

4. Click the **Add** button to store the shortcut in your Favorites list.

To read a saved topic, double-click its entry in the Favorites list, or select the entry and click the **Display** button. If you no longer want an item in the Favorites list, click the **Remove** button. You can't rename a topic; instead, add it using the new name, then remove the entry under the old name.

The Web changes

Don't be surprised if the page you see looks a little different from the one shown here. Microsoft regularly redesigns all its Web pages to make them more usable. Even if the look changes, however, the information in the Knowledge Base remains the same.

Pick one newsgroup

Microsoft's public news servers offer dozens of newsgroups that cover Windows 2000 topics. When you have a question, find the one newsgroup that seems like the best match for your question, and post it there. Do not send your question to several newsgroups (a practice called cross-posting), in hopes that you'll find the right one. If you do, expect to receive sharp criticism (or even *flames*) from other newsgroup participants for your breach of *Netiquette*.

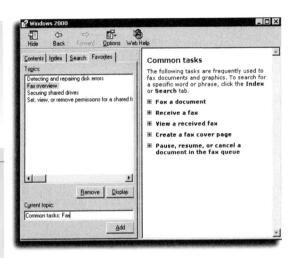

Use custom names

Get in the habit of saving useful Help topics to the Favorites list, and don't be afraid to rename them. Because the list is sorted in alphabetical order, you can use your own naming scheme to group related topics. Enter a prefix such as **Fax:**, for instance, to make sure all topics related to faxing appear consecutively in the list.

Paste problems?

Because Help topics are written in HTML, the information you copy and paste is also in this format. If email software on either end of the connection—yours or the person to whom you're sending the message—can't interpret HTML, some parts of the topic may not appear correctly. (Outlook Express, Outlook 98, and Outlook 2000 all handle HTML just fine.) Also, pop-up definitions and hyperlinks won't work correctly when pasted into another program.

Copying and Printing Help Topics

Do friends, family members, or co-workers ever call you for help with Windows questions? If an online Help topic answers their question with exactly the right wording or detail, try giving them a copy of the topic instead of trying to describe the solution yourself. You can copy the topic and paste it into an email message, or you can print one or more topics on paper.

Copying a Help topic to email

1. Open the Help topic you want to copy.
2. To copy only a portion of the topic, use the mouse to make a selection. To copy the entire Help topic, right-click and choose **Select All**.
3. Right-click and choose **Copy** from the shortcut menu.
4. Open your email program, create a new message, address it and give it a subject line.
5. Paste the copied information into the body of the message, add any notes of your own, and send the message.

Windows 2000 also allows you to print Help topics complete with all formatting and graphics (although hyperlinks obviously don't work). Open the topic you want to print, click the **Options** button on the toolbar, and then choose **Print**. If the Contents pane is visible, you'll see the dialog box shown in Figure 3.7. The default option prints a single topic, although you can also choose the paper-gobbling option to print all topics in a given heading.

FIGURE 3.7
Avoid the second option here unless you're certain you know how many topics are in the current heading.

SEE ALSO

➤ *For help setting up a new printer, see "Setting Up a Local Printer," p. 208.*

➤ *For information on how to manage print jobs, see "Managing Print Queues," p. 219.*

Print a portion

You can choose to print just a selection from a Help topic. This option is helpful if the topic has a useful set of step-by-step instructions that you want to tape to your monitor or pin on your bulletin board, but you don't need the explanation leading up to those instructions. Use the mouse to select the portion you want to print; then right-click and choose **Print** from the shortcut menu.

Controlling Access to Your Computer

How the Logon Process Works ●

Managing Users and Groups ●

Creating and Managing Passwords ●

Locking Your Computer ●

How the Logon Process Works

Why Ctrl+Alt+Del?

If you've used Windows 95 or MS-DOS, you know better than to press Ctrl+Alt+Del, because that key combination restarts the computer. Windows 2000, like previous versions of Windows NT, uses this combination of keys to eliminate the possibility that someone could display a Windows 2000-style logon dialog box on a computer running another operating system; by doing so, they could capture logon information from unsuspecting users and use it to break into systems. Pressing Ctrl+Alt+Del guarantees that the logon dialog box is genuine.

Who are you? In essence, that's the question you have to answer every time you start a computer that uses Windows 2000 as its operating system. The correct answer doesn't involve deep philosophical issues—all you have to do is enter a correct username and password when Windows 2000 displays the logon dialog box.

If your system is not connected to a Windows 2000 *domain*—if you're using Windows 2000 on a computer at your home or small business, for example—you can configure the system so that it logs you on automatically. In this configuration, you see the logon box flash by as your computer starts up, but Windows automatically enters the default username and password for you. For all other configurations, however, Windows 2000 displays a dialog box at startup, requesting that you press **Ctrl+Alt+Del** to log on. When you press these three keys simultaneously, you see the logon dialog box shown in Figure 4.1.

SEE ALSO

> To learn how to configure logon options when you first set up Windows 2000, see "Choosing a Network Configuration," p. 40.

You can't just pick a username and password out of the blue, nor does Windows 2000 allow you to bypass the logon dialog box by pressing Esc, as you can with Windows 95 and Windows 98. Instead, when you enter a username and password and click OK, Windows checks the values you entered against those stored in its database of authorized user accounts. If it finds a match, you get to log on. However, if you enter an invalid username or password, you see an error message and you have to try again.

FIGURE 4.1
You must enter an authorized username and password here before you can use a Windows 2000 computer.

This security step has two profound benefits:

- It keeps your data safe from unauthorized users. The only way someone can open files stored on your computer is to log on with your username and password.

- It allows two or more authorized users to share a computer without having to share data or personal settings. With minimal effort, you can set up your computer for access by another person and control that person's access to other users' data.

By default, Windows 2000 assumes you want to log on using an account on the local machine—that is, the computer you're sitting in front of right now. When you enter a username, Windows 2000 looks in the database of usernames stored on that machine. On a corporate network, however, you might be required to log in using an account stored on a network server. In that case, you need to enter not only your username, but the name of the domain as well.

SEE ALSO

➤ *For more details on the differences you encounter on a network, see "Windows 2000 and Your Corporate Network," p. 25.*

➤ *To learn more about using the Administrator's account or managing your user profile, see "Who's Managing Your Computer?" p. 20.*

Choose either of two ways to enter the domain when you log on:

- In the **User name** box, type in your username followed by @ and the domain name: bianca@marketing, for example, or ebott@phoenix.example.com.

- Click the **Options** button to display the expanded dialog box shown in Figure 4.2. Choose the correct domain (or the name of the local computer) from the **Log on to** list. If the username you entered in the first box contains the @ symbol, this box will be grayed out.

Three strikes, you're out?

In theory, a would-be data thief could sit down in front of your computer, enter your username, and then try one password after another, hoping to stumble onto the right one. (The thief's job would be even easier if you chose an easy password, such as your dog's name.) That's why, on many corporate networks, administrators define rules that lock users out after a certain number of failed attempts. If you forget your password and make too many incorrect guesses, the system will assume someone's trying to break in and lock out your account. If that happens, you'll have to go to your administrator and have the account unlocked. (If you're the administrator and you forget your password, however, you're out of luck!)

FIGURE 4.2
To log in with a user account set up on your corporate network, use this expanded dialog box.

69

Trouble logging on?

Does Windows refuse to log you on even though you know you're entering the correct password? The problem could be that you have two accounts with the same name but with different passwords—one on the network and the other on the local computer— and you've inadvertently selected the wrong location. Click the **Options** button to make sure the correct location is selected in the **Log on to** list.

When you've finished working on a shared computer, or when you want to log on as another user, press **Ctrl+Alt+Del** again and choose the **Log Off** option. Click **Yes** when asked if you're sure you want to log off. Windows shuts down all programs you're currently running, giving you the chance to save any open data files. When the process is complete, the machine is available for a new logon.

Managing Users and Groups

Every Windows 2000 computer includes a built-in Administrator account. As part of the initial setup process, you typically add at least one *user account*. Later, you can add more user accounts, assigning each to one or more *group accounts* to define the rights and permissions for each user.

Creating a New Local User Account

Groups help you manage

By definition, user accounts *inherit permissions* based on their membership in a group. Any member of the Backup Operators group, for example, has special access rights to files so that they can make backups without actually seeing the contents of a file. Group accounts are a time-saving management tool. If you assign rights every time you create a new user account, you'll spend hours going through dialog boxes and checking options. With groups, you set those options once and then move users in and out of groups to change all permissions at one time.

If you have *administrative rights* on your computer, you can log on and create or edit new user accounts on your local machine at any time. Say you're about to go on a vacation or a business trip, and while you're away, a co-worker needs to use your office. By setting up an account on your machine, you can give that person access to the computer while still keeping your personal settings and data safe.

Creating a new user account

1. Open Control Panel and double-click the **Users and Passwords** option.

2. If you're currently logged on as an ordinary user, Windows prompts you to enter the username and password for an account that belongs to the Administrators group on the local machine. After you enter the correct information and click **OK**, you see a list of all user accounts currently established on the local machine, like the one shown in Figure 4.3.

3. The next step is slightly different, depending on whether the local computer is part of a domain.

FIGURE 4.3
You can add, remove, and edit user accounts here, but only after you log on with an administrator's name and password.

No need to log off

If you're in the middle of another project, you can open the Users and Passwords utility without having to disturb any of your existing work. When you open the Users and Passwords option, Windows checks to see whether you're a member of the Administrators group. If you're not, you must enter an administrator's username and password to continue.

Are you on a domain?

It isn't always obvious whether the local machine belongs to a Windows 2000 domain. If you're not sure, open Control Panel, double-click the **System** icon, and look on the network identification tab. This dialog box displays the computer's full name and the name of the domain it belongs to, if any. If you see only a workgroup name, the computer doesn't belong to a domain.

- If the computer is not part of a domain, click the **Add** button to start the Add New User Wizard shown in Figure 4.4.

- If the computer is part of a network and the user you want to add already has a domain account, click the **Add** button. This starts a slightly different version of the Add New User Wizard, which allows you to add an account from the network directory to your local machine.

- If the computer is part of a network but the user you want to add does not have a domain account, don't click the **Add** button. Instead, go to the **Advanced** tab in the Users and Passwords dialog box. Click the **Advanced** button to open the Local Users and Groups window, click the **Users** icon in the left pane, and then choose **Action**, **New User**. This opens the dialog box shown in Figure 4.5. Unlike the Add New User Wizard, you enter all information in one location.

4. Enter the name you want the new account to use; if you're adding a domain account to your local machine, include the domain name, too. The username must not be currently in use on the machine. Usernames are not case sensitive, so you can safely enter any combination of capital and lowercase letters.

FIGURE 4.4
This wizard steps you through the process of creating a new user account.

FIGURE 4.5
This version of the Add New User dialog box appears if you begin with the Local Users and Groups utility.

Pick a different machine name

You may be tempted to use the same name for your machine as for your main user account. Don't do it. Although Windows 2000 will allow you to create this configuration, you're almost certain to run into trouble later when the rest of the network has trouble figuring out the difference between JANEDOE the machine and JANEDOE the user. Try JANEDOE-PC as the computer name instead.

5. In the Add New User Wizard, click the **Next** button and enter a password for the account. Set other password options at this step, if you want. (If you used the Local Users and Groups option to create a new user, password options are on the same dialog box as the username.)

6. If the wizard is available, click the **Next** button to specify which group you want to use for the new account, as shown in Figure 4.6, and click **OK** to create the account. If the wizard is not available, click **OK**; the new account is automatically added to the Users group.

FIGURE 4.6
When you create a new user account with the wizard's help, you can specify which group the new account belongs to.

SEE ALSO

➤ *For advice on how to create effective passwords, see "Creating and Managing Passwords," p. 75.*

Assigning Users to Groups

Are you puzzled by which group to specify when creating a new account? Follow these guidelines for using the built-in Windows 2000 group accounts:

- Choose the **Standard User** option if you want to allow anyone who logs on with the new account to save data, install new programs, and reset system options such as the date and time. This option adds the user account to the Power Users group. A user in this group cannot open other users' data files if those files are stored on an *NTFS volume*.
- Choose the **Restricted User** option to allow anyone who logs on with the new account to run programs and access his or her own data. This option adds the user account to the built-in Users group. Users in this group cannot install new programs or change system settings.

What's in a name?

A username can be up to 64 characters long (although I strongly recommend that you keep usernames to 15 characters or fewer) and can consist of any combination of letters, numbers, and most symbols (but not the @ sign). Although it's perfectly legal to use a space as part of a username, I strongly recommend that you not do so. Spaces can wreak havoc with programs and network protocols that pass this information back and forth in ways that are different from the Windows 2000 standard. Instead of a space, try using the underscore character: Ed_Bott, for example.

**Restricted means
just that**

Use the **Restricted User**
option when you want to
prevent an inexperienced
user from getting into trouble accidentally. Because
users in this group can't
install programs, another
user in the Administrators
or Power Users group must
set up all programs.

**Remove or disable
unused accounts**

If you're concerned enough
about security to create
separate accounts for different users, then you
should also take care to
promptly remove accounts
that are no longer needed.
If you set up an account for
use by an employee,
remove the account when
that employee leaves.
Removing the account pre-
vents that user from log-
ging on later, when they
have no right to do so.
Disabling an account is a
good idea when you have
an account that is used
infrequently. For example,
if you have a temp come in
every quarter to help with
accounting chores, create
an account for that person,
but leave it disabled.
Enable the account while
the user is in the office,
and disable it again after
the temporary task is
finished.

- In most cases, you should avoid the **Other** option. One noteworthy exception is when you want to add the new account to
  the Administrators group—for example, so that you can delegate
  management duties to another person.

SEE ALSO

➤ *For advice on when to use the Administrators group, see "Who's Managing Your Computer?"*
  p. 20.

Editing, Deleting, and Disabling User Accounts

As an administrator, you can view all local user accounts at any time.
With Control Panel's Users and Passwords option, you can change
the settings for an account (including its password) or remove it permanently. It's also possible to disable an account temporarily,
although this option takes extra work.

- To change an account's settings, select its entry in the list of user
  accounts and click **Properties**. You can change the group to
  which an account belongs or change the password for any
  account except the one you're currently using.

- To remove an account permanently, select its entry in the list of
  user accounts and click **Remove**.

To disable an account temporarily, you must use the Local Users and
Groups management utility.

Disabling an account temporarily

1. Open the **Users and Passwords** option in Control Panel. You
   may be required to supply the name and password of an account
   in the Administrators group.

2. In the Users and Passwords dialog box, click the **Advanced** tab;
   then click the **Advanced** button to open the Local Users and
   Groups utility.

3. In the left tree pane, select the Users icon. In the right pane,
   select the account you want to disable.

4. Right-click and choose **Properties**. The Properties dialog box
   for the selected account appears, as shown in Figure 4.7.

FIGURE 4.7
Disable an account if you want it to be unavailable now but expect that you might want to reuse it later.

5. Check the **Account is disabled** box and then click **OK** to save the changes.

When an account is disabled, its icon appears in the Local Users and Groups window with a red X over it. Anyone trying to log on to a disabled account sees an error message that instructs them to contact the system administrator.

Working with the Guest Account

Windows 2000 includes a built-in Guest account, designed to allow a casual user to log on to a machine without the need to get his or her own account. This option might be useful if you set up a computer in a central location for visitors to use when accessing the Internet.

By default, the Guest account is disabled. If you want to turn it on, follow the procedures listed in the previous section for disabling an account; in the final step, clear the **Account is disabled** check box.

Creating and Managing Passwords

Your password functions as the key that unlocks your personal settings and data files. If another person learns your password, he or she has the capability to log on to your account. In a one-person office,

Locked out?

Just below the **Account is disabled** box in the user account's Properties dialog box is a check box labeled **Account is locked out**. This setting is not directly controlled by an administrator; instead, it kicks in when the administrator sets a *group policy* that governs unsuccessful logon attempts. If your administrator has turned on this policy and someone repeatedly tries to access your account with an incorrect password, the system automatically turns on this option. Only an administrator can turn it off.

that might not be important. On a corporate network, however, giving a stranger access to your account could put confidential data at risk. If security is an issue for you, pay close attention to password settings.

What Makes a Good Password?

Ideally, a password should be impossible for another person to guess, but easy enough for you to remember, The most common mistake people make when selecting a password is to choose a word that exists in a standard dictionary—even the most inexperienced hacker can use a password "cracker"—software that runs through all the entries in a dictionary looking for a match. An even worse password is the kind that anyone who knows about you could guess: your name or the name of your spouse, a child, or a pet; your birthday; your favorite sports team; or the word *password*.

Security experts recommend that you follow these guidelines to create safe passwords:

- Make it at least 7 characters long. Anything shorter is too easy to guess.

- Include a mix of capital letters, lowercase letters, numbers, and symbols. A password like **3Yz$1ptn** is nearly impossible to "crack."

- If you must write down your password, put it in a safe place where only you can access it, such as your wallet or purse. Don't leave a note containing your password in a desk drawer or stuck to your monitor.

- Avoid the temptation to share your password with another person. If you have to do so because of an emergency, change it as soon as you can.

- If you have an account in the Administrators group and a regular user account, use different passwords for each one. Never use the administrative password for any other purpose, especially for access to Web sites.

One password for all logons

Windows 2000 uses a "single logon" system—when you log on to a domain using an authorized username and password, you unlock access to all resources on the network. Although this eliminates the hassle you might face if you had to keep entering a password every time you accessed another server, it increases your responsibility to keep your account details secure.

Check the Caps Lock key

Is Windows telling you your password is incorrect? Passwords are case sensitive; if you inadvertently press the Caps Lock key, you'll enter the password in ALL CAPS and it won't match the version stored in the user database. Turn off the Caps Lock key and try again.

- Change your password frequently—at least every 90 days. If you suspect that another person may know your password, change it immediately.

- Some Windows and Internet Explorer dialog boxes offer to store your password for reuse later. Never choose this option to save the password for your network logon or local Administrator account.

Choosing Initial Password Settings

As part of the process of creating a new user account, Windows 2000 allows an administrator to set some password options. When logged on as Administrator, you can change any local user's password, and you can also specify what happens the first time a user logs on with that account.

Look at the four check boxes in the New User dialog box, shown previously in Figure 4.5. Use these check boxes according to the following guidelines:

- **You want to give the new user a temporary password and force them to select their own password.** Enter a password and check the **User must change password at next logon** box. The first time the user logs on using the password you created, Windows 2000 will display the Change Password dialog box and require the user to choose a new password.

- **You want to give the new user a secure password, without allowing them to replace it with an easier one.** Enter a password and check the **User cannot change password** box. If the user tries to use the Change Password option, Windows will display a dialog box informing the user that he or she doesn't have permission to do so.

- **You want to force the user to change passwords at regular intervals.** Clear the **Password never expires** check box. With this check box cleared, users are required to change the password every 42 days. This option is not available if you check the **User must change password at next logon** box.

Choose one option only

The first two password check boxes are mutually exclusive. If you check the **User must change password at next logon** box, the **User cannot change password** box is grayed out, and vice versa.

77

Changing Passwords

To change your own password, log on and press **Ctrl+Alt+Del**. In the Windows Security dialog box, choose the **Change Password** option. This opens the Change Password dialog box shown in Figure 4.8. Enter your old password as well as the new one and click **OK** to confirm the change.

FIGURE 4.8
When you log on using a network account, the Change Password dialog box lets you choose between local and network user accounts.

To change the password for a different local user account, log on using an administrative account and open the **Users and Passwords** option in Control Panel. Select the name of the user account from the list and then click the **Set Password** button. Enter the new password and click **OK** to record the change. This change is effective the next time a user logs on with that account.

Locking Your Computer

After you log on with your username and password, you have access to all your personal data and user settings. Unfortunately, if you walk away from your desk, anyone who sits down in front of your computer also has access to that data. If you plan to be away for more than a few minutes, it's always a good idea to lock your computer.

To lock your computer, press **Ctrl+Alt+Del** and click the **Lock Computer** option. Windows 2000 displays the dialog box shown in Figure 4.9, preventing anyone else from getting to your work. To regain access to your computer, press **Ctrl+Alt+Del** and enter your password when prompted.

Log off or lock?

What's the difference between logging off and locking your computer? Logging off closes all programs and data files. When you return to your desk, you can't just get back to work—you have to log on again and restart all your programs. By locking your computer, however, you keep all running programs in memory. When you return and enter your password, you can get right back to work.

FIGURE 4.9
Lock your computer
when you plan to step
away for more than a
few minutes.

SEE ALSO

➤ *For instructions on how to automatically lock your computer after a set interval, see "Using a Screen Saver," p. 205.*

part

II

WORKING WITH WINDOWS 2000

chapter

5

Installing and Running Programs

Before You Install a New Program...

Look for the logo

Before purchasing new software, check its specifications carefully. In particular, look for the Windows 2000 logo on the box or on the software company's Web site. That logo means the product has been tested by Microsoft and is certified to run correctly with Windows 2000. If you don't see the logo, the software may still run correctly, although you may need to install a *patch* or update to resolve minor incompatibilities. Check the manufacturer's Web site before trying to install any software without a Windows 2000 logo.

If you've recently upgraded from Windows 95 or Windows 98 to Windows 2000, you're probably accustomed to installing new software programs with relative ease. (Getting them to work properly, of course, is another issue.) With Windows 2000, you have two hurdles to overcome before you can even think about installing a new program:

- **Compatibility.** Many programs that work just fine under Windows 95 or 98 will fail when you try to run them under Windows 2000. Communications programs, games, and disk utilities are especially likely to fall into this category.

- **Permissions.** System administrators can typically install any software program on any computer running Windows 2000. If you don't have administrative rights on your PC, you might get an error message when you try to install certain programs, or the installation might fail to complete properly. In some cases, you may find that certain features of a program don't work properly if you install it using an account that doesn't have administrative rights.

SEE ALSO

➤ *For an overview of what a system administrator can and can't do, see "Who's Managing Your Computer?" p. 20.*

➤ *To learn how Windows 2000 user accounts work, see "Managing Users and Groups" p. 70.*

How does it know?

Windows 2000 uses a simple test to determine that you're trying to install a program. If you run a program named `Setup.exe` or `Install.exe` (either by double-clicking an icon or inserting a CD that automatically runs a program), it steps in and displays the warning dialog box shown here. When the setup routine starts with a different program name, however, such as `Setupw.exe`, Windows 2000 doesn't get involved at all.

In some cases, the setup routine for a new program will notice that you're using Windows 2000 and will pop up a warning dialog box or even prevent you from installing the program at all. Even when setup goes smoothly, however, you may see a compatibility dialog box like the one shown in Figure 5.1—it warns that Adobe PhotoDeluxe version 1.0 (PD.EXE, as identified in the title bar) requires an upgrade to run properly.

If you try to install a new program while you're logged on without administrative rights, you may see the dialog box shown in Figure 5.2.

FIGURE 5.1
If a program is incompatible with Windows 2000, you'll see this dialog box when you try to run it. Click the **Details** button for suggestions on how to fix the problem.

FIGURE 5.2
Whenever possible, run software installation programs using an administrator's account rather than an ordinary user account.

Use the defaults

As a general rule, I recommend that you use the default location specified by the Setup routine unless you have a good reason for changing it. If the folder is already in the Program Files hierarchy, leave it there. However, you can and should overrule programs that insist on dumping their files in top-level folders—if Adobe Acrobat wants to create folders called `C:\Acrobat`, you have every right to specify `C:\Program Files\Acrobat` as the new location instead. Choosing that location keeps your disk from getting cluttered.

Installing and Running Windows Programs

For all but the simplest applications, the setup process involves five separate steps. When you run a program called Setup or Install, it handles the following details:

- The setup routine creates one or more folders to store the files that actually run the program. Logically enough, this location is usually a subfolder beneath the Program Files folder, located on the same drive as the Windows 2000 system files.

- Next, it copies the collection of files that actually run the program. This includes not only the executable file, but support files, sample data, fonts, and other elements that the program needs.

- Most setup routines make entries in the *Windows Registry* that control how the program runs and define default preferences for you.

SEE ALSO

➤ *To learn about the Windows Registry and how to safely view and edit it, see "Working with the Windows Registry," p. 451.*

- Setup creates *associations* between the program and its *file types*. As part of the installation routine, for example, Microsoft Word orders Windows to open Word whenever you double-click a Word document file that uses the extension .doc.

SEE ALSO

➤ *To learn how to view and edit all file associations, see "Changing Associations Between Files and Programs," p. 156.*

- Finally, Setup creates one or more *program shortcuts* you use to start the program. Typical setup routines add shortcuts to the Programs menu. Really aggressive setup routines also splatter shortcuts on the desktop and the Quick Launch bar and install icons in the tray at the right of the taskbar.

SEE ALSO

➤ *To learn how to customize the Start menu, see "Organizing the Start Menu for Maximum Efficiency," p. 187.*

➤ *For instructions on how to add, remove, and change shortcuts on the Quick Launch bar, see "Putting Favorite Programs on the Quick Launch Bar," p. 193.*

Moving any but the simplest program is next to impossible. You can't just copy a folder full of program files from one computer to another, or even to another location on the same hard disk. If you want to install a program on a new computer, find the original installation disks and run the setup routine again. To move a program's files from one location to another on your computer, uninstall it first, and then run the Setup program again.

Installing a Program from CD or Floppy Disks

Some installation programs run automatically, as soon as you insert the CD into the drive. The AutoPlay feature works because the CD contains a file called Autorun, which Windows 2000 recognizes and runs automatically.

If nothing happens when you insert the CD, or if the program is on floppy disks, you'll have to find the setup program (it's typically called Setup or Install) on the CD or floppy disk and run it yourself.

Settling Setup duels

It's all too common for two programs to fight over the rights to a given file type. Netscape Navigator and Internet Explorer are notorious for grabbing file associations so that each opens every conceivable type of Web page. Typically, the winner is whichever setup program ran most recently. That's why, when file associations need repair, your first step should be to reinstall the program that controls those associations.

Use Control Panel's Add/Remove Programs option to automate this process. Although it takes an extra step or two, this option can be a lot less hassle when the setup program is hidden among hundreds of files on the CD.

Installing a new program

1. Click the **Start** button, open the **S̲ettings** menu, and click **C̲ontrol Panel**.

2. Double-click the **Add/Remove Programs** icon to open the Add/Remove Programs dialog box.

3. Click the **Add New Programs** icon in the left pane of the dialog box to display the Add New Programs screen shown in Figure 5.3.

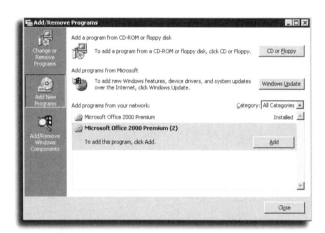

4. Click the **CD or F̲loppy** button and follow the wizard's prompts as it looks for the setup program. If the wizard can't find the program (because it's in a subfolder on the CD, for example, or because it's stored on a local or network drive), click the **B̲rowse** button on the final screen to specify the folder where the setup program is located.

5. Click the **Finish** button to run the setup program you found.

SEE ALSO

➤ *For details on how to install and uninstall Windows 2000 options, see "Adding and Removing Windows Components," p. 449.*

This works for down-loads, too

Don't let the wording of the **CD or F̲loppy** button fool you. You can also use this feature to set up a program that you've downloaded to your own hard drive or to a shared folder on a network server.

FIGURE 5.3
Click the **CD or F̲loppy** button to search for a setup program.

How to turn off AutoPlay

If you don't want a setup program to run automatically when you insert a CD, temporarily disable AutoPlay by holding down the **Shift** key as you place the disk in the drive. Because AutoPlay is the default action for that CD, don't double-click its icon in the My Computer window, either—instead, right-click the **CD** icon and choose **O̲pen** or **E̲xplore** from the shortcut menu to view all the files on the CD.

Installing a Program from the Network

On a corporate network, your administrator can eliminate the need for floppy disks and CDs and allow you to install programs from a central location on the network. If any such programs are available to you, you'll see them listed in the box at the bottom of the Add/Remove Programs dialog box (shown previously in Figure 5.3). In fact, some programs configured this way will install automatically on your computer. The exact behavior you see depends on how your network administrator has configured the installation program.

Your network administrator may have made two types of program files available on the network:

- *Published programs* are available to you if you want or need them. To install a program, select its entry from the Add/Remove Programs list and click the **Add** button. The program installs automatically if you double-click a file associated with that program; if someone sends you an Excel worksheet and Excel isn't available on the system where you try to open it, Windows will find the Excel setup files on the network, install the program for you, and open the file. Be patient—with some programs this process can take 10 minutes or more.

- *Assigned programs* are those that the system administrator has decided are essential to members of a group or users of a particular machine. Each time you log on to a Windows *domain*, the server checks the list of currently available programs with those assigned to your user account; if any are missing or damaged, Windows installs or repairs them automatically before letting you log in.

Running Programs

To run a program, use the shortcut that its setup routine created—typically on your Programs menu. If you know the name of the program's executable file, you can type it into the Run box or in a Command Prompt window. To start the Windows Calculator without using the Programs menu, for example, click the **Start** button and choose **Run**. In the Run dialog box, type `calc`, and click **OK** or press **Enter**.

Installing and Running MS-DOS Programs

Older programs written for MS-DOS require special considerations at installation time. As with Windows programs, incompatibility is a common problem. In particular, many games and system utilities will not work. Other programs have problems because they were designed to run on machines that are slow by today's standards, and their timing routines fail to run properly.

MS-DOS programs run in an MS-DOS emulation window, sometimes called a "DOS box."

Like earlier Windows versions, Windows 2000 stores configuration information for MS-DOS applications in Program Information Files (often called PIFs). To change any of these options, right-click the program's icon and choose **Properties**. Figure 5.4 shows the Program tab of a typical PIF; settings here let you change the name of the shortcut and the executable file to which it refers, set a different startup folder, and specify whether to run in a window or in full-screen mode.

Other tabs on the PIF Properties dialog box let you set memory, multitasking, and font options. The Font tab is especially useful for character-based MS-DOS applications you plan to run in a window. By selecting a different font size here, you can compress a full-screen program into a small window or bump up the font size so that it's easier to read.

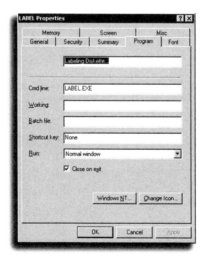

Choose full screen or window

Normally, MS-DOS programs run in a window; to expand the program window so that it fills up the entire screen, press **Alt+Enter**. To restore the program to a window, press **Alt+Enter** again. When a program is running in full-screen mode, you can switch to other running programs or open windows using the **Alt+Tab** shortcut.

Use the Troubleshooter

If an MS-DOS program is giving you fits, try using a troubleshooting utility built into the online Help. Search for the **MS-DOS programs Troubleshooter** and run through its exhaustive diagnostic routines and its list of suggested fixes.

FIGURE 5.4
Shortcuts to MS-DOS programs include extra tabs that allow you to adjust memory, fonts, and other settings not required by Windows programs.

Stay away from the Repair folder

You'll also find copies of `Autoexec.nt` and `Config.nt` in the Repair folder, under C:\Winnt (along with many other system files). Do not modify any files in this folder! These files are intended for use by Windows 2000's Emergency Recovery Disk utility, and changing these copies will have no effect on programs you run.

What do the % signs mean?

Windows 2000 includes a large number of *system variables* that programs use as a form of shorthand. The `%systemroot%` variable is a convenient way to find the folder that contains your Windows 2000 program files, regardless of which drive it's on or what the folder is actually named. On a typical system, those files are in `C:\Winnt`; if you customize your Windows 2000 installation, however, the equivalent folder might be in `F:\Windows2K`. By entering the variable name, you can count on Windows to find and open the right folder, regardless of where it's located.

If your MS-DOS program normally requires special settings in the `Autoexec.bat` and `Config.sys` files, you need to make some special adjustments for Windows 2000. If you want these settings to be available to all MS-DOS programs, edit the `Autoexec.nt` and `Config.nt` files; you'll find these two files in the System32 folder, beneath the folder that contains your system files (typically `C:\Winnt`). To add MS-DOS configuration settings that apply to only one program, follow these instructions:

Creating a custom MS-DOS configuration

1. Click the **Start** button and choose **Run**. In the Run dialog box, type `notepad` and click **OK** or press **Enter**.

2. In the Notepad window, pull down the **File** menu and choose **Open**. In the **File name** box, enter `%systemroot%\System32\Autoexec.nt` (be sure to include the percent signs). Click the **Open** button.

3. Make any required changes to the `Autoexec.nt` file.

4. Pull down the **File** menu and choose **Save As**. In the **Save in** box, choose the folder that contains the files for your MS-DOS program, and then click the **Save** button. Be careful that you don't replace the original file!

5. Repeat steps 2 through 4 for `Config.nt`.

6. Right-click the PIF icon for the MS-DOS program and choose **Properties**. In the Properties dialog box, click the **Program** tab, and click the **Windows NT** button.

7. Edit the paths shown in the Windows PIF Settings dialog box so that they point to the two new files you just saved. Note that you must enter the full paths manually; no Browse button is available.

8. If your MS-DOS program runs erratically, check the **Compatible timer hardware emulation** box. Click **OK** to close the dialog box. Your custom MS-DOS program is now ready to run.

Creating Shortcuts to Favorite Programs

The easiest way to start a program is to use one of the shortcuts created when you first set it up. It's not always the fastest way, however—especially when the shortcut is buried under three or more layers of cascading menus. The worst example in Windows 2000 is the group of programs that collectively makes up the Fax group. It takes six clicks to create a one-page fax: Click the **Start** button, open the **Programs** menu, and then work your way through the Accessories, Communications, and Fax groups before you finally reach the shortcuts. If you send several faxes a week, that's way too many clicks.

SEE ALSO

➤ *For more details about Windows 2000's fax capabilities, see "Using Windows to Send and Receive Faxes," p. 222.*

To make yourself more productive, I recommend two simple steps: First, gather the shortcuts you use most often and put them where you can get to them quickly. Next, rearrange the shortcuts to programs you use less frequently so that they're accessible without cluttering things up.

In general, you can choose from four common locations for program shortcuts:

- **The Start menu.** When you drag an icon and drop it on the Start button, Windows adds a shortcut at the top of the Start menu.

- **The Programs menu.** Most setup routines create their own folder within the Programs menu and organize all their shortcuts within this group. (Microsoft Office is a noteworthy exception; by default, it dumps all its shortcuts into the Programs menu itself.) Feel free to move, copy, and delete these shortcuts so that their organization helps you work more productively.

- **The Quick Launch bar.** This area, located just to the right of the Start button, holds pint-sized shortcut icons that are always visible.

- **The Desktop.** Windows 2000 stores system objects such as the My Computer and My Documents icons here. You can add your own shortcuts as well.

Careful with those keys!

Assigning keyboard shortcuts is a great way to access the handful of programs you use regularly. Be careful with the key combinations you use, however. If another program uses a key combination you assign to a program shortcut, it will no longer be available in that program. For instance, Microsoft Word uses Ctrl+Alt+*number* to apply the styles Heading 1, Heading 2, and so on. Likewise, Microsoft Excel uses Ctrl+Alt+F9 to calculate all sheets in the current workbook. If you use a particular program's keyboard shortcut regularly, don't use that shortcut for a program.

You can also define shortcut key combinations that let you start a program shortcut without using the mouse. For instance, you might want to pop up the Windows Calculator by pressing **Ctrl+Alt+C**. Here's how:

Assigning a shortcut key to a program

1. Locate the program shortcut on the Start menu, the Programs menu, or the desktop. (If you try to assign a key combination to a program shortcut in any other folder, Windows will ignore it.)

2. Right-click the shortcut icon and choose **Properties**.

3. Click in the **Shortcut key** box and press the key combination you want to use to launch the program. All such keyboard shortcuts use Ctrl+Alt plus a letter, number, punctuation mark, or function key. You can use the Shift key, but not the spacebar, Esc, Enter, Tab, Print Screen, or Backspace keys.

4. Click **OK** to save the new shortcut key.

5. Test the key combination to make sure it works. To change a shortcut key, repeat steps 1 through 4. To remove a shortcut key, click in the **Shortcut key** box and press the spacebar.

SEE ALSO

➤ For step-by-step instructions on how to rearrange the Start menu, see "Organizing the Start Menu for Maximum Efficiency," p. 187.

➤ For advice on how to make best use of the desktop, see "Personalizing the Windows Interface," p. 170.

➤ To learn how to customize the Quick Launch bar, see "Putting Favorite Programs on the Quick Launch Bar," p. 193.

If you've successfully installed a program, but you can't find its shortcut—perhaps because you deleted it by accident—you can easily re-create it. To do so, you need to know the name of the program's executable file.

Finding a program file

1. Click the **Start** button, click the **Search** option, and choose **For Files or Folders** from the cascading menu.

2. If you know all or part of the program name you're looking for, enter it in the **Search for files or folders named** box. Otherwise, enter `*.exe` here.

3. Click the drop-down arrow at the right of the **Look in** box and choose **Browse** from the bottom of the menu. In the Browse

dialog box, select the folder that contains the program you installed; this location is usually (but not always) in the Program Files folder.

4. Click the **Search Now** button. Files that match the criteria you specified appear in the Search Results pane at the right.

5. Select the icon for the program's executable file, hold down the right mouse button, and drag the icon onto the desktop. Choose **Create Shortcut(s) Here**.

6. If you prefer, move the shortcut from the desktop to another location—on the Start menu or the Quick Launch bar, for example.

If you're not certain what the program's executable file is called or where it's located, search for files named *.exe on all local hard drives. The list will be huge, but you can narrow it down with three logical tests:

- First, look at the program icons in the Search Results window to see if you recognize the one you're looking for.

- Second, sort the list alphabetically and focus on those that begin with the same name as your program.

- Third, if you suspect that a file is the right one but you're not sure, right-click, choose **Properties**, and check the Version tab. Figure 5.5, for example, shows that the file called Pm40nt is actually Partition Magic for Windows NT.

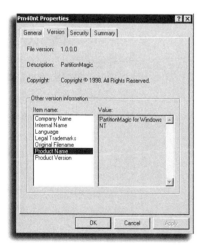

Try the tray, too!
Many programs add tiny icons in the *notification area* (sometimes referred to as the *system tray*) at the right of the taskbar, just to the left of the system clock. These icons typically provide quick access to the programs they work with; for example, Real Networks' RealPlayer utility adds a tray icon that allows you to open the RealPlayer and tune in to *streaming media* broadcasts from the Internet. Right-click any tray icon to see its shortcut menu; double-click the icon to choose the default menu option (shown in bold on the right-click shortcut menu).

FIGURE 5.5
Puzzled by a program icon? Find its name and other important details on the Version tab of this dialog box.

Changing the Way a Program Shortcut Works

You can customize any program shortcut, regardless of whether you created it or a setup routine placed it in your Programs menu. To see the options available to you, right-click the shortcut icon and choose **Properties**. Figure 5.6 shows the Properties dialog box of a typical program shortcut.

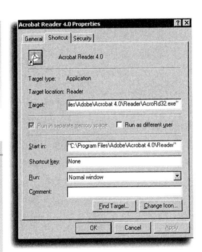

FIGURE 5.6
Adjust these options to change the way a program shortcut works.

Quick access to properties

If a shortcut is anywhere on your Start menu, you can get access to its properties directly, without having to open a new folder window. Click the **Start** button and find the shortcut you want to adjust; if necessary, click the **Programs** menu and look in individual program groups until you find the right icon. Point to the shortcut, right-click, and choose **Properties**.

- **Target.** The name and (optionally) *path* of the file to which the shortcut points. You should never need to edit this setting; if you move the target file for any reason, it's usually easier to re-create the shortcut.

- **Start in.** Defines the folder that the program uses for opening and saving files. By default, most programs open the folder that contains the program files; customizing this option can save you time and frustration when you're ready to open or save data files.

- **Shortcut key.** Defines a key combination you can use to start the program.

- **Run.** Allows you to specify whether you want the program to start minimized as a taskbar icon or maximized to a full screen. The default setting, Normal window, remembers the window size you last used for that program.

- **Comment.** Text in this box appears as part of the *ScreenTip* (sometimes referred to as a *ToolTip*)—the description that pops up when you let the mouse pointer hover over a shortcut icon.

- **Find Target.** Click this button to open a window showing the contents of the folder that contains the target file.

- **Change Icon.** Allows you to specify a different icon for a short-cut. Figure 5.7 shows some of the alternate icons available for Norton AntiVirus 2000, for example.

FIGURE 5.7
Pick an icon, any icon. Use this dialog box to assign a new icon to a shortcut, using any of the icons stored in the target file.

- **Run in separate memory space.** Choose this option only if you have problems with an older Windows program that crashes frequently. It won't stop the crashes, but it will keep the program crash from affecting other programs.

- **Run as different user.** Allows you to enter a different username and password so that you can run a program with a different set of *user rights*. This option is most useful for utilities that will run properly only when you have administrative privileges.

Running More Than One Program at a Time

Windows allows you to open one program after another until you run out of memory. On the one hand, that's a big advantage, because you can switch back and forth between projects without having to go through the hassle of shutting down and restarting programs. On the other hand, it can be confusing when you have 10 or 20 windows open at a time.

Go ahead, open another window...

If you've recently upgraded from Windows 95 or Windows 98 to Windows 2000, you probably have at least one painful memory of a system crash that wiped out every running program. Windows 2000 is far more reliable than those other Windows versions. Its basic design makes it nearly impossible for one program to crash the entire system, which means you can safely open as many windows as your available memory will allow. Of course, it's still a good idea to save files often and back up data regularly.

Windows 2000 includes some convenient shortcuts to help you switch from one program to another. It also includes several useful ways to arrange windows on the screen so that you can work with two windows at the same time.

Switching Between Running Programs

Every running program has its own taskbar button. Click any button to bring that window to the front and begin working with it. Click again to minimize the selected window.

To switch quickly among all running programs, hold down the **Alt** key and tap the **Tab** key. As long as you continue to hold down the Alt key, you'll see a window like the one shown in Figure 5.8, with icons representing each taskbar button. Tap the **Tab** key again to move to the next icon in the list—the text at the bottom of the window identifies each icon. Release the **Alt** key to switch to the selected window.

Which button is which?

If you have more than a handful of windows open at one time, the taskbar can become so crowded that you can't tell which window goes with a given button. When that happens, use the ScreenTips to get more information. Let the mouse pointer hover over a taskbar button for a second or two, and a text box will pop up, displaying the contents of the window's title bar.

FIGURE 5.8
Hold down the **Alt** key and press **Tab** to cycle through all open windows.

Resizing and Arranging Program Windows

Every Windows program can be arranged in one of three configurations:

- **A normal window.** Click and drag the title bar to move a window around on the screen. Aim the mouse pointer at any border until it turns to a double-headed arrow and drag it to resize the window.

- **Maximized.** In this configuration, the window occupies the entire screen. You can't move it or resize it, although you can switch to other windows, which then appear in front of the maximized window.

- **Minimized.** When you minimize a window, it is no longer visible on the screen; however, its taskbar button remains.

The three small buttons at the right edge of the title bar let you minimize, maximize, or close a window. If a program is maximized, the middle button lets you restore it to a normal window.

You can also use shortcut menus on the taskbar and on individual taskbar buttons to minimize, maximize, and restore program windows. However, these menus are much more useful when you want to arrange two or more windows next to one another so that you can work with their contents simultaneously.

Like previous Windows versions, Windows 2000 lets you right-click any empty portion of the taskbar and display the shortcut menu shown in Figure 5.9. Choose either of the **Tile Windows** options to arrange all currently visible windows horizontally or vertically. (The **Cascade Windows** menu choice arranges all windows in a stack, with only the title bars of the windows in back visible; for all practical purposes, this option is useless.)

The trouble with tiling windows using the taskbar menu is that you have to make sure every window is minimized, then restore only those you want to tile, and then (finally) tile the windows. With Windows 2000, unlike previous Windows versions, there's an easier way. This technique comes in handy when moving or copying files between two windows; it's also useful when you want to display two browser windows side by side so that you can compare the contents of similar Web pages. Follow these steps:

Arranging two windows side by side

1. Select the taskbar button for the first window you want to tile.

2. Hold down the **Ctrl** key and click the taskbar button for each additional window you want to tile.

3. Right-click any of the selected buttons to display the shortcut menu shown in Figure 5.10.

Use the title bar

Many longtime Windows users are unaware of one of the most useful Windows shortcuts of all: Instead of squinting to hit the tiny boxes in the top-right corner of a window, just double-click anywhere on the title bar. On a normal window, this shortcut maximizes the window. If the window is already maximized, double-clicking the title bar restores the program to a window that you can move or resize.

FIGURE 5.9
Choosing either **Tile** option rearranges all visible windows (those that aren't minimized). Be sure to minimize windows you don't plan to work with.

Undo to the rescue

If you use one of the **Tile** options from the taskbar shortcut menu with more than two or three windows visible, the result is usually a mess, resulting in a bunch of windows that are too small to work with comfortably. When this happens to you, press the Undo shortcut, **Ctrl+Z**, to restore all windows to their previous size and position.

4. Choose **Tile <u>H</u>orizontally** to arrange the selected windows, one on top of the other; choose **Tile <u>V</u>ertically** to arrange them side by side.

FIGURE 5.10

This shortcut menu, new in Windows 2000, appears only when you select two or more taskbar buttons by holding down the **Ctrl** key and clicking.

Using the Keyboard to Manage Program Windows

If your keyboard includes a Windows key, use it in the following combinations to save a surprising number of keystrokes:

Table 5.1 Windows key shortcuts

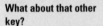

Press the Windows Key +	To Perform This Function
By itself	Display the Start menu
D	Minimize/restore all open windows
E	Open My Computer
F	Open the Search window
F1	Open Windows Help
R	Open the Run dialog box

What about that other key?

Some keyboards, such as the Microsoft Natural Keyboard, include a pair of Windows keys, one on either side of the spacebar; they may also include an extra key, usually to the right of the right-side Windows key, that contains an icon resembling a mouse pointer and a menu. This key pops up the shortcut menu for the currently selected object. Unless you're a keyboard whiz, you'll rarely need to use this key—the right-mouse button is quicker.

Troubleshooting Problems with Programs

It's a fact of life: all programs contain bugs. Most of the time, the bugs are minor and crop up only in rare circumstances. Sometimes, however, a bug can cause a program to run very slowly or even to stop responding completely. When this happens, you should immediately try to save any data you're working on and close the program. If it stops responding completely, you'll need to use the Windows 2000 Task Manager to shut it down.

The Task Manager is a three-tabbed dialog box that displays information about all running programs and services, as well as statistics about the amount of memory and processor time your system is currently using. The quickest way to display the Task Manager is to right-click any empty part of the taskbar and choose **Task Manager** from the shortcut menu. Click the **Applications** tab to see a list such as the one shown in Figure 5.11.

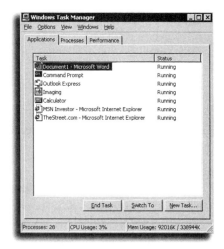

FIGURE 5.11
The Task Manager shows this list of all running programs. When a program stops responding, use the **End Task** button to close it immediately.

Look at the entry in the Status column for the program that's giving you trouble. If you see **Not Responding**, Windows has stopped receiving information from the window, and you will probably have to end the task manually. Select the program name from the Task column and click the **End Task** button.

For more detailed information about what's running on your system, click the **Processes** tab. This list (an example is shown in Figure 5.12) is usually much longer than the list of programs because it includes hidden tasks and services that Windows runs.

The best use of the Processes tab is to identify programs that are using too much of your system's resources (memory or processor) and slowing down the performance of other programs. On the Processes tab, double-click the **CPU** or **Mem Usage** heading to sort by the value in that column. Values in the CPU column represent the percentage of your CPU used by that process, with the total always equal to 100. Values in the Mem Usage column represent the actual amount of memory the process is using, in kilobytes.

Slow switcher

Although you can use the Task Manager's **Switch To** button to move between programs, it's much easier to use taskbar buttons or the **Alt+Tab** shortcut instead.

Fast access

If you use the Task Manager regularly, learn its keyboard shortcut: **Ctrl+Shift+Esc**.

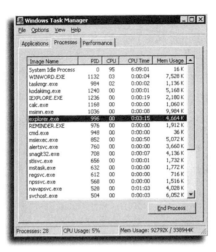

FIGURE 5.12
Use this dialog box to identify programs that are using more than their fair share of processor time.

System Idle Process? What's that?

Under normal circum-环境 stances, an entry called System Idle Process is at the top of the list when you sort the Processes list by CPU use. That entry is a placeholder that represents the part of your CPU that isn't being used. If you have two programs that are each consuming 5% of CPU time, the System Idle Process should read 90, meaning that 90% of your CPU is free for other tasks.

End a process only as a last resort

Use the **End Process** button only when all else fails and you can't close a program using its menus or the **End Task** button. If you're not certain which program goes with which process, be extra careful. Generally, you're better off closing all programs (if possible), logging off, and then logging on again (or restarting Windows) rather than trying to kill individual processes.

Here's what you can do with the Task Manager:

- Has a program stopped responding? If you see the words Not Responding next to an entry in the list on the Applications tab, wait a reasonable amount of time for the program to finish what it's doing, and then click the **End Task** button. For programs that are truly stuck, Windows may display a confirmation dialog box before actually ending the program.

- Is a program using up more than its share of memory? If you're having trouble running one program because you're out of memory, sort by Mem Usage on the Processes tab and find the processes at the top of the list that are using the most. Close those programs normally to free up memory.

- Is a program using up more than its share of the CPU? Sorting by the CPU heading lets you see which processes are draining the CPU. In some cases, high CPU usage is normal, especially when a program is working in the background; if a program that should be idle is consuming a large amount of your CPU, however, you may want to close it.

After opening Task Manager, you can leave it open for quick access. When you minimize Task Manager, an icon appears in the notification area at the right of the taskbar, which you can double-click to restore Task Manager. Use the **Options** menu to specify whether you want to hide the Task Manager button when you minimize it and to control whether Task Manager stays on top of all other windows when you use it.

Uninstalling Programs Safely

Setting up a new program is a complicated process—at least from the point of view of Windows 2000—so it stands to reason that getting rid of an installed program is equally complex. You may choose to uninstall a program if you no longer need it and want to free up the disk space it occupies. If you've discovered that a program doesn't work as you expected or has unpleasant side effects, you may be even more anxious to get rid of it. In any case, don't just delete its sub-folder from the Program Files folder. Instead, use the **Add/Remove Programs** option in Control Panel to undo all the changes that the program's Setup routine did in the first place.

When you open the **Add/Remove Programs** option, you see a list of installed programs, similar to the list shown in Figure 5.13. This window includes a wealth of information about installed programs, including the amount of disk space the program's files consume and how often you've used it in the past 30 days; some programs, including Microsoft Office, include hyperlinks that display support information as well.

FIGURE 5.13
All installed programs show up in this window. Click the **Change/Remove** button to begin uninstalling the program.

Click the **Change/Remove** button to start the Setup program and begin uninstalling the program. Before you can remove a program, you may need to log on with administrative rights. For the most part, this process is completely automatic. Typically, uninstall programs remove the program files and settings without erasing any data files you've created. As always, though, you should back up data files before uninstalling a program.

SEE ALSO

➤ *For instructions on how to back up some or all of your files, see "Rules for (Nearly) Painless Backup," p. 281.*

Running Programs with a Different User Account

As noted earlier in this chapter, Windows looks for programs named Setup and Install, offering to run them under an administrator's account if you supply the correct password. You can do the same with other programs at any time. You may want to run a program under another user's account to gain access to files stored in a folder that's not available to your regular account, for example, or to adjust settings that require an administrator's privileges.

Find the program shortcut and hold down the **Shift** key as you right-click. From the shortcut menu, choose **Run as**. The dialog box shown in Figure 5.14 appears.

FIGURE 5.14

When you need to run an application under another user's account, use this dialog box. Of course, you need to enter the correct password before the program will run!

Note that this trick works with most options in Control Panel, which is useful when you want to adjust system settings. However, it does not work with Windows Explorer or with Control Panel options that are actually special-purpose system folders—Fonts, Scheduled Tasks, Network and Dial-Up Connections, and Administrative Tools, for example.

chapter
6

Browsing for Files

How Windows Organizes Your Files

If you've used MS-DOS or earlier versions of Windows, you already understand the basic organization of a local disk drive. Each *drive* (identified by a letter—c:, for instance) contains one or more folders, starting with the root folder (c:\). When you install Windows 2000, it creates a set of folders to store program and data files. On a new computer, for example, Windows 2000 puts its own program files in c:\Winnt and a group of subfolders; each local user gets a set of folders within C:\Documents and Settings to store preferences and data files. (Each user's set of folders is called a *user profile*.)

However, Windows also uses folders to display objects that don't correspond to directories on a hard disk. In fact, every time you open an Explorer window, you see a consistent hierarchy of folders that collectively give you access to every resource on your system and network. In many cases, these folders are partly or completely virtual:

Are they folders or directories?

If you've used MS-DOS for any length of time, you may be more comfortable referring to folders and subfolders as *directories* and *subdirectories*. True MS-DOS veterans, in fact, remember when the CD (Change Directory) and DIR (Directory) commands were the starting point for every file management task. In the case of data and program files, Windows folders and subfolders are directly equivalent to MS-DOS directories and subdirectories. On the other hand, Windows *system folders*, such as My Computer and the Windows desktop, don't correspond directly to DOS-style directories. In this book, I use the term *folder* whenever possible because it's more technically accurate; if you prefer to mentally substitute the term *directory*, be my guest.

- **Desktop.** This essential system folder is the first thing you see when you start Windows; fittingly, it has a permanent position at the top of the folders list. The desktop includes all the "My" system icons (My Documents, My Computer, My Network Places) and the Recycle Bin. You can save files and create folders on the desktop, too—Windows stores objects you create in the Desktop folder under your user profile.

- **My Documents.** On the desktop and in the Folders list, this icon is a shortcut to the actual folder you use for data files. By default, double-clicking this shortcut opens C:\Documents and Settings\Username\My Documents (where *Username* is your logon name); however, as I explain a little later in this chapter, you can change this setting so that the My Documents icon points to any local or network folder.

- **My Computer.** Displays icons for all local drives, any shared network drives that have been *mapped* to a drive letter, and the Control Panel icon (see Figure 6.1). This folder is completely virtual—you can't save files or create folders in My Computer.

FIGURE 6.1
You'll find icons for all
your local drives in the
My Computer folder.
Use Control Panel to
adjust system settings
of all types.

Uncluttered view

Compared with Windows 95
and Windows 98, the
Windows 2000 interface
is much cleaner. In those
older Windows versions,
for instance, the My
Computer folder contains
icons for Printers,
Scheduled Tasks, and Dial-
Up Networking connec-
tions. Windows 2000
makes much better use of
Control Panel than its predecessors—if you're not
sure where your favorite
icons have gone, open
Control Panel first. Chances
are good that you'll find the
missing icon there.

SEE ALSO

➤ *To learn how to work with drives and drive letters, see "Setting Up a Hard Disk," p. 232.*

■ **My Network Places.** This virtual folder includes icons for all
the networked computers (servers and workstations) in your
workgroup or *domain*. Every time you open a network folder,
Windows creates a shortcut to that location and adds it to this
folder. My Network Places replaces Windows 95's Network
Neighborhood.

SEE ALSO

➤ *To learn how to use network resources, see "Opening and Editing Shared Files," p. 340.*

■ **Recycle Bin.** This icon, which appears on the desktop and in
the Folders list, is actually a pointer to a group of hidden folders
that store files you've deleted recently. When you double-click
the **Recycle Bin** icon, Windows displays a list of deleted files
and gives you the opportunity to restore one or more.

SEE ALSO

➤ *To learn how to use and customize the Recycle Bin, see "Recovering Deleted Files," p. 164.*

- **Internet Explorer.** This is the one oddball icon in the Folders list. It shows up in Explorer windows when you display the Folders pane, but it doesn't appear in the drop-down Address list at the top of the window. Basically, this icon appears for only one reason—to let you switch with one click from Windows Explorer to Internet Explorer.

One of the least known and most useful system folders in Windows 2000 is the All Users folder. Any objects you create in the Desktop or Start Menu folders here will be visible to anyone who logs on to the computer. When you install a program while logged on as an administrator, Windows usually puts program shortcuts in the All Users folder. Any user who is a member of the Power Users or Administrators group can add or delete icons from these folders, too. To open this folder, click the **Start** button, choose **R**un, enter `%allusersprofile%` (be sure to include the percent signs), and press **Enter**.

Changing the location of My Documents

1. Right-click the My Documents icon on the Windows Desktop and choose **P**roperties.

2. In the Properties dialog box (see Figure 6.2), click the **M**ove button.

3. In the Browse for Folder dialog box (see Figure 6.3), select the folder you want to use as your main storage location for documents. If the folder doesn't exist, click the **New Folder** button to create it. Click **OK** to enter your choice in the **T**arget box.

4. Click the **A**pply button. A confirmation dialog box asks if you really want to move all your documents to the new location. Click **Y**es to make the change; click **N**o to back out without making any changes.

5. Click **OK** to close the Properties dialog box. Now, whenever you use a program's **F**ile menu and choose **O**pen or **S**ave, you can click My Documents to view the contents of the folder where you prefer to store your documents.

Keep the desktop clean

Any folders you create on the Windows desktop appear at the bottom of the Folders list. If you create too many folders here, you may discover that the clutter makes it harder to find the folders you're looking for. I recommend that you put no more than two folders on the desktop; put any additional folders in the My Documents folder instead, where they're never more than two clicks away.

The All Users folder is smart

What happens when you put an icon in the Desktop or Start Menu folder of the All Users folder and it has the same name as an icon in your personal Desktop or Start Menu folder? Relax—you won't start seeing double. Windows detects the conflict and shows only the personal version.

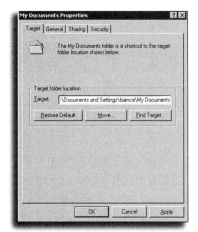

FIGURE 6.2
Where do you want to store your everyday working files? Use this dialog box to specify the location you want to use as the default document folder.

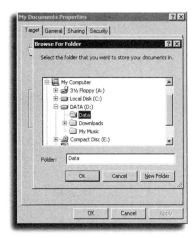

FIGURE 6.3
This browse dialog box appears in Windows whenever you need to pick a folder. Click the plus sign at the left of a drive or a folder to see its subfolders.

Change the name, too

Does the name My Documents make you cringe? Go ahead and change it, if you want. Right-click the My Documents icon, choose **Rename**, and enter any name you prefer—
**Bianca's Data
Files**, for example, or
Ed's Documents, or even plain ol' **Data**. Click **OK** to save your change.

If you decide later that you want to restore the My Documents folder to its original location, open the Properties dialog box for the My Documents folder and click the **R**estore **D**efault option. Click **Y**es in the confirmation dialog box that asks if you want to move all your files.

Browsing Files with Windows Explorer

For everyday file management tasks, the tool you'll use most often is the Windows Explorer. This all-purpose system utility lets you do just about anything you need with program and data files, from organizing files in folders and subfolders to searching for documents based on their contents, to opening files for editing.

Depending on the task at hand, you can choose either of two views of the Windows Explorer. *Single-folder view* displays only the contents of the current drive or folder. The two-pane *Explorer view*, on the other hand, includes the *Folders pane*, a tree-style view of all the drives, folders, and resources on your computer and your network. The contents of the current drive or folder are visible in the pane on the right. Figure 6.4 shows an Explorer window in which the Folders pane is visible.

FIGURE 6.4
Click the **Folders** button to show or hide the Folders pane. Use this pane to quickly navigate through local drives, system folders, network servers, and even pages on the World Wide Web.

1. Up button
2. View button
3. Address bar
4. Browse list (drop-down)
5. Folders pane
6. Info pane
7. Folder contents
8. Status bar
9. Expand/collapse indicator

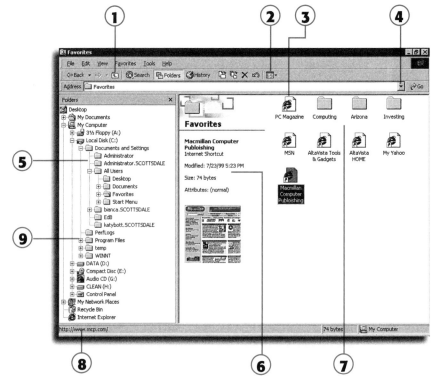

110

As I'll demonstrate later in this chapter, a cleverly disguised version of Explorer appears in the Open and Save As *common dialog boxes* in every Windows program, as well.

Browsing Through Drives and Folders

In single-folder view, Explorer shows you the contents of one folder at a time.

To drill down into subfolders, just keep double-clicking. From the My Computer window, for example, double-click a drive icon to view its contents; then double-click a folder within that drive, double-click a subfolder within that folder, and keep drilling down until you find the folder you're looking for.

 How do you go back up through the hierarchy of folders? Press the **Backspace** key to move up one level at a time. If you prefer to use the mouse, click the **Up** button on the standard toolbar. When you reach the Desktop icon, however, you're at the top of the tree; the Up button is grayed out, and pressing **Backspace** no longer has any effect.

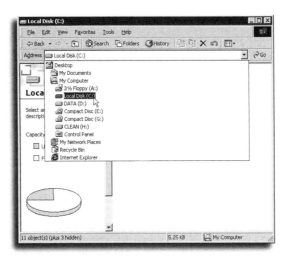

FIGURE 6.5
In single-folder view, use this browse list to quickly jump to system folders such as My Documents or to begin working with files on another drive.

In single-folder view, Explorer has one handy shortcut that lets you jump quickly to any drive or system folder, even if you're currently three or folders deep in another drive. Click the drop-down arrow at the right side of the Address bar to display a browse list like the one shown in Figure 6.5. Choose a starting location, and then double-click folder and drive icons to open each one and burrow deeper into subfolders.

Because the Explorer window typically displays only the name of the current folder, it's sometimes hard to tell where you are in the hierarchy. Use the browse list to see your exact location at a glance. In Figure 6.6, for example, you can easily see which project and department the current set of files belongs to.

FIGURE 6.6

Lost in a maze of sub-folders? Drop down this browse list to get your bearings in a hurry.

Pause to refresh

When you view the contents of a floppy disk in an Explorer window, the display doesn't update automatically when you change disks. Likewise, if another user adds, renames, or deletes files in a shared network folder, these changes do not automatically appear in an open window on your system. In both cases, you need to *refresh* the display to see the most up-to-date contents. To reread the contents of the disk, click the **Go** button to the right of the Address bar, or pull down the **View** menu and choose **Refresh**, or press **F5**.

Normally, when you double-click a folder icon, its contents replace the contents of the current window. Most of the time, that's the right behavior—if each new folder opened in its own window, you'd quickly be buried in folder windows. But sometimes you want to open a folder in a new window, perhaps so that you can compare its contents with those of another window. In that case, hold down the **Ctrl** key and double-click a folder or drive icon.

When the Folders pane is visible, it's much easier to move through the hierarchy of drives and folders. A plus sign to the left of an icon means it contains additional folders. Click the plus sign to expand that branch and see additional folders. A minus sign to the left of an icon means that branch is already expanded; click the minus sign to collapse the branch again.

Expanding or collapsing a branch in the Folders pane doesn't change the contents shown in the right pane. To display the contents of a different folder, you have to click its icon in the All Folders pane.

Browsing with Path Names

Is DOS dead? Technically, yes, but little bits of DOS history keep popping up where you least expect them. If you're comfortable with MS-DOS path names, for instance, you can use the same syntax to open drives and folders directly, without double-clicking. Enter the path name in the Address bar of any Explorer window, or click the **Start** button, choose **Run**, and enter the path of the folder you want to open.

As I mentioned earlier, the default Explorer settings show only the name of the current folder in the Address bar. That can be terribly confusing when you're working with two identically named folders on different drives or even on different computers. For instance, I keep a backup copy of all my document files on a network server, using the same folder structure as on my computer. If I open the Projects folder on my computer and on the server, and then arrange the two windows side by side, I have no way of knowing which is which, and I risk accidentally opening an older file or replacing a new file with an earlier draft.

To avoid that problem, I've configured Explorer so that it shows the full path name of any folder. From any folder window, pull down the **Tools** menu and choose **Folder Options**. Click the **View** tab, and then check the box labeled **Display the full path in the address bar**. Click **OK** to save your changes. The next time you open an Explorer window, you'll see the full path of the current folder, as shown in the example in Figure 6.7. When you arrange two folder windows side by side, the drive letter or server name at the beginning of the path tells you exactly where that folder is located.

The case of the phantom plus sign

In some cases, clicking a plus sign to the left of an icon in the Folders pane causes the indicator to disappear completely. Don't be alarmed—Windows is actually doing you a favor. When you display the Folders pane, Windows checks the contents of all local hard drives and adds the plus sign next to any icon that contains subfolders. However, it does not automatically check for subfolders on removable drives (such as floppy disks) or network connections because doing so might slow down the performance of your system. Instead, it places the plus sign next to each such icon and doesn't actually check for subfolders until you click that icon. If it finds no subfolders, it removes the plus sign.

Look, ma—no mouse!

I use the Run box more than most people, I'll bet, because I dislike having to move my hand back and forth between the keyboard and the mouse. Instead of double-clicking through one folder after another, I tap **Windows+R**, type in the path of the folder I want to open, and press **Enter**. If you don't have a Windows keyboard, press **Ctrl+Esc** to pop up the Start menu, and then press **R** to open the Run dialog box.

113

FIGURE 6.7
Where is that file, exactly? Turn on the option to display full paths to see full details about the location of the current folder.

Which slash is which?

In DOS-style pathnames, the backslash (\\) is the separator character between directories—oops, I mean folders. In Internet addresses, the slash (/) is used to separate parts of an address. In most cases, Windows is intelligent enough to change slashes to backslashes, or vice versa, if you enter the wrong type for the current address.

Entering path names doesn't have to be tedious, either. The AutoComplete feature in Windows 2000 can fill in much of the detail for you, all the way down to the filename. AutoComplete works in the Address bar and in the Run dialog box. After you type the first few letters of the path, Windows finds the first matching name and offers to finish entering it for you. The path name shown previously in Figure 6.7, for example, is 84 characters long; you can enter the full path by pressing fewer than 20 keys.

Using AutoComplete to enter path names

1. Open the **Run** dialog box, click in the **Open** box, and type the first few letters of the folder you want to open—`c:\D`, in this example.

2. Just below the **Open** box, Windows displays a drop-down list of all the folders in the root of drive C: that begin with the letter D. `C:\Documents and Settings` is at the top of the list. Press the down arrow to add that entry to the Run box.

3. Press the backslash key (\\) to begin displaying the next group of files and folders, and enter as many characters as you need to jump to the next folder you want to open. In this example, we enter **B** to jump to `Bianca.SCOTTSDALE`.

4. Press the down arrow to highlight the folder name in the **Open** box.

5. Continue this way, using the backslash, the down arrow, and an occasional letter or number to jump to the exact file or folder you're looking for. When the entire path name is visible in the <u>O</u>pen box, press **Enter** to open that folder or file.

Using AutoComplete effectively takes some practice, but accomplished keyboard users will get into a productive rhythm in no time, and the savings in keystrokes can be profound.

Searching for Files and Folders

The Search bar isn't just for looking up information on the Internet. You can also use it to find a file—or hundreds of files for that matter—anywhere on a local drive or a shared network drive. To start a search from scratch, click the **Start** button and choose **Sear<u>c</u>h**, **For <u>F</u>iles or Folders**. If you want to reuse an Explorer window that's already open, click the **Search** button. Regardless of which technique you use, Windows opens the Search Assistant; like the Folders pane, it takes over the left side of the Explorer window, as shown in Figure 6.8.

Be patient

The first time you use AutoComplete in a given Windows session, you may notice a delay of a few seconds before the first AutoComplete suggestion appears. That's because Windows has to go out and physically read the directory on the hard disk, a process that can be slow. The next time you enter an address, however, Windows is able to look at the copy of the directory in RAM, which is many times faster, and you probably won't notice any delay at all.

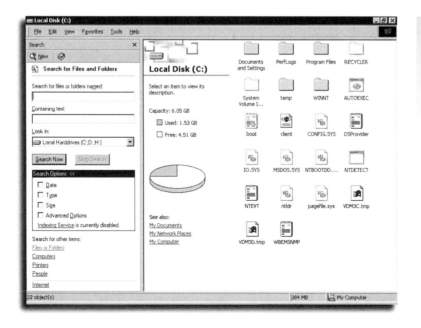

FIGURE 6.8
Use the Search Assistant to find files by name, date, or their contents.

Most of the options in the Search Assistant are fairly self-explanatory. The secret to finding lost files quickly is combining criteria in the Search Assistant so that only the files you're looking for show up in the Search Results pane on the right. Three fields at the top of the Search pane are generally most useful:

- **Search for files or folders named.** Enter any character or group of characters that you want to search for in the list of file-names for the selected location. If you enter more than one text string, with each entry separated by a space, the Search Assistant looks for filenames that match any of the entries in the list. In effect, the Search Assistant separates the terms with a logical OR. Thus, entering `house office` here turns up files named `Invitation to housewarming party` and `Office procedures manual`. If you leave this box blank, the Search Assistant returns all files that match other criteria you specify.

- **Containing text.** Enter any text string—typically a word or a phrase—and the Search Assistant will look in the selected location for files that contain that exact text. If you enter more than one word, the Search Assistant treats it as a phrase and returns a matching file only if the text you entered appears in the precise order you entered it.

- **Look in.** Allows you to specify a location where you want to search. By default, the Search Assistant looks in every folder on every local drive. Use the drop-down list to narrow the search to a single drive or just to the My Documents folder. Click **Browse** at the bottom of the drop-down list to choose a specific folder. You can enter multiple locations here—separate each entry with a comma. To search for files only within a specific folder and its subfolders, right-click the folder icon and choose **Search** from its shortcut menu; that automatically puts the name of the selected folder into the **Look in** box.

After entering these criteria, click the **Search Now** button to begin looking for files. As it works, the Search Assistant displays matching files in the Search Results pane to the right.

If the file you're looking for has popped up in the Search Results pane, but the Search Assistant is still chugging along, click the **Stop**

Search button. This option is also useful if the search is taking too long and you want to narrow the range of files in the search criteria.

Want more search options? The four check boxes under the **Search Now** button let you add details to narrow down your search. When you check one of these boxes, the Search Assistant displays additional options that are specific to that data type. Figure 6.9 shows all four options fully expanded.

FIGURE 6.9
Use these additional search options to zero in on a particular file.

By carefully combining criteria, you can perform some fairly sophisticated searches. Table 6.1 describes some common search scenarios and lists the settings you might use to track down matching files.

Table 6.1 Common solutions to everyday search problems

Problem	Solution
You're looking for one important file. You know part of its name, and you know you last worked on it in January.	In the **Search for files or folders named** box, enter a word or a few characters that you're certain are in the filename. Check the **Date** box and choose the **Files Modified between 1/1/2000 and 1/31/2000**.
You've sent letters to several of your most important clients about a specific project and you want to see all those letters.	Click in the **Containing text** box and enter a word or phrase that you know appears in all the letters— the project name, for instance.

continues...

One bar at a time, please

When the Search Assistant bar is visible, the Folders pane is hidden, and vice versa. There is no way to display both Explorer bars at once. When you no longer need to use the search results, click the **Folders** button to display the Folders pane again.

Table 6.1 Continued

Problem	Solution
Your My Documents folder is taking up too much disk space, partly because you've created a lot of documents that contain embedded graphics files.	Check the **Size** box and enter **at least 200KB** (or whatever value you decide to use as your minimum). In the **Look in** box, choose **My Documents**.
You've created dozens of Excel workbooks, and they're scattered all over your hard drive. You'd like to gather them all in one place and organize them by project.	Check the **Type** box and choose **Microsoft Excel Worksheet** from the drop-down list. Or enter ***.xls** in the **Search for files or folders named** box.

The Search Results pane looks and acts much like a regular Explorer window. From the Search Results pane, you can switch to any view, including Details view. You can look at a file's properties; rename a file or a folder; delete one file, a group of files, or an entire folder; move or copy files; or open any selected file for editing.

As Figure 6.10 illustrates, however, the Search Results pane also includes information you won't find in an ordinary Explorer window. If you select a single icon, the top of the pane displays information about that file, folder, or shortcut, including a hyperlink that allows you to jump to the folder containing that file. For some files, including shortcuts to Web pages, this region also displays a thumbnail preview.

Sometimes, finding one folder is just the start of the file management process. For instance, if your search turns up a draft of last year's annual report, you might want to open the folder containing that file so that you can copy graphics, Web pages, charts, and other supporting files for this year's version.

If you select an icon and then click the hyperlink at the top of the Search Results pane, Explorer opens the folder in the current window, replacing the Search Results. Use the **Back** button to return to the Search Results pane. If you prefer to open a new window, right-click the icon instead and choose **Open Containing Folder** from the shortcut menu.

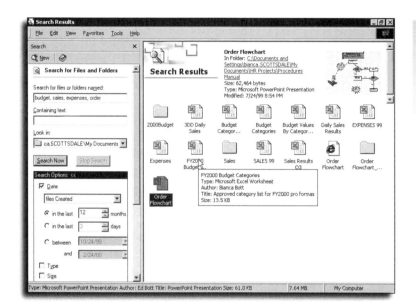

FIGURE 6.10
Look at the top of the Search Results pane for more details about the selected icons.

Do you find yourself performing the same searches again and again? At the end of each week, for instance, you might want to copy all the Word documents you produced during the week to a backup disk for safekeeping. Here's how:

Saving and reusing a search

1. Use the Search Assistant to find the right group of files: check the **D**ate box and enter the criteria `files modified in the last 7 days`; then check the **T**ype box and choose **Microsoft Word document** from the drop-down list.

2. Click the **Search Now** button to perform the search. It is not necessary for the search to find any matching files.

3. Click in any empty space in the Search Results pane. Then pull down the **F**ile menu and choose **S**a**ve Search**.

4. Enter a name and location for the Saved Search icon and click the **S**ave button.

5. To reuse the search, double-click the **Saved Search** icon. Modify the search criteria, if you want, and click the **Search Now** button.

Gathering Information about Files and Folders

When you open a folder window, you can see, at a minimum, the name of each icon in the folder. You can also see how many items are in that folder. Sometimes that's all the information you need to find the file you want to start working with. But you may need more particulars before you can get to work. Knowing the creation date of each file, for example, can help you arrange the list of files for an important project in chronological order so that you can recover an important paragraph that was deleted from an early draft. Switch to Details view to see all the standard details stored with each file in the current folder—the date and time the file was created, when it was last saved, its size, and much more.

You can also peek into the contents of files in a folder, seeing a thumbnail image of the file's contents and even adding notes or keywords to make it easier to search for files later.

Viewing Details About a Folder's Contents

How many files are in a given folder? How much space are they taking up? When was the last time you opened any of these files? The answers to these questions can help you decide when it's time to delete old data files or store them in a different location.

For a quick overview of a folder's contents, click the **Views** button and choose **Details** from the drop-down list. This view displays a grid like the one shown in Figure 6.11, in which each file is represented by a single line. By default, four fields are visible: the self-explanatory Name and Size fields; Type, which specifies the program Windows will open if you double-click the file icon; and Modified, the date when the file was last changed and saved.

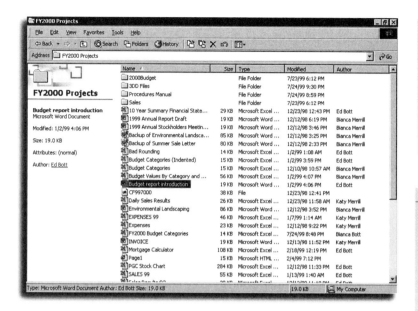

FIGURE 6.11
Details view displays basic file facts like a DOS-style directory view. You can also customize it to show extra information, such as the Author field at right.

All new for Windows 2000

If you've recently switched to Windows 2000 from Windows 95 or Windows 98, the capability to customize Details view should be a welcome surprise. For Microsoft Office users who are already in the habit of adding comments and categories to Word documents and Excel workbooks, the payoff is immediate—you can view those extra details (and even sort by individual fields) in an Explorer window.

SEE ALSO

➤ *For a detailed discussion of how to manage file associations, see "Changing Associations Between Files and Programs," p. 156.*

To add extra columns to Details view, right-click any column heading and choose items from the shortcut menu shown in Figure 6.12.

Click the **More** option at the bottom of the shortcut menu to see a dialog box (see Figure 6.13) with a lengthy list of additional columns you can add to Details view.

FIGURE 6.12
Check any of these options to add extra columns of data to Details view.

FIGURE 6.13
Although you can arrange the layout of columns using the buttons here, it's easier to drag them into position directly.

Invisible columns

What does it mean when a column is checked on the list, but you can't see it in Details view? Most likely you resized the column's width to zero, which makes it disappear. To restore the default column widths, right-click any column heading and choose **More** from the shortcut menu. In the Column Settings dialog box, select the name of the column. Make sure a check mark is in the box to its left, then check the value in the box at the bottom of the dialog. If it says the selected column should be 0 pixels wide, change the value to at least 20. After you click OK, the column will be visible again.

Buttons in the Column Settings dialog box allow you to change the order and width of visible columns. It's much easier, however, to use the mouse to customize Details view:

- To change the width of columns, point to the dividing line between column headings. When the pointer changes to a two-headed arrow, click and drag in either direction.

- To automatically adjust the width of a column to match the widest entry it contains, double-click the dividing line to the right of a column heading.

- Click any column heading to sort the folder's contents by that column. Click again to sort in reverse order—something you can't do in any other view.

Some of the extra columns you can choose in Details view are specific to a particular type of data and frankly are not much use in most folders. One group of columns displays information on programs—Module Description, Module Version, and so on—and is of most use to developers. The block of columns at the end of the list—Frame Rate, Video Compression, Audio Sample Size, and the like—are useful in folders that contain collections of multimedia files, such as `C:\Winnt\Media`.

Viewing Details About Individual Files

What's inside that file? The name, unfortunately, doesn't always give you enough information to figure out a file's contents, especially when they have names like `Report1.doc` and `Report2.doc`. The slow and tedious way to find out exactly what's in a given file is to open it. Before you go through that process on a folder full of files, however, try using the extra information that's close at hand.

In any Explorer window, you can get a quick overview of some file details just by pointing and clicking. Point at a file and Windows displays a ScreenTip that contains information about the file's contents. Select a single icon and the information pane at the left side of the window shows that same information, as well as a thumbnail preview for certain data types. Figure 6.14 shows examples of both.

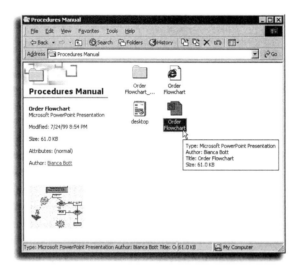

FIGURE 6.14
When you select the icon for an Office document, a graphics file, or a shortcut to a Web page, Explorer displays a preview in the info pane at left.

Need more information? Your next stop is the Properties dialog box. Point to the file in question, right-click, and choose **Properties** from the shortcut menu. The General tab (see Figure 6.15 for an example) displays all the basic details of the file, including its name, size, and date created.

Extra details for Office documents

If you and your co-workers use Microsoft Office 97 or Office 2000, you may already have access to extended file information without even knowing it. For years, Office documents have included extended properties boxes that you can use to track details about files, including a document's title, author, categories, and number of pages. Windows 2000 is the first operating system that allows you to easily view and edit all these details. For more information about working with Office, check out *Using Microsoft Office 2000* (by Ed Bott) or *Special Edition Using Microsoft Office 2000* (by Ed Bott and Woody Leonhard), both published by Que.

FIGURE 6.15
The General tab shows basic details about a file or a folder. Unlike previous Windows versions, you can rename a file by editing its name here.

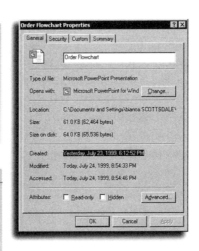

Tell your co-workers

Advanced properties are a great way to tag files with information, particularly in shared folders where a group of people are constantly posting new work. If your co-workers are also using Office 2000, show them how to edit the Advanced Summary properties of every file they create or edit; if everyone gets into the habit of entering this information, the whole team will be more productive.

Still not enough information? Open the Properties dialog box again and click the **Summary** tab. The exact details you see vary, depending on the file type and the format of the disk where the file is stored. Figure 6.16, for example, shows the Summary properties of a Windows bitmap file stored on an *NTFS volume*. The information at the top of the dialog box describes the file's attributes; these entries can't be changed except by editing the image itself. You can add and change any details in the fields at the bottom of the dialog box, however. Click and begin typing to add your own comments or other details.

FIGURE 6.16
By entering extra details for files like this graphic, you can make it easier to find out about the file without having to open it.

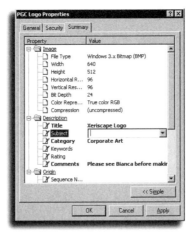

Overwhelmed by the sheer volume of detail in this dialog box? The Summary tab typically offers two levels of detail. To switch to a less cluttered view (like the one in Figure 6.17), click the **Simple** button; to restore the full details, click the **Advanced** button.

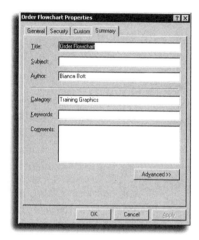

FIGURE 6.17
This simplified view of the Summary tab shows only the most important file details and hides custom properties.

Working with Advanced properties entails one big "gotcha," however. These properties are available only when the file is stored on an NTFS volume. When you move the file from an NTFS drive to one formatted with FAT or FAT32, you will lose important information. By displaying the dialog box shown in Figure 6.18, Windows 2000 warns you if this is about to happen. If the extra details are important, cancel the move and make sure to keep the file on an NTFS drive.

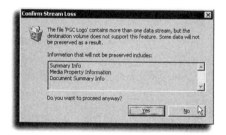

FIGURE 6.18
Moving a file from an NTFS volume to a FAT-formatted drive may mean losing important details.

Gathering Information About a Group of Files

When you select two or more icons in an Explorer window, you can no longer view properties of each individual file. Instead, the info pane and the Properties dialog box display collective statistics—the number of files you selected and the amount of disk space they occupy. Use these properties when you need to know whether a group of files will fit on a removable disk, such as a floppy or a zip disk.

Previewing Pictures in an Explorer Window

Keeping track of a large collection of graphics files can be a nightmare because pictures tend to be large files that are slow to load. It's often hard to describe a picture with a meaningful name, too, especially when trying to use short filenames for compatibility with other programs.

What? Another system folder that begins with the word *My*? As the name implies, the My Pictures folder (located in the My Documents folder) is the preferred location for all kinds of images, including those that are scanned and downloaded. What makes the My Pictures folder special is the Image Preview control in the lower-left corner. When you select a graphics file, this small window instantly displays it, as shown in the example in Figure 6.19.

FIGURE 6.19
Many scanning and image-editing programs use the My Pictures folder as their preferred storage location because its previewing capabilities are so impressive.

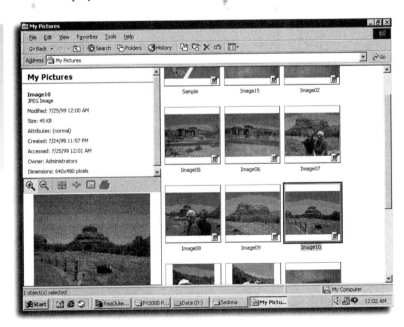

SEE ALSO

➤ *To discover how to add the Image Preview pane to any folder window, see "Customizing Explorer's Appearance," p. 131.*

Use the buttons on the Image Preview window to zoom in or out on an image, to see it in a full-screen preview, or to send the image directly to the printer.

Opening and Saving Files in Program Windows

Typically, when you use the **Open** or **Save As** choices on a program's **File** menu, you open one of the *common dialog boxes* in Windows 2000. As the name suggests, these dialog boxes are the same in all programs, making it possible for you to use the same techniques to open and save files, regardless of which program you're using. Look closely at the dialog box in Figure 6.20, for example, and you'll see that it's actually a scaled-down Explorer window with a few unusual features.

Limited file support

Thumbnails view and the Image Preview control use slightly different techniques. As a result, some file types that are visible in Thumbnails view don't show up properly in the Image Preview control. Web graphics (*JPEG* and *GIF* files) and Windows bitmaps display properly in either location. PCX files, however, show up only in Thumbnails view.

FIGURE 6.20
This common dialog box is actually an Explorer window; the Places bar at the left makes it easy to jump to the locations where you're most likely to find data files.

When working with common dialog boxes, keep the following general principles in mind:

- As in a full Explorer window, you can use the **Up** and **Back** buttons to move back through higher-level folders.

- The View button at the right of the toolbar lets you choose any of the common Explorer views, including **Thumbnails** and **Details** views.

Uncommon dialog boxes?

Not all programs use the common dialog boxes shown here. Older Windows programs in particular may use dialog boxes that lack the Places bar, and some programs replace the common dialog boxes with their own versions, ostensibly to add features. Microsoft Office is the most notable example—although its dialog boxes closely resemble those in Windows 2000, you'll see subtle differences if you look closely.

- Click icons in the Places bar at the left side of the window to jump to common locations such as the My Documents folder or to begin browsing a different drive with My Computer.

- The History icon lets you see and open shortcuts for files and folders you've used recently.

- Unlike a full Explorer window, common dialog boxes allow you to filter the list of files so that you see only those of a certain type. If the icon you're looking for isn't visible, try choosing **All files** from the Files of type list.

Changing the Way a Folder's Contents Appear

In every Explorer window, you can choose a broad range of display options that control how icons appear in an Explorer window. You can specify the size (large or small) and arrangement (rows, columns, or freeform) of icons. You can arrange icons in order by name, size, type, or date. All the View options described here work the same in single-folder windows and in the Explorer windows where the Folders pane is visible.

SEE ALSO

➤ *To learn how to control advanced Explorer options, including the capability to see normally hidden files, see "Customizing Folder Options," p. 151.*

Choosing a View

For every folder, Windows gives you a choice of five icon arrangements. Each type of view has its advantages, depending on the task you're trying to accomplish. For instance, large icons are useful in folders that contain a relatively small number of files of several types; the larger icon images let you quickly distinguish between different file types. Details view, on the other hand, is particularly useful when you have a long list of files that were created at different times and you want to sort by date.

To apply a new view to the current folder, click the **View** button and select one of the following choices from the drop-down list:

- **Large Icons.** This view uses full-size icons with a text label that shows as much of the filename as will fit. Best suited for folders that contain a small number of icons, such as My Computer; it's much less useful in folders that contains hundreds of icons, unless you enjoy scrolling.

- **Small Icons.** Displays icons that are one-fourth the size of those in the Large Icons view. The filename appears in a label to the right of each icon. Like Large Icons view, the initial arrangement of icons is in rows, going from left to right, and you can move icons anywhere within the folder. This view is most useful in folders that contain a large number of files.

- **List.** This view uses the same size icons and labels as Small Icons view; however, icons are arranged in columns, starting at the top left of the contents window, going down, and then to the right. You cannot rearrange the position of icons. This view is most useful in common dialog boxes.

- **Details.** From left to right, each row in this view includes the file's icon, name, size, type, and the date the file was last modified. Details change slightly for different types of windows; if you open the Recycle Bin in this view, for example, you see the Original Location and Date Deleted columns that are unique to this folder. You cannot move or reposition icons in Details view; as we'll see shortly, however, you can add or remove columns from this view.

- **Thumbnails.** For folders that contain mostly graphics, switching to this view can make the task much easier. In this view, every file occupies a space roughly four times the size of the default Large Icons view, and Windows fills this space with a small preview image of the graphic, as shown in Figure 6.21.

Drag at will

In Large Icons view, you can drag file, folder, and shortcut icons anywhere in the folder window. You don't have to be neat or follow any particular order. Moving icons around in this fashion can help you group files that you plan to copy or move. Explorer remembers the arrangement of icons the next time you open that folder.

Refreshing graphics

If a thumbnail doesn't display properly, right-click the icon and choose **Refresh Thumbnail** from the shortcut menu.

FIGURE 6.21
What's in this folder that's full of digital photos? With Thumbnails view turned on, you don't need to guess.

Arranging File and Folder Icons

As I noted in the previous section, you can choose any order and arrangement for folders in which you use Large Icons or Small Icons view. If you want to move your favorite icons to the top of the window and you don't mind if they line up unevenly, just drag them into position. However, if you prefer to let Explorer keep things tidy, you have two options:

- Want all your icons lined up neatly at all times? Pull down the **View** menu, choose **Arrange Icons**, and then check the **Auto Arrange** option. Move icons into any order you want—other icons will shift position to make room for the icons you move. When you resize the window, the icons automatically shift position so that they're visible within the window.

- Want to clean up a messy folder without changing the order of icons? First move the icons into the order you want; then pull down the **View** menu and choose **Line Up Icons**. Explorer "snaps" the icons into position along an imaginary grid. In some cases this may leave empty spaces within the folder window. If you resize the window, some icons may shift out of view; you'll need to scroll to the right to view them.

Not just for Web pages

Thumbnails view is not particularly useful in folders filled with boring business documents because all you end up with is icons that take up four times as much space as normal without providing any extra information. Two types of documents translate well to this view, however. If you have a folder filled with shortcuts to Web pages, try switching to Thumbnails view and watch as Explorer extracts a tiny preview of each Web page. Microsoft Office documents, especially PowerPoint presentations, also work well as thumbnails, although Word and Excel require that you check a box on the document's Properties page to save a preview picture.

Sorting Files and Folders

Regardless of the view you choose, you can sort the contents of folder window by name, type, size, or date.

To sort files within a folder, pull down the **View** menu and choose **Arrange Icons**. (You can also right-click and choose **Arrange Icons** from the shortcut menu.) Choose one of the following options from the submenu:

By Name. Sorts in ascending alphabetical order by filename, with folders grouped at the top of the list.

By Type. Sorts in ascending alphabetical order by file type.

By Size. Sorts folders first in ascending alphabetical order by name, and then arranges files by size, with the smallest files at the top of the list.

By Date. Moves all the subfolders to the top of the list and sorts them by date in descending order, then sorts files the same way; in both cases, the most recent files appear at the top of list.

In Large Icons, Small Icons, List, and Thumbnails view, sorting by anything other than name is guaranteed to give you a headache because the information used for sorting is hidden. If you plan to sort files and folders by any other column, switch to Details view first. In this view, click the column headings to sort by that column. Click again to sort in reverse order—something you can't do in any other view.

> **Not for Lists or Details**
>
> The Auto Arrange option is grayed out when you use List or Details view. In either of these views, Explorer automatically sorts icons based on their filename or a column you select; the Auto Arrange option is unnecessary.

> **File Type is not file extension**
>
> When you sort by file type, Explorer uses the registered file type, not the file's extension. Web pages with the .htm or .html extension, for instance, use the default file type of Microsoft HTML Document 5.0. Although it's hardly intuitive, that means in a long list of files, the way to find Web pages is to sort by File Type and then scroll to the middle of the list.

Customizing Explorer's Appearance

Like most parts of Windows, Explorer contains a wide array of customization options.

Changing the Width of Panes

When the Folders pane is visible, you can change the proportions between it and the Contents pane. For instance, you might want to widen the Folders pane to search through a long branch of nested folders; when you find the right one, make the Folders pane narrow again so you can see more files. To change the width of panes, point to the vertical dividing line between the panes. When the mouse pointer changes to a two-headed arrow, click and drag in either direction. Release the mouse button when the panes are the size you want.

Changing the Width of Columns

In Details view, Explorer uses columns to display information about files, folders, and system objects. To change the width of columns, point to the dividing line between column headings. When the pointer changes to a two-headed arrow, click and drag in either direction.

Showing and Hiding the Status Bar

The status bar, which appears along the bottom of every Explorer window, displays information about the current folder. If no file is selected, it tells you the number and total size of all objects in the folder. If you select a single icon, it displays details about that file. And if you select multiple icons, it tells how many are selected and how much space they occupy. Most of the time, you should leave the status bar on. If you don't see the status bar in a folder window, it may just be hidden. Pull down the **View** menu and click **Status Bar** to make it reappear.

Showing and Hiding Toolbars

By default, the Address bar and the Standard Buttons toolbar (with full text labels) appear in all Explorer windows. The Address bar is a crucial part of Explorer because it shows you which folder is currently displayed and lets you enter the name and path of another folder to display. Standard toolbar buttons are also useful, especially those that let you show and hide the Search Assistant and Folders pane and switch views.

Let Explorer choose the width

Want Explorer to automatically resize a column in Details view so that the widest entry in the list fits perfectly? Double-click the dividing line to the right of any column heading.

If you want to maximize the amount of space available for files and folders, you can temporarily hide the Address bar, the Standard toolbar, or both. Pull down the **View** menu, choose **Toolbars**, and check or uncheck the appropriate menu choices to show or hide either element.

I recommend a much better way to make more room for files without losing access to toolbar buttons. Change the oversized toolbar buttons to a smaller, streamlined version that is half the height. Pull down the **View** menu, choose **Toolbars**, and click the **Customize** option. This opens the Customize Toolbar dialog box, shown in Figure 6.22. From the **Text options** list, choose either **Selective text on right** or **No text labels**. From the **Icon options** list, choose **Small icons**. Click **Close** to save your changes. Options you choose here apply to all Explorer windows.

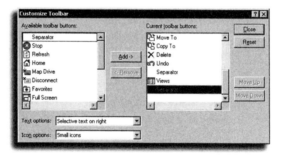

FIGURE 6.24
Want your Explorer toolbars to take up less space? Choose these options.

Figure 6.23 shows what the revised toolbar looks like. Because I chose the **Selective text on right** option, some of the toolbar buttons have labels, whereas others don't.

Customize toolbars, too

In previous Windows versions, Explorer didn't permit you to customize toolbar buttons. In Windows 2000, however, you can add or remove buttons to show only those you use most frequently. I like having the Properties button on the toolbar, for example, because it allows me to display the Properties dialog box with one click instead of two.

FIGURE 6.23
To conserve space in Explorer windows, shrink toolbar icons to a smaller size and hide the text labels that normally appear under toolbar buttons.

Saving Folder Display Options

When you change the view options for a folder, Windows remembers that setting and restores it the next time you view that folder. If you create a custom Details view for a folder that contains audio files, for example, Explorer will remember and reuse that view. As you move from folder to folder, the view changes to reflect the settings you last used. If you prefer to view all folder windows in a view other than the default Large Icons view, Windows 2000 enables you to set all Explorer windows to a single view.

Setting view options for all folders

1. Open any Explorer window and choose the view options (view type, arrangement, and so on) you want to use for all folders. (This option ignores toolbar settings and the sort order you define.)

2. Pull down the **Tools** menu, choose **Folder Options**, and click the **View** tab. The Folder Options dialog box appears (see Figure 6.24).

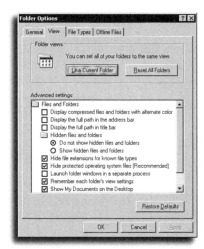

FIGURE 6.24
Use this dialog box to
change the view for all
folders at once.

3. In the Folder views area, click the button labeled **Like Current
   Folder**. Click **Yes** when asked to confirm that you want to
   change settings.

4. Click **OK** to save your changes.

To restore folder windows to their default view settings, open the Folder
Options dialog box, click the **View** tab, and click the button labeled **Reset
All Folders.** This restores all folders, including system folders such as My
Computer and Control Panel, to the default Large Icons view.

chapter 7

Managing Files and Folders

Organizing Files

What's the secret of being able to find files when you need them? The most important element is a good filing system, and the Windows Explorer is the tool you'll use most often to organize your files. By opening folder windows, you can create new folders, copy and move files between folders, delete files and folders you no longer need, and rename files so that they describe their contents clearly and accurately.

In Windows, every drive, file, folder, and system object is represented by an icon. Although keyboard shortcuts exist for many operations, most people find it more convenient to manage by mouse. By clicking and dragging icons, for example, you can copy or move file icons from several folder windows into a new folder window to organize a group of related files by project, drag a program icon onto the Start menu to create a shortcut, or drag a file icon into an open program window to open that file immediately.

Selecting Icons

Before you can manage a single file, you first have to click its icon to select it. To move, copy, or delete a group of files in one operation, use any of the following techniques to select the files you want to work with.

SEE ALSO

➤ *For advice on how and when to change folder options, see "Customizing Folder Options," p. 151.*

- To select multiple icons that are adjacent to one another in a folder window or on the desktop, click to select the first one and then hold down the **Shift** key and select the last icon. All the icons in between the two will be selected, as well.

- To select multiple icons that are not adjacent to one another, select the first one, then hold down the **Ctrl** key and select all additional icons. To deselect an icon, continue holding down the **Ctrl** key and select it again.

Taskbar buttons need one extra step

Surprisingly, if you drag an icon onto a taskbar button and drop it, Windows protests with a dialog box. The solution? Drag the icon onto the taskbar button and hold it there for a second or two; after a brief pause, the program window opens, allowing you to drag the icon into it. Release the mouse button to open the file.

Point, click, or double-click?

In this book, I assume that you're using the Classic-style interface, in which you click to select and double-click to open a file. If you've set your system to use the Web-style interface, in which you point to select and single-click to open, you need to make a mental conversion when reading some instructions in this book. When the instructions say to click, you should point to select; when I ask you to double-click, you need to click just once (although Windows is smart enough to respond properly if you accidentally double-click in this configuration).

- Use the mouse to draw an imaginary rectangle around a group of files. Point to one corner of the rectangle and hold down the left mouse button as you drag the selection to the opposite corner. Watch the dotted line that appears as you drag the mouse pointer; all icons within this box are selected. This technique works no matter which icon view you've selected.

- To use the keyboard to select a group of adjacent icons, select the first one, hold down the **Shift** key, and press the arrow key to select additional icons. To use the keyboard to select icons that are not adjacent to one another, select the first one, hold down the **Ctrl** key, and use the arrow keys to move through the list; press the spacebar for each file you want to select.

- To quickly select all the files in a folder, press **Ctrl+A** (or pull down the **Edit** menu and choose **Select All**).

If you make a mistake and want to clear all selections, click any empty space in the current folder window or on the desktop.

It's easy to spot files that you've selected, because they appear in a different color than normal. (In the Windows standard color scheme, selected objects are blue.) When you drag one or more files, you see an outline or a ghostly image of the selection, depending on the color settings you've selected.

Creating a New Folder

To create a new folder, follow these steps:

1. Double-click the icon for the drive or folder in which you plan to create the new folder.

2. Right-click any empty space in the contents pane. From the shortcut menu, choose **New** and then choose **Folder**.

3. Windows adds a folder icon at the current location with the generic name New Folder. Because this name is already selected, just start typing to change it immediately.

4. Press **Enter** to save the new folder.

Sort, then select

What's the easiest way to select related icons? Switch to Details view and sort by the column that contains the icons you want to select. Scroll to the first item that matches your criteria and click to select it; then hold down **Shift** and click the last item in the list.

Fast selections

Windows includes a neat shortcut that lets you select all but a few icons within a folder—and even Windows experts sometimes forget it exists. For instance, you might want to delete 20 early drafts from a project folder, leaving only the final version and a few supporting files. Instead of clicking to select all the files you want to delete, select only the handful of files you want to keep, and then pull down the **Edit** menu and choose **Invert Selection**. Windows selects all the files in the current folder except those you marked, after which you can move, copy, or delete the selected objects.

Dragging and Dropping Icons

What happens when you drag an icon from one folder and drop it into another? If you select icons for data files or folders, Windows moves or copies the selected icons, depending on the destination you select. For program files and system objects, you will typically end up creating a shortcut in the new location. Table 7.1 shows what happens when you drag and drop different types of icons to common destinations.

Table 7.1 Default drag-and-drop actions

When You Drag and Drop...	Windows Does This...
File or folder icon(s) to a destination on the same drive	Moves files from the original location to the destination folder
File or folder icon(s) to a destination on a different drive	Copies files to the destination folder; the original files remain intact
Program file icon to destination folder on any drive	Creates shortcut; the original file remains unchanged
Any file icon to Start button	Creates shortcut at the top of the Start menu; the original files are unchanged
Any folder or drive icon to Start button	Creates cascading shortcut menu at the top of the Start menu; the original files are unchanged
System icon (printer, Control Panel icon, and so on) to any destination	Creates shortcut; the original icon remains intact

If you're confused by all those possible drag-and-drop outcomes, that's completely understandable. One excellent way to figure out exactly what will happen when you drag an icon from one location to another is to look at the mouse pointer before you release the mouse button. A plain arrow-shaped pointer means you're about to move the selected icons. If you see a plus sign just to the right of the pointer (see Figure 7.1), you can expect Windows to copy the selection; a small curved arrow in a box next to the pointer (see Figure 7.2) means you'll end up with a shortcut. If the pointer you see doesn't match the result you want, press **Esc** before releasing the mouse button to abort the move or copy procedure.

FIGURE 7.1
The small plus sign next to the mouse pointer means you're about to make a copy of this file.

FIGURE 7.2
The shortcut arrow here tells you that dragging this icon will create a shortcut.

Of course, you can override these default actions:

- To change a default move to a copy, press the **Ctrl** key before releasing the mouse button. This technique is useful when you want to make a copy of a file in the current folder.

- To change a default copy to a move, press the **Shift** key before releasing the mouse button. Use this technique when you want to archive files on a different drive, such as a network server or a Zip drive.

- To create a shortcut without changing the original file, hold down the **Alt** key while dragging.

Frankly, I've never had much luck memorizing these shortcuts, which is why I prefer a much easier drag-and-drop alternative. After selecting one or more icons, hold down the right mouse button and drag them to the destination where you want to move or copy the files. When you release the mouse button, Windows pops up a short-cut menu like the one shown in Figure 7.3. The default action appears in bold type, but you can choose any of the three actions or cancel the whole operation, if you prefer.

SEE ALSO

➤ *For instructions on how to arrange two folder windows side by side, see "Resizing and Arranging Program Windows," p. 96.*

Perfect copies

When you drag a file from one folder to another to make a copy, Windows uses the same filename in both locations, and the two files are absolutely identical. If you hold down **Ctrl** while dragging to make a copy in the same folder as the original file, however, Windows knows that you can't have two files with the same name in a single folder; therefore, it tacks the words `Copy of` to the front of the filename. After creating the copy, rename it if you prefer a different label.

Drag folders, too

You can drag an entire folder to move or copy it from one place to another. When you do, all files and subfolders within the folder come along for the ride. Be certain you have enough room in the destination folder before you try moving an entire folder.

Quick copy to a floppy

To quickly copy one or more files to a floppy disk, select the icon(s), right-click, and choose **Send To** from the shortcut menu. Then choose the floppy drive from the submenu. This menu also includes short-cuts for the My Documents folder and the desktop (where it creates a short-cut).

Moving and Copying Files

To move or copy files from one folder window to another, drag the icons to any empty space in the destination folder. This technique is easiest when you view the destination folder in Large Icons view. Be careful not to drop the selected icon(s) on another icon! If you do, the results will vary, depending on the type of icon you inadvertently use as the drop target. Dropping a group of icons onto a program icon, for instance, causes Windows to open the program and attempt to load every one of the dropped icons. If the target is a subfolder icon, Windows will move or copy the files into that subfolder instead of the folder that's currently open. If you accidentally move or copy a group of files to the wrong location, press Ctrl+Z immediately to undo your action.

To move or copy files using a two-pane window that includes the Folders pane, follow these steps:

1. Open an Explorer window and browse to the folder that contains the file or files you want to work with. If the Folders pane is not visible, click the **Folders** button ▣ on the toolbar.

2. In the right contents pane, select the icon or icons you want to move or copy.

3. Hold down the right mouse button and drag the selected icon(s) over the top of the folder icon in the left pane. If the icon for the destination folder is not visible, let the mouse pointer hover over the icon belonging to its parent folder for a second or two, and the branch will expand automatically.

4. When the pointer is over the icon for the destination folder, release the mouse button.

5. Choose the appropriate action—**Copy Here**, **Move Here**, or **Create Shortcut(s) Here**—from the menu.

You can also use two built-in shortcuts to move and copy files without dragging and dropping. After making a selection, click the **Move To** [icon] or **Copy To** [icon] buttons on the toolbar and select the destination folder from the Browse For Folder dialog box.

You can also use the Windows Clipboard to cut, copy, and paste files between folders and drives, the same way you copy text and graphics between documents. This is one of my favorite techniques because I have no trouble remembering the Ctrl+C, Ctrl+X, and Ctrl+V keyboard shortcuts. To copy, move, or create shortcuts using the Clipboard, follow this procedure:

Using the Clipboard to move or copy files

1. Select the file(s) or folder(s) you want to move or copy.

2. Place the selected icons on the Clipboard using any of the following mouse or keyboard techniques:

    ▪ Pull down the **Edit** menu and choose **Copy** or **Cut**.

    ▪ Right-click the selected icon(s) and choose **Copy** or **Cut**.

    ▪ Press **Ctrl+C** (Copy) or **Ctrl+X** (Cut).

3. Open the destination folder and use any of the following techniques to complete the move or copy:

    ▪ Pull down the **Edit** menu and choose **Paste**.

    ▪ Right-click the folder icon or anywhere in the contents pane and choose **Paste**.

    ▪ Right-click the folder icon or anywhere in the contents pane and press **Ctrl+V**.

Renaming Files

To rename a file, a folder, or a shortcut, start by selecting its icon. Then use any of the following options to highlight the name for editing:

▪ Right-click the icon and choose **Rename** from the shortcut menu. This technique works on any icon in any location, including the Start menu and the Quick Launch bar.

▪ From within a folder window, pull down the **File** menu and choose **Rename**.

Copy and paste to email, too

The Clipboard techniques work just fine in email messages, as well. Copy the files using the techniques I describe here, and then paste them into a mail message as *attachments*.

Where are those buttons?

If you're used to a previous version of Windows that included Internet Explorer 4.0, you may wonder where Explorer's Cut, Copy, and Paste buttons went. They're not gone, just hidden by default. If you really want them back, open any Explorer window, pull down the **View** menu, choose **Toolbars**, and click the **Customize** option. Select the **Cut**, **Copy**, and **Paste** options in the left pane and click the **Add** button to put them in your toolbar.

- Press the **F2** key. This shortcut works for icons on the desktop or in a folder window, but not with icons on the Start menu or the Quick Launch bar.

One at a time

From within the Windows shell, you can rename files only one at a time. If you want to change the names of a group of files, you need to open a Command Prompt window and type DOS-style commands. Look for more details in Appendix B, "Using the Command Line."

By default, Windows selects all the text in an icon's name when you highlight it for editing. To wipe out the old name and enter a completely new one, just start typing. If you want to preserve part or all of the old name—to change `Annual Report First Draft` to `Annual Report Second Draft`, for instance—click again, or use the arrow keys to move the *insertion point* to the correct location. To save the new name, press **Enter** or click any empty space on the desktop or in a folder window.

Deleting Files and Folders

To delete one or more files or folders, select the icons you want to get rid of and then use any of the following techniques:

Click, pause, click...

Yet another way to rename an icon is to click on the name twice, once to select the icon, and the second time to select the text for editing. The problem with this technique (and the reason I don't recommend it) is that you have to click, pause, and click again. If the pause in the middle isn't long enough, you end up double-clicking and inadvertently open the file you selected. If the pause between clicks is too long, on the other hand, Windows forgets the first click and selects the icon again. I strongly recommend using the right-click **Rename** menu, which requires only two clicks.

- Press the **Del** key.
- Pull down the **File** menu and choose **Delete**.
- Right-click and choose **Delete** from the shortcut menu.
- Drag the selected icon(s) and drop them on the Recycle Bin icon.

When you use any of these techniques on files stored on a local hard drive, Windows moves the selected files or folders to the Recycle Bin. This extra step provides you with some security because you can usually recover files from the Recycle Bin if you discover you deleted them by mistake.

Don't be lulled into a false sense of security by the Recycle Bin, however, because in some common circumstances Windows ignores it completely. If you open a shared folder on another computer, for example, and delete files stored there, Windows deletes the files immediately without moving them to the Recycle Bin. Likewise, if you delete files on a floppy disk or on removable media such as a zip disk, Windows does not store those files in the Recycle Bin. (In both cases, you see a warning dialog box first.) Using the **DEL** command from an MS-DOS Prompt window removes the files permanently, without storing safe copies in the Recycle Bin and without warning you.

And if you overwrite a file with another file of the same name, the old file does not go into the Recycle Bin.

SEE ALSO

➤ *For more information on recovering deleted data, see "Recovering Individual Files," p. 164, and "Recovering Deleted Folders," p. 165.*

In some cases, you might be certain you want to delete a file without storing it in the Recycle Bin. If you're getting rid of a particularly large file, for example, you might want to bypass the Recycle Bin; that way, Windows doesn't have to empty a bunch of old files from the Recycle Bin to make room for it. To delete a file immediately, first select its icon and then press **Shift+Del**. Or hold down the **Shift** key, right-click, and choose **Delete** from the shortcut menu.

By default, when you choose to delete files or folders rather than moving them to the Recycle Bin, Windows displays the Confirm File Delete dialog box shown in Figure 7.4, which forces you to click **OK**. This is the same dialog box that appears when you delete files on a shared network folder or a floppy disk.

SEE ALSO

➤ *For details on how you can customize the Recycle Bin, see "Changing the Way the Recycle Bin Works," p. 165.*

Undoing Changes

Windows 2000 lets you undo actions you perform when managing files. If you inadvertently delete a file, move it to the wrong location, or make a mistake when renaming a file or folder, click the **Undo** button [Undo] on the standard toolbar or press **Ctrl+Z**.

Windows remembers the last five file-management actions you took, such as deleting, moving, or renaming files, and can undo any of the five actions, beginning with the most recent one. Unfortunately, it's not always easy to tell exactly what Undo will accomplish, and no Redo option is available to restore your original action, either. If you

---

A better Recycle Bin?

If you want more protection against inadvertent file deletion than the Windows 2000 Recycle Bin offers, check out utility programs from other vendors. Symantec's Norton Utilities (www.symantec.com) and PowerQuest's Lost & Found (www.powerquest.com) both offer enhanced versions of the Recycle Bin to give you greater protection.

FIGURE 7.4
When you hold down the **Shift** key and delete one or more files, Windows bypasses the Recycle Bin after asking you to confirm that's what you really want to do.

Careful with folders!

When you delete a folder, you also delete all files and subfolders within that folder. Check the contents carefully before you drag a folder icon into the Recycle Bin.

delete a file in one folder, for example, and then move to a different Explorer window and press Ctrl+Z, Windows will restore the file you deleted; however, you can't be sure it worked until you open that folder window again. For a clue about what Undo will do, pull down the **E**dit menu and look at the choice at the top of the menu. You'll see **U**ndo Delete, **U**ndo Move, or **U**ndo Rename—the exact choice varies depending on which action you took most recently.

Using Shortcuts

Even in the most orderly filing system, the files you use most often are scattered across your hard disk. Whether you organize data files by the program that created them, by project, or by date, you will invariably want quick access to related files that are located in different folders. If you're starting to create a new annual report, for instance, you might want a Word document from your My Documents folder, a handful of logos from a network server, and a copy of last year's report from your Archive folder. Drilling down into each of those folders and subfolders every time you want to work on this project can take many mouse clicks—even if you can remember where all those files are located.

You don't want to move those files into a new folder, however, because their current organizational scheme makes perfect sense (and your network administrator would have a fit if you moved the shared corporate files). Nor do you want to create copies of each one, because then you would end up with different versions of the same file in different locations, and you would risk using an outdated version in an important document. Fortunately, there's a solution that lets you preserve your orderly filing system and still keep programs and documents readily accessible. By creating a shortcut to each of the files you want to work with, you can create a temporary group of icons in one location.

How Shortcuts Work

As the name implies, a shortcut is a pointer to an object stored elsewhere. You can create a shortcut for almost any object in Windows, including programs, data files, folders, drives, Dial-Up Networking

---

Undo works on the desktop, too

The Undo shortcuts described in this section also work if you make a mistake with a file or folder on the Windows desktop. For example, if you accidentally delete a file from the desktop or move it to the wrong folder, press **Ctrl+Z** immediately to recover the file.

Shortcuts save space, too

Shortcuts have one other attractive characteristic— they save space. A shortcut file is typically only a few hundred bytes in size and occupies about 4KB of disk space. If you make five copies of a 1MB graphics file, you use up an extra 5MB of disk space; in contrast, five shortcuts occupy about 20KB of disk space, or less than one half of one percent of the space of all those copies.

connections, printers, and Web pages. The *target*—the term Windows uses for the file or folder that the shortcut refers to— might be on your local hard disk, on a network server, or on the Internet. Using shortcuts effectively can save you tremendous amounts of time every day.

Shortcuts are small files that contain all the information Windows needs to create a link to the target. The shortcut uses the same icon as the target file, with one crucial difference: a small arrow in the lower-right corner that identifies the icon as a shortcut instead of an original. After creating a shortcut, you can move or copy it anywhere; the target file remains in its original location.

When you right-click a shortcut, the menu choices are the same as those you would see when you right-click the target file. Likewise, double-clicking the shortcut has the same effect as opening the target file. However, if you right-click a shortcut and choose **Pro̲perties**, the dialog box shows the properties of the shortcut rather than those of the target file, as the example in Figure 7.5 demonstrates.

> **Rename or delete at will**
>
> If you see the shortcut arrow on an icon, you can delete or rename it without fear. Deleting a shortcut has absolutely no effect on the target file, which remains intact in its original location. Likewise, changing the name of a shortcut does not change the name of the target file.

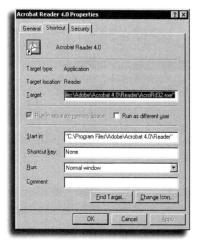

FIGURE 7.5
The Properties dialog box for a shortcut provides important information. Click the **Find Target** button to open the folder that contains the target file and look at its properties.

When you double-click a shortcut, the effect is the same as if you had double-clicked the target file. But what happens if you've moved or renamed the target? If you renamed the file or moved the file to another folder on the same drive, Windows can usually reestablish the link between the shortcut and the target. It looks in the same folder for a file with the same date and time stamp but a different

Use shortcuts freely
You can create multiple shortcuts to a single file— a technique you can use to organize your work more effectively. Suppose you organize your work by project, and you incorporate work from your corporate art department into each project. If the art department stores logos and other graphics in a common location on a file server, put a shortcut to that shared folder in each of the project folders you're working on. When you need to find an up-to-date logo, you won't have to drill down through dozens of folders to find it—just double-click the shortcut to open that folder immediately.

name. If no such file exists in the original folder, Windows looks in subfolders and then on the entire drive where the target file was originally stored. If it finds a match, the shortcut changes the link to point to that file automatically. This all happens quickly—usually so quickly you might not even notice that the shortcut stopped working briefly.

If you moved the target file to a different drive, however, Windows won't be able to find it, and the shortcut will break. If Windows can't find the target file, it tries to identify the nearest matching file. As it chugs through your entire hard drive or server, it displays the dialog box shown in Figure 7.6. If you see this dialog box for more than 30 seconds, chances are good that Windows will not be able to find the target. If you know where the target file is located, I recommend that you click the **Browse** button and find it yourself.

If you let the search go on, eventually Windows displays the closest match it can find, using a dialog box like the one in Figure 7.7. In my experience, Windows is nearly always wrong. If you got lucky and Windows found the right file, click the **Fix It** button. If the suggested file is the wrong one, click **Delete It** to get rid of the shortcut. Then use the Search Assistant to find the correct file and create a new shortcut from scratch.

FIGURE 7.6
If you see this dialog box, Windows can't find the target file for your shortcut.

FIGURE 7.7
If Windows can't locate the target for a shortcut, it suggests the closest matching file—usually the wrong one.

SEE ALSO

➤ *For details on how to use Internet shortcuts, see "Saving Links to Your Favorite Web Sites,"* p. 381.

➤ *To learn how to use the Search Assistant to find files, see "Searching for Files and Folders,"* p. 115.

Creating a New Shortcut

As I noted earlier, the easiest way to create a new shortcut is to use the right mouse button to drag an icon to a new location, and then choose **Create Shortcut(s) Here** from the menu that appears. The second-easiest way is to use the Create Shortcut Wizard.

When should you create a shortcut by dragging and dropping, and when should you use the Create Shortcut Wizard? If you can see the file for which you want to create a shortcut, use the right-mouse-button drag-and-drop technique to create a shortcut. If, on the other hand, you want to create a shortcut to a file or folder that is buried several folders deep, use the wizard—its Browse for Folder dialog box is the fastest way to link to a drive, file, or folder icon.

Creating a new shortcut

1. Right-click any empty space in a folder window or on the Windows desktop. From the shortcut menu, choose **New**, and then click **Shortcut**. The Create Shortcut dialog box appears (see Figure 7.8).

> **Fast desktop shortcuts**
>
> Want to create a shortcut on the desktop? If you can see a file or folder icon, you can create a desktop shortcut with just a few clicks—and this trick even works from the Open or Save As dialog box in a Windows program. Right-click the file or folder, choose **Send To** from the shortcut menu, and click **Desktop (create short-cut)**. Move the shortcut to another location later, if you prefer.

FIGURE 7.8
Use this wizard to create a new shortcut in two easy steps.

2. If you know the exact name and path of the file you want to use, enter it into the box. Or click the **Browse** button to open the

Browse for Folder dialog box. Don't be fooled by the name—from this dialog box, you can select a document, a program file, a folder, or a drive icon. Click **Next** to continue.

3. Give the shortcut a descriptive name and click **Finish**. Test the shortcut to make sure it works correctly.

Changing a Shortcut's Properties

To change a shortcut after you've created it, right-click its icon and choose **Properties**. In the Properties dialog box, click the **General** tab to see basic information about the shortcut file itself, such as the shortcut's name and when it was created. Click the **Shortcut** tab (see Figure 7.9 for an example) to change the target file (or add *switches* or other details to the target information), specify a different startup folder, define a keyboard combination that you can use to launch the shortcut, or add a *comment* to describe the shortcut.

FIGURE 7.9
Use this dialog box to change a shortcut's settings. Comments appear as part of the ScreenTip.

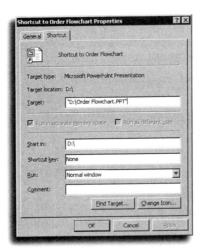

To associate a different file with the shortcut, click in the **Target** box and enter a new filename, including its full path. Because no Browse button is available, it's usually easier to create a new shortcut than to edit this field.

SEE ALSO

➤ *For details on how to use the startup folder and assign key combinations to shortcuts, see "Creating Shortcuts to Favorite Programs," p. 91.*

Customizing Folder Options

By default, Windows 2000 configures Explorer so that it behaves much like its predecessor in previous Windows versions. However, you can make several changes in the overall behavior of folder windows. To get to all these settings, open any Explorer window, pull down the **Tools** menu, and choose **Folder Options**. Three of the four settings on the **General** tab (see Figure 7.10) let you make sweeping changes to the appearance of icons and the way the mouse works. (Strictly speaking, the *Active Desktop* options shouldn't be in this dialog box at all because they affect only the desktop and not folders.)

SEE ALSO

➤ *To learn how to use different Explorer views, see "Customizing Explorer's Appearance," p. 131.*

➤ *For details on how and when to set Active Desktop and customization options, see "Taming the Active Desktop," p. 182.*

Sharing shortcuts is OK

When you create a shortcut to a file on your own hard disk, Windows stores it with a reference to that disk's drive letter—C:, for instance. However, it also stores information that identifies your machine by name. If you send that shortcut to another user (through email, for example), Windows translates the target location so that it points to the correct address. As long as you allow the other person access to the folder that contains the target file, he or she can open it by double-clicking the shortcut.

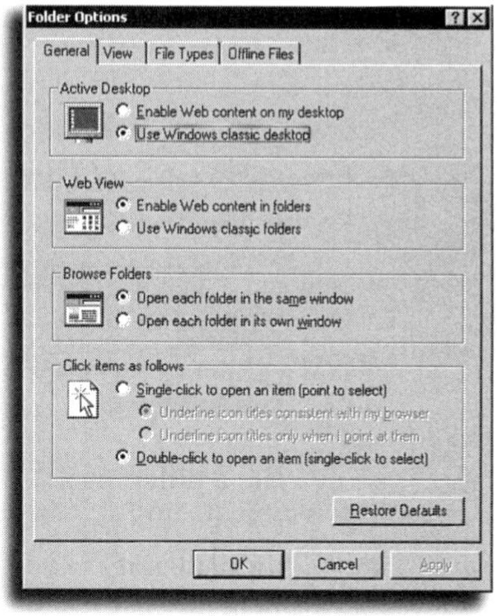

FIGURE 7.10
The options shown here let you control the behavior of the mouse and the display of icons in folder windows.

Viewing Folders as Web Pages

Your settings may be different…

If you upgraded to Windows 2000 from a previous version of Windows, your folder settings may be different. Microsoft has been wildly inconsistent as it introduced various versions of Explorer in Windows 95 and Internet Explorer. Your system may be set up to use the Web-style interface even if you never made that choice yourself. To use the default settings for Windows 2000, open the **Folder Options** dialog box, go to the **General** tab, and click the **Restore Defaults** button.

Web View = HTML

When Windows says Web view, you can take it literally. In Web view, Explorer uses *HTML templates* to store instructions about what kind of content appears in the info pane. A *list control* embedded in this template defines where the filenames appear. One of the options in the Customize This Folder Wizard lets you edit this template. If you speak fluent HTML, be my guest, but don't expect any help from Windows—the wizard opens the template in Notepad, and if you want to customize anything, you have to enter tags by hand. Unless you're a Web whiz, it's not worth the headache.

Windows 2000 gives you the option to display each folder as if it were a Web page. With this option (which is on by default), Explorer includes a Web-style info pane to the left of each folder window. What you actually see in the info pane for each folder varies slightly because different folders use different Web view templates. Typically, this pane includes the name of the folder, details about the currently selected files or folders, and buttons you can click to change options specific to that folder.

You can turn this feature on or off for all folders using the two Web view options on the **General** tab of the Folder Options dialog box. Check **Enable Web content in folders**, the default setting, to specify that you want the info pane to be available at all times for all folders. Select **Use Windows classic folders** if you want to see only a simple list of icons, without Web content.

In most system folders (My Computer, Control Panel, and Recycle Bin, for example), Web view provides useful information. If you want to leave Web view on for these folders but turn it off for folders that contain data files, try customizing individual folders instead.

To begin customizing a folder, pull down the **View** menu and choose **Customize This Folder**. Follow the wizard's prompts to make changes to the current folder only. After the opening screen, for instance, the wizard lets you choose any or all of three options, as shown in Figure 7.11.

- You can select an HTML template from the list of built-in choices that Windows provides. As Figure 7.12 demonstrates, you can choose any of four built-in templates. Use the Classic template if you want to hide Web content for this folder only, without turning off Web view completely. Choose the Standard template to restore the default Web view to a folder.

- Modify the background picture. Normally, folder windows have no background at all. You can add a graphical image in JPEG or BMP format to make the folder look more interesting.

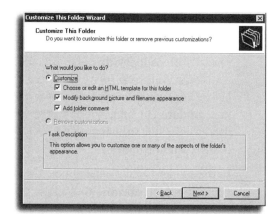

FIGURE 7.11
Use this wizard to customize the look of any folder window; this wizard is not available for system folders.

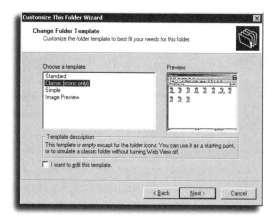

FIGURE 7.12
Use one of these four templates to change the appearance of a folder in Web view. Don't bother trying to edit a template unless you're an HTML expert.

- Change the color that Windows uses for filenames in an Explorer window. Use this option if you've selected a background picture for the folder—custom colors can make it easier to read the filenames against the background image.

- Add a comment that appears in the info pane. This option is most useful if you're responsible for managing a shared folder, either on your computer or on a network server, and you want other users to see a description of the contents of the folder.

Graphics sometimes get in the way

Use background graphics sparingly in folder windows. Generally, a background image makes it more difficult to see icons and labels; if you must use a background picture, try a light gray or pastel image that is subtle and doesn't interfere with the folder's contents.

How Many Windows?

Try these shortcuts

Most of the time, you'll want to use a single window to browse for files and folders. Occasionally, however, you might want to open a folder in a separate window. If you hold down the **Ctrl** key and double-click a folder icon, Windows uses the opposite of the current Browse Folders setting. Therefore, if you've set Explorer to use a single window for browsing, **Ctrl+click** to open a new window. If you use the multiple-windows option, **Ctrl+click** to open a folder in the current window.

In the original version of Windows 95, double-clicking a folder icon caused a new window to open. If you started with My Computer, double-clicked the C: drive icon, and then went a few folders deep; before you knew it, your screen was cluttered with six or more separate windows. In later Windows versions, Microsoft changed this default behavior so that clicking a folder icon replaced the contents of the current window.

In the Folder Options dialog box, the Browse Folders section lets you choose one of two settings:

- Select **Open each folder in the same window** if you prefer the default behavior, which replaces the contents of the current window whenever you double-click a folder or a drive icon.

- Choose **Open each folder in its own window** if you want to open a new window every time you double-click a folder or a drive icon.

One Click or Two?

Windows lets you choose one of two procedures for selecting icons. If you stick with the default Classic-style interface, you click each icon to select it and double-click it to open it. On the other hand, if you've chosen the Web-style interface, you point at a file to select it and you click once to open it, the same as you would in a Web browser.

The options in the **Click items as follows** section let you switch from the default Classic style to Web style and back. With the single-click option on, a typical folder window will look like the one in Figure 7.13.

When you switch to the Web-style interface, the change is effective throughout Windows—even Open and Save As dialog boxes are affected. Unfortunately, some programs don't use the common dialog boxes, and as a result, you'll occasionally find yourself having to click and double-click. Most users find the Web-style interface too clumsy for everyday use; I don't recommend it.

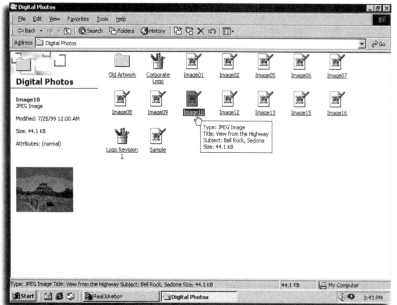

FIGURE 7.13
Using the Web-style
interface, all filenames
are underlined and the
mouse pointer resem-
bles a pointing hand, the
same as in a browser
window.

**Need help? Click the
question mark**

If you're baffled by any of
the check boxes on the
View tab of the Folder
Options dialog box, get a
quick explanation from the
online help. Click the small
question-mark icon in the
title bar to change the
pointer to an arrow-and-
question-mark combination.
Then point to any entry in
the list of options and click
to pop up a helpful
ScreenTip.

Advanced Folder Options

Aside from the basic options, you can also choose from an assortment of advanced folder options. Click the **View** tab in the Folder
Options dialog box to display the selection shown in Figure 7.14.

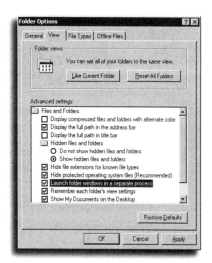

FIGURE 7.14
These options let you
fine-tune some of
Explorer's more obscure
options.

After installing Windows 2000 for the first time, I recommend that you open this dialog box and make any necessary changes. For example, I prefer to display the full path of a file or a folder in the Address bar (but I don't display the title bar). I also like to see hidden and system files in folder windows. These options and others are easy to set by checking and unchecking boxes here. It takes only a few seconds to run through the entire list, and you'll notice the benefits every time you browse for files.

Changing Associations Between Files and Programs

Every time you double-click an icon—in a folder window, on the Start menu, or on the desktop—Windows has to figure out what to do next. If the icon represents a program or a Web page, the choice is easy: run the program or load the Web page in your default browser. But if you selected a data file, the task is trickier: Windows has to figure out which program is responsible for that type of file, open that program, and then load the file.

To make this job simpler, Windows keeps a master list of *registered file types*. For each file type, Windows keeps track of the default file extension and the program it should use to open or edit that file type. Windows sets up a large number of default *associations* between file types and programs on its own. For instance, Windows knows that any file with the extension TXT is a text document; if you double-click this file type, Windows opens the file in Notepad.

Most Windows programs add their own associations. For example, the superb archiving utility WinZip (available on the Web from Nico Mak software at www.winzip.com), registers a large number of extensions, including ZIP, ARJ, and UUE, as WinZip files.

When you install two programs that use the same file extensions— for example, two programs that you use to edit GIF or JPEG graphic images—the one you installed most recently is usually the one that Windows recognizes for file associations.

To view the master list of all file associations, open the **Folder Options** dialog box and click the **File Types** tab. Figure 7.15 shows a typical set of entries. By default, this list is sorted by Extension. Click the **File Types** heading to sort by file type instead, in alphabetical order.

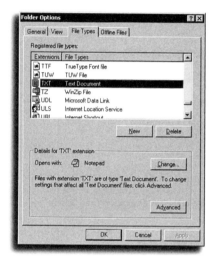

FIGURE 7.15
This master list of file associations defines which program Windows uses when you double-click an icon.

Although it's possible to use this master list to change the association between a program and a file type, it's much easier to do so directly from Explorer. You can override the default association on a one-time basis, or you can make the change permanent.

Say you're working with a JPEG graphics file, and you want to use the Windows 2000 Imaging program to edit it. Double-clicking the file causes it to open in Internet Explorer, which is not what you want. But changing the association permanently would mean that all such files open in Imaging—that's not what you want, either. Fortunately, Windows offers a way to choose which of several programs you want to use with a particular file type.

Choosing which program opens a data file

1. Point to the icon and right-click to display its shortcut menu.

2. Choose **Open With** from the shortcut menu. If the file type is already associated with more than one program, choose the program you want from the cascading menu or click **Choose Program**.

Extension? File type?

The relationship between file extensions and file types does not involve a direct, one-to-one correspondence. In fact, it's not unusual for a single file type to use several file extensions. For instance, Windows knows that any document with the extension HTM, HTML, or HTW is a Web page of the file type Microsoft HTML Document 5.0. If you change the settings for that file type, your changes apply to all documents of that type, regardless of their extension.

3. Browse through the list of registered programs in the Open With dialog box (see Figure 7.16) and select the program you want to use to open the data file. If the program is not listed here, click the **O̲ther** button and browse to select its *executable file*.

FIGURE 7.16
Right-click a data file and choose a program from this list. Check the box at the bottom of the dialog box to make the change permanent.

It's easier the second time

After you've used an alternate program to open a given file type, that option appears on the **Open With** menu. Instead of having to go through the dialog box, all you have to do is choose the program name from the cascading menu.

4. If you want the program you selected to run whenever you double-click files of this type in the future, check the **A̲lways use this program to open these files** box.

5. Click **OK** to open the file.

To permanently change associations between a file type and the program Windows uses to open it, start by selecting a file of that type. Right-click and choose **P̲roperties** from the shortcut menu, and then click the **General** tab. You see a dialog box like the one in Figure 7.17.

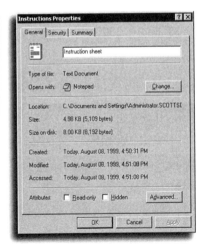

FIGURE 7.17
Click the **C̲hange** button to choose a different program for use with this file type.

Near the top of this dialog box, you'll find two important pieces of information: the file type and the program registered to handle that file type. To permanently change the program associated with this file type, click the **<u>C</u>hange** button. In the Open With dialog box, select the program you want to use and click **OK**.

The Long and Short of Filenames

When you create a new file or folder in Windows, you have to give it a name. Windows gives you a tremendous amount of flexibility in choosing a descriptive name, but you must abide by the following rules:

- A file or folder name can consist of up to 255 characters, including spaces.

- You can use any letters (A–Z) or numbers (0–9) in any combination.

- You can use most punctuation marks and special characters, including periods and commas, semicolons, exclamation points and ampersands, parentheses, single quotation marks, and square brackets. However, Windows will display an error message if you try to use any of the following characters:

  \ / : * ? " < > |

- The filename you enter must be unique in the current folder. Windows does not consider case (upper- and lowercase letters) in filenames, so Report2.doc is the same as REPORT2.doc.

When you enter a descriptive filename, Windows 2000 stores the name exactly as you entered it. In most cases, it also creates a short filename to go along with the name you entered. This step is crucial for compatibility with older Windows and MS-DOS programs, which do not recognize long names for files and folders. Short filenames may also be required on a network. If you share files with people who use older operating systems that don't recognize long filenames, such as Windows 3.1, they will see only the short filename.

How long is too long?

Although the theoretical maximum length of a file or folder name is 255 characters, I strongly recommend that you restrict names to no more than 30 or 40 characters. Windows counts the full path name in the 255-character limit; if you create a very long filename and move it to a location several folders deep, you'll encounter error messages. It's also nearly impossible to read extra-long filenames in an Explorer window.

When to use short names

If you routinely share files with other people who use MS-DOS or Windows 3.1, or if you routinely open a particular file type in an older Windows program that doesn't recognize long filenames, you should avoid using long filenames whenever possible. Restrict filenames to eight characters or fewer, and don't use spaces. That way, the filename you see in Explorer windows will be the same as the ones others see when they browse for files.

Hunting down duplicates

If you routinely store backup copies of important data files, you'll end up with duplicate filenames scattered all over your system. That can cause problems if you inadvertently open an older version of a file. To quickly find duplicates, use the Search Assistant. Click the **Start** button, choose **Search**, and select **For Files or Folders**. In the **Search for files or folders named** box, enter part or all of the filename you want to match, and then click **Search Now**. Pull down the **View** menu and choose **Details** to see all the duplicate files grouped together, with the name of each one's folder in a column to the right of the name.

Not like Windows 95

The process by which Windows 2000 generates short filenames is similar to the one that Windows 95 and Windows 98 use, but it is not identical. If you learned the rules for those older Windows versions, read this section carefully.

Suppose you've just created a Word document and named the file `Annual Report Draft 11-01-2000`. When you open a folder window or use the Open dialog box in Word, you see the filename exactly as you created it. But if you try to open that file using an older Windows program, you'll need a secret decoder ring to find the right file—the short file equivalent of that file may look something like `AN3A43~1.DOC`, which is far from intuitive.

Where does the short name come from? When you create a file, Windows checks the name you entered against the rules for MS-DOS files. If the name uses eight or fewer characters, with no more than three characters in the extension and no spaces or extra periods, the short name and the long name are identical. Thus, if you call a file `Report14.doc`, Windows stores the same name in both the long and short list.

However, if the name you enter includes more than eight characters, if you use more than three characters in the extension, or if the name includes a space or an extra period (which is not legal under MS-DOS file-naming rules), Windows 2000 generates a short name automatically. Windows stores the long name you entered and the short name it created as part of the directory information for that file.

Suppose you use Microsoft Word to create a daily report for publication over your company's intranet. You store all the files in a single folder, and you use a consistent naming scheme in which each file starts with the words *Sales Report* followed by the current date. For the first file you create, `Sales Report 01-01.doc`, Windows determines that it needs to generate a short name because the file is longer than eight characters and contains spaces. First, it strips away all spaces and grabs the first six characters of the long name. Next, it adds a tilde character and the number 1. Finally, it tacks on the extension from the original long name. The result is the short name `SALESR~1.DOC`.

For the next three files you create using this naming scheme, Windows follows the same procedure, tacking on the numbers 2, 3, and 4, respectively, to avoid creating duplicate filenames. Thus, on the fourth day your long filename `Sales Report 01-04.doc` becomes `SALESR~4.DOC`. After the fourth such file, however, the rules change.

Rather than use ~5, ~6, and so on, Windows uses only the first two characters of the long filename, tacking on four characters it generates at random, followed by ~1 and the extension. Thus, on the fifth day, your long filename `Sales Report 01-05.doc` may become `SA2C19~1.DOC`.

Most of the time, you won't have to deal with short filenames. On the rare occasions that you do, however, it helps to know how Windows works.

SEE ALSO

➤ *For directions on how to use the* DIR *command to see short filenames, see "Viewing Directory Listings," p. 463.*

Working with Hidden and System Files

Every file and folder includes four special *attributes* that Windows uses for access control. On new files and folders you create, these four attributes are always off. Windows and Windows programs may reset attributes on specific files and folders as part of the setup process.

- **System.** Windows marks some files and folders with the System attribute, which makes them invisible in folder windows unless you specifically choose the option to display such files. You cannot change this attribute from an Explorer window.

- **Archive.** Marks files that have been changed since they were last backed up. Most backup programs use the Archive attribute to decide which files need to be copied as part of a partial backup. You cannot change this attribute from an Explorer window, either.

- **Read-only.** Prevents users from changing a file or folder. You can turn this attribute on and off for any file or folder you create; depending on your user privileges, you may also be able to do this for other files.

- **Hidden.** Prevents users from seeing a file or folder in a normal folder window or directory listing. (Anyone can open or change the file, however, if they can find its icon or type its name in an Open dialog box.) If you change folder options to make hidden files visible, their icons appear lighter than the icons for normal files and folders.

Short names are hidden

Explorer windows do not offer any way to see the automatically generated short names for files you create, nor are these names visible in the Properties dialog box for a given file. The only way to view short filenames from Windows 2000 is to open a Command Prompt window and use the DIR command with the /X switch. See Appendix B, "Using the Command Line," for details.

Change System files with care!

Windows marks files with the System attribute for a good reason—to prevent you from inadvertently modifying or deleting files that Windows requires. The only way to turn this attribute on or off for a given file or folder is to open a Command Prompt window and use the ATTRIB command. (Enter **ATTRIB** /? at the prompt for details of the syntax for this command.) Generally, I recommend that you avoid messing with the System attribute unless you absolutely must do so—to manually replace a damaged file, for example. After turning off the system attribute and making repairs, always be sure to turn this attribute on again.

161

To change the Read-only or Hidden attribute for a file or folder, select its icon, choose **Properties** from the shortcut menu, and click the **General** tab. Use the check boxes at the bottom of this dialog box to turn either attribute on or off.

To see all attributes for all the files and subfolders in a given folder, first switch to Details view; then pull down the **View** menu, click **Choose Columns**, check the **Attributes** box, and click **OK**. The letters A, R, H, and S appear in this column to indicate files and folders with special attributes. (Of course, you can see System and Hidden files in folder windows and directory listings only if you've used the Folder Options dialog box to override the default settings.)

For the most part, Windows and Windows applications adjust file attributes automatically. You might want to manually adjust file attributes, however, to protect important files from accidental modification. For instance, if you copy your corporate logo to a shared folder on a network server, you might want to set its Read-only attribute so that you or other users don't accidentally change the file. To do so, right-click the file's icon, choose **Properties**, and on the **General** tab, check the **Read-only** box.

If you hide a single file or set it to be read-only, Windows applies your change immediately. However, if you turn on the Read-only or Hidden attribute for a folder that contains other files or subfolders, Windows displays the dialog box shown in Figure 7.18. Think carefully before you choose!

FIGURE 7.18
To provide maximum protection for files and folders, choose the second option when marking a folder as Read-only or Hidden.

- The first option, **Apply changes to this folder only**, might not have the effect you expect. This action displays a warning dialog box, but it doesn't stop you (or any other user) from renaming or deleting the folder, nor does it prevent changes to files and subfolders within that folder.

- The second option, **Apply changes to this folder, subfolders and files**, causes Windows to go through the contents of the folder you selected and change the attributes on every icon stored there. It's an all-or-nothing proposition—if you want only some of the files and folders to be marked read-only, you must repeat this process individually for each icon. However, if you later create a new file or subfolder in that folder, it will not be marked with the same attribute!

A word of caution: If you set the Read-only attribute for a file or folder, any user can still delete it. By default, Windows displays a warning dialog box before proceeding with the deletion, but it's all too easy to click right past it—and if you have turned off the Confirm File Deletion dialog boxes, you won't even receive this warning. If you have a file that is truly important, make sure you keep a backup copy in a safe location.

If you're confident that you can work with hidden and system files without crashing your computer, you may want to adjust Explorer's options so that you can see these files in folder windows.

Making hidden files visible

1. Open any folder window (My Computer works nicely), pull down the **Tools** menu, and choose **Folder Options**.

2. In the Folder Options dialog box, click the **View** tab. Under **Hidden files and folders**, select the **Show hidden files and folders** option.

3. If you also want to be able to see System files and folders, click the box to the left of the **Hide protected operating system files** option to remove the check mark. A warning dialog box asks you to confirm that you really want to do this; click **OK** to continue.

4. Click **OK** to save your changes and close the Folder Options dialog box.

> **Don't rely on attributes**
>
> If you're really concerned about protecting files and folders from unauthorized changes, don't rely on the Read-only and Hidden attributes. Instead, use file permissions to restrict users from modifying or deleting particular files.

> **Or start with Control Panel**
>
> Unlike previous Windows versions, Windows 2000 includes the Folder Options icon in Control Panel. To adjust Explorer settings without opening an Explorer window, open **Control Panel** and double-click this item.

If you pull down the **Edit** menu and choose **Select All** (or use the **Ctrl+A** keyboard shortcut), you might think you've selected all the files in the current folder. If that folder contains hidden files, however, you'll see a warning message like the one in Figure 7.19. There is no way to manage hidden files from Explorer unless you make them visible.

Recovering Deleted Files

When you delete a file or folder stored on your own hard disk, it doesn't actually disappear; instead, Windows moves it to a special system folder called the Recycle Bin. The file remains there until you empty the Recycle Bin or until the Recycle Bin becomes full and Windows starts tossing out old files to make room for new ones. As long as the file or folder you deleted remains in the Recycle Bin, you can recover it intact.

Recovering Individual Files

Restore all? Just say no!

If you use the Web view option with the Recycle Bin, the info pane at the left side of the window contains one particularly dangerous button. If no files are selected, the info pane shows two buttons: **Empty Recycle Bin**, which is potentially useful, and **Restore All**, whose consequences can be disastrous. I strongly recommend that you never, ever click the **Restore All** button—especially if the Recycle Bin contains more than a handful of files. This option is guaranteed to make a mess of your filing system, and in some cases, it could even replace a newer file with an old, outdated version.

To recover a deleted file, double-click the **Recycle Bin** icon on the desktop, or select its icon in the Folders pane of an Explorer window or from the drop-down list in the Address bar. Browse through the contents until you find the file or files you're looking for. To return the file to its original location, right-click and choose **Restore** from the shortcut menu. To restore the file to a location other than where it came from originally, drag the icon out of the Recycle Bin and drop it anywhere you like—on the Windows desktop, for example.

If you use the Web view option with the Recycle Bin, the info pane at the left side of the window contains all kinds of useful information, as well as buttons you can click to perform different actions. Select a single file and you can see the name of the folder in which it was originally stored, its size, and when it was deleted. If you choose multiple files, you lose some of these details, but you can see the total size of the files you selected. Click the **Restore** button to quickly move the selected file(s) back to their original location.

Recovering Deleted Folders

When you delete a folder that contains files and subfolders, Windows keeps a copy of the entire folder in the Recycle Bin. You can't see individual files that might be in the folder, nor can you restore files one at a time. In fact, if you inspect the properties of the folder icon, you get no information at all—whether you switch to Details view, pop up the Properties dialog box, or use the info pane, Windows tells you the folder contains 0 bytes.

To restore an entire folder from the Recycle Bin, use the same options that you would with individual files: right-click and choose **Restore** from the shortcut menu, or drag the folder to the desktop so that you can look through all the files it contains.

Changing the Way the Recycle Bin Works

When I install Windows 2000, one of the very first things I do is make a few adjustments to the way the Recycle Bin works. For example, Windows 2000 insists on displaying the Confirm File Delete dialog box every time I move a file to the Recycle Bin. Because I find this dialog box annoying, I like to turn it off.

I also like to adjust the amount of space the Recycle Bin uses. In a normal Windows 2000 installation, the Recycle Bin sets aside 10% of the space on every local disk partition for storing deleted files. On a 5GB volume, that means the Recycle Bin is using 500MB of space, which is far more safety net than I need. I prefer to cut its appetite down to size. (Don't make the Recycle Bin too small, however. I recommend that you allow at least 50MB of room in the Recycle Bin—more if you regularly work with extra-large files such as graphics and sound files.)

Customizing the Recycle Bin

1. Right-click the **Recycle Bin** icon and choose **Properties** from the shortcut menu. The Recycle Bin Properties dialog box appears (see Figure 7.20).

2. If you have more than one drive, each one will have its own tab in the dialog box. Use the option at the top of the Global tab to specify whether you want to **Configure drives independently** or **Use one setting for all drives**.

> **Watch those dialog boxes!**
>
> If you turn off the confirmation dialog box, Windows gives you no warning when you delete a file permanently, as is the case when you select files on a shared network folder and press the **Del** key. If you choose to disable this feature, you must be extremely careful every time you delete a file; you may not get the chance to bring it back.

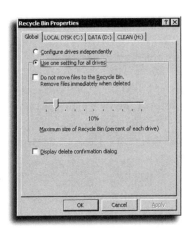

FIGURE 7.20
Normally, the Recycle Bin sets aside 10% of each drive for storing deleted files. Use this dialog box to adjust this setting.

What's the right setting?

How much space should you reserve in the Recycle Bin? The correct answer depends on your personal comfort level and on the type of files you produce most often. If you typically create word processing files of 50KB or so, a 100MB Recycle Bin leaves you enough room for 200 documents, which should be plenty. On the other hand, if you routinely create and delete large graphics files and desktop publishing documents that are 5–10MB in size (or more), consider increasing the size of the Recycle Bin so that it will hold a few weeks' worth of work.

3. Use the slider control on the Global tab to change the percentage of disk space reserved for the Recycle Bin (if you chose the **Configure drives independently** option, click each drive tab in turn to adjust this setting for individual drives). You can choose any setting between 0% and 100%, but the most realistic settings are between 3% and 20%.

4. If you do not want to use the Recycle Bin at all, check the box labeled **Do not move files to the Recycle Bin. Remove files immediately when deleted.** If you chose to configure each drive independently, you'll need to adjust this check box on each drive's tab. (Unless you are extremely low on hard disk space, I do not recommend this option.)

5. To avoid having to deal with the confirmation dialog box every time you delete a file, clear the check mark from the box labeled **Display delete confirmation dialog**.

6. Click **OK** to save your changes and close the dialog box.

Emptying the Recycle Bin

Under normal circumstances, you shouldn't need to delete the Recycle Bin. When it fills up, Windows automatically deletes the oldest files to make room for new files you delete. If you run short of hard disk space—when installing a new program, for example—

you may decide to clear out the Recycle Bin to make room for the new program. To delete all files from the Recycle Bin, right-click its icon and choose **Empty Recycle Bin** from the shortcut menu.

SEE ALSO

➤ *For details on how to use the Disk Cleanup Wizard to empty the Recycle Bin automatically, see "Removing Unneeded Files," p. 277.*

Drive-by-drive settings

If you organize files using multiple disk partitions, each with its own drive letter, setting separate Recycle Bin properties for each drive may make perfect sense. For instance, suppose you have all your system and program files on C:, your data files on D:, and a small F: partition you use only for temporary files. In that case, it makes sense to keep a small Recycle Bin on C:, a large one on D:, and disable the Recycle Bin completely on F:.

chapter

8

Customizing Windows 2000

Personalizing the Windows Interface

When you install Windows 2000 on a freshly formatted drive, Windows uses default settings for all kinds of interface elements, including the color of the *desktop*, fonts and colors used in the *title bars* of windows and dialog boxes, the size of text in menus, the size and spacing of icons and scrollbars, and more. By default, for example, the Windows desktop uses a soft blue background, and the text on pull-down menus and taskbar buttons appears in the Tahoma font at 8 points.

If you don't mind that your computer looks like every other off-the-rack Windows PC in the world, you can skip this section. However, tweaking the look of the Windows interface can help to make you more productive. If you have trouble reading text, for example, you can bump up the size of the text used in menus and title bars. Changing the colors of text and backgrounds can improve readability as well. And adding scanned or saved graphical images to your desktop can personalize your PC in the same way as hanging framed photos on your office walls.

The gray flannel desktop?

In some corporations, excessive personalization is discouraged. In extremely restricted environments, a network administrator may use *group policies* to prohibit users from customizing the Windows interface. Before you add personal pictures to your desktop, check to be sure you're not violating a corporate policy. If you get an error message when you try any of the techniques listed in this chapter, ask your network administrator for a list of policies that govern the use of your computer.

Changing the Desktop Background

In lieu of the basic blue background, you can choose to personalize the desktop in any of the following ways:

- Change to a different background color. Your exact choice of colors depends on your display adapter and color settings.

SEE ALSO

➤ *For instructions on how to change the number of colors visible in Windows, see "Setting Display Options," p. 43.*

- Use a repeating *pattern* to add a geometric design to the background color.

- Display a single image as *wallpaper*, centered on the desktop. If the image is smaller than your screen resolution, you can stretch it so it fills the entire desktop space.

- Use a single image, repeated on the desktop in a tile pattern that starts at the top left.

- Let Internet Explorer's home page fill the right side of the desktop, leaving room to the left for desktop icons. This option requires that you enable the Active Desktop option, which is covered in the next section.

- Add multiple images and Web-based objects to the desktop, moving them around to create a collage of images. This option also requires that the Active Desktop be turned on.

Windows allows you to use most popular graphic file formats on the desktop, including bitmaps (.bmp or .dib file extensions), GIF files (.gif), and JPEG images (.jpg). You can also create or save a Web page and use it as wallpaper—just be sure to use the .htm extension.

Using a saved Web page as your desktop may seem like a strange idea; however, if you know the basics of Web design, you can create an attractive desktop with custom backgrounds, precisely placed images, and links to your favorite Web pages.

Changing the desktop background

1. Open Control Panel and double-click the **Display** option, or right-click any empty space on the desktop and choose **Properties** from the shortcut menu. In either case, the Display Properties dialog box opens.

2. On the **Background** tab (see Figure 8.1), select a background picture from the wallpaper list. If the graphic file you want to use does not appear in the list, click the **Browse** button to locate it.

Wallpaper and patterns together?

If you choose to center a graphical image as wallpaper and the image is smaller than your screen resolution, Windows displays the background color and any pattern you've chosen in the space around the wallpaper image. If you tile or stretch the graphic so it covers the entire desktop, the pattern button is grayed out.

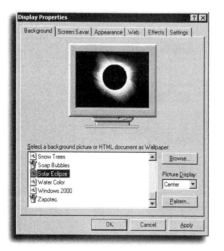

FIGURE 8.1
As you select background options from the Display Properties dialog box, the preview pane shows approximately what the image will look like.

When to tile and stretch

Tiling a graphic image is most effective with simple images that form a pattern. The larger the image and the more detail in it, the sillier it's likely to look when tiled. Likewise, stretching a graphic file to fill the entire desktop often makes part of the image look distorted. Experiment with either setting; if you don't like the result, change it back.

Where's the wallpaper?

Windows stores its own collection of wallpaper files in a standard location. Regardless of how your system is set up, you can open this folder by clicking the Start button, choosing **Run**, and entering `%windir%\Web\Wallpaper`. (Be sure to include the percent signs.) Add your own graphical image files or saved Web pages here and they'll appear in the list of choices for every user of the computer.

3. From the **Picture Display** list, choose **Center**, **Tile**, or **Stretch**. (These options are not available if you selected a Web page as the wallpaper.) The preview window shows what your screen will look like if you use a *resolution* of 800×600 pixels; if you use a higher resolution, the preview is only approximate.

4. Click **Apply** to change the background immediately without closing the dialog box.

5. If you're not satisfied with the results, repeat steps 2 through 4. When you've changed the background to your liking, click **OK** to close the Display Properties dialog box.

If you're a skilled graphic artist, you can make your own wallpaper using a painting or drawing program. Even if you're not a skilled artist, you can turn a scanned or saved image into wallpaper. When creating your image, it's often a good idea to leave a neutral area on the left side, so that desktop icons such as My Computer and the Recycle Bin don't get lost in the image. The Solar Eclipse wallpaper file, included with Windows 2000, does this nicely at 800×600 resolution, as Figure 8.2 shows.

SEE ALSO

➤ *To learn how to create a two-row taskbar, see "Making Taskbar Buttons Easier to Read,"* p. 196.

You can accomplish the same effect by saving the image using a size that's slightly smaller than the resolution you normally use. If you normally set your screen resolution to 1024×768, for instance, crop the image to 824×668, which leaves a 50-pixel border around all four edges of a centered image. Then set the desktop color to one that blends smoothly with the edges of the image, and you can arrange your desktop icons in this area rather than on top of the image itself.

If you're tired of the current wallpaper and want to return to a standard background, scroll to the top of the **Picture Display** list and choose (None).

If any portion of the desktop is visible, you can add a desktop pattern to jazz up the standard background color. Patterns are small arrangements of black dots and white space, 8 pixels on each side. When you specify that you want to use a pattern, Windows displays the black dots in a repeating pattern on your desktop, using your default background color in place of the white space. Because each pixel is so small, the overall effect is to add the illusion of texture to the desk-top surface.

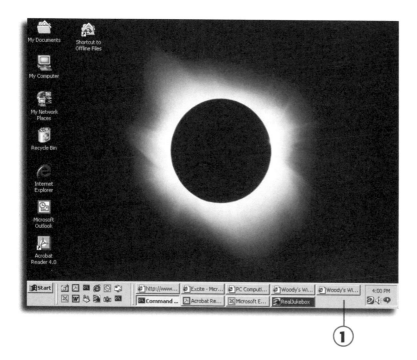

FIGURE 8.2
The neutral background makes it easy to see icons and their labels. If you use this wallpaper image at a higher resolution, set the desktop color to black.

(1) This two-row taskbar lets you see more text on buttons. See page 196 for details on how to make this change.

From Web to wallpaper

If you find an attractive graphic image on a Web page, you can easily add it to your desktop, either as wallpaper or as an Active Desktop item. Open the page in Internet Explorer and right-click the graphic. Choose **Set as Wallpaper** to automatically replace the current wallpaper with this image; choose **Set as Desktop Item** to add the image as an Active Desktop item.

Changing the desktop pattern

1. Open the Display Properties dialog box and click the **Background** tab.

2. Click the **Pattern** button to open the Pattern dialog box (see Figure 8.3). (If this button is grayed out, you must change your wallpaper settings, as described in the previous section.)

3. Choose any entry from the **Pattern** list. Look at the Preview area to the right of the list to see a small sample of the pattern using your current background color.

4. To customize the design of a pattern, click the **Edit Pattern** button. In the Pattern Editor dialog box (see Figure 8.4), click any of the 64 blocks (one per pixel) to toggle it between black and white. Watch the Sample box to see the effect of your changes. Enter a new name in the **Name** box, click **Add** to save

the new pattern, and click **Done** to return to the Pattern dialog box.

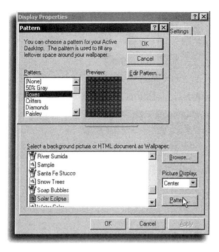

FIGURE 8.3
The pattern you select repeats across your desktop, as in the small Preview box shown here.

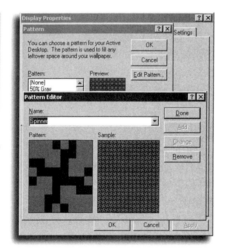

FIGURE 8.4
Use this editing window to create your own pattern by starting with an existing one.

Removing a pattern

If you're not happy with any entry in the Pattern list, you can easily remove it. Open the Pattern Editor, select the entry you want to zap, and then click the **Remove** button.

5. Click **OK** to save your changes.

Changing Fonts and Colors Used Throughout Windows

As I mentioned at the beginning of this chapter, Windows 2000 allows you to adjust the colors, fonts, and other settings of 18 separate interface elements, including windows, icons, menus, and title bars. Although you can tinker with each one of these settings individually, the best starting point is to choose one of the predefined schemes that Windows supplies. Open the Display Properties dialog box, click the **Appearance** tab (see Figure 8.5), and scroll through the list of available schemes.

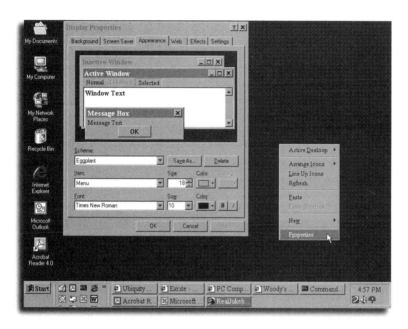

FIGURE 8.5
Not surprisingly, the background color for the desktop is purple in the Eggplant scheme. Unlike the Windows Standard scheme, this one uses the Times New Roman font for menus and title bars.

When you select a scheme, Windows previews its colors and fonts in the window just above the scheme's name. To switch to the selected scheme, click the **Apply** button.

Don't like the scheme you chose? On the **Appearance** tab, choose the **Windows Standard** scheme to restore all colors, fonts, and other settings to their defaults. In fact, you can return to this setting any time you want to undo all your customizations and start with a clean slate.

If you don't mind messing with individual interface elements, you can create your own scheme and save it under any name you like.

SEE ALSO

➤ *For details on how to adjust color settings for your display adapter, see "Setting Display Options," p. 43.*

Schemes for special needs

Some of the predefined schemes in Windows 2000 have been specifically designed to make it easier for users with visual impairments to read text on the screen. If you see the word *large* in parentheses at the end of a scheme name, that means the text in menus and title bars is noticeably bigger than the Windows Standard scheme. *Extra large* means the text is extremely large—typically too large for a user with average vision to tolerate. The 12 schemes that begin with High Contrast mix black and white with a variety of bright colors to make it easier to distinguish text.

Making Menu and Window Text More Readable

Although tweaking all 18 interface elements may seem like a waste of time, I've found that selective customizations make it easier to work with Windows. For example, I typically set the resolution on my large-screen monitor to 1280×1024. That setting lets me maximize the number of windows I can open at once; unfortunately, because I'm squarely on the far side of 40 years old, it also forces me to squint to make out the text in menus, messages, and title bars. The solution? I bump up the size of the fonts used in each of these desktop items. In fact, because I find the Verdana font more readable than Tahoma, I like to change all font settings from 8-point Tahoma to 10-point Verdana.

Increasing text size throughout Windows

1. Open the Display Properties dialog box and click the **Appearance** tab.

2. From the drop-down **Item** list, choose **Active Title Bar**.

3. Select a new font from the drop-down **Font** list, and then select a font size from the drop-down **Size** list to its right. (This setting also affects the size of the text in taskbar buttons.) Do not adjust any other settings in this dialog box.

4. Repeat steps 2 and 3, using the Icon, Menu, Message Box, and Selected Items choices from the drop-down **Item** list.

5. Click **Apply** to make your changes effective.

6. To save the changes you just made so that you can reapply them at any time, click the **Save As** button to open the Save Scheme dialog box. Enter a name for the new scheme (**Easy Reading**, for example), and click **OK**. Close the Display Properties dialog box if you're finished making changes.

Figure 8.6 shows what a typical program window looks like with the Windows Standard settings (left) and the larger customized fonts (right).

How many colors?

Many of the customization options available here depend on the color settings you selected for your display adapter. If you set your system to run with 256 colors, many colors will appear as patterns of dots rather than smooth colors. Likewise, you must set your system to High Color or better before you can set a gradient pattern on title bars, in which Windows blends two colors in a pattern that fades from left to right.

Smart settings

When you customize the Windows interface, many of the settings are interrelated. For instance, when you change the font for the Active Title Bar, your changes apply to the Inactive Title Bar as well—the only difference between those two settings is the color of the title bar. Likewise, if you increase the font size for the Active Title Bar, Windows automatically increases the size of the title bar so the text will fit properly.

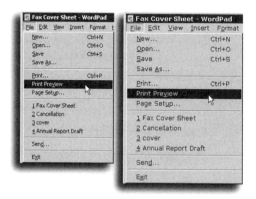

FIGURE 8.6
At high resolutions, the default fonts used in the Windows Standard scheme (left) are hard to read. Increasing the size (right) can help you avoid eye strain.

Making Buttons and Borders Bigger

Do you have trouble distinguishing between small objects when you point and click? If so, adjust another group of settings to make the targets a little larger.

- **Active Window Border/Inactive Window Border.** Normally, the edge of each window is a mere 1 pixel wide. Increasing its size to 3 or 4 pixels may make it easier for you to resize windows. Adjust the color of the Active Window Border from the default gray to a solid black to make it easier to pick out the window you're currently using.

- **Caption Buttons.** These are the three buttons (Close, Minimize, and Restore/Maximize) at the right side of every title bar. Increasing their size from the default 20 pixels to 22 or 24 can make it easier to hit these elusive boxes. Unfortunately, this change also bumps up the size of icons on the taskbar.

- **Icon Spacing (Horizontal and Vertical).** If icons are too close together for comfort, try moving them further apart than the default setting of 43 pixels.

- **Scrollbar.** By default, scrollbars are 16 pixels wide. Increasing this number makes the scrollbar wider and also increases the height and width of its controls.

Some settings are grayed out

The exact options available for each item (color, font, and size) differ slightly, depending on the type of item you selected. Remember, though, just because you *can* change something doesn't mean you *should*.

Clean out the list

The list of predefined schemes in Windows 2000 is long, and most of the choices represent color combinations you would never want to use. (Lilac? Rose? Sorry, not for me.) To clear unwanted entries off the list, select each one and then click the **Delete** button.

Don't resize icons

Avoid the temptation to change the size setting for icons. Icon images are fixed at 32 pixels in size, and making them larger or smaller usually makes them look worse.

Changing Colors

Many items in the Windows interface have color settings you can adjust. When you choose a predefined scheme or use one you've saved yourself, Windows applies all these changes at once. If you want to create your own color scheme, adjust each setting individually, and then save the results under a new scheme name.

Adjusting colors of desktop items

1. Open the Display Properties dialog box and click the **Appearance** tab.

2. From the **Item** list, select the Windows element whose color you want to change. (See Table 8.1 for a list of editable color settings.)

3. The square below the **Color** button shows the current setting for the selected item. Click the drop-down arrow to display the basic palette, as shown in Figure 8.7.

Choose a scheme first

To modify an existing scheme, be sure that scheme's name is visible on the Appearance tab of the Display Properties dialog box. (The name disappears from the list as soon as you make the first change.) After you finish making changes, be sure to save them; enter any existing scheme name to replace the current scheme with the new settings.

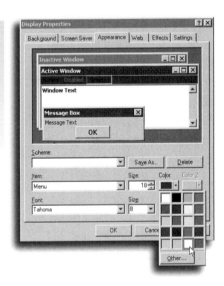

FIGURE 8.7
This set of 20 colors is the basic Windows palette. To choose from a much wider selection of colors, click the **Other** button.

4. Click any color square to assign that color to the selected element. If you don't see the color you want, click the **Other** button to open the full Color dialog box shown in Figure 8.8. Click any color square or create a custom color to assign it to the selected item, and then click **OK**.

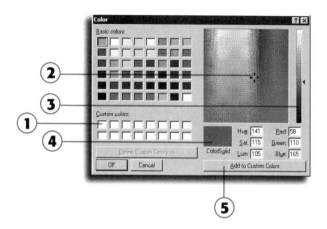

FIGURE 8.8
The expanded selection of colors in this dialog box gives you more choices, including these options:

(1) First, click here to select the square where you want the custom color to appear.

(2) Move the pointer in this *color matrix* to choose a color.

(3) Slide this control up or down to lighten or darken the color.

(4) Watch the preview area to see how your color will look.

(5) Click this button to save the custom color.

5. Repeat steps 2 through 4 for other items whose colors you want to edit.

6. Click **Apply** to make your changes effective.

7. Save your changes as part of a new or existing scheme, and close the Display Properties dialog box.

Table 8.1 Desktop items with color properties

Item	What You Can Adjust
Desktop	Changes the background color for the desktop.
Window	Changes the background color and the color of default fonts used in all windows, including those for Explorer and for Windows programs; avoid using anything other than white or a light color for the background color and black or a dark color for text.
Application Background	Controls the background color you see behind document windows in programs that use separate document windows in a single program window, such as Microsoft Excel.
3D Objects	Sets the background color and font color for objects that pop up in windows and on the desktop; this setting controls the look of taskbar buttons, for example.

continues...

Color confusion

For some items, you have two or even three color options available. The Active and Inactive title bars, for example, let you specify two colors to blend together for the background of the title bar, plus another color for the text. Be sure you use the right color box for the setting you want to change. To make your title bars one solid color, choose the same color in each one.

Table 8.1   Continued

Item	What You Can Adjust
Active Title Bar/Inactive Title Bar	Sets the background color and font color for the title bar; if your display adapter is set to High Color or better, you can specify two colors for the title bar and Windows will blend them in a gradient that fades from left to right.
Selected Items	Specifies the color of the background and font used for icons you select in Explorer windows and system folders such as Control Panel or My Computer.
Menu	Determines the background color and font color of pull-down menus and shortcut menus that appear when you right-click.
Message Box	Sets the default color of fonts used for text in dialog boxes and in many program windows.

Changing Icons and Visual Effects

If you want total control over every aspect of the Windows interface, open the Display Properties dialog box and click the **Effects** tab (see Figure 8.9). Using the options here, you can adjust even the most subtle attributes of menus, pointers, and icons. Although most of these settings are trivial, two offer the potential to make you slightly more productive.

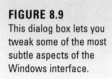

FIGURE 8.9
This dialog box lets you tweak some of the most subtle aspects of the Windows interface.

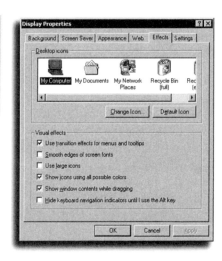

Ignore the top section of the Effects dialog box, which allows you to change which icon is associated with My Computer, My Documents, the Recycle Bin, and other desktop icons. Instead, focus on the six check boxes at the bottom of the dialog box:

- **Use transition effects for menus and tooltips.** This option allows you to choose whether you want menus to fade or scroll into place instead of just popping up or down. It's most noticeable (sometimes annoyingly so) on older, slower PCs. If you find these effects distracting, clear the check box to disable the feature.

- **Smooth edges of screen fonts.** At large sizes, some fonts have distinctly jagged edges. Check this box and Windows will add gray pixels along the rough edges to give the fonts a smoother appearance. This option is only effective when you have chosen High Color or True Color settings—it has no effect if you run your display adapter with 256 colors.

SEE ALSO

➤ *To learn how to increase the number of colors visible on your screen, see "Setting Display Options," p. 43.*

- **Use large icons.** By default, this option is unchecked, and I recommend that you leave it that way unless you have a visual impairment and need to see icons at a much larger size.

- **Show icons using all possible colors.** Leave this option checked so that Windows can automatically display the correct desktop and folder icons for your display resolution and color depth.

- **Show window contents while dragging.** With this option checked, you should find it much easier to position windows on the screen. Clear this check box only if you experience performance problems when moving windows around.

- **Hide keyboard navigation indicators until I use the Alt key.** In every Windows program, you can select menu options by pressing the Alt key and a letter. The exact letter to press for a given menu choice is indicated by an underlined character. On a clean installation of Windows 2000, these underlined characters are hidden until you tap the Alt key. Clear this check box to

---

Where did themes go?

Some earlier versions of Windows allowed you to install and use collections of interface elements called *desktop themes*. (The Windows 95 Plus! package and Windows 98 both support themes.) If you upgraded from a system that had themes installed, Windows 2000 will allow you to continue using any themes that are currently installed, using the Desktop Themes option in Control Panel. If you install Windows 2000 from scratch, the Control Panel does not include the Themes option; instead, you run the program by typing **Themes** into the Run box.

No effect on printed pages

Font smoothing makes text look better on the screen only; it has no effect on printed pages. Because printers typically operate at a much higher resolution than your screen, you shouldn't notice jagged edges on printed output, even if they appear on the screen.

instruct Windows to display the underlined characters at all times in all menus.

Taming the Active Desktop

Of all the pieces of the Windows interface, the Active Desktop is the most confusing and controversial. The first incarnation of the Active Desktop, in Internet Explorer 4.0, was noteworthy for the Channels bar, a mostly useless collection of links to Web pages that took up precious desktop space for no apparent reason. In Windows 2000, the Channels bar is gone and the Active Desktop actually has a few useful features.

The basic idea of the Active Desktop is that you can view your desktop as if it were a Web page. You can add graphics, resize them, and move them around to form a collage. You can turn your home page (or any Web page, for that matter) into your desktop wallpaper, complete with hyperlinks that you can use to open Web pages. You can also add components written in Web formats such as HTML and Java to your desktop—Microsoft's gallery of Active Desktop components includes clocks, weather maps, and stock tickers, for example.

To turn the Active Desktop on or off, use any of the following three switches:

- Open Control Panel's Display Properties dialog box, click the **Web** tab, and check **Show Web content on my Active Desktop**.
- Right-click any empty space on the desktop and choose **Show Web Content** from the shortcut menu.
- Open Control Panel's Folder Options dialog box, click the **General** tab, and check **Enable Web content on my desktop**.

Using Your Home Page as a Desktop Item

Do you want to use your Web browser's home page as the dominant part of your desktop image? Microsoft is betting they can convince some people to say yes to this curious configuration. Not surprisingly, they've designed the default Internet Explorer home page,

Keyboard users, take note!

Whenever possible, I try to use keyboard shortcuts rather than shifting my hand between the keys and the mouse. As a result, I use the Alt+*key* shortcuts regularly. When I set up Windows 2000 on a new machine, one of the first things I do is to change this default so I can see at a glance which key I need to press.

Give the Active Desktop a chance

If you decided long ago that the Active Desktop does nothing useful and makes your system run slower and crash more often, I understand completely. But I suggest that you skim through this section anyway. You may find that some of the features in the Active Desktop, such as the capability to use JPEG files as wallpaper, are actually useful. More importantly, I'll show you how to turn off the parts of the Active Desktop you don't like.

Or let Windows do it for you…

Windows will offer to turn on the Active Desktop for you if you choose a JPEG image as your wallpaper. It will also turn on the Active Desktop if you right-click the desktop and choose **Customize My Desktop** from the shortcut menu.

msn.com, so that it fits perfectly on the desktop. However, I've found that any portal-style page will do as a desktop background; see Figure 8.10 for an example of what the desktop looks like when Yahoo! is set as the background.

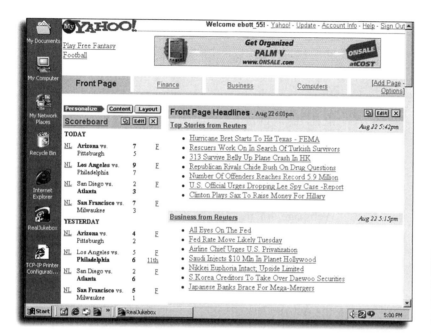

FIGURE 8.10
When you set your current home page as a desktop element, Windows uses as much space as possible without covering any desktop icons.

To use your browser's home page as an Active Desktop element, right-click any empty space on the desktop and choose **Active Desktop** from the shortcut menu; then check the **My Current Home Page** option. (If this option is not visible, click the **Show Web Content** option first.)

Do you want to use a Web page as wallpaper, without any trace of desktop icons? To set a Web page so that it takes over the entire desktop, right-click an empty space on the desktop and choose **Active Desktop**; then clear the check mark next to the **Show Desktop Icons** menu choice. If you choose this option, you can still access icons on the Desktop from an Explorer window.

Browsing takes some getting used to when you use a Web page as an Active Desktop element. Portal pages usually launch links in a new window, but some pages replace the desktop contents with a new page, making it difficult to get back to your preferred home page.

Best at full speed
Using a Web page as your desktop is only effective when you have a full-time Internet connection. If you have to dial up to download pages, don't bother with this option. Likewise, the best type of Web page to use as part of an Active Desktop is one that updates itself regularly. Most so-called portal pages, including Yahoo! and Excite, are set up to automatically update news headlines, sports scores, and other details every 10–15 minutes.

183

Getting back to the desktop

One problem with using a Web page as the desktop is that it's hidden while you work with other windows. To quickly minimize all open windows so you can see the desktop, click the Show Desktop icon on the Quick Launch bar (just to the right of the Start button).

To return home on an Active Desktop Web page, right-click and use the **Back** choice on the shortcut menu.

SEE ALSO

➤ *For details on how to change your home page, see "Changing Your Start Page," p. 404.*

Adding New Desktop Items

If you're not sold on the benefits of using your home page as a desktop item, how about creating a collage of pictures on the desktop? Unlike Windows wallpaper, which allows you to choose only one picture for the desktop, you can add as many images to the Active Desktop as you want, resizing and rearranging them to fit the available space. You can also add small HTML-based items that let you view information or perform specific tasks.

To add pictures and saved HTML documents from a location on a local drive or shared network folder, enlist a wizard's help.

HTML items? Why?

Placing an HTML object on the desktop may sound like a parlor trick with no useful purpose. For most Web pages, that's true because banner ads and other clutter make the pages too big to work on a desktop. If you have even basic Web authoring skills, however, you can easily create pages that run scripts so you can look up information (such as Zip codes or shipping rates) using online databases.

Adding new Active Desktop items

1. Right-click any empty space on the desktop and choose **Active Desktop**; then click **New Desktop Item**.

2. In the New Active Desktop Item Wizard, click the **Browse** button. Locate the image file or saved HTML page and click **Open**.

3. The wizard fills in the full name and path of the file you selected in the **Location** box. Click **OK** to add the object to the desktop.

4. The wizard places the new item in an arbitrary location on the desktop. To move it to the location you prefer, click the image or HTML object and move the mouse pointer to the top border until a thick border pops up. Click the border and drag the image to a new location.

5. Repeat steps 1–4 for any additional desktop items you want to add.

Figure 8.11 shows the border around a selected desktop item—use the top border to move the image, or click and drag any border to resize the object.

FIGURE 8.11
Point to the top border of any Active Desktop item to display this title bar.

Adding a Web page or a Web-based graphical file as an Active Desktop item is a simple drag-and-drop operation. If you see a graphical image on a Web page that you want to add to your desktop, right-click the image and choose **Set as Desktop Item** from the shortcut menu. Follow the prompts to set up a synchronization schedule for the image. One common use for this technique is to add a satellite weather map to your desktop. Web sites such as the Weather Channel (http://www.weather.com) include a wide selection of international and regional maps that make great "live" desktop images.

SEE ALSO

➤ *For full details on how to synchronize offline Web pages and Active Desktop items, see "Browsing the Web Without an Active Internet Connection," p. 380.*

Finally, you can add components from Microsoft's Active Desktop gallery to your desktop. Start the New Active Desktop Item Wizard and click the **Visit Gallery** button, which opens your Web browser and takes you to a collection of HTML and Java-based components at Microsoft's Web site. It takes a few minutes to poke through the collection and see if anything piques your interest. Figure 8.12 shows what the desktop looks like after adding a Java clock from the Gallery and a weather map from the Weather Channel Web site.

Arranging Items on the Active Desktop

As I noted in the previous section, you can drag Active Desktop items to a new location by clicking the thick border along the top of the item. To temporarily hide or show individual items, right-click anywhere on the desktop and use the shortcut menu—each item gets its own entry at the bottom of the menu.

Copy or synchronize?

If you want to add an image to your desktop because you like its looks, don't bother creating a link to the Web-based graphic. Instead, copy the image to a local drive and use the New Active Desktop Item Wizard to add it to your desktop. Reserve the synchronization option for images that change over time, where you want Windows to periodically update the image file for you.

185

To remove or change individual items, right-click the desktop and choose **Customize My Desktop**. That opens the Web tab of the Display Properties dialog box, which contains a full list of all the Active Desktop items you previously defined, as shown in the example in Figure 8.13.

FIGURE 8.12
This Active Desktop collection includes several pictures from a local drive, a Web-based image, and a Java component.

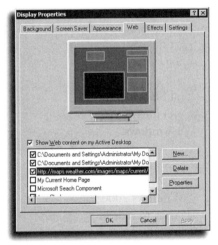

FIGURE 8.13
Use this dialog box to adjust or remove Active Desktop items.

- A check mark next to any item means it's currently visible on the desktop. Clear the check box to hide the item.

- When you select an item in the list, its position in the preview window in the top half of the dialog box changes color to show you its approximate position.

- Click the **Delete** button to permanently remove an Active Desktop item.

- Select any item and click the **Properties** button to adjust its settings, including the schedule that Windows uses for automatic updates to the item.

How do you keep items from moving around after you've positioned them precisely where you want them? Right-click the desktop and choose **Lock Desktop Items** from the shortcut menu.

Organizing the Start Menu for Maximum Efficiency

When you want to tackle virtually any Windows task, click the **Start** button. The built-in shortcuts on the Start menu give you quick access to programs, documents, Control Panel settings, and Help. To make this menu even more useful, customize it with your own shortcuts and fine-tune the arrangement of system shortcuts to suit your preferences.

You can add items to the top of the Start menu or anywhere on the **Programs** menu. Other parts of the Start menu are customizable as well, but only in strictly defined ways. For example, you can't remove the **Help** or **Run** choices, but you can add a prompt that makes it easier to log off. You can also turn several Start menu choices (Control Panel and Favorites, for example) into *cascading menus* instead of menu choices that open folder windows.

Changing the Appearance of the Start Menu

Unlike all previous Windows versions, Windows 2000 incorporates a feature called *Personalized Menus*, which tries to reduce the inevitable clutter on the Programs menu by showing you shortcuts only for

Resizing an image

By dragging the border of an Active Desktop item, you can adjust its size. Unfortunately, there is no way to preserve the aspect ratio of the object. As a result, you may inadvertently distort an image when resizing it. Fixing it is no problem. Aim the mouse pointer at the top of the image until you see the thick border. Click the down arrow at the left edge of the top border to reveal a pull-down menu. Choose **Reset to Original Size**. Now you're ready to try again.

Love/hate cascading menus?

There are two kinds of people in the world: those who love cascading menus, and those who want to obliterate every trace of them. Personally, I find cascading menus annoying, especially when they extend more than one level. As a result, I go to a lot of trouble to reorganize my Programs menu to be "flat," and I shun all the options that put extra cascading menus on the Start menu.

programs you've used recently and hiding those you haven't clicked lately.

When using this feature to create a shorter Programs menu, Windows doesn't delete shortcuts or program groups. Instead, it hides the less-frequently used choices. Your only indicator that some menu choices are hidden is a double arrow at the bottom of the Programs menu, as shown in Figure 8.14. If you leave the Programs menu open for a few seconds or double-click the double arrow, the full menu appears (see Figure 8.15).

FIGURE 8.14
Where's the rest of the Programs menu? With Personalized Menus enabled, Windows hides shortcuts you haven't used lately.

(1) Click here to expand the menu and show all available shortcuts.

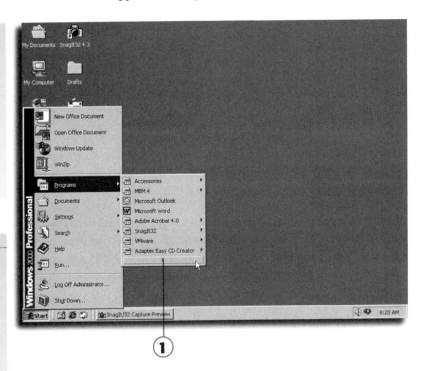

Office did it first
Like so many Windows interface elements, the Personalized Menus feature first appeared in another Microsoft program—Office 2000. If you use Office, chances are you've already had to deal with this feature. If you use Office and Windows 2000 and you prefer to see all menu choices all the time, you'll need to change menu settings in two places.

Although the basic concept behind the Personalized Menus feature makes sense, in practice it can be confusing. Some users complain that they waste as much time searching for hidden menu items as they save. If that describes your feelings, too, go ahead and turn off Personalized Menus. Click the **Start** button, chose **Settings**, and select **Taskbar and Start Menu**. On the General tab of the Taskbar and Start Menu Properties dialog box, clear the check mark from the **Use Personalized Menus** option. Click **OK** to make the change effective immediately.

FIGURE 8.15
After you click the double arrow at the bottom of the menu (or wait a few seconds), Windows displays the full menus.

Adding New Items to the Start Menu

Windows 2000 lets you add items to the Start menu in any of three ways:

- To add, edit, or remove items using a conventional folder window, right-click the **Start** button and choose **Open** or **Explore**. The Start Menu folder that opens contains shortcuts that are part of your personal profile and not available to other users.

- Click the **Start** button, choose **Settings**, and click the **Taskbar & Start Menu** option. Click the **Advanced** tab and use the **Add** and **Remove** buttons to manage shortcuts one at a time. The **Advanced** button opens a special-purpose Explorer window containing only the Start menu and its subfolders.

SEE ALSO

➤ *For an overview of how to create and manage program shortcuts, see "Creating Shortcuts to Favorite Programs," p. 91.*

- Finally, you can drag icons directly to the Start button and drop them to create shortcuts. The original file remains in its current location, and the new shortcut appears at the top of the Start menu.

Small icons give you more room

If you've added more than seven icons to the top of the Start menu, you should definitely change the default configuration of the Start menu from large icons to small. (You'll find this setting on the General tab of the Taskbar and Start Menu Properties dialog box.) The small icons are slightly harder to see, but they give you easily twice as much room at the top of the menu. The effect is especially striking at low screen resolutions—800×600 and smaller.

You're not restricted to program icons on the Start menu. You can create shortcuts for files, folders, and system objects (such as Dial-Up Networking shortcuts) here as well. In Windows 2000, dropping a folder on the Start button creates a shortcut that behaves differently than in any other Windows version. As Figure 8.16 shows, the resulting folder shortcut turns into a cascading menu that displays the entire contents of the folder.

FIGURE 8.16
Dropping a folder on the Start menu creates a folder shortcut, which displays the contents of the folder in a cascading menu.

Of course, if you want more cascading menus, Windows is only too happy to oblige. The list of check boxes at the bottom of the Advanced tab of the Taskbar and Start Menu Properties dialog box (shown in Figure 8.17) lets you add a number of items to the Start menu, as outlined in Table 8.2.

FIGURE 8.17
Use the options at the bottom of this dialog box to add multiple cascading lists to the Start menu.

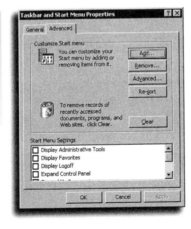

Table 8.2 Advanced Start menu settings

Option	What It Does
Display Administrative Tools	Adds the Administrative Tools option to the Programs menu. Make this choice if you administer the local machine and you're tired of going to the Control Panel to open Administrative Tools.
Display Favorites	Adds a cascading Favorites menu to the Start menu. Can be annoying, especially if your Favorites list is long.
Display Logoff	Adds a **Log Off** *username* command to the Start menu. Extremely useful on shared machines or if you're in the habit of logging out when you leave your computer.
Expand Control Panel	Turns the Control Panel choice on the <u>S</u>ettings menu into a cascading list.
Expand My Documents	Displays the contents of the My Documents folder as a list off the Start menu rather than opening a folder. The more files you have in this folder, the less likely you'll want to make this change.
Expand Network and Dial-Up Connections	Shows all your connections in a cascading menu instead of a window. Useful if you rely on a dial-up connection for Internet access.
Expand Printers	Shows all defined printers in a cascading menu rather than in a folder window. Worth checking this option if you routinely use multiple printers.
Scroll the Programs Menu	If your Programs menu is too tall to fit in one screen, this option adds scroll arrows at the top and bottom of the list; clear the check box to see the column continue to the right.
Use Personalized Menus	Enables or disables this controversial feature, which hides menu choices you haven't used lately.

Rearranging Items on the Start Menu

Every new program you install typically adds at least one shortcut to the Programs menu—in some cases, programs add their own group to the Programs menu, with multiple shortcuts. Windows 2000 doesn't automatically add new shortcuts in alphabetical order.

> **Direct shortcut editing saves time**
>
> Get in the habit of working directly with shortcuts on the Programs menu. When you select any shortcut on the menu and right-click, you see the same shortcut menu that you would see in a folder window. Using this technique, you can copy, remove, or change the properties of any shortcut, any time.

Windows 95 users, take note!

Of all the changes in the Windows interface since Windows 95, this one is perhaps the most confusing. New Windows 2000 users complain loud and long that their Start menu isn't sorted properly. If this feature bugs you, get in the habit of watching where each program puts new shortcuts, and move them immediately to the location you prefer.

Instead, it drops them at the bottom of the Programs menu. Over time, because of this behavior, the order of the Programs menu can practically become random.

If you prefer to keep your Programs menu organized in alphabetical order, try either of these two techniques to keep things manageable.

1. Click the **Settings** button and choose **Taskbar & Start Menu**; click the **Advanced** tab and click the **Re-sort** button. This step instantly rearranges the Programs menu, placing all folders at the top and shortcuts at the bottom and sorting both groups into alphabetical order.

2. Use the mouse to drag shortcuts and groups directly into a new position. Open the Programs menu, click any shortcut or group, and drag it to a new location.

Reopening Documents You've Edited Recently

Windows 2000 keeps track of every file you open from an Explorer window (including the common Open dialog boxes in program windows). For each such file, it creates a shortcut and stores it in a folder called Recent, which is a part of your personal profile.

These shortcuts aren't smart

If you open a file and save it under another name, or if you delete a file after opening it, the shortcuts in the Recent folder don't change. When you click a shortcut on the Documents menu and get an error message in return, the most likely explanation is that you deleted the original target file.

- To reopen any of the 15 files you opened most recently, click the **Start** button and choose **Documents**.

- From a program window, you can see a filtered list of all the files and folders you've opened. Click the **History** button in the Places bar, and use the **Files of type** list to select which type of file you want to see.

SEE ALSO

➤ *For more details on how to use common dialog boxes, see "Opening and Saving Files in Program Windows," p. 127.*

- To open an Explorer window with shortcuts to all the files and folders you used recently, click the **Start** button, choose **Run**, and enter `%userprofile%\Recent` in the Run dialog box.

An obscure option lets you clear the contents of the Recent folder and the Documents menu. Why would you want to do this? Maybe you don't want another user to see which files you've been working on lately. Or perhaps you're about to start a big new project that involves a large number of files, and you want the contents of the Documents menu to reflect only your current work. Or maybe you just hate clutter.

You can clear out individual items from the Recent folder by opening the file and deleting each one. To quickly empty the entire contents of the Recent folder (and thus the Documents menu), click the **Start** button, choose **Settings**, and click the **Taskbar and Start Menu** option. On the Advanced tab, click the **Clear** button. This option also eliminates entries you typed into the Address box of Explorer windows and in the Search Assistant.

Putting Favorite Programs on the Quick Launch Bar

Every time you install a new program, it typically adds at least one shortcut—and often an entire group of shortcuts—to the Programs menu. Eventually, your Programs menu is cluttered with dozens of groups, and it can take four or five clicks plus a bit of searching every time you want to start a program.

Instead of suffering through all those clicks, use the Quick Launch bar to organize icons for your favorite programs. This efficient little toolbar appears just to the right of the Start button, where it gives you one-click access to the programs you use most often. By default, the Quick Launch bar includes only a few icons—a Show Desktop button and shortcuts for Internet Explorer and Outlook Express. You can add and remove icons at will, however. Each icon takes up only a tiny amount of space.

To copy any shortcut from the Programs menu to the Quick Launch bar, hold down the right mouse button and drag the shortcut directly from the Programs menu to a location on either side of an existing icon on the Quick Launch bar. (Don't use the left mouse button

Missing the Quick Launch bar?

If the Quick Launch bar isn't visible on your desktop, it's probably just hidden. To make it reappear, right-click any empty space in the taskbar, click the **Toolbars** menu choice, and click **Quick Launch**.

unless you want to move the shortcut off the Programs menu completely.) When you see a thick black line, release the mouse button and choose **Create Shortcut(s) Here**. The new icon appears in the location where you clicked, pushing any existing icons to the right.

To move any icon to a new position on the Quick Launch bar, drag it to the location you want. If you add more items than will fit in the space available, Windows shows as many icons as it can, and then adds a double arrow at the right of the Quick Launch bar. To adjust the width of the Quick Launch bar, point to the vertical line just to the right until the mouse pointer turns to a double-headed arrow; drag to the right to make additional room for Quick Launch icons or drag to the left to make more room for taskbar buttons.

For maximum productivity, I suggest that you make the Quick Launch bar wide enough to show five icons. Go ahead and add more program icons if you want, and arrange them in order so that the programs you use most often are visible, then click the double arrow to display a pop-up list of additional icons, as shown in the example in Figure 8.18.

<table>
<tr><td colspan="2">

Keep the Show Desktop icon

By default, the Show Desktop icon is the first one on the Quick Launch bar. I recommend that you keep this tiny button in that preferred position, just to the right of the Start button; that way you can always clear all open windows out of the way and get to the desktop with just one click.

</td></tr>
</table>

FIGURE 8.18

For one-click access, put the programs you use most often at the beginning of the Quick Launch bar. Use the double arrow to display hidden icons in a pop-up menu.

Because Quick Launch items are nothing more than shortcuts, you can manage them using the same techniques you use with shortcuts anywhere in Windows. If you don't use Outlook Express, for example, feel free to clear it off the taskbar: right-click its icon and choose **Delete** from the shortcut menu. To change the settings for any Quick Launch item, right-click and choose **Properties**.

SEE ALSO

➤ *For details about how you can customize shortcuts, see "Changing the Way a Program Shortcut Works," p. 94.*

➤ *If you change your mind and want to restore a deleted shortcut, see "Creating Shortcuts to Favorite Programs," p. 91.*

Every user on a Windows 2000 computer has a personalized set of Quick Launch icons. To open your personal Quick Launch folder in an Explorer window, right-click any empty space in the Quick

Launch bar and choose **Open** from the shortcut menu. In the resulting folder window, you can create new shortcuts, remove existing ones, or copy shortcuts from other folders, including the Programs menu.

SEE ALSO

➤ *For more details on how to manage files and folders, see "Organizing Files," p. 138.*

Arranging the Taskbar and Other Toolbars

The taskbar is an essential part of the Windows interface, allowing you to switch between programs and open windows with a single click. Windows includes an assortment of customization options that let you decide how much space the taskbar should occupy and whether it's visible at all times or slides out of the way when not in use. These options allow you to strike a balance between making the most of your screen real estate and making it as easy as possible to switch between programs.

Changing the Appearance of the Taskbar

By default, the taskbar takes over a portion of the real estate at the bottom of your screen. If you increase its height to two or three rows (details are in the next section), it takes up even more room that you could be using for programs. At low screen resolutions in particular, you may want to slide the taskbar out of the way so you can use as much of the screen as possible for programs. To control the appearance of the taskbar, click the **Start** menu, choose **Settings**, and select **Taskbar & Start Menu**. Figure 8.19 shows the settings available here.

Three settings in this dialog box have a direct impact on the taskbar:

- **Always on top.** This setting, which is on by default, ensures that the taskbar is always visible. If you clear this check box, program windows will cover up the taskbar when you maximize them. I strongly recommend that you leave this box checked.

- **Auto hide.** Specify that the taskbar should slide out of the way at all times. With this option checked, you will not be able to see which programs are running unless you move the mouse pointer

---

Don't move the taskbar

Although the taskbar is normally docked at the bottom of the screen, you can move it to the top of the screen (with the Start menu dropping down) or to either side of the screen. Macintosh users may prefer the up-top arrangement, but I don't recommend moving the taskbar from its default location. Putting the taskbar on the side of the screen makes buttons too hard to read, and docking it at the top confuses some programs, which either cover up the title bar or hide behind it.

The taskbar moved by itself!

It's all too easy to accidentally move the taskbar to the side of the screen, just by clicking and dragging in the wrong place. If this happens to you, it's a simple matter to drag it back where it belongs. Point to the region just to the right of the clock, click, and drag the taskbar to the bottom of the screen. You don't need to be precise: The taskbar snaps into position automatically when you get in the right vicinity.

to the bottom of the screen—that signals Windows that you want to raise the taskbar. Use this option only if you absolutely must maximize screen space—on an old notebook PC with extremely limited resolution, for example.

- **Show clock.** Clear this check box to hide the clock. If you use a one-row taskbar, this recovers a bit of space that Windows can use for taskbar buttons.

FIGURE 8.19
Use these options to hide the taskbar automatically and reserve more screen space for programs.

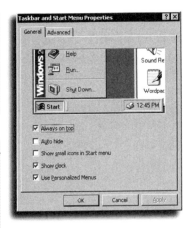

Try full screen instead

Some programs offer a full-screen viewing mode that lets you work with as much data as possible by hiding most parts of the Windows interface. When browsing Web pages with Internet Explorer, for example, you can press F11 to switch to full-screen mode. (Press F11 again or click the Full Screen button to restore the normal Windows view.) In this view, the title bar, status bars, menus, and all but the Standard toolbar are hidden, allowing you to use the full screen to view the current page. Office 97 and Office 2000 offer a similar feature.

SEE ALSO

➤ *For more details on how to customize the system and taskbar clock, see "Adjusting the Date and Time," p. 46.*

Making Taskbar Buttons Easier to Read

The more windows you open, the harder it becomes to figure out what each taskbar button does. At a resolution of 800×600, for example, the text on the taskbar buttons is nearly impossible to read after you open five or six windows—all you see is the first few letters in the title of each window. As you open more and more windows, eventually all you see on each taskbar button is the program icon, with additional buttons scrolling off the taskbar completely.

How can you make the taskbar easier to read? Start by increasing your screen resolution to the maximum size you can tolerate. If you use a notebook computer, your choices are restricted by the design of the LCD screen, but on any desktop monitor of 15 inches or more, you should be able to comfortably work at a resolution of 1024×768 or higher.

SEE ALSO

➤ *For instructions on how to adjust the screen resolution, see "Setting Display Options," p. 43.*

Next, increase the number of rows on the taskbar so you can see more buttons. At a screen resolution of 1024×768, you should have room for at least two rows of buttons; if you run at a higher screen resolution, you can comfortably increase the taskbar height to three or even four rows.

Aim the mouse pointer at the top of the taskbar until it turns to a two-headed arrow; then drag up to add one or more extra rows. By default, Windows insists on using the top row for the Quick Launch bar and the bottom row for taskbar buttons. Aim the mouse pointer at the vertical bar to the left of the taskbar until it turns to a two-headed horizontal arrow, and then click and drag the taskbar to the right of the Quick Launch bar. Now you have two rows of taskbar buttons.

Figure 8.20 shows a typical taskbar with 10 windows open. With one row of buttons at the screen resolution of 800×600, it's literally impossible to see what each button represents, because only the first letter of each window title is visible. With two rows of buttons, however, you can clearly read several words on each button, making it easy to see which button goes with which window.

> **Practice makes perfect**
>
> Moving toolbars around takes a bit of practice, and the individual toolbars have a maddening way of positioning themselves in odd places. If your first attempt doesn't succeed, try it again. After you get the taskbar into position, don't forget to slide it to the left, against the Quick Launch icons, so you have as much room as possible for buttons and text.

> **FIGURE 8.20**
> Increasing the taskbar to two rows makes it much easier to see which window each taskbar button represents.

After you've finished rearranging the taskbar into two or more rows, you'll discover another space-saving bonus: all the icons in the Quick Launch bar and in the system notification area (the "tray" at the right of the taskbar) use the extra rows as well. Because these icons stack up neatly instead of creeping onto the taskbar, you should have even more room for buttons.

Adding, Removing, and Rearranging Toolbars

Windows lets you choose any or all of four system toolbars that you can display as part of the taskbar. In addition, you can create your own toolbars from any existing drive or folder. The Quick Launch toolbar is visible unless you choose to turn it off; to use the other toolbars, you need to choose them from the taskbar's pop-up menu.

To add another toolbar, point to any empty space on the taskbar, right-click, and choose **Toolbars** from the shortcut menu. The menu offers the following choices:

- **Address.** The same as the Address bar in an Explorer window. When this toolbar is visible, you can enter a Web address or the path of a local or network drive or folder. When you press Enter, Windows opens a Web browser or Explorer window.

- **Links.** This is the same toolbar that you'll find in an Internet Explorer window. If you've customized the Links toolbar with shortcuts to your absolute favorite Web pages, you might want to add it in the taskbar region for quick Web access

- **Desktop.** Shows all the system objects (My Computer and its friends) and shortcuts you add to the desktop, in a toolbar format. If you use the desktop as a holding area for files and folders, you might find a use for this folder.

- **Quick Launch.** Hides or shows the toolbar that contains shortcuts to your favorite programs. An absolutely essential productivity tool for Windows users. I can't imagine anyone wanting to hide this toolbar.

- **New Toolbar.** Lets you turn any drive or folder into a toolbar. Read on for details about how you can use this feature most effectively.

Does anyone need all these toolbars? Absolutely not. In fact, most of them take up too much room, and it takes careful planning and positioning to get them arranged properly. Figure 8.21, for example, shows how I've used three rows on the taskbar to arrange four toolbars for maximum effectiveness.

Why would you want to create a toolbar from a folder? One excellent use of this feature is to make it easier to browse for files. If you add the My Computer toolbar to your taskbar and position it properly, you can turn it into a pop-up menu that lets you view all the files on any local or mapped network drive until you find exactly the one you're looking for—and you don't have to open an Explorer window.

Web page as toolbar?

Some of the ways you can use extra toolbars are downright strange. For instance, you can create a new toolbar using an Internet address. Of course, trying to view a Web page through a tiny toolbar is challenging, to say the least. When I see strange and useless features like this, I want to ask Microsoft's designers what they were possibly thinking.

This isn't the Run box

Don't confuse the Address toolbar with the Run box on the Start menu. The big difference between the two is that in the Run box, you can type the name of a program and Windows will start that program if it can. You can't use the Address bar to launch a program.

FIGURE 8.21
To use multiple toolbars, spend the time to arrange them properly. The Links toolbar at the right actually functions as a pop-up menu.

1. Click and drag this region to move a toolbar.

2. Click here to see hidden choices on a toolbar.

Creating a My Computer toolbar

1. Right-click any empty portion of the taskbar. Choose **Toolbars** from the shortcut menu and click the **New Toolbar** option.

2. In the New Toolbar dialog box, select My Computer and click **OK**. The new toolbar appears on the taskbar.

3. Point to the toolbar's *sizing handle* (the vertical line at the left of the My Computer label) until the mouse pointer turns to a two-headed arrow; then click and drag as far to the right as possible, until all you see is the My Computer label and a double arrow.

The My Computer toolbar appears with separate icons for every object in the My Computer folder—local drives, mapped network drives, and the Control Panel. Because you've pushed the toolbar to the far right edge of the taskbar, none of these icons are visible until you click the double arrow. Click each entry on the pop-up menu to unfurl a cascading menu that shows the contents of that drive or folder, as I've done in Figure 8.22. When you find the file or folder you're looking for, click to open it.

These steps work for any folder

The My Computer folder makes a particularly useful toolbar, but you can use these same techniques with any drive or folder icon, or even a network server. Try it with the My Documents folder or My Network Places, for example.

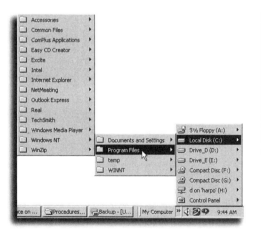

FIGURE 8.22
When you add the My Computer toolbar to the taskbar and push it to the far right, it works especially well. Click the double arrow to use it as a pop-up toolbar.

Use a two-row taskbar

If you decide to add extra toolbars to your taskbar, I strongly recommend that you increase its height to at least two and preferably three rows. That's the only way to prevent the new toolbars from rendering the taskbar buttons unreadable.

Right-click any toolbar to adjust display options. This shortcut menu allows you to hide or show the text for each shortcut on the toolbar and use large icons instead of small, for example.

If you don't mind giving up a big chunk of the space your programs normally use, you can drag a toolbar to any edge of the screen and dock it there. You can also open a toolbar and let it "float" on the desktop. The effect is a little strange, but it works well with simple, uncluttered folders such as My Computer, as shown in Figure 8.23. To allow a toolbar to float, drag it off the taskbar and drop it on any empty desktop space.

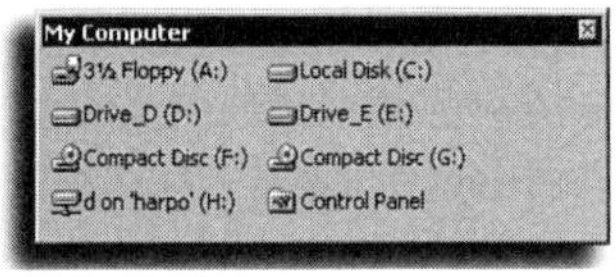

FIGURE 8.23
If you drag a toolbar off the taskbar, it can float on the desktop. Don't like the effect? Click X to close it, or drag it back onto the taskbar.

Managing Fonts

Fonts control the look of text and special characters on the screen, on printed output, and on Web pages. Each font includes a set of characters (typically numbers, letters, punctuation, and symbols) with a distinctive look and style. Windows 2000 includes a basic selection of fonts; you can add fonts, which then become available for use in all Windows programs.

Viewing All Fonts on Your Computer

Sharing fonts

When you create a document or a Web page, other people may not see things exactly as you intended. If you share a file with another person (such as an email attachment or on a Web server), Windows checks the list of fonts you specified against the list of fonts installed on the other person's machine. If a font you used is not available, Windows substitutes the closest matching font. You can use any fonts for printed output; for shared documents, however, you should stick with fonts that are widely available.

To view a list of all fonts installed on your machine, open Control Panel and double-click the **Fonts** option. Figure 8.24 shows a Windows 2000 system with a number of additional fonts installed.

Windows 2000 supports three types of fonts:

- **Outline fonts.** These fonts are the ones you see most commonly in Windows and in Windows programs. As the name implies, the font file contains instructions that define the outline for each character in this type of font. Using these instructions, Windows can scale the font up or down to any size between 1 and 1638 points and rotate it in any direction. Windows 2000 comes with a large number of OpenType fonts and also allows you to use *TrueType* and *Adobe Type 1* outline fonts. Windows 2000 includes the following *OpenType* fonts: Arial, Courier New, Lucida Console, Times New Roman, Symbol, and Wingdings.

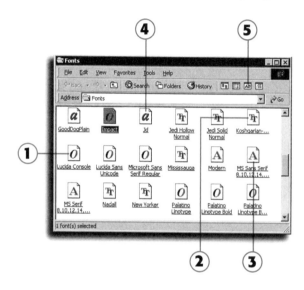

FIGURE 8.24
Open the Fonts folder to see a full list of all fonts installed on your computer.

(1) OpenType font

(2) TrueType font

(3) Vector or raster font

(4) Adobe Type 1 font

(5) Use these toolbar buttons to choose a different view of installed fonts.

- **Raster fonts.** Raster fonts are stored in files as bitmap images of a fixed size and can't be scaled or rotated. Windows 2000 includes five raster fonts (Courier, MS Sans Serif, MS Serif, Small, and Symbol), which are primarily used for compatibility with older Windows programs.

- **Vector fonts.** Windows 2000 also includes three vector fonts, which are used primarily with plotters (special-purpose printers that use pens to produce line drawings, such as blueprints). These fonts—Modern, Roman, and Script—are not used for any other purpose.

Although the Fonts folder looks at first glance like any other Explorer window, this system folder includes one capability you won't find anywhere else: you can group fonts according to how similar they are to a font you select. If you're tired of the Arial font, for example, you might want to find another installed font that has the same characteristics. Open the Fonts folder, pull down the **View** menu, and choose **List Fonts By Similarity**. Choose your standard of comparison from the drop-down list at the top of the window, and

No need for Adobe Type Manager

Adobe Type 1 fonts were originally designed for use with PostScript printers. In previous Windows versions, the only way to install and use these fonts was with a utility program called Adobe Type Manager. This program is not required in Windows 2000 because the operating system can manage Type 1 fonts directly.

Windows displays all your fonts with the description Very Similar, Fairly Similar, or Not Similar.

Viewing Individual Fonts

Do you know the difference between Haettenschweiler and Trebuchet? The names don't offer even a hint of what these fonts look like, and most fonts have similarly unhelpful names. When you want to see what an individual font looks like, double-click its icon in the Fonts folder. That opens a preview window, as shown in the example in Figure 8.25.

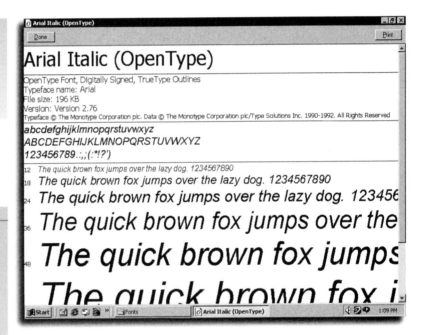

> **OpenType = TrueType+**
>
> The OpenType standard is new in Windows 2000, but it's not dramatically different from the old TrueType standard. All the OpenType fonts that come with Windows 2000 are functionally identical to their TrueType equivalents.

> **FIGURE 8.25**
> To see a sample of any installed font, double-click its icon in the Fonts folder.

> **Courier versus Courier New**
>
> Don't confuse the raster font Courier with the OpenType font Courier New. Despite the similar names, the two fonts look very different. The old-style font looks acceptable on the screen only at a handful of smaller point sizes. At higher point sizes (36 point, for example), the Courier font looks jagged and downright ugly, whereas the same text formatted in Courier New looks just fine.

The preview window provides three important categories of information about the selected font: its name and copyright information (OpenType fonts also show whether the font is digitally signed); the complete character set available for the font; and samples at various sizes.

To print a font sample so you can see what it looks like on paper, click the **Print** button. When you finish working with the preview window, click the **Done** button.

Installing New Fonts and Keeping Them Organized

How many fonts can you install on a Windows 2000 computer? Maybe a better question is, How many fonts *should* you install? In theory, there is no limit to the number of fonts you can install. In practice, each font you add consumes system resources (such as memory), and if you add more than a few hundred fonts you may notice irritating delays every time you open a program or pull down a font list.

With that caveat in mind, feel free to add all the fonts your heart desires. Where do you find new fonts? The Internet, of course. Literally hundreds of sites specialize in fonts—some freely downloadable, others available as shareware, and still others for sale by professional designers. Here are four sites I recommend for starters:

- Hewlett-Packard maintains a list of links to the world's top commercial font designers at `http://www.fonts.com/fontlinks.htm`.

- The True Type Resource page has hundreds of interesting links; find it at `http://members.aol.com/jr9er/index.html`.

- Choose from hundreds of downloadable fonts at the Font Foundry, `http://www.fontfoundry.com`.

- Media Builder (`http://www.mediabuilder.com`) is packed with clip art, animated GIFs, banner-making software, and other resources for Web builders. The site includes a font of the day and nearly a thousand downloadable TrueType fonts.

If you downloaded an OpenType, TrueType, or Type 1 font to a convenient location, you can install the font by dragging its icon to the Fonts folder. If the Fonts folder is already open, use its Install routine to add fonts.

Installing a new font

1. Open the Fonts folder, pull down the **File** menu, and choose **Install New Font**.

2. In the Add Fonts dialog box (see Figure 8.26), select the drive and folder that contain the fonts you want to add. If you downloaded a group of fonts from the Internet, for example, choose the folder where you saved the downloaded files.

Whittle down the list

Some fonts come in multiple styles—Arial, Arial Bold, Arial Italic, and so on. When you are searching through the Fonts folder, all these extra files can be a distraction. To hide some of the clutter, pull down the **View** menu and choose **Hide Variations (Bold, Italic, etc.)**.

Free fonts with favorite programs

Many new programs automatically install new fonts as part of their installation routine. Microsoft Office, for example, installs dozens of fonts, and graphics programs such as CorelDRAW typically include hundreds of TrueType fonts. In some cases, you can find still more fonts by running the Setup program again and searching through additional options.

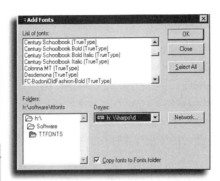

Organize fonts into groups

Most business users have no need to go overboard with fonts. In fact, to keep your system running smoothly I recommend that you install no more than 200 fonts at one time. Graphic designers, however, often need to keep hundreds or thousands of fonts available to handle special-purpose jobs such as headlines and body text in flyers, ads, and newsletters. If your job description includes these tasks, consider investing in font management software that allows you to organize fonts into groups so that you can load and unload them as needed. You can find many programs in this category; I recommend Printer's Apprentice, from Lose Your Mind Software (http://www.loseyourmind.com).

3. In the **List of fonts** box, select the font(s) you want to add. To select multiple fonts, hold down the **Ctrl** key and click each one. To select all fonts in the folder, click the **Select All** button.

4. In general, you should check the **Copy fonts to Fonts folder** box. However, if you want to add fonts from a shared network drive without using disk space on your computer, clear this check box.

5. Click **OK** to add the fonts.

To delete an installed font, open the Fonts folder and select the font you want to delete; then pull down the **File** menu and choose **Delete**.

Managing Printer Fonts

When you pull down the font list in a program (such as Windows 2000's built-in word processor, WordPad), you will normally see all the fonts available in your Fonts folder. In addition, you may see some fonts that aren't listed in your Fonts folder. As the example in Figure 8.27 shows, these fonts use an icon that resembles a printer; not surprisingly, these are *printer fonts*, which are not actually installed on your computer but instead are available in your printer's memory.

If my currently selected printer is a Hewlett-Packard LaserJet 4 Plus, as in the example shown in Figure 8.27, I can format text using any of these printer fonts, but the results on the screen will not match the printed output. If I choose the Marigold font, for example, the onscreen text appears in Arial (the closest matching font), whereas the printed version is a handsome script font.

FIGURE 8.27
In program windows, fonts that use the printer icon are installed only in your printer's memory, not on your computer.

Does this mismatch bother you? Then try either of these two options:

- Contact the company that manufactured your printer and see if they have TrueType fonts that match the printer fonts. When you install these fonts, what you see on the screen will match what you see on the page.
- Change Windows settings so printer fonts are no longer visible in program windows. Open the Fonts folder, pull down the **Tools** menu, and choose **Folder Options**. Click the TrueType tab and check the box labeled **Show only TrueType fonts in the programs on my computer**. After you restart your system, the printer fonts will no longer be visible on the menu. Instead, you will see only those OpenType and TrueType fonts installed on your computer.

Special note for PostScript printers

If you have a *PostScript printer*, your printer has 17 or 35 Adobe Type 1 fonts built in, and you can use special utilities to download additional fonts into the printer's memory. To get *WYSIWYG* output, you must install matching screen fonts for each printer font. Do not choose the option to show only TrueType fonts, which hides all your PostScript fonts!

Using a Screen Saver

Screen savers date back to the PC equivalent of the early Jurassic era, when text-based programs ran on green and black screens. In those days, leaving a program up could actually burn a pattern into the phosphor dots of the monitor, damaging the screen beyond repair. Today's high-resolution color monitors don't suffer from the same problem as those old green screens, but screen savers survive anyway, as a way to keep your data private.

If you step away from your desk, a screen saver keeps nosy passers-by from snooping at whatever you happen to be working on right now. Or go a step further and add password protection to prevent even the most determined snoop from breaking in to your files.

This password really works

Under Windows 95 and Windows 98, password-protected screen savers offer only the illusion of security. In Windows 2000, however, this protection is tied directly to the system login, which means your data is truly safe, even if someone decides to restart your PC.

To set or change a screen saver, open Control Panel, double-click the **Display** option, and click the **Screen Saver** tab (see Figure 8.28). Choose a screen saver from the list, and choose how many minutes you want Windows to wait before covering up the screen.

FIGURE 8.28
Check these options to lock your system up tight if you go 10 minutes without using the keyboard or mouse.

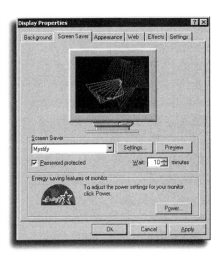

How many minutes?

A password-protected screen saver can drive you slowly mad if you make the waiting interval too brief. Try to strike a balance between security and convenience; instead of relying on the screen saver, get in the habit of locking your machine every time you leave for an extended period of time. Press Ctrl+Alt+Del and choose **Lock Computer** to protect your PC without waiting for the screen saver.

To view all settings for the screen saver you selected, click the **Settings** button. Figure 8.29, for example, shows color, shape, speed, and other options for the Mystify screen saver. Click the **Preview** button to see how the selected screen saver will appear on your monitor. Move your mouse or press any key to end the preview. If you're happy with the screen saver you selected, click **Apply** or **OK** to begin using it.

FIGURE 8.29
Remove the check mark from the **Clear Screen** box to allow the Mystify screen saver pattern to slowly erase the data on your screen—it's a striking effect.

SEE ALSO

➤ *For an overview of the Windows login process, see "Locking Your Computer," p. 78.*

➤ *To automatically turn off your monitor instead of displaying a screen saver, see "Changing Power Options," p. 51.*

To restore the normal display after the screen saver kicks in, move the mouse or press any key. If you checked the **Password protected** box, you see a logon prompt at this point, and you have to enter your password to resume.

Printing and Faxing

Setting Up a Local Printer

Virtually every Windows program includes a Print function. Before Windows 2000 can put any of your work on paper, however, you have to provide some details about your printer. To install a new printer or configure an existing one, start by opening the Printers folder. Click the **Start** button, choose **Settings**, and then choose **Printers**. The resulting dialog box lists all the printers currently available to you, including those that are connected directly to your computer as well as shared computers on your corporate network. Figure 9.1 shows what the Printers folder might look like on a busy network.

FIGURE 9.1
This system folder lists all printers currently set up for use with your computer. Switching to Details view, as I've done here, provides maximum details about each one.

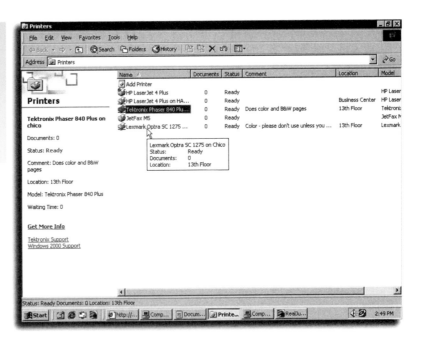

 Of course, the first time you open the Printers folder, the only icon you see is Add Printer. This is the starting point to add any printer's icon to the Printers folder, although the exact steps required differ slightly, depending on the type of printer and whether it's connected directly to your computer or attached to another computer on your network.

Before you can set up a new printer, you must first log on using an administrator's account. For printers that conform to Plug and Play standards (as most recent models do), all you have to do is connect the printer to your computer, turn it on, and start the computer. The Plug and Play software handles all the details of installing the printer *driver* software.

If Windows doesn't automatically detect your computer, or if you don't want to restart your computer, use the Add Printer icon in the Printers folder to set up the printer *port* and install the required driver.

As a general rule, newer is better when it comes to printer drivers. If a driver for your printer model is available as part of Windows 2000's collection of drivers, use it to get started. Check the Web for more recent drivers, either from Windows Update or from the printer manufacturer, but beware of drivers that arrive on floppy disks—if the printer in question sat in a warehouse for any length of time, the disk may be out of date. If you have two driver files to choose from, check the file dates to see which one is more recent.

Setting up a local printer

1. Connect the printer to your parallel (printer) port and turn on its power.

2. Open the Printers folder and double-click the **Add Printer** icon to start the Add Printer Wizard.

3. Follow the wizard's prompts to begin the installation process. Be sure to select the **Local printer** option, and make sure the **Automatically detect my Plug and Play printer** check box is selected (as I've done in Figure 9.2). Click **Next**. If Windows successfully detects your printer and installs its driver, skip ahead to Step 6. If Windows is unable to detect your printer model, you'll see an error message. Click the **Next** button to continue.

4. Select the port to which the printer is connected. Most computers have a single printer port, called LPT1. If your computer has more than one printer port, check the computer's documentation to see which is which. Additional ports will typically be numbered LPT2, LPT3, and so on. Click **Next** to continue.

Easiest setup of all

If you install a printer that connects to the Universal Serial Bus (USB), IEEE 1394 (FireWire), or infrared ports, Windows 2000 automatically starts the Found New Hardware Wizard as soon as you connect the printer. You don't have to restart your computer, and in most cases you can start printing virtually immediately.

Parallel port occupied?

The overwhelming majority of personal printers connect to a PC through the *parallel port*. (The rare exceptions are usually plotters, designed to print out mechanical drawings such as blueprints; these typically connect to a serial port.) If you already have another device, such as a scanner, connected to your printer port, you may need to use a pass-through adapter so that the printer can share the port. Check the documentation for the other device to see how to proceed.

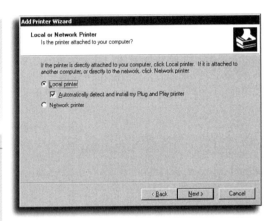

FIGURE 9.2
Check this box to force Windows to try to detect your printer and install the correct software.

No driver? Don't just guess...

If you don't see your exact printer model in the list of supported drivers, resist the temptation to choose a model that sounds close to yours. The result could be odd errors when printing. When in doubt, check with the printer manufacturer to see if the driver file for another printer model is compatible with your hardware.

5. In the list of supported printers (see Figure 9.3), select the name of the printer manufacturer on the left and the printer model on the right. If you have an active Internet connection, click the **Windows Update** button to check Microsoft's Web site for a supported driver. If you downloaded an up-to-date driver from the manufacturer's Web site, click the **Have Disk** button and specify the location where the driver file is stored. Then click **Next**.

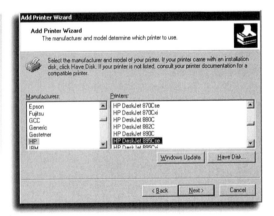

FIGURE 9.3
Windows 2000 includes drivers for literally thousands of printers—unless your printer is very new or very old, chances are it's listed here.

6. Give the printer a name and specify whether you want it to be the default printer that Windows programs use automatically.

7. Follow the wizard's prompts to finish installing the printer. Choose whether you want to share the printer and be sure to print a test page to verify that the installation was successful.

SEE ALSO

➤ *For instructions on how to give others access to your printer, see "Sharing Printers," p. 345.*

8. Finally, the wizard displays a dialog box that lists all the settings you chose (see Figure 9.4 for an example). If you need to adjust any of these settings, click the **Back** button; otherwise, click **Finish** to continue.

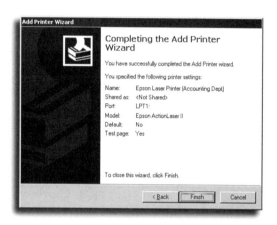

FIGURE 9.4
After running through the Add Printer Wizard, check all your settings here. If everything looks right, click **Finish** to complete the installation.

After you click the **Finish** button, Windows 2000 copies any necessary files (prompting you for a CD or the location of Setup files, if necessary) and adds the printer icon to your Printers folder.

If you install more than one printer (local or network), a small black check mark appears above the icon for the default printer. This designates the printer that your Windows programs will use automatically unless you specify a different printer for a particular job. To change the default printer, right-click the icon of the printer you want to use and choose **Set as De̲fault Printer** from the shortcut menu.

Connecting to a Network Printer

Plug and Play works great on local printers, but it can't help you connect to a shared printer on a network. Instead, you have to get the process started manually. If you know the exact name and location of the printer, you can perform the entire installation in just a few steps with the help of the Add Printer Wizard. If your network is

Use any name you want

When setting up a printer, the name you give the printer is the one that appears under its icon in the Printers window. By default, Windows suggests the model name of the printer, just as it appears in the list of drivers. However, you can name the printer anything you want—Ed's LaserJet, for example. I recommend that you keep the name short, no more than 15 characters, including spaces and punctuation marks. If you enter a descriptive name, you can still see the model name for any installed printer: open the Printers folder and switch to Details view.

a simple workgroup without a Windows 2000 domain, you can browse through a list of computers and find shared printers. Either way, you use the Add Printer Wizard.

Connecting to a workgroup printer

1. Open the Printers folder, double-click the **Add Printer** icon, and follow the wizard's prompts.

2. In the Local or Network Printer option, choose **N<u>e</u>twork printer** and click **Next**. The wizard displays the Locate Your Printer dialog box, shown in Figure 9.5.

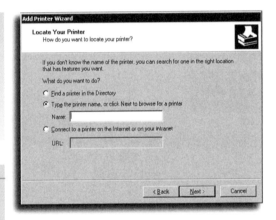

Every printer has a name

Confusingly, every shared printer has two names. One is the name you entered when you first set it up; by default, this is the same as the printer's model name. When you share a printer over a network, you also have to give the share itself a name. By default, Windows uses the first eight characters of the printer's name as the share name. When you connect to a network printer, remember that these two names are usually different.

3. Select the middle option, **Typ<u>e</u> the printer name,** or click **Next** to browse for a printer. If you know the exact name of the printer and the computer to which it's attached, enter it here using the format *computer_name**share_name*. If you don't know the exact name, click **Next**.

4. In the Browse for Printer dialog box, you see a tree-style list of all the computers in your workgroup, as shown in Figure 9.6. Double-click the name of any computer to see which shared printers are available on that computer, and then double-click the name of the printer. Click **Next** to continue.

5. Follow the remaining steps in the wizard to complete the installation. When you click **Finish**, Windows copies driver files, if necessary, and adds the icon to your Printers folder.

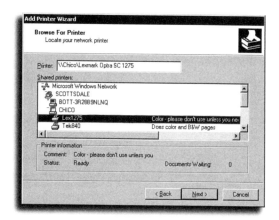

Printing over the Web?
If a shared printer is connected to a Windows 2000 server, you may be able to connect to it by entering its URL. To see all printers connected to a server, open your Web browser and enter `http://server_name/printers`. If you want to connect to a printer in the resulting list, click its name to open the printer's Web page and then click **Connect**. Although you can theoretically use this capability to print over the Internet, this option is really intended for use on corporate intranets.

If you're connected to a Windows 2000 *domain* and your network administrator has set up printer entries in the *Active Directory*, you can skip the wizard and let Windows do all the work of searching for a printer. Connecting to a shared printer with this technique is ridiculously easy.

Using the Active Directory to set up a printer

1. Open the **Start** menu, click **Search**, and choose **For Printers**. The Find Printers dialog box (see Figure 9.7) appears.

2. Enter all or part of the printer's name in the **Name** box. (Leave this box blank to see a list of all available printers on your network.) Click **Find Now**.

3. The results of the search appear in a box below the search criteria you typed. To connect to any printer you see here, double-click its entry in the list. The printer is now available in any Windows program.

Are you looking for a specific type of printer? In most offices it's easy to find a laser printer, but not so easy to find a printer that can produce color output, do two-sided printing, or handle oversized paper. In an ordinary search, the printer name might not tell you which printer has the capabilities you want. To narrow your search, click the **Features** tab in the Find Printer dialog box (see Figure 9.8) and check any of the options you see there. (Unless you're a network administrator, skip the Features tab in the Find Printer dialog box—options available here are strictly for experts.)

FIGURE 9.7
Double-click any entry in this list to connect to it instantly, with no further configuration required.

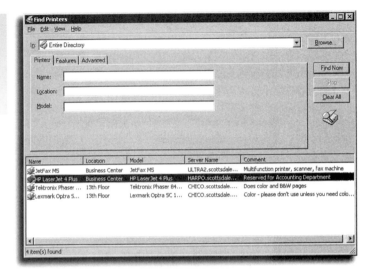

FIGURE 9.7
Double-click any entry in this list to connect to it instantly, with no further configuration required.

FIGURE 9.8
Looking for a color printer that can print at least 12 pages per minute? Choosing these options helps find exactly the right printer, even on a large network.

Find the perfect printer

In a large corporate network, you may have access to hundreds of printers. Most of them are useless to you because they're on another floor or even in a different building. To filter the list of printers so you see only those near you, enter text in the Location box before you click the Find Now button. This option is only effective if the person who set up each printer remembered to fill in the Location field.

After you connect to a shared network printer, you can use it the same as if it were attached directly to your computer.

Printing Perfect Pages

To print a document from within any program, use the Windows standard menu technique: Pull down the **File** menu and choose **Print**. Many programs (for example, Internet Explorer, Netscape

Navigator, Adobe Acrobat Reader, and every Microsoft Office program) also include a Print button on the standard toolbar. If you prefer to keep your hands on the keyboard, try pressing **Ctrl+P**— a surprising number of programs use this standard shortcut to send the current document to the printer.

Most newer Windows programs, including Windows 2000 utilities such as WordPad, use the multitabbed dialog box shown in Figure 9.9. (The selection of tabs differs, depending on the program from which you're printing.)

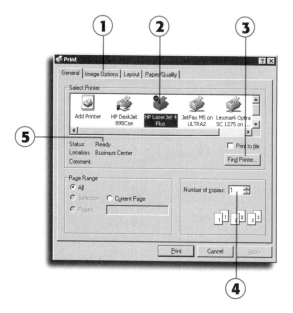

FIGURE 9.9
The standard Print dialog box gives you control over all aspects of printing a document.

1. Click any of these tabs to adjust options for the current print job.

2. Select a printer by clicking its icon; right-click to open the printer window or set options.

3. Click here to install a network printer.

4. Use this control to print extra copies.

5. If the printer has a problem (low toner, out of paper, paper jam), a status message appears here.

Some Windows programs (especially older programs not written specifically for Windows 2000) use a slightly different Print dialog box, like the one shown in Figure 9.10. Again, the exact arrangement of options on this type of dialog box varies depending on the program.

In either style Print dialog box, you can check the **Print to file** option, which lets you store a printed document as a file instead of sending it directly to the printer. When you're ready to print, drag the output file and drop it on the printer icon. This option is available mostly for compatibility with older versions of Windows; generally, as I'll demonstrate later in this section, you'll get better results choosing the *offline printing* option.

FIGURE 9.10
To choose a different printer than the current default, use the drop-down **Name** list.

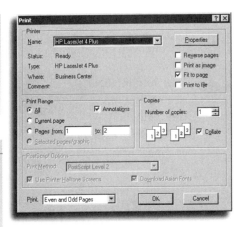

When to print to a file

In one specific case, it makes sense to print to a file. Suppose you have a form you use regularly, and every few days you print a few copies. If you never need to edit the form, you can print it to a file and store that file on your desktop along with a shortcut to the printer. When you need a fresh copy, drag the file icon and drop it on the printer icon.

Create a printer shortcut

Want fast access to your favorite printer? Open the printers folder, right-click, and choose **Create Shortcut**. Windows creates the shortcut on the desktop where it's most useful. Double-click the shortcut to open the print queue and view pending documents. Or drop document icons directly on the shortcut to quickly print them.

After you send a document to the printer, Windows displays a printer icon in the notification area on the right side of the taskbar (next to the system clock). When this icon vanishes, your document has finished printing. To see how many documents are waiting to print, let the mouse pointer hover over this icon for a few seconds and look for the ScreenTip.

Sending a File Directly to the Printer

You don't have to open a document to print it. Instead, drag a document icon and drop it directly on a printer icon in the Printers folder, or on a shortcut to a printer icon on your desktop. You can also right-click any document icon and choose **Print** from the shortcut menu.

If this sounds too good to be true, you're right. Yes, this technique has the time-saving advantage of not requiring you to open a program window just to print a document. However, it also has a few risks: You can't preview the document before printing it, and in the case of documents created by Microsoft Word and other programs that support scripting languages, printing directly can cause macros and macro viruses to run without warning. I recommend using this shortcut only when you're certain you know exactly what's in the document you're printing. Never use drag-and-drop printing with a document someone else sends you.

Setting Print Options

Depending on the type of printer you're using, you can adjust a dizzying array of print options. From within a program, pull down the **File** menu and choose **Print**. If you see a multitabbed Print dialog box, click the appropriate tab to see the options available in that section; if you see the single-tab Print dialog box, click the **Properties** button to reach print options. In either case, your changes apply only to the current job. To adjust printer settings so they apply to all jobs you or any other user sends to a printer, open the Printers folder, right-click the printer icon, and choose **Printing Preferences** from the shortcut menu.

When printing, always check the layout options, especially the orientation of the paper. For many printers, this dialog box (see Figure 9.11) also includes an extremely cool paper-saving option that lets you print multiple pages on a single sheet. You can place from 2 to 16 pages on a single sheet of paper. Obviously, shrinking pages like this makes them more difficult to read, but the effect can still be useful if you simply want to check the layout of a long document, such as a newsletter.

Permission, please

Before you can change default printing preferences, you must have the Manage Printers permission. If your network or system administrator has given you only Print permissions, you will be able to adjust a small number of settings in the Printing Preferences dialog box, but these changes will apply only to jobs you print and not to other users.

FIGURE 9.11
Pick a number between 2 and 16, and Windows will shrink your printed pages to fit more data on a single sheet of paper.

Next, choose paper and print quality options. For a no-nonsense laser printer, you may see only one option on this tab; more sophisticated printers typically include more options. Figure 9.12, for example, shows options for a color printer. In this case, selecting the manual feed option lets me print a high-quality scanned photo without wasting time or expensive custom paper.

FIGURE 9.12
For printers that use expensive supplies, always check these options before printing.

Although you needn't do so with every print job, for some special situations you may need to adjust printer-specific options. Click the **Advanced** button to display settings that apply to the printer model you're working with. Figure 9.13 shows options for a Hewlett-Packard color inkjet printer; options for a plain black LaserJet would be different.

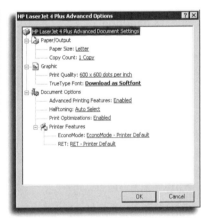

FIGURE 9.13
Click the **Advanced** button to choose any of these printer-specific options. Changes apply only to the current document.

Each setting in the Advanced Options dialog box appears as a hyperlink. When you select a link, it changes to a drop-down list of available options. If you change a setting and then move to another entry in this dialog box, your changes appear in bold type.

Managing Print Queues

When you click the Print button or use the Print menu in most Windows programs, the print job doesn't necessarily go straight from your PC to the printer. If the printer is connected directly to your computer, Windows *spools* the print job to a file on your hard disk rather than sending it directly to your printer. Although it might seem like an extra step, spooling actually makes you more productive. For most documents, the spooling process happens quickly; after the print job is safely stored on your hard drive, Windows can feed pages to the printer in the background while you continue to work with the program.

When you print to a shared printer on the network, your print job goes to the *print server* to which the printer is attached; that machine typically handles the details of spooling.

Because printers are mechanical devices, they operate much more slowly than a computer's memory. As a result, it's possible to create a backlog of print jobs. If you open a dozen Web pages, for example, and send them to the printer in rapid-fire succession, Windows has to keep track of each file and print all the pages in order. If several network users send jobs to a printer while it's handling another job, Windows holds the new jobs in the order in which they were received and sends them, one at a time, to the printer.

At any time, you can view the status of all jobs in the *print queue* for a given printer. Is the printing process taking too long? Is there a paper jam or another problem with the printer? The print queue window lets you identify these and other problems. You can pause the printer while you fix the problem, placing all pending print jobs on hold; you can also pause or cancel a single print job, or cancel all print jobs in the queue—if you have permission to do so.

To view all documents currently in the print queue, open the Printers folder and double-click the icon for the printer in question. As Figure 9.14 shows, each job in the print queue gets its own entry, with complete status information on the document and its progress.

Some servers aren't even PCs

A network printer doesn't have to be connected to a computer. Several hardware manufacturers (including Hewlett-Packard and Intel) make dedicated print servers; these small boxes contain one or more printer ports as well as a network jack. Dedicated print servers get a network name or an *IP address*, the same as a PC-based print server would. To connect to a printer on one of these devices, you use the same techniques as you would with any other network printer.

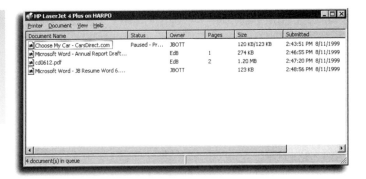

FIGURE 9.14
In the print queue window, each waiting job gets its own entry. Right-click any entry to manage that document.

Quick check on the queue

If you currently have a document waiting to print, double-click the printer icon in the notification area at the right of the taskbar. That opens the printer window and shows all current documents.

To manage individual documents, select one or more documents, right-click, and use the shortcut menu. If you sent the job to the printer, you have complete control over that job as part of the default permissions, and you can pause, resume, or cancel the job at any time before it reaches the top of the list and begins going to the printer. If another user sent the job to the printer, you can delete the job only if you have the Manage Documents permission.

- **Pause.** Temporarily stops the selected document from printing.

- **Resume.** Begins printing a document that was previously paused.

- **Restart.** Prints a document again, from the beginning. This option is usually useful only for very large documents because short ones don't sit in the queue long enough to restart.

- **Cancel.** Deletes the current job from the queue. If the job has already begun printing, you may end up with one or more pages of gibberish from the printer.

- **Properties.** Displays detailed information about any job in the print queue, including its size and who sent it to the printer. Figure 9.15 shows an example of one such job. Note that if you want to move a job ahead of another in the queue, you can do so by increasing its priority using the sliding control here.

Manage multiple jobs

To cancel multiple print jobs in a single action, hold down the **Ctrl** key as you select each print job. Then right-click and choose **Cancel**.

FIGURE 9.15
Want to move your job ahead of others in the queue? Move the **Priority** slider to the right.

To manage the printer itself, open the Printers folder, right-click the printer icon, and use the shortcut menu. If the window for that printer is already open, the same choices are available from the **Printer** menu.

- Choose **Pause Printing** if you want to stop the flow of documents from the print queue to the printer. This option is useful if you need to make a change to the printer, such as changing the paper in the default tray.

- Choose **Cancel All Documents** if you want to kill all the pending documents without printing any of them. This option has no effect on documents that have already been sent to the printer and are waiting in its memory.

- Choose **Use Printer Offline** if you're not currently connected to a printer—for example, if you're using a notebook computer on an airplane. This option is also useful if your printer is noisy and you want to run all the queued print jobs later, while you're in a meeting or at lunch. When you're ready to print, right-click the icon again and remove the check mark from this menu choice.

Finally, for printers connected to a Web server, you can view the print queue using a Web-style interface. Figure 9.16, for example, shows the print queue for a printer connected to a Windows 2000 Server. The choices available here are identical to those available in a conventional printer window, except that you can manage the printer by using the Web browser rather than by opening a printer folder.

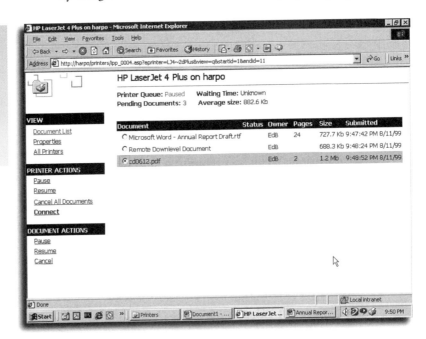

FIGURE 9.16
Use this Web-style printer window to manage documents on a shared network printer connected to a Windows 2000 Web server.

No sharing

Although the Fax icon appears in the Printers folder, Windows 2000 enforces one crucial difference between its virtual fax machine and local printers: You can't share a fax printer with other network users. Although the Properties dialog box for the Fax icon includes a Sharing tab, it contains only the message that sharing is not supported.

To connect to a Web-style print queue, click in the browser's Address bar and enter the address http://server_name/printers (substituting the name of the Web server). The resulting Web page displays a list of all printers on that computer, the same as if you had opened the Printers folder. Click the hyperlink for the printer you want to manage to see all pending jobs for that printer.

Using Windows to Send and Receive Faxes

What's the difference between a printer and a fax machine? Not as much as you might think. In fact, if you install a modem with fax capabilities—and these days, that includes nearly all modems—Windows 2000 automatically installs the fax service and adds a Fax icon in the Printers folder. After you complete some relatively simple configuration steps, you can "print" a text document or an image file to a remote fax machine; you can also receive incoming faxes and view them on the screen or send them to your own printer.

In addition to the Fax printer icon, Windows 2000 installs a group of icons you can use to configure the Fax service. To view this group of icons, click the **Start** button, and then drill down through the **Programs** menu to **Accessories**, **Communications**, and finally **Fax**. This program group consists of five icons, including a Fax Queue that lets you view pending faxes and cancel, pause, or resume any item in the list; a shortcut to the My Faxes folder; and a Fax Service Management icon, which lets you configure various fax options.

Should you use Windows 2000's built-in fax capabilities? If you've struggled with the half-baked fax features in previous Windows versions, I don't blame you for being skeptical. Surprisingly, however, this feature really works, especially for outgoing faxes. Except for a few minor quirks, sending a fax is easy and nearly idiot-proof. Receiving faxes is a bit trickier, but after you configure your system correctly it works flawlessly—and you never run out of paper.

Setting Up the Fax Service

If you want to use the Fax service exclusively to send faxes, you can skip the setup process completely. The first time you use the Send Fax Wizard, Windows displays the dialog box shown in Figure 9.17.

My Faxes? Not exactly...

Although the name of the My Faxes folder would suggest that it contains only faxes you send and receive, that's not the case at all. The My Faxes folder is actually contained in the All Users profile, and it contains all faxes sent or received by any user logged on to the current machine. Although you can change the location where Windows stores faxes, you can't do so on a per-user basis. If you send or receive a confidential fax and you don't want any other user to be able to see it, be sure to move it out of this folder and into a location accessible only to you, such as the My Documents folder.

FIGURE 9.17
The first time you send a fax, Windows prompts you to enter basic setup information and then hands you to the Send Fax Wizard.

If you choose the default option, **Edit the user information now**, Windows opens the Fax Properties dialog box shown in Figure 9.18; after you enter information about yourself, you're ready to send a fax. Take the time to fill in this section completely; as I'll explain shortly, the Fax service uses this information to create personalized cover pages automatically.

FIGURE 9.18
Don't skip this step: Information you enter in this dialog box automatically appears in cover pages when you send a fax.

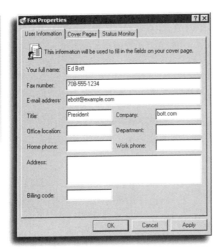

If you want to be thorough when setting up the Fax service, you must go to several different locations:

- By default, Windows 2000 disables the capability to receive faxes. To enable this feature, open the **Programs** menu, and then click **Accessories**, **Communications**, and **Fax.** Open the Fax Service Management console, double-click the Devices tree, and select your fax modem. Right-click and choose **Properties** to view the dialog box shown in Figure 9.19; check the **Enable receive** box and, optionally, adjust the number of rings you want Windows to wait before answering.

- While this dialog box is open, edit the text in the **TSID** box—this line, which appears on all your outgoing faxes, typically contains your fax number and company name. Edit the **CSID** box to change the text that appears at the top of all incoming faxes.

- To change the location where Windows stores incoming faxes, click the Received Faxes tab and choose a folder.

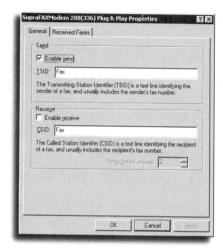

FIGURE 9.19
By default, Windows disables the capability to receive faxes. Check the box in the bottom half of this dialog box to enable this feature.

■ To set the number of retries the Fax service uses when the number you're calling is busy, open the Fax Service Management console and select the **Fax Service on Local Computer** item in the Tree pane at left. Pull down the **Action** menu and choose **Properties** to display the dialog box shown in Figure 9.20.

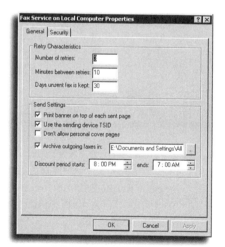

FIGURE 9.20
Normally, if you get a busy signal when faxing, Windows tries three more times, with a 10-minute wait between tries. Adjust settings here to change the retry options.

■ Use this same dialog box to set the number of rings Windows listens for before answering an incoming fax.

■ Click the **Security** tab to set permissions for all fax options. By default, members of the Administrators and Power Users groups can use and configure fax features; add or adjust these permissions if you want other users to be able to send and receive faxes.

Sending Faxes Through Your Modem

To send a fax, you don't need to go through an elaborate setup routine. Pull down the **File** menu, choose **Print**, and select the **Fax** icon from the list of available printers. Click the **Print** button to start the Send Fax Wizard.

The Send Fax Wizard marches you through three steps:

First, it opens the Recipient and Dialing Information page (see Figure 9.21), in which you enter the name and phone number of the person or persons to whom you're sending the fax. Be sure to click the **Add** button to insert the name in the box at the bottom.

<table>
<tr><td>How many rings?</td></tr>
</table>

How many rings?

If you have a dedicated fax line, you can leave the default settings at two rings; Windows will always pick up incoming calls quickly. For shared voice/fax lines, don't check the **Enable receive** box; instead, use the manual answering procedure I describe later in this chapter.

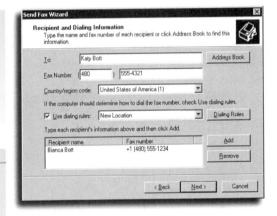

FIGURE 9.21
Enter a name and phone number at the top of this page; then click the **Add** button to insert the name in the box at the bottom.

Accidental fax?

If you have not yet set up a printer on your computer, Windows displays a message asking whether you want to fax the current document or print it. Click the **Fax** button to open the Send Fax Wizard; if you wanted to print the document and not fax it, click the **Install Printer** button to add a new printer and use it.

The next step of the wizard, Adding the Cover Page (see Figure 9.22), lets you select one of four ready-made cover pages. Select a template from the drop-down list, and fill in the Subject and Note lines. The text you enter will appear in the corresponding fields on your cover page. If you don't want to send a cover page with your fax, clear the **Include a cover page** check box. This option is most useful when the first page of your faxed document includes all the information you need to identify the recipient.

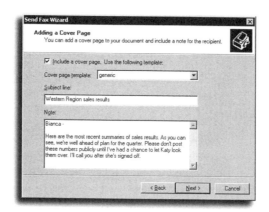

FIGURE 9.22
Always fill in a subject for your fax. The note text is optional, but it can be useful if you want your fax to have special handling at the receiving end.

Finally, on the **Scheduling Transmission** page, select the time when you want to send the fax (the default is **N̲ow**), and add a billing code if you want. (The code will appear in the fax log.) Click the **N̲ext** button to review all the choices you made. If everything is correct, click the **Finish** button to send your fax.

Windows also includes an option that lets you send a one-page fax that consists of only a cover page. This option is handy when you want to send a quick note to someone who doesn't have access to email. Click the **Start** button, and then choose **Programs**, **Accessories**, **Communications**, and **Fax**, Click the **Send Cover Page Fax** option to open the Send Fax Wizard and follow the steps outlined earlier.

To send a scanned document via fax, use the Imaging program (found in the **Accessories** group on the **P̲rograms** menu). To add pages after scanning the first page, pull down the **P̲age** menu and choose **A̲ppend**. After you have scanned all the pages you want to fax, click the **Print** button and send the document to the fax printer, as you would with any other document.

Receiving Faxes

To set up your fax modem so you can decide when to receive faxes on a voice line, open Control Panel's **Fax** option and click the **Status Monitor** tab. Check the **E̲nable manual answer for the first device** check box and click **OK**.

Number confusion

After you click the **Add** button, check the name and number in the list of recipients at the bottom of the dialog box. In some cases you'll find the number is incorrect—dialing 1 plus an area code where none is required, for example. If this happens, click the **Remove** button, clear the **Use dialing rules** check box, and enter the number exactly as you want it dialed, with or without prefixes and area codes.

Make your own cover pages

Buried in the Fax group is a small applet called the Fax Cover Page Editor, which allows you to create and modify cover pages for the fax service. Although you can create a cover page template from scratch, it's easier to customize one of the four cover page templates installed with Windows 2000. The applet is relatively easy to use, and the online help is clear and straightforward.

With this option set, every time the phone rings, you see a dialog box that asks whether you want to answer the call. Pick up the phone and determine whether the incoming call is voice or fax. If it's a voice call, click **No**; if you hear the screeching sound of a fax, click **Yes**.

Viewing Faxes You've Received

To view and print a fax, open the **My Faxes** folder and browse through the proper folder: **Received Faxes** or **Sent Faxes**. Double-click the fax you want to view or print. Windows opens the file using the Imaging Preview program. To print the fax, pull down the **File** menu and choose **Print**.

part

III

WINDOWS 2000 AND HARDWARE

Managing Disks and Drives

Setting Up a Hard Disk

Compressing Files to Save Disk Space

Working with Floppy Disks

Setting Up a Hard Disk

Handle disks with care

Partitioning and formatting a hard disk is not a task for the faint-hearted. By definition, the process destroys any data that might be on the current disk. If you wipe out the partition that holds your system files, you must reinstall Windows 2000. Before you even think of working with local disks and partitions, make sure you have an up-to-date backup and a set of emergency disks.

Whether you upgrade to Windows 2000 from an earlier version of Windows or install a clean copy on a new system, the Setup program typically handles all the details of preparing a hard disk so you can store data on it. If you add a second hard disk, however, or if you want to rearrange partitions on your existing disk, you need to work with a special tool called the Disk Management Utility.

Using the Disk Management Utility

To run the Disk Management Utility, you must be able to supply a username and password with administrative rights. (And even that may not be enough if your network administrator has restricted access to Disk Management by setting up a group policy that affects your user account.)

SEE ALSO
➤ *To read more about logging in as an administrator, see "Who's Managing Your Computer?" p. 20.*

Starting the Local Disk Manager

Better safe than sorry

Before you begin working with any kind of system utility, get in the habit of closing all programs. That simple precaution guarantees that you don't inadvertently corrupt data in an open file. Before you do major disk surgery, such as partitioning a disk or formatting a volume, I strongly recommend that you fully back up all data.

1. Open Control Panel, right-click the **Computer Management** icon, and choose the **Run as** option.

2. In the Run As Other User dialog box, enter the username and password of an account that is a member of the Local Administrators group. (In the **Domain** box, use the name of your computer.) Click **OK**.

3. In the left (tree) pane of the Computer Management window, click the **Disk Management** option under Storage.

Figure 10.1 shows what the Disk Management window looks like on a typical system. (Of course, the exact details you see will be slightly different from those shown here, depending on the number of physical disks installed in your system and how each one is configured.)

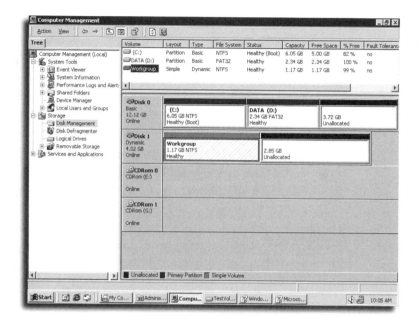

FIGURE 10.1
The Disk Management window is Mission Control for any task involved with physical disks installed in your computer.

When working with the Disk Management Window, you need to understand the following terms and concepts:

- **Disks.** Physical storage devices attached to a computer. Windows 2000 allows you to set up hard disks in two ways. *Basic disks* are most commonly used in Windows 2000 Professional; if you boot with Windows 95/98 or an MS-DOS startup disk, you can see these disk types. *Dynamic disks* enable you to take advantage of advanced features, such as the capability to combine two or more disks using the same drive letter.
- **Partitions.** On basic disks only, these are subdivisions of a physical disk that function as though they were separate disks. You can create up to four *primary partitions* on a basic disk, each of which can have its own drive letter, or you can create up to three primary partitions and one *extended partition*. If your computer includes a 27GB physical disk, for example, you might subdivide it into three primary partitions of 8GB, 6GB, and 5GB, and then create an extended partition from the remaining 8GB.

Not as easy as 1-2-3

For a variety of obscure technical reasons, disk numbering always starts at 0, rather than 1. Thus, if your system includes two hard disks and one CD-ROM drive, Windows identifies them as Disk 0, Disk 1, and CD-ROM 0, respectively. Your computer's startup files generally must be on Disk 0, although you can install the Windows 2000 program files on any hard disk.

- **Volumes.** Portions of a dynamic disk that function as though they were separate disks. Unlike disk partitions, you can create an unlimited number of volumes on a single physical disk and assign a different drive letter to each one.

- **Logical drives.** Subdivisions of an extended partition that function as though they were separate disks, each with its own drive letter. Only basic disks can contain logical drives.

- **Disk format.** Before you can store data on a disk, you have to prepare it by running a formatting utility. As part of the process of formatting a hard disk, you also have to choose a *file system*.

- **Drive letters.** On a basic disk, you can assign a drive letter to each primary partition and each logical drive within an extended partition. On a dynamic disk, each volume can have its own drive letter. In the My Computer window, each partition or volume that has a drive letter appears as a local drive with its own icon.

Basic or Dynamic Disk?

When you install a new disk in a computer and run the Disk Management Utility, Windows 2000 detects your new disk and starts up the Write Signature and Upgrade Disk Wizard automatically (see Figure 10.2). Stop and read every screen carefully as you go through this wizard! If you click quickly through the default settings, you will upgrade the disk type from basic to dynamic and write disk configuration information called a *signature* to the disk. That can cause enormous headaches later. If you decide you want to set up the new disk as a basic disk, click the **Cancel** button.

SEE ALSO

➤ To learn more about the disk types you see in the Upgrade Disk Wizard, see "Creating and Managing Volumes on Dynamic Disks," p. 239.

Should you allow this wizard to complete the upgrade process? For most users of Windows 2000 Professional, a basic disk configuration is good enough. Most of the technical options described on the opening screen of this wizard are only appropriate for computer professionals setting up a server, so it's somewhat baffling that this wizard even appears at all. In fact, a dynamic disk can cause serious problems on some systems.

FIGURE 10.2
Beware of this wizard, which can configure a disk so that other operating systems won't recognize it.

- If Windows detects that you're running on a portable computer, the option to upgrade to a dynamic disk is unavailable.

- If you have set up your system so that it lets you choose from a menu of operating systems at startup, do not upgrade a basic disk to dynamic. Windows 95, Windows 98, and Windows NT 4.0 will not recognize volumes on a dynamic disk.

- If you have only one physical disk, Windows 2000 will set it up as a basic disk when you run Setup. Although you can later upgrade this basic disk to a dynamic disk, there is usually no practical benefit to doing so, because these advanced features typically require two or more physical disks.

If you've already upgraded a basic disk to a dynamic disk, you can change it back to a basic disk, but only if you first remove all volumes from the disk. In the Local Disk Manager, find the dynamic disk in the graphical portion of the window. Right-click the icon at the left of the disk (where you see the description Dynamic Disk) and choose **Revert to Basic Disk** from the shortcut menu.

Creating and Managing Partitions on Basic Disks

When setting up a new disk, how many partitions (or volumes) should you create? No single answer is right for everyone. Use the following general guidelines to help decide on the right configuration for you.

- **One disk, one partition**. When installing Windows 2000 on a PC with a single disk, the simplest setup is to create one large partition with the drive letter C:. This option prevents you from having to juggle multiple drive letters, but it adds some management headaches. For example, to run CHKDSK (the Windows disk-checking utility), you must restart your system.

SEE ALSO
➤ *For details on how to use CHKDSK, see "Checking Disks for Errors," p. 275.*

- **One disk, multiple partitions**. With a large enough physical disk, this option gives you maximum flexibility. For instance, you might choose to create two equal-size partitions on a 13GB disk; use the C: drive for Windows and program files, and reserve the second drive (D:) for data files, pointing the My Documents folder to this location. If you use multiple operating systems, you must install each one on a separate partition.

SEE ALSO
➤ *For step-by-step instructions on how to point the My Documents folder to any location you want, see "How Windows Organizes Your Files," p. 106.*
➤ *To learn more about using Windows 2000 with other operating systems on a single PC, see "Keeping Your Old Operating System," p. 32.*

- **Multiple disks**. Adding a second disk (or a third or a fourth disk, if your system has room for it) is a great way to add storage capacity without having to reinstall Windows 2000. If you work with very large files, such as video clips or graphical images, I recommend a single partition on the largest drive you can find. On a Windows 2000 computer that is shared by several users, you might want to create separate storage areas for each user. In that case, create an extended partition and then create a series of logical drives, one for each user.

Creating a new partition

1. In the bottom pane of the Local Disk Manager window, right-click on the Unallocated region and choose **Create Partition**. The Create Partition Wizard opens. As with all wizards, you click the **Next** button to move from one step to the next.

2. Select the partition type you want to create: **Primary partition** or **Extended partition**.

3. Specify a size for the new partition. By default (see Figure 10.3), Windows suggests using the maximum available size; enter a smaller number if you want to create multiple partitions, and click **Next** to continue.

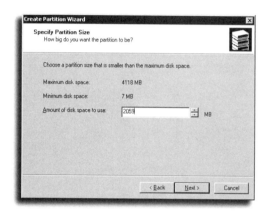

FIGURE 10.3
The wizard assumes you want to create a single partition using all available space; if you want multiple partitions instead, enter a smaller number here.

- If you created an extended partition, you've reached the end of the wizard. Click **Finish** to create the partition. To begin creating logical drives, right-click the extended partition and choose **Create Partition**; choose **Logical drive** as the partition type and specify the size of the logical drive you want to create (the default is to use the entire extended partition as a single logical drive). At this point, you can continue with the remaining steps in the wizard.

- If you created a primary partition, continue with the remaining steps in the wizard.

4. Assign a drive letter or path to the newly created partition. The wizard gives you three options, as shown in Figure 10.4.

- **Assign a drive letter.** The default choice is the next available unused drive letter. Use the drop-down list to choose a different letter.

- **Mount this volume at an empty folder that supports drive paths.** Use this option to display the contents of the selected partition using a drive letter and folder name from an existing drive. In the next section, I explain how to use this feature.

Bye-bye, FDISK

If you've used MS-DOS or Windows 95 to manage disks, you're probably used to firing up the FDISK utility to create and manage partitions. That utility is not available in Windows 2000. To manage partitions and volumes, you must use Disk Management. Although you can theoretically boot with an MS-DOS floppy disk and use FDISK to view partitions on a Windows 2000 system, resist the temptation to change partitions using this older tool! Volumes on dynamic disks will not be visible at all, and you run the risk of damaging data beyond repair if you try to make changes with FDISK.

237

- **<u>Do not assign a drive letter or drive path.</u>** Choose this option if you want to hide a partition. If you have set up your system so you can choose different Windows versions at startup, for example, you might want one partition to be invisible to Windows 2000 so that you don't inadvertently tamper with the other operating system's program files.

FIGURE 10.4
Most of the time, you will choose the next available drive letter from this dialog box.

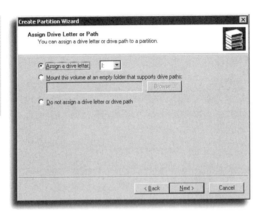

5. Before you can store data, you must format the partition or logical drive. The wizard lets you choose a file system and other formatting options, as shown in Figure 10.5. (I explain the differences between NTFS and FAT32 a bit later in this chapter.)

FIGURE 10.5
On a new drive, leave the **Perform a <u>Q</u>uick Format** box unchecked so Windows fully tests for bad sectors.

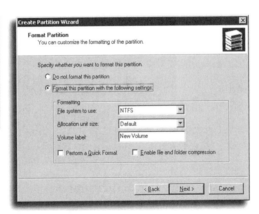

6. In the wizard's final step, it displays a summary of the settings you selected. If you made any mistakes, click the **Back** button to adjust options as needed. Otherwise, click **Finish** to create the partition or logical drive and return to Disk Management.

After creating a partition, return to the Local Disk Manager and create additional partitions or logical drives, if any unallocated space remains.

Creating and Managing Volumes on Dynamic Disks

If you've upgraded a basic disk to a dynamic disk, the procedures for setting up a new disk are slightly different. And if your system has two or more dynamic disks, you have even more options. On dynamic disks, instead of creating partitions and logical drives, you create *volumes*. As with a basic disk, you start by right-clicking on Unallocated space in the graphical display at the bottom of the Disk Management window, and then choose **Create Volume** from the shortcut menu.

The Create Volume Wizard works much like the Create Partition Wizard. Instead of creating primary and extended partitions, however, you create one of the following three types of volumes:

- **Simple volumes** are similar to primary partitions, with one important difference: you can *extend* a simple volume using free space on the same disk or on another dynamic disk. If you run out of room on drive S:, for example, add another hard drive to your system and set it up as a dynamic disk. Now you can open Disk Management, right-click the S: volume, and choose **Extend Volume** from the shortcut menu. Follow the prompts to add unallocated space from the new disk to the existing volume, and you now have the storage you need.

- **Spanned volumes** are made up of unallocated space on two or more dynamic disks. This option is available only if you have at least two dynamic disks with free space on them.

- **Striped volumes** are also made up of unallocated space on two or more dynamic disks. When you save data to a striped volume, Windows alternates data between the two drives, which has the effect of speeding up disk access dramatically.

How does it work?

Why are striped volumes faster? Think about the way disk drives work—a magnetic head moves from place to place on a disk coated with a magnetic film, reading bits of data encoded on the surface of the disk. If you want to read, for example, 100 pieces of data, the head has to physically move 100 times from one location to the next. In a striped volume, you have two magnetic heads doing the work. So at the exact time the first disk is grabbing data from the first location, the second disk is grabbing data from the second location. Each disk, working independently, needs to grab only half the data, and you get the whole file much faster.

Compression box grayed out?

Is the **Enable file and folder compression** box grayed out in the Create Partition Wizard? Make sure you've specified NTFS as the file system; FAT32 drives can't be compressed.

239

Dynamic disks can be daunting

As soon as you begin working with dynamic disks, you cross over the line that separates casual Windows users from Windows-experts-in-training. Extending or spanning volumes can be tremendously useful ways to increase available storage without having to back up and reinstall Windows, but the technical challenges are daunting. The Disk Management window offers a wealth of detailed online help—don't be afraid to use it if you get stuck. And pay careful attention to dialog boxes and error messages you see when working with dynamic disks, because they can help prevent you from inadvertently deleting or damaging data.

Yes, there's a catch...

Not all simple volumes can be extended. If you originally created a partition on a basic disk and then upgraded it to a dynamic disk, Windows converted the partition to a volume. However, this volume cannot be extended. You must follow a specific order to successfully extend a volume: Create a dynamic disk first and then create a simple volume—you can successfully extend that volume to space on any dynamic disk. No, the process doesn't work in reverse: You can't make a volume smaller, unfortunately.

What's the difference between a spanned and a striped volume? For starters, the space you use on two different disks for a spanned volume doesn't have to be equal. If you have 3.72GB free on Disk 0 and 4.08GB free on Disk 1, you can combine them in a single spanned volume to create a single volume with 7.8GB of space and a drive letter of your choosing. When you open the My Computer folder and double-click the drive icon for that volume, you see its contents the same as if they were on a single disk or partition.

A striped volume, on the other hand, must consist of an equal amount of space on both disks. With 3.72GB free on Disk 0 and 4.08GB free on Disk 1, you can use all the space on the first disk but only 3.72GB from the second, for a total of 7.44GB. Figure 10.6 shows what the striped volume looks like in Disk Management.

Choosing the Right File System

When you format a hard disk, Windows asks you to specify which file system you want to use. Choose carefully because the wrong choice can have serious consequences:

- **FAT** is the least powerful but most compatible option. If you use Windows 2000 and the original version of Windows 95 on the same machine, you must format the system drive using the FAT file system. On drives more than 1024MB in size, the FAT file system is incredibly wasteful; switching to FAT32 or NTFS can easily give you 30% more storage space because these file systems are so much more efficient. Using the FAT file system, you cannot specify individual access permissions for files and folders.

- **FAT32** is an improved 32-bit version of the FAT file system that stores data with less wasted space. On systems where you choose between Windows 95B or Windows 98 and Windows 2000, this file system is your best choice. Like the FAT file system, FAT32 does not allow you to set access permissions on files and folders.

- **NTFS** is the preferred choice on systems that run only Windows 2000, especially on systems that are shared by multiple users. NTFS includes features that help repair disk errors automatically, and it allows you to secure individual files and folders with strong password protection. If you use Windows NT 4.0 and Windows 2000 on the same machine, you must install Service Pack 4 or later on the NT4 machine so that both operating systems can read and write data properly.

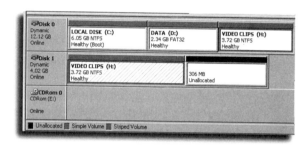

FIGURE 10.6
With two dynamic disks, you can combine space from two or more physical disks using a single drive letter. Here, drive H: is a striped volume that uses equal blocks of space on two disks.

As I noted in the previous section, the Create Partition and Create Volume Wizards handle formatting chores for you. However, you can reformat a drive at any time if you want to start from scratch. If you created an NTFS drive, for example, and you decide you want to format it as FAT32 instead, you need to reformat it. Open the My Computer folder, right-click the drive icon, and choose **Format** from the shortcut menu. Figure 10.7 shows the choices available when you select this option.

If you want to convert a FAT or FAT32 drive to the NTFS file system, a simple Windows utility can handle the job without requiring you to back up, reformat, and restore. To perform the conversion, first open a Command Prompt window (you'll find a Command Prompt shortcut in the Accessories group on the Programs menu); then type the following command (substituting the correct drive letter) and press **Enter**:

```
CONVERT drive_letter: /fs:ntfs
```

Shared files are fine

Don't confuse local access to a disk with shared access over a network. If you create a partition, format it using the NTFS file system, and then restart the system using Windows 95 or 98, that partition will be invisible—those Windows versions don't speak NTFS. However, if you share the NTFS drive over the network, any Windows 95 user who has the proper access permissions can read and write files on that drive with no problems. Your computer takes care of the local access while the network handles the job of transferring files between machines.

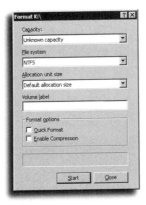

FIGURE 10.7
The Format dialog box allows you to choose a file system and other options.

Changing Drive Letters and Paths

In Windows 2000, drive letters are persistent—after you specify that you want a drive to go by a specific letter, it stays that way until you change it. That's true even if you add or remove partitions, volumes, and removable drives. That's a huge change from Windows 95 and 98, where drive letters change dynamically every time you boot. And unlike those older Windows versions, you can also access files stored on a disk partition or volume without assigning a letter.

Typically, you choose drive letters at the same time you create a partition or volume. But you can reassign drive letters at any time. Why would you want to do this? Suppose you have one physical disk that consists of two partitions: C: for program files and D: for data. Your CD-ROM drive uses E:. Unfortunately, your D: drive is only 2GB in size, and it's bursting at the seams. If you purchase a 20GB drive, create one huge partition, and add it to your system, Windows 2000 will suggest that you assign it the next available drive letter—in this case, F:.

Go ahead and use F: as the drive letter for now. After you've formatted the drive, copy all your old data files from D: to the new F: drive. Close all programs and Explorer windows, and then follow these steps to swap the drive letters for the two drives:

Reassigning drive letters

1. Open the Disk Management window, right-click the old drive, and choose **Change Drive Letter and Path**.

Formatting is destructive

For all intents and purposes, formatting a drive has the same effect as feeding all your data into a shredder. When the formatting is complete, all data that had been stored on the drive in question is gone for good. Fortunately, it's nearly impossible to format a hard drive by mistake. You must be logged on as an administrator to tackle the job, and Windows displays several warning dialog boxes and gives you ample chance to back out before completing the operation. As with all disk operations, back up crucial data before you click the **OK** button!

2. In the Change Drive Letter and Paths dialog box (see
Figure 10.8), click the **Remove** button.

FIGURE 10.8
Use this dialog box to
assign a new letter to a
drive. After you make the
assignment, the letter
stays with the drive until
you change it.

3. Windows displays a dialog box warning you that changing drive
letters may cause problems with programs. Click **Yes** to continue, and then click **Close**. The original drive no longer has a
drive letter.

4. In the Local Disk Manager, right-click the new F: drive and
choose **Change Drive Letter and Path**.

5. In the Change Drive Letter and Paths dialog box, click the **Edit**
button.

6. In the Edit Drive Letter and Paths dialog box, select D: from
the drop-down **Assign a drive letter** list.

7. Once again, Windows displays a warning dialog box; click **Yes** to
continue, and then click **Close**. The new drive now uses the letter D:.

8. Return to Disk Management one more time, right-click the former D: drive (which currently has no letter), and choose
Change Drive Letter and Path.

9. In the Change Drive Letter and Paths dialog box, click the **Add**
button and choose F: from the drop-down **Assign a drive letter**
list.

10. Close all dialog boxes and close the Local User Manager.

After completing this sequence, your new 20GB drive has all the data
from the old drive, with plenty of room for new data. Best of all, you
and your programs can find the data exactly where you've both
grown accustomed to finding it: on the D: drive. After you verify

Use letters as hints

The drive letter you assign
to a partition or logical
drive can serve as a clue to
the contents of that drive.
For instance, I've created a
separate partition where I
store programs I download
from the Internet; naturally,
I use the letter P: to remind
me that I can find programs
there. You might choose S:
for shared files, or W: for
Web pages you've created.

that you can access all your old data on the new drive, delete the old copies and use the F: drive for another purpose.

Of course, you don't have to use drive letters at all if you don't want to. Instead, you can create a path (a drive letter and folder name) on an existing drive. In the previous section, for example, you might not want to assign F: to the leftover 2GB drive. Instead, you could tell Windows that you want to see files stored in that location whenever you open the C:\Backups folder.

Assigning a path to a drive

1. Open Disk Management and right-click the partition, volume, or logical drive you want to assign to a path. From the shortcut menu, choose **Change Drive Letter and Path**.

2. Click the **Add** button and click in the **Mount in this NTFS folder** box.

3. Click the **Browse** button to display the dialog box shown in Figure 10.9.

4. Select a drive icon and click the New Folder button to create an empty folder that will refer to the selected partition, volume, or logical drive.

5. Replace the generic New Folder name (see Figure 10.10) with the name you want to use and click **OK**. Click **OK** to close the Add New Drive Letter or Path dialog box and make the change effective.

FIGURE 10.9
Browse for a folder (or better yet, create a new one) to use when referring to a specific partition.

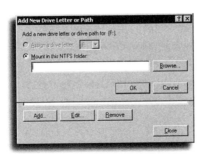

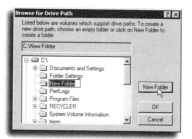

FIGURE 10.10
Use this dialog box to create a new folder and assign it as a drive path.

If you open an Explorer window and display the contents of drive C:, you'll notice a change: the icon for the Backups folder uses a drive icon instead of a folder icon. That's your only clue that this folder is different. As far as programs are concerned, files stored on this partition act as though they're in a regular folder on the C: drive.

Compressing Files to Save Disk Space

Like its predecessor, Windows NT 4.0, Windows 2000 is capable of storing files using *disk compression* so that they take up significantly less room. This can be an excellent way to squeeze more space out of a drive, as long as you understand its limitations.

- Compression is available only on drives formatted with the NTFS file system. If you format a drive with FAT or FAT32, you can't compress it.

- Some files don't compress well. MP3 audio files and zip archive files, for instance, are already highly compressed—if you store them on a compressed NTFS drive, you'll barely notice a difference in size. Bitmap graphics and database files, on the other hand, are capable of significant compression.

- Windows has to work a bit harder to compress and decompress a file or folder each time you save and open it. If you're unhappy with your system's current performance, you shouldn't turn on compression.

- Before you can compress a drive, you need a fair amount of free space. If your current drive is packed to the gills, you may not be able to compress it until you delete some files and clear out some space.

Use several paths

Windows lets you assign only one drive letter to each partition, volume, or logical drive. However, you can assign as many drive paths as you want. If you have three NTFS drives on your system—C:, D:, and E:—you could create paths on each one that point to another volume or logical drive. Regardless of which drive path you work with, the contents are always the same.

It's not DriveSpace

Older versions of MS-DOS and Windows (including Windows 95) used a crude compression system called DriveSpace; in early MS-DOS versions, this feature was called DoubleSpace. This compression system is completely incompatible with Windows 2000, which uses a more modern and reliable compression procedure. If you have a disk partition that uses DriveSpace, Windows 2000 will not be able to read or write files to that drive letter.

The easiest way to maximize space on your system is to compress an entire drive. Open the My Computer folder, select the NTFS drive you want to compress, and right-click. From the shortcut menu, choose **Properties**. On the General tab (see Figure 10.11), check the **Compress drive to save disk space** box.

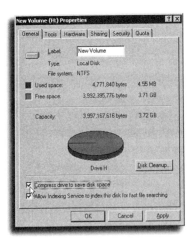

FIGURE 10.11
Check this box to compress an entire drive.

By default, Windows will compress only the files in the *root folder* of the selected drive. To compress every file and folder on the drive, you must change the default option in the Confirm Attribute Changes dialog box (see Figure 10.12), which appears when you select compression for an entire drive.

FIGURE 10.12
Choose the bottom option to compress all files and folders on a drive. If the drive contains a lot of data, the compression process can take a long time.

Compressing an entire drive is a radical step. In some cases, you can accomplish the same space-saving goal by compressing one or more files or folders. Suppose you have a folder filled with hundreds or even thousands of bitmap images, each greater than 100KB in size.

By compressing that folder, you can reduce the storage requirements for those files to a fraction of their uncompressed size. Remember, though, to compress a file or folder, it must be stored on an NTFS drive.

Open an Explorer window and select the icons for the files or folders you want to compress. Right-click and choose **Properties**. On the General tab, click the **Advanced** button. In the Advanced Attributes dialog box (see Figure 10.13), check the **Compress contents to save disk space** box.

FIGURE 10.13
Choose this option to compress files and folders individually.

After you turn on compression for an NTFS drive or folder, how does Windows deal with new files you create in that location? What happens to files you copy or move to the compressed drive or folder?

- If you create a new file in a compressed folder, it is compressed automatically.
- If you copy a file to a compressed folder, Windows compresses it, regardless of where it comes from.
- If you move a file from a different NTFS drive into a compressed folder, it is stored in compressed format, regardless of its original format.
- If you move a file into a compressed folder from another folder on the same drive, however, the file retains its original state.

No Advanced button?

If you don't see the **Advanced** button when you inspect the properties for a file or folder, you can't compress it. The most likely explanation is that the file or folder is not on an NTFS drive. Remember, disk compression works only on drives formatted with the NTFS file system.

Working with Floppy Disks

Like hard disks, floppy disks require formatting before you can store data on them. That's true of conventional 1.44MB floppy disks in the

3 1/2-inch format, as well as older 5.25-inch disks, which hold 1.2MB of data. Newer format floppy disks hold much higher capacities. LS-120 drives, for example, use disks that are the same size and shape as a 3 1/2-inch floppy disk, but they hold 120MB of data.

Formatting a floppy disk is a straightforward task. Insert the disk into the drive and open the My Computer folder. Right-click the floppy drive icon (typically A:) and choose **Format** from the shortcut menu. Unlike hard disks, which offer a choice of file systems, you can format a floppy disk only with the FAT file system. Figure 10.14 shows other options in the Format dialog box.

Special drives required

LS-120 disks may look like standard floppy disks, but inside they're quite different. If you put one of these high-capacity disks into a standard floppy drive, nothing will happen. To read and write the high-capacity disks, you need a special drive.

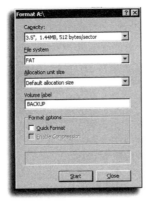

FIGURE 10.14

If you simply want to erase a floppy disk, check the **Quick Format** box and click **Start**.

It's impractical to copy an entire hard disk or CD-ROM, but it's easy to create a duplicate of a floppy disk. Windows includes a utility that handles the whole process in two passes—one for the source (original) disk and the second for the destination (copy) disk.

To copy a floppy, make sure you have a disk the same size as the one you plan to copy. Insert the original disk in the floppy drive, open the My Computer folder, right-click the floppy drive icon (normally A:), and choose **Copy Disk**.

Because most systems have only one floppy drive, the same drive letter typically appears in both sides of the Copy Disk dialog box, as shown in Figure 10.15. Click **Start**, and Windows reads the entire contents of the disk into memory.

Formatting not required

If the destination disk isn't formatted, Windows handles this chore automatically as part of the Copy Disk process. You don't need to format disks beforehand.

FIGURE 10.15
Follow the prompts to duplicate a floppy disk.

When the Copy From phase is complete, Windows prompts you to remove the original disk, insert the destination disk, and click **OK**. When the copy is complete, you'll see a message at the bottom of the Copy Disk dialog box.

Use write protection

When you copy floppy disks, Windows erases any data on the destination disk without any warning to you. That can be disastrous if the destination disk contains important data files. If you store crucial data on floppy disks, always slide the write-protect tab to the locked position to prevent disasters.

chapter

11

Adding and Configuring Hardware

Before You Add New Hardware...

When you first set up Windows 2000, the Installer program goes through a lengthy process of detecting all the hardware currently connected to your system. On a system made up of reasonably new, reasonably standard parts, this routine finds all or most components—including keyboards and mice, display adapters and monitors, network adapters, hard disks, and even your computer itself.

SEE ALSO

➤ *For a full explanation of how the Windows 2000 setup program works, see "Setting Up Windows 2000, Step by Step," p. 33.*

To see a full list of all the hardware currently installed on your computer, use the Device Manager in Windows 2000. As Figure 11.1 shows, this Explorer-style utility shows all devices, organized by category, with special icons that help you quickly spot devices that aren't working properly.

FIGURE 11.1
The yellow exclamation point over devices in this list means you need to make some repairs before the hardware will work.

(1) This device is not working properly

(2) These devices need new drivers.

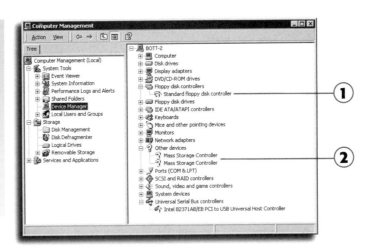

Using Device Manager

1. Log on using the Administrator account.

SEE ALSO

➤ *To learn more about the special privileges assigned to the Administrator account, see "Who's Managing Your Computer?" p. 20.*

2. Right-click the **My Computer** icon on the desktop and choose **Manage** from the shortcut menu. The Computer Management window opens.

3. In the left pane, click the **Device Manager** option. A list of all installed devices appears in the right pane.

4. To see details about the devices in each category, click the plus sign to the left of that category. If Windows detects any problems with a device, it automatically expands that category's listing and displays a yellow exclamation point.

5. To see details about an individual device, change its settings, or update its driver, right-click the device name and choose **Properties** from the shortcut menu.

After the initial setup process, you can add hardware to your system. Before you can use it with Windows 2000, however, you generally have to install a *driver* file, which provides the software instructions that allow Windows to control the flow of data to and from the device.

For the most part, hardware upgrades fall into one of the following three scenarios:

- **Replacements for internal components, such as a display adapter or a network card.** If an administrator installs the drivers for the new device before physically installing it in the computer, Windows will usually detect the device automatically the next time you start up.

- **New internal devices, such as a SCSI adapter or a tape drive.** In this case, you can typically install the device driver after physically installing the device.

- **New external devices, such as a printer or a scanner.** In most cases, you can install an external device without shutting down the power to your PC. Devices that connect to the *Universal Serial Bus (USB)* will be detected automatically; with devices that connect to a parallel or serial port, you may need to force Windows to scan for hardware changes. Devices that hook up to your computer through a *Small Computer Systems Interface (SCSI)* adapter will work properly only if they're connected and powered up when you start your computer.

Do you get an error message?

When you try to open Device Manager while logged in as an ordinary user, Windows displays an error message warning you that you will be unable to uninstall devices or update drivers. If you just want to look at the inventory of installed devices, you can safely ignore this message. However, if you need to troubleshoot a hardware problem, close Device Manager and restart it using the Administrator account.

This isn't Windows 95

Although the Windows 2000 version of Device Manager superficially resembles the utility of the same name in Windows 95 and Windows 98, experienced users will notice some crucial differences. If you've recently upgraded to Windows 2000, don't just breeze through the Device Manager when troubleshooting hardware problems—take the time to look carefully at each tab.

To force Windows 2000 to scan your system and detect newly added hardware, log on as Administrator and run the Add/Remove Hardware Wizard (described in the next section).

Checking Compatibility

Without the correct driver software, most devices simply won't work with Windows 2000. The effect can be extremely frustrating if you go to a lot of trouble to install a new device only to discover it doesn't work properly. How do you avoid wasting time and money on incompatible hardware? For starters, check Microsoft's official *Hardware Compatibility List* (HCL) at `http://www.Microsoft.com/hcl`. Choose a category from the drop-down list to see all compatible products; enter a portion of the product name to filter the list further. Logos on the HCL search result page (Figure 11.2) help you determine whether a product is compatible with Windows 2000 and whether drivers are available for download.

Power down first!

When installing a new internal device, always shut down Windows and turn off the power to your computer first. Only then is it safe to take the cover off the computer and add a new device or replace an existing one. Be especially careful around the power supply, and never, ever remove its cover. Even after you physically disconnect the cord from the power outlet, your PC's power supply packs a wallop that can knock you halfway across the room and possibly kill you. Don't take chances.

FIGURE 11.2
These logos help you sort out whether an upgrade is compatible with Windows 2000.

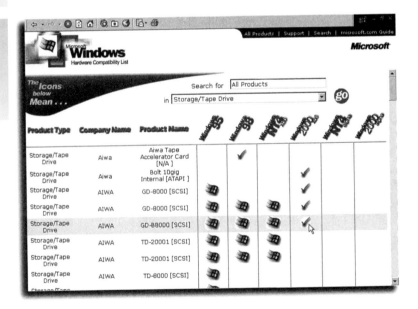

Is the HCL perfect? Hardly. The list contains only products that have been thoroughly tested by Microsoft, and it's often out of date. If a product you're thinking of purchasing isn't on the list, you may be able to successfully install and use it under Windows 2000. Check the manufacturer's Web site for claims of compatibility, and insist on a money-back guarantee if it turns out you can't get it to work with Windows 2000.

Whenever you add or replace a piece of hardware, I strongly recommend that you follow these three guidelines:

- First, find the latest drivers and download them from the Web if necessary. Often, the floppy disks that come with new hardware packages contain out-of-date drivers; you'll save yourself a potential headache if you download the newest version and save it to a floppy disk before you try installing the device.

- Back up all data before you do even the simplest upgrade, and be especially vigilant when replacing crucial hardware, such as disk controllers. A botched upgrade can render your system unbootable; if that happens to you, you'll appreciate having ready access to your data files.

SEE ALSO

➤ *For details on backing up safely, see "Rules for (Nearly) Painless Backup," p. 281.*

- Finally, create an Emergency Rescue Disk and make sure the Windows 2000 Setup disks are close at hand before starting any hardware upgrade. If your system loses the capability to boot properly, you can use these tools to recover quickly.

SEE ALSO

➤ *For more information on how you can use an Emergency Rescue Disk to minimize the potential for lost data, see "Preparing for Disaster," p. 272.*

How Plug and Play Works

In the best of all possible worlds, hardware would install itself, without requiring any effort on your part. Surprisingly, Windows 2000 is up to that challenge—well, most of the time, anyway—thanks to its *Plug and Play* feature.

Hardware, software, firmware?

For some types of hardware, drivers aren't enough. You may need to download and install a *firmware* update as well. Firmware is software code contained in a chip on the device itself, and firmware updates are sometimes required to enable new features or fix bugs. Check the manufacturer's Web site for details on how to perform a firmware update.

Your old drivers may work

For some categories of hardware, older drivers that were written for Windows NT 4.0 may work under Windows 2000. This is usually not the case with network adapters and tape drives, but it should work with display adapters and printers. Always look for a Windows 2000–compatible driver first; if one isn't available, try the Windows NT 4.0 driver and see if it works.

The opposite of Plug and Play?

In Microsoft's jargon, any piece of hardware that doesn't follow Plug and Play standards is a *legacy device*. Any add-in card that plugs into an *Industry Standard Architecture (ISA) slot* is a legacy device. Configuring legacy devices can be a nightmare because you often have to set jumpers and switches and then enter configuration details into a dialog box. Avoid using these older components, especially sound cards and network adapters, which are notoriously tricky to set up properly.

Do you need a new BIOS?

The BIOS handles all the details of starting up the computer, establishing communications with hardware, loading the operating system startup files, and turning over control to the operating system. On modern computers, the BIOS program is in an electronically programmable memory chip on the computer's *motherboard*. Like all software, this code can contain bugs. It's not uncommon for a BIOS to go through several revisions to fix problems and fully enable features. If you find that a specific piece of hardware isn't working properly even after you've loaded the correct driver, check with the system manufacturer: You may need a BIOS upgrade to make things work together properly.

Plug and Play is an industry-wide standard that defines how computers and peripherals interact with one another. For Plug and Play to work properly, three conditions must be true:

- The device itself must follow the Plug and Play standard. Today, any device that plugs into an internal *PCI slot*, an external USB connector, or a PC Card slot is virtually certain to meet this test.

- The computer's Basic Input/Output System (*BIOS*) must be capable of automatic configuration. Any computer made in 1998 or later will usually pass this test.

- The operating system must be capable of recognizing the device and automatically configuring it. Windows 2000 fully supports the Plug and Play standard.

When you add a Plug and Play device to your system, Windows 2000 automatically detects it and attempts to load the proper driver for it. If you see the Found New Hardware dialog box (see Figure 11.3), that's a surefire indicator that the process is going smoothly.

Next, Windows tries to find driver files for the new hardware, looking in its own cache of signed drivers and also checking to see whether you've installed an updated driver. If it finds a signed driver, it installs the new driver automatically; if no compatible driver is installed on your computer, Windows opens the Found New Hardware Wizard and asks you to specify a location for the driver file. Figure 11.4 shows the choices Windows offered when I plugged a new network adapter into the USB port on a notebook computer.

Choose the **Search for a suitable driver for my device** option if you're not certain where the appropriate driver file is located. You can select any or all of the following four choices:

- **Floppy disk drive.** Choose this option and clear all others if you have a floppy disk that contains the correct drivers.

- **CD-ROM drives.** Choose this option and clear all other if drivers for your new device are on a CD.

- **Specify a location.** Use this option and clear all others if you've downloaded a driver file from the Web; you can browse to find the correct location.

FIGURE 11.3
If Windows finds the correct driver for a Plug and Play device, it loads it automatically.

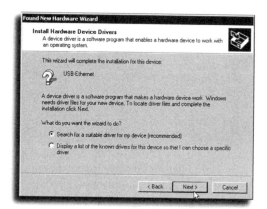

FIGURE 11.4
If Windows can't find a driver for your new device, use this wizard to specify the correct location.

- **Microsoft Windows Update.** This option checks Microsoft's Web site for updated drivers. This option is always appropriate because if drivers are available here, you can be certain they've been thoroughly tested for compatibility.

In some cases, Windows installs a driver that works properly with the new device, but it's not the best one. For instance, Windows may be unable to distinguish between several models of a network adapter that all use the same basic parts. In this case, choose **Display a list of the known drivers for the device so that I can choose a specific driver**. This option lets you select a category and manufacturer, and then choose from all compatible drivers in that category, as shown in Figure 11.5.

Where are the drivers?

During Setup, Windows 2000 automatically creates a folder called Driver Cache and copies a huge compressed file called `Driver.cab` there. As the name suggests, this file contains driver files—thousands of them, all tested and digitally signed by Microsoft to verify that they work properly with Windows 2000. If the device you're trying to install has a driver in this location, Windows installs it automatically.

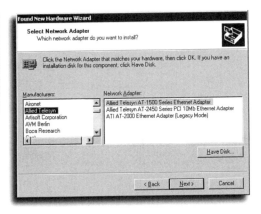

FIGURE 11.5
To pick the best driver for your device from a list, choose the category and manufacturer first.

Which Upgrades Can Users Install?

Policies may affect you

If you're on a corporate network, you may not be able to install any piece of hardware without an administrator's assistance, even if the signed driver is right there on your machine. This will be true if the network administrator has set up your network with a *group policy* that restricts the ability of users to install hardware.

Normally, you must log on using an account with administrative rights before you can install a new device. However, an ordinary user may be able to install driver software for a device if signed drivers for that device are available on the computer—either in the driver cache that Windows creates during Setup, or in a separate location set up by an administrator. Thus, if you plug in a USB scanner with built-in Windows 2000 drivers, it will work without an administrator's help. On the other hand, if the correct driver for a new device is on a floppy disk or CD-ROM, you must log on with an administrator's account to complete the installation.

Using the Wizard to Add or Remove Hardware

Control Panel's Add/Remove Hardware Wizard is the logical starting point any time you want to install or uninstall a device. It's not necessarily the most efficient way to add a new device, and the interface can be confusing at times, but it's your best choice if you don't know a shortcut.

To add drivers for a new device, choose the first option, **Add/Troubleshoot a device**. Click the **Next** button to search for new Plug and Play compatible devices; if Windows doesn't find any, it displays a list of installed devices, as shown in Figure 11.6. Choose the top option, **Add a new device**, and click **Next**.

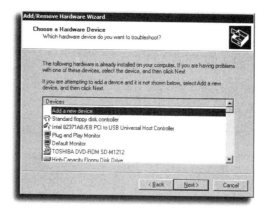

FIGURE 11.6
To install a new device, select the top choice in this list.

In the succeeding dialog boxes, follow the same steps I outlined in the previous section, pointing to the location where the correct driver is stored.

When should you uninstall a device? If you've replaced one internal device—a network adapter, for example—with another, it's a good idea to remove the old driver from your system.

To uninstall a driver, choose the second option in the Add/Remove Hardware Wizard, **Uninstall/unplug a device**. Figure 11.7 shows the list of devices that appears when you click **Next**. Choose an entry from the list and click **Next** to remove it.

Uninstall to get a fresh start

Are you having trouble with a device driver that just isn't working properly? Sometimes the problem is a file that was damaged in copying, and the solution can be easy: remove the existing driver, restart your system, and let Windows redetect and reinstall the driver.

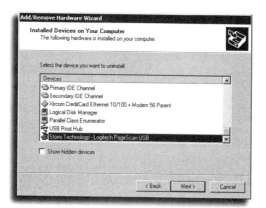

FIGURE 11.7
Choose a device from this list and click **Next** to permanently remove it from your system.

What are hidden devices?

If you look carefully in the Add/Remove Hardware Wizard, you'll see an unassuming check box that lets you **Show hidden devices**. Never, ever check this box! Hidden devices are typically hidden for a good reason—because Windows requires them to run properly. You don't need to update their drivers, and uninstalling such a device can cause a disaster.

What if you don't want to remove a device driver permanently? I can think of two common situations where you might want to temporarily disable a device: If the device is causing a conflict with another device driver or program, you might want to disable it temporarily while you use the other program or try to install the other device. To do so, find its entry in Device Manager, right-click, and choose **Properties**. On the **General** tab, find the drop-down **Device usage** list and select **Do not use this device (disable)**.

In the case of external devices, such as a digital camera or a network card in your notebook computer, you might want to eject the device when you no longer need it. Before unplugging a device, it's a good idea to tell Windows you're about to do so. When you do that, Windows unloads the drivers, warns you of any open files where you risk losing data, and then tells you it's OK to unplug the device.

If you normally leave a device plugged into your computer and need to unplug it only occasionally, use the second option in the Add/Remove Hardware Wizard, **Uninstall/unplug a device**. After selecting the device from the list, choose the **Unplug/Eject a device** option and follow the wizard's prompts to prepare the device for unplugging.

If you frequently connect and disconnect one or more devices, check the **Show Unplug/Eject icon on the taskbar** option in the final panel of the Add/Remove Hardware Wizard. With this option enabled, you see a small icon in the taskbar. Click this icon once to see a list of all devices you can safely remove; click any item on the list to stop it. Or double-click the taskbar icon to open the Unplug or Eject Hardware dialog box, as shown in Figure 11.8.

FIGURE 11.8
Before disconnecting a PC Card or other removable device, it's a good idea to let Windows shut it down gracefully.

Installing and Configuring Common Upgrades

As I noted in the previous section, the Add/Remove Hardware Wizard is an all-purpose tool useful for installing just about any kind of device. In some categories, however, you can choose a more direct option to add, remove, and configure devices. Whenever you can choose one of these options, I recommend that you do so because the device-specific options typically give you more control over features that are unique to that category.

Printers

To add drivers for a new printer, double-click the **Add Printer** icon in the Printers folder (available from Control Panel or from the **Settings** option on the **Start** menu).

SEE ALSO

➤ *For detailed instructions on how to set up a new printer connected to your computer, see "Setting Up a Local Printer," p. 208.*

➤ *For help with sending pages to a printer connected to your corporate network, see "Connecting to a Network Printer," p. 211.*

Modems

Most newer modems—internal and external—are Plug and Play devices. When you plug in the new device, Windows should recognize it and load the driver automatically. Windows 2000 supports a huge number of modem types, too, so there's an excellent chance that the correct driver will load automatically.

Windows 2000 requires that you enter some basic dialing information, including your area code, the first time you install a modem. If the Setup program detects a modem, you can complete this step when you install Windows 2000. If you add a modem to your system after setup, you'll see the same dialog box, shown in Figure 11.9.

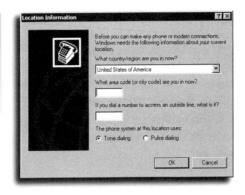

FIGURE 11.9
The first time you set up a modem, Windows asks for some basic dialing information.

Why enter an area code?

A surprising number of Windows features offer to connect to the outside world through a phone line. Dial-up Internet connections and the built-in fax service (described in Chapter 9) are two examples. By entering your area code, you allow Windows to set up *dialing rules*, which let the operating system decide how to dial the number based on your location and the area code of the number you're calling. If you use Windows 2000 on a notebook computer, you can set up alternate locations and Windows will automatically know how to complete your call.

If Windows fails to detect your modem automatically, you can force the process. Open Control Panel's Phone and Modem Options dialog box and click the **Modems** tab. Use the **Add** and **Remove** buttons to install or uninstall a modem. Clicking the **Add** button starts the Add/Remove Hardware Wizard, with options customized for modems. Normally, this wizard tries to detect your modem automatically; check the **Don't detect my modem; I will select it from a list** box if you want to skip detection. Even if your modem doesn't include a Windows 2000 driver, you can usually get it to work properly by selecting one of the options in the **[Standard Modem Types]** category, as shown in Figure 11.10.

The most common cause when a modem fails to dial out is a misconfigured port. Modems communicate by way of the serial port. Most PCs have two serial ports, typically set up as COM1 and COM2. If the physical connector on the back of the PC isn't labeled and the modem doesn't work, open the Phone and Modem Options dialog box, select your modem, and click the **Properties** button; then try selecting the other port to see if that's the problem. Internal modems often configure your system for COM3 or COM4. Here, too, try changing port assignments until you find the right one.

Scanners and Cameras

Scanners and digital cameras offer a convenient way to capture image files and store them for later viewing or editing. Many such devices install themselves automatically through Plug and Play. If your scanner or digital camera is connected and turned on but isn't working, open Control Panel and double-click the **Scanners and Cameras** option. The Scanners and Cameras dialog box (see Figure 11.11) shows a list of all currently installed devices in this category.

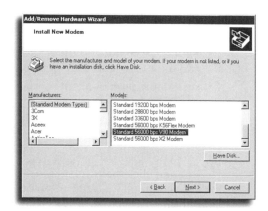

FIGURE 11.10
No modem driver? Try one of these generic options.

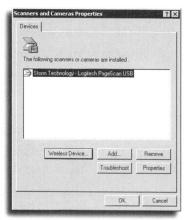

FIGURE 11.11
Use this dialog box to set up a scanner or trou-bleshoot problems.

Most of the options in this dialog box are fairly straightforward. Use the **Add** and **Remove** buttons to install or uninstall a driver. Click the **Troubleshoot** button to launch a step-by-step wizard that can help you diagnose and fix most common problems.

56K confusion

Most recent-vintage modems enable you to make a dial-up connection at a maximum speed of 56,600 bits per second, or 56KB. Of course, this is a theoretical maximum—your actual speed is usually less, depending on the quality of your phone line, the modem on the other end of the connection, and some esoteric technical factors. Windows includes three generic 56KB drivers. Use the V90 option if your modem is relatively new and you're certain it supports the V.90 standard. Older 56KB modems may use one of two technologies that were popular before the V.90 standard was adopted: K56Flex or X2. Check the documentation to see which one will work with your system.

When is a modem not a modem?

Informally, some people refer to advanced communication devices such as ISDN terminal adapters and ADSL connection devices as modems. Some are; some aren't. To set up many such high-speed devices, you need special drivers that configure the device for a network connection. When in doubt, ask your telecommunications provider for help.

Click the **Properties** button to open a dialog box that lets you perform either of the following tasks:

- **Test your scanner or camera.** On the **General** tab of the Properties dialog box, click the **Test Scanner or Camera** button. This lets you check the connection between your computer and the device in question when troubleshooting.

- **Choose which program goes with an action.** Some scanners and most compatible cameras can respond to specific events, such as the push of a button when you're ready to take a picture. On the **Events** tab (see Figure 11.12), you can specify how Windows should respond to each such event.

Display Adapters and Monitors

Setting up a display adapter is typically a straightforward process. Shut down your computer, replace the old card, and then restart. If Windows recognizes the new adapter and has a suitable driver, it should install automatically. If Windows can't automatically install a driver, the procedure is slightly more complicated.

Installing a new display adapter

1. Restart your computer. Because Windows can't recognize your new adapter, it installs the Standard VGA adapter to allow your adapter to work at the most basic level.

2. If your adapter includes a Setup program, run it here to install the correct drivers and any additional utilities. If this procedure installs the correct driver software as well, you're finished.

3. If your adapter includes a driver disk, or if you downloaded a new device driver from the Internet, use the Add/Remove Hardware Wizard to install a driver for the device. (See the previous section for instructions on how to use this wizard.)

After installing a new adapter, don't forget to adjust settings such as display resolution and color depth.

Under normal circumstances, you should never need to install drivers for a monitor. Windows 2000 uses generic drivers called Default Monitor and Plug and Play Monitor for all monitors. To add a special driver for a monitor that requires it, open Device Manager, find the Default Monitor entry, open its Properties dialog box, and update the driver as described later in this section.

FIGURE 11.12
If you have multiple pro-
grams capable of han-
dling input from a
scanner or camera,
specify which one
responds to specific
actions, such as pushing
a button.

If you have room for a second display adapter in your computer and a second monitor on your desk, you can also take advantage of one of the coolest features in Windows 2000 to extend your workspace over both monitors. You can drag windows from one monitor to another, even running the two monitors at different resolutions (one at 1152×864 and the other at 800×600, for example).

To set up multimonitor support, both display adapters must support this feature (check the Hardware Compatibility List at `http://www.microsoft.com/hcl` before buying the second card). After you install the second card, connect it to a second monitor. Restart your computer, log on, right-click the desktop, and choose **Properties**. On the Settings tab of the Display Properties dialog box, you should see settings for two monitors, as shown in Figure 11.13. At first, only one monitor is active; you must go through several steps to enable the second monitor.

Hands-free connection

If you have a digital camera that includes an infrared port, you may be able to send images to your com-puter without having to hassle with cables. Look for a **Wireless Device** button on the Scanners and Cameras Properties dialog box; that tells you your computer has the correct support. Click to open the Wireless Link dialog box and use the **Image Transfer** tab to set up the connection.

Using two monitors at once

1. In the Display Properties dialog box, click the monitor that is grayed out.

2. Check the **Extend my Windows desktop onto this monitor** box and click **Apply**.

3. Adjust resolution and color depth for the second monitor.

SEE ALSO

➤ *For details on how to adjust display settings, see "Setting Display Options," p. 43.*

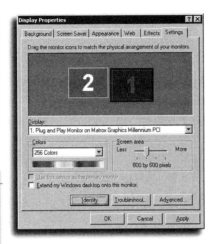

FIGURE 11.13
With two display adapters and monitors, you can double the amount of screen space available to you.

Multimonitor is addictive

The capability to use multiple monitors was originally developed for financial analysts and stockbrokers who need to keep track of several information displays at all times. But anyone whose job involves large amounts of information can benefit from adding a second (or even third) monitor to the desktop. I keep a Web browser and the controls for my PC's CD player in one window while I use Word and Excel in the other. I switch between windows far less often than I used to.

Which is which?

If you're not sure which physical monitor goes with which icon in the Display dialog box, click the **Identify** button. This displays a huge number on the monitor so you can distinguish the monitors unmistakably.

4. Click the icon for the first monitor and adjust its resolution and color depth.

5. Drag the dialog box to the edge of the screen and onto the other monitor. If the monitors aren't positioned correctly (in other words, if you drag a window to the right side of the right monitor and it appears at the left side of the left monitor), click and drag either monitor icon to its correct location.

6. Click **OK** to save your changes.

Multimedia Devices

Sound and full-motion video devices used to be extraordinarily difficult to configure. Now, thanks to Plug and Play, most such devices literally configure themselves. To adjust additional settings, open the **Sounds and Multimedia** option in Control Panel.

Click the **Hardware** tab to see a list of all currently installed devices, with buttons you can click to troubleshoot the device or adjust its properties. Click the **Audio** tab (see Figure 11.14) to see a series of boxes you can use to adjust the specific settings of each device.

FIGURE 11.14
Click the **Advanced** button under a device to set specialized options.

For instance, some sound cards allow you to specify the type of speakers you're using (from basic stereo speakers to a theater-quality quadraphonic sound system). If you're an audiophile, click the **Advanced** button under the playback device and adjust settings as necessary.

SEE ALSO

➤ *For an explanation of how to associate sounds with Windows events, see "Setting Sound and Multimedia Options," p. 49.*

Updating Hardware Drivers

Device drivers are just software. That means they're prone to bugs and glitches, ranging from the trivial to the catastrophic. Of course, if your current driver doesn't work, or if it causes your system to crash or slow down unacceptably, a driver update is essential. Otherwise, consider updating if a newer version enables features you want to use, or if it fixes bugs you've already encountered.

SCSI troubles?

If your scanner is hooked up to a SCSI port, troubleshooting problems is far trickier than it is with devices attached to a USB or a parallel port. Make sure the device is turned on when you start your computer and that the SCSI adapter lists the device on the screen that appears before Windows starts. You may also need to adjust the ID number (a SCSI setting) for the device. If you're still stumped, try the excellent Troubleshooter tool for more help.

Where's my DVD player?

If you have a Windows-compatible DVD drive with a decoder card, Windows 2000 automatically installs the DVD Player applet as part of Setup. This program lets you watch movies (in DVD format) on your computer screen. If you don't have a supported decoder, the DVD player isn't installed. Can't find the DVD player program? Just pop a DVD into the drive and it should start automatically.

Most manufacturers post updated drivers on their Web sites; typically, you can go to the manufacturer's home page and click a link called Support or Downloads to see if any updates are available. After downloading the new driver, save it to an easy-to-remember location (if the driver files are stored in a compressed file, uncompress them first).

Updating a device driver

1. Log on as Administrator and open Device Manager.

2. Double-click the category in which the device is listed and select its entry from the list of installed devices.

3. Right-click and choose **Properties** from the shortcut menu. A dialog box such as the one shown in Figure 11.15 appears.

4. Click the **Driver** tab and click the **Update Driver** button to start the Upgrade Device Driver Wizard.

5. Follow the wizard's prompts, choosing **Display a list of the known drivers for the device so that I can choose a specific driver.**

6. In the screen that lists currently available drivers, click the **Have Disk** button and browse to the location where you stored the new driver.

7. Select the correct driver and click **OK**, and then follow the wizard's prompts to complete installation.

FIGURE 11.15
Need details about the driver for an installed device? Look no further.

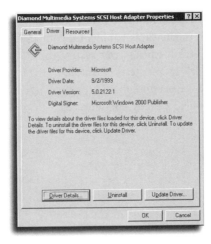

Troubleshooting Hardware Problems

What should you do when a hardware device suddenly stops working? The first thing you should suspect is a problem with the hardware itself. Is it turned on? Is it receiving power? Is it plugged in securely to the computer? After verifying the physical connection, try using the built-in troubleshooting tools in the Add/Remove Hardware Wizard. Log in as Administrator, open Control Panel, and start the wizard. Choose the first option, **Add/Troubleshoot a device**, and click the **Next** button. After Windows searches for new Plug and Play-compatible devices, it displays a list of installed devices.

Look for the device that isn't working properly. Do you see a bright yellow question mark over its icon? If so, double-click to open its Properties dialog box. On the **General** tab, look for any information from Windows that may point to the problem. In Figure 11.16, for example, Windows found the problem and clearly identified the solution—which, unfortunately, requires contacting the equipment manufacturer for updated software.

Newer doesn't always mean better

"If it ain't broke, don't fix it." That bit of folk wisdom perfectly describes the proper philosophy toward driver upgrades. Is your hardware doing what it's supposed to do? Are all features enabled? Does your system run smoothly? If the answer to all three questions is yes, resist any temptation to update to the latest driver for that device. Paradoxically, new drivers can sometimes introduce bugs and cause conflicts with other installed devices. If you're not certain whether you need a new driver update, do your homework first.

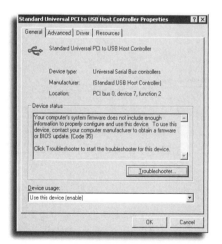

FIGURE 11.16
Always look here first to see whether Windows can diagnose a problem for you.

Do you need to restart?

In general, when you install a new hardware driver, you have to restart your system to load the updated driver. This isn't true for all devices, however. If you're not prompted to reboot, you don't have to do so.

If you don't see a possible explanation, click the **Troubleshooter** button, if one is available. This opens the appropriate topic from online Help, which offers suggestions that might help you get back on track. Figure 11.17, for example, shows the extensive Help available if you're having problems with a scanner.

FIGURE 11.17
Need Help? Use the online troubleshooters.

Check those connections!

An external device may look securely plugged in, but looks can be deceiving. Before assuming that a connection is good, try unplugging and replugging the device at both ends of the connection. Sometimes even a tiny bit of dirt at either end can spell the difference between a solid connection and one that doesn't work properly.

chapter 12

System Maintenance and Troubleshooting

Preparing for Disaster

Virus alert!

Windows 2000 is packed with diagnostic tools and system maintenance utilities. Surprisingly, though, the operating system doesn't include an antivirus program. Unfortunately, you can't afford to be without this essential protection. Viruses are real, and Windows 2000 isn't immune to them. Take your pick of several excellent antivirus tools; just make sure the version you install is compatible with Windows 2000. If you don't know where to start, I suggest a quick trip to www.symantec.com— follow the links to information about Norton AntiVirus.

Let the network do it

If you're on a corporate network, your network administrator probably has a routine backup program in place for all data stored on servers. In that case, all you need to do is keep copies of all your important files on the server, where they'll be backed up automatically.

Over the course of months or years, you will inevitably amass a collection of data that is both irreplaceable and indispensable. Letters and contracts, sales spreadsheets, email, names and phone numbers, digital photos—the sheer variety of data on the average hard disk is breathtaking. It's all held together on your hard disk by a film of magnetic material literally a few molecules thick, and it can vanish in an instant.

Accidents happen. People make mistakes. A power surge, lightning, fire, even a stray speck of dust can trash every bit of your data in less than a heartbeat. I can't show you how to prevent every disaster, but I can recommend a regular maintenance program that will let you spot some data disasters before they happen, and I can tell you how to recover quickly from accidents you didn't see coming.

If your system is running properly right now, congratulations! The best possible time to put together a comprehensive emergency plan is when everything is working just fine. Here are the four basic steps:

- Check your hard disk and verify that it contains no errors. Schedule follow-up checks once a week so that you can spot potential disk problems before they have a chance to corrupt large amounts of data.

- Back up your data files and schedule a full backup once a week. If your day-to-day documents are irreplaceable, consider performing an *incremental backup* at the end of each day.

- Develop a routine maintenance plan and stick with it. At a minimum, you should run the Windows Disk Defragmenter utility (described later in this chapter) at least once a month. You should also install a good antivirus program and keep it up-to-date.

- Have an emergency kit at hand. At a minimum, you need the four setup disks from Windows 2000 Professional and an Emergency Recovery Disk for your system.

Cleaning Up and Repairing Disks

Most common Windows 2000 errors are disk related. That shouldn't be surprising because the hard disk typically contains more moving parts than the rest of your PC put together, and you use it nearly nonstop.

Gathering Information about Disks

Before you can maintain or troubleshoot disks, you need to gather some information. The most basic information about local drives is available in the My Computer window. As Figure 12.1 shows, this view displays the total drive size and free space available in no fewer than four locations: the info pane at the left of the window, the status bar at the bottom of the window, columns in Details view, and ScreenTips that appear when you let the mouse pointer hover over a drive icon.

For more detailed information about an individual drive, right-click its icon in the My Computer window and choose **Properties**. The resulting dialog box (see Figure 12.2) provides slightly more detail than the My Computer window.

Disks? Drives?

What's the difference between a *disk* and a *drive*? Although the terms are often used interchangeably, there is a distinction. In this book, I use the term *disk* to refer to the physical piece of hardware in your computer. I use the term *drive* to refer to the *partitions* or *logical volumes* on each disk, typically identified by drive letters. In the simplest setup, your computer contains one disk with only one partition, and thus one drive letter; however, it's not unusual to see systems with two or more disks divided into multiple partitions, each of which has its own drive letter—C:, D:, E:, and so on.

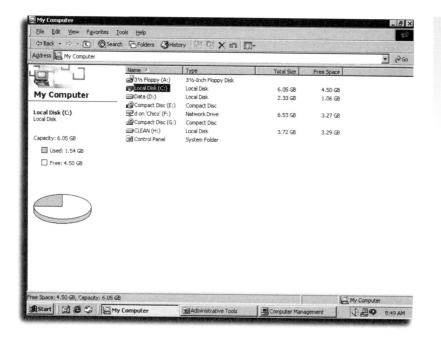

FIGURE 12.1
Do you have enough free space on that drive? This window gives you an overview of free space on all drives.

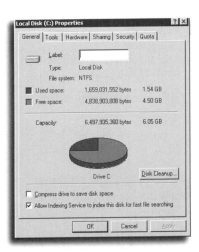

FIGURE 12.2
Check the properties of any drive to see its disk format, the exact amount of free space, and whether compression is enabled.

Free space minimums

How much free space do you need on a drive? More is better. In general, I recommend that you always keep at least 10% of the drive space free. If you have too little free space on a drive, Windows is likely to slow down noticeably; when you run out of space, you risk losing data, and you're likely to see random error messages that appear when Windows and Windows applications are incapable of creating and saving temporary working files.

This dialog box tells you which disk format is in use on the highlighted drive—NTFS, FAT32, or FAT. If you're concerned about the integrity of your data, you should use NTFS on all local disks. This disk format is considerably more reliable than FAT or FAT32; in fact, the NTFS format can detect and automatically repair many common disk errors, making it more reliable day in and day out.

To see information about the physical disks installed on your computer, open the Properties dialog box for any drive and click the **Hardware** tab. The resulting dialog box (see Figure 12.3 for an example) shows a description, including the manufacturer and model number, for all physical disks in the computer, including hard disks, floppy drives, CD drives, and other removable storage.

SEE ALSO

➤ *For more details on disk management, see "Setting Up a Hard Disk," p. 232.*

If you're experiencing a problem with a hard disk, try using Windows 2000's built-in Troubleshooter to diagnose the problem. From the Hardware tab of the Properties dialog box for any drive, click the **Troubleshoot** button; then follow the prompts as the Windows Help system walks you through the diagnostic process.

SEE ALSO

➤ *For more information about this and other troubleshooters, see "Searching for Answers in Windows Help," p. 56.*

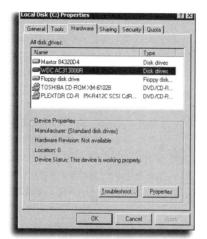

FIGURE 12.3
If Windows detects a problem with a physical disk, it displays a warning message here; click the button to begin troubleshooting.

Checking Disks for Errors

At regular intervals, you should use Windows 2000's Check Disk utility to inspect your disk for errors. This utility examines the organization of your hard drive at a more detailed level than the file system, looking for errors that can prevent you from reading or writing information properly. Any user can check a disk for errors; however, you must be logged on as Administrator before Windows will allow you to repair any errors it finds.

Checking for disk errors

1. Close all running programs and open the My Computer window or the Disk Manager tool.

SEE ALSO

➤ *For more details on working with My Computer, see "Browsing Files with Windows Explorer,"* p. 110.

2. Point to the drive you want to check, right-click, and choose **Properties**.

3. On the Tools tab (see Figure 12.4), click the **Check Now** button.

It doesn't add up...

The Properties dialog box for an individual drive lists the exact amount of available and free space, in bytes, as well as a rounded version in megabytes (MB) or gigabytes (GB). If you notice an apparent discrepancy between the two numbers, here's the simple explanation: A megabyte is not a million bytes; rather, it's 1,024 kilobytes, each of which consists of 1,024 bytes. Likewise, a gigabyte is 1,024 megabytes. To calculate the rounded value, Windows divides the exact number of bytes by 1,024 to produce the number of kilobytes, divides by 1,024 again to get megabytes, and then divides by 1,024 one more time to figure out the number of gigabytes.

FIGURE 12.4
This built-in diagnostic utility looks for errors on local hard disks and repairs them, if you're logged on as an administrator.

Use Disk Manager

If you're logged on with your everyday user account and you want to check a disk, your best bet is to run the Disk Management tool as an administrator. This option gives you access to the complete set of Disk Management functions without forcing you to close all programs and log off first. Open Control Panel and double-click the **Administrative Tools** icon; right-click the **Computer Management** icon and choose **Run as** from the shortcut menu. In the Run as Other User dialog box, enter the name and password of your Administrator account. In the tree pane at the left, choose **Disk Management**. Now right-click any drive in the right pane, choose **Properties**, and click the **Tools** tab.

4. In the Check Disk dialog box (see Figure 12.5), you can specify which actions you want to take:

   ▪ **A̲utomatically fix file system errors.** This option looks for mistakes in the index of files on your hard disk. If it finds, for example, that the actual size of a file is different from the listing in the disk directory, it will correct the directory information.

   ▪ **Sca̲n for and attempt recovery of bad sectors.** This option looks for damage to the physical structure of the disk itself. If the Check Disk utility finds a bad sector, it attempts to move any data currently stored there and then marks the sector as "bad" so that Windows no longer attempts to store data there.

5. Click **S̲tart** to begin checking the disk.

SEE ALSO

➤ *For more details about the Administrator account, see "Who's Managing Your Computer?" p. 20.*

➤ *To learn how to run a program with administrative rights without having to log off and log back on, see "Running Programs with a Different User Account," p. 102.*

If you see an error message when you try to check a disk, the most likely explanation is that you tried to perform this task from an account without administrative rights. Or you may have one or more data files open, in which case the Check Disk utility displays the dialog box shown in Figure 12.6 and offers to reschedule the disk-checking operation. To run Check Disk immediately, click **N̲o,** close any program that's holding a file open, and then check the disk. If you're simply performing routine maintenance, however, and you plan to restart your computer in the next 24 hours, it's OK to click **Y̲es** and reschedule the task for later.

FIGURE 12.5

In general, you should check both options and let Windows fix any mistakes it finds.

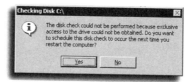

FIGURE 12.6

For routine disk maintenance, it's perfectly safe to defer disk checking until the next time you restart your computer.

The Check Disk utility displays a fairly simple progress bar as it works; when it finishes, it displays a report of any problems it found and fixed. While the utility is running, it's best to keep your hands off the keyboard and mouse—be sure not to open or save any files on a disk as it's being checked.

Removing Unneeded Files

Windows 2000 creates a huge number of temporary files on your hard drive, and it doesn't always clean up after itself. If you can get rid of this excess baggage, you can free up significant amounts of hard disk space. Don't just randomly delete files, however; instead, use the Windows 2000 Disk Cleanup Wizard to make extra room on your hard disk.

To start Disk Cleanup, use either of these techniques:

- On the Start menu, click **Programs**, open the **Accessories** group, click the **System Tools** menu, and select **Disk Cleanup**. Choose a drive from the list in the Select Drive dialog box and click **OK**.

- Open the **My Computer** window, select any drive icon, and right-click. Choose **Properties** from the shortcut menu. On the General tab, click the **Disk Cleanup** button.

Local drives only

Windows 2000's disk-checking options work only with local drives. You can check any hard drive volume, as well as floppy disks and other removable media, such as Zip and LS120 disks. However, you can't check a CD or a shared network volume for errors.

Check these options

For routine maintenance, I recommend you always check both options when running the Check Disk utility. If you suspect that your disk contains serious errors, however, leave both boxes unchecked. This option allows you to see a report of errors and then choose whether to correct them.

As its first order of business, the Disk Cleanup Wizard scans the disk in question, looking for locations where it can typically recover space. Figure 12.7 shows a dialog box that includes several options.

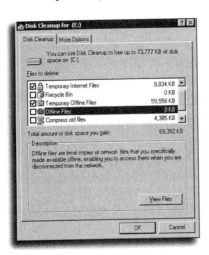

FIGURE 12.7
The Disk Cleanup Wizard suggests places where you can safely delete files, and it keeps a running total of the disk savings for each option you check.

What should you do with the list of categories the Disk Cleanup Wizard presents? Follow these general guidelines:

- **Downloaded Program Files.** Unless the amount of space shown here is enormous, leave this box unchecked. These files are *ActiveX programs* that work with Web pages, and if you delete a file here you'll just have to download it again the next time you visit the page that uses that program.

- **Temporary Internet Files.** This cache of Web pages you've viewed recently can take up as much as 10% of your hard drive. Clearing it up can recover plenty of disk space. On the down side, you'll pay a performance penalty the next time you use your browser, because Internet Explorer will have to retrieve pages it would otherwise have plucked from the cache.

- **Recycle Bin.** This system folder holds all the files you've recently deleted, up to the maximum size specified in its properties.

SEE ALSO
➤ *To learn about other Recycle Bin options, see "Recovering Deleted Files," p. 164.*

Faster check

The only way to open the graphical version of Check Disk described here is from the Properties dialog box of a disk. However, you can use the CHKDSK command to run a character-based version of the same utility. To check drive C:, for example, open a Command window from an administrator's account and enter the command **CHKDSK C: /F**. Leave off the **/F** (fix) switch if you just want to check for errors without fixing them automatically.

- **Temporary Offline Files.** This collection, which can grow surprisingly large, consists of copies of files you access over your company's network. If you have a notebook and a network connection in the office, you might want to look through this cache of files first; otherwise, you can safely delete all files here.

- **Offline Files.** This group consists of Web pages and network files you specifically marked for offline use. Delete only if you're certain you no longer need the offline copies.

SEE ALSO

➤ *For an overview of how offline Web browsing works, see "Browsing the Web Without an Active Internet Connection," p. 380.*

- **Compress old files.** Unlike all other options the wizard presents, this one doesn't involve deleting any files. Instead, checking this box tells Windows to look for files you haven't accessed in at least 50 days and mark them for compression. Note that the amount of saved disk space is approximate because the exact level of compression varies by file type.

- **Catalog files for the Content Indexer.** If you've enabled indexing on your hard drive, Windows builds an index of all the files stored there. Left to their own devices, these indexes can grow huge. If you delete an index using the wizard, you can easily re-create it later.

Finally, you can recover disk space the hard way—by removing programs. Click the **More Options** tab to display two buttons that let you remove programs and optional Windows components.

SEE ALSO

➤ *For advice on how to uninstall a program, see "Uninstalling Programs Safely," p. 101.*

Reorganizing Data for Faster Access

When Windows stores a file on a hard disk, it chops the file into small units, called *clusters*, for storage. If each cluster is 4KB and a file is 400KB in size, Windows splits it into 100 pieces for storage. On a newly formatted drive, those 100 clusters will probably all end up arranged consecutively on the disk, where Windows can retrieve them in one smooth motion. As you add, edit, and delete files, however, free space stops being smooth and continuous and becomes

---

You can't clean up a CD

The Disk Cleanup Wizard works by deleting files, so it stands to reason that you can't run this utility on a CD or other read-only device. In fact, when you select a read-only drive, the Disk Cleanup button doesn't even appear on the General tab of the Properties dialog box.

Lift the lid first...

Before you let the Disk Cleanup Wizard empty the Recycle Bin for you, click the **View Files** button and scan through the list of files. After you empty the Recycle Bin, it's nearly impossible to recover a deleted file.

What's an old file?

By default, Windows considers any file you haven't accessed in at least 50 days to be a candidate for compressing. If you want to compress more space, set this number to a lower value, such as 30.

Upgrade available

The defragmentation utility included with Windows 2000 is actually a "light" version of a program called Diskeeper, from Executive Software (www. execsoft.com). If you purchase the full version you can defragment your system's swap file; more importantly, you can sched-ule the degragmenter to run unattended.

fragmented. When you create a new 400KB file, Windows may store it in 8, 10, 12, or 20 separate groups of clusters on the drive. The result is slower performance when you read data, because the disk head, which reads magnetic information stored on the magnetic sur-face of your disk, has to move from place to place to assemble the entire file.

To rearrange the data on the disk, use Windows 2000's built-in Disk Defragmenter. As the name implies, it gathers fragments of files from all over the drive and rearranges them in contiguous chunks for better access.

To run the Disk Defragmenter, open the My Computer window, right-click, and choose **Properties**. On the Tools tab, click the **Analyze** button. After Windows completes the analysis, you see a dialog box like the one shown in Figure 12.8.

FIGURE 12.8
A fragmented disk slows down your system.

Click the **View Report** button to see details about the level of frag-mentation on the selected drive, including names of files and folders that are heavily fragmented. Figure 12.9 shows a typical report.

FIGURE 12.9
This report shows you which files and folders are most fragmented.

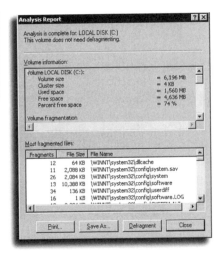

To begin reorganizing data on the hard drive, click the **Defragment** button—this option is available from several places within the Disk Defragmenter program. As the utility goes about its business, you see a display like the one shown in Figure 12.10.

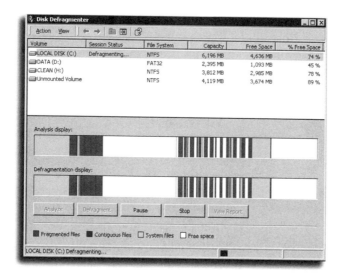

FIGURE 12.10
You see this visual feedback as the Disk Defragmenter works.

How often should you defragment your local hard drives? I recommend that you go through this system maintenance chore at least once a month. If you routinely create and delete large numbers of files, try defragmenting more often. I also recommend that you run the Disk Defragmenter first before you install a major software program.

Before running the Disk Defragmenter, it's a good idea to close all running programs. That makes it easier for the utility to move data without worrying about locked files. Try running the utility just before you leave for a long lunch or for the evening. While the Disk Defragmenter is doing its thing, it consumes most of your system's resources, making performance painfully slow for other programs.

Why view a report?

Although the information in the Disk Defragmenter's report window may look intimidating and overly technical, it's easy to put it to good use. When you scroll through the report, you may discover that a handful of large files dominate the list. If you know that you no longer need some of those files, delete the files or move them to a different drive before you begin defragmenting. That speeds up the entire process and increases the likelihood that you'll be able to successfully defragment the drive.

Rules for (Nearly) Painless Backup

If you can't remember the last time you did a full system backup, what are you waiting for? Murphy's Law of Large Hard Drives says that sooner or later you *will* lose precious work to a hard disk crash.

When that happens, you'll realize that even a slightly out-of-date backup is better than none at all. Windows 2000 includes an excellent backup program—you only have to supply a location to store the backup files, such as a network hard drive, a tape drive, or a stack of Zip or LS-120 disks. No backup strategy is painless, but you can keep the hassle factor to a minimum (and sleep better at night) by following this program:

- Organize all your current working files in a single location (the My Documents folder is ideal for this purpose). Use subfolders in the My Documents folder, for example, to help organize data by project or category. Keep scrupulous backups of this folder—a full backup every week and daily incremental backups.

SEE ALSO

➤ *For detailed instructions on how to sort files into folders, see "Organizing Files," p. 138.*

- Do you have older files you need to access infrequently? To minimize the amount of data you need to back up every week, store these files in a location other than the My Documents folder. Create a new folder in the root of the drive that contains your data files (usually C:, but you can choose any drive), and name it `Archive` (or `Old Files`, or any name that works for you). When you finish a project and no longer expect to edit any files associated with it, move the entire subfolder out of your My Documents folder and into the Archive folder. Back this folder up in full every month, and do incremental backups once a week.

- Look for programs that store data in hidden locations so that you can include this data in your backups. Email programs are notorious for hiding mail in out-of-the-way places: Outlook Express stores its data files in a hidden folder in your Windows *user profile*. Netscape Messenger buries your messages and address books several subfolders beneath the `\Program Files\` `Netscape` folder. Every version of Outlook (97, 98, and 2000) has a different default location for its data files.

SEE ALSO

➤ *For instructions on how to move Outlook Express data to a folder where you can easily and safely back it up, see "Backing Up and Restoring Your Messages and Address Book," p. 434.*

- Let Windows 2000 do backups automatically, on a regular schedule. The built-in backup utility includes a scheduler that lets you set up backup jobs to run when you're not likely to be at your computer. If you work regular business hours, for example, you might schedule your daily backups for late evening and your weekly backups for Saturday or Sunday. When you show up for work in the morning, the backup should be complete.

- For critical data, keep multiple backup sets. If something goes wrong during the backup process, you can lose everything on that set. Likewise, if you discover that the files on your most recent backup are corrupted or infected with a virus, you'll need to roll back a few days or weeks. For serious backup programs, such as those for your crucial business data, I recommend four complete sets of backup media, one for each week. In Week 5, reuse the tapes or disks from Week 1. This strategy lets you recover (at least partially) from any disaster, even if it takes three weeks to discover the damage.

- Finally, store important backups away from your office. If your hard drive crashes, it's handy to have a backup tape in your desk drawer. But if your office burns down, you'll have a hard time recovering data from the melted backup tape next to the charred PC. Tossing the most recent backup tape into the briefcase you take home every night is a good strategy.

Before you can use the Backup program to do a complete system backup, you must log in as a member of the Administrators or Backup Operators group.

Backing Up Your Files

The Backup program is almost completely wizard driven. To get started, open the **Programs** menu, expand the **Accessories** group, choose the **System Tools** group, and click the **Backup** icon.

All backup functions are available on the four-tabbed dialog box shown in Figure 12.11. To start a backup, click the **Backup Wizard** button on the Welcome tab. (The following steps assume you're backing up to a file on a network server; if you use a tape drive, be sure to read the next section for details on how to set up each tape before you begin backing up.)

Data treasure hunt

A surprising number of programs store important data in subfolders beneath the Program Files folder. Many customization settings for Windows programs are actually stored in a subfolder called Application Data, which is hidden in your user profile folder (Documents and Settings*username*). Trying to figure out where each program stores its data can be a mystery, but the effort may be worth it. Ask yourself how long it would take to re-create the data a program creates. The answer to that question should dictate how thoroughly you search for buried data files.

Close files before backing up

If you schedule Backup to run when you're not around, remember to shut down all running programs before you leave. If another program has a data file open, most backup programs (including the one in Windows 2000) will skip over that file completely. This caveat is especially true of email programs; if you leave your email client running every night, Backup may never have a chance to save a copy of your messages.

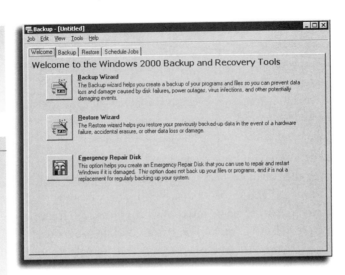

FIGURE 12.11
Use the Backup Wizard to walk you through the steps of backing up data.

Make Backup easy to reach

The Backup icon is buried three layers deep on the Start menu, which hardly qualifies as convenient. If you use the Backup utility regularly, create a shortcut on the Start menu itself or on the Quick Launch bar.

Got disks?

Use the full system backup option only if you have a destination that can comfortably hold that much data. Tape drives and large network shares are ideal; removable drives are less desirable. If you have 5GB of files to back up and the destination is a Zip drive with 100MB capacity, you'll need 50 Zip disks to hold all your data, and you'll spend the better part of an afternoon swapping disks.

To keep things simple, the wizard asks for just the essentials:

- **What to Back Up.** Choose **Back up everything on my computer** if you want to create a full system backup that you can restore in the event of a hard disk crash. To select a subset of files, choose **Back up selected files, drives, or network data**. The last option, **Only back up the System State data**, is grayed out unless you log on as Administrator or as a member of the Backup Operators group.

- **Items to Back Up.** If you chose the middle option in the previous step, the wizard displays the dialog box shown in Figure 12.12. Click the check boxes to the left of items you want to include in the backup. You can select an entire drive, or click the plus sign to the left of any item in the left pane to choose specific folders. You can also check individual files in the right pane, although it's usually safer and more efficient to select entire folders.

- **Where to Store the Backup.** If the Backup utility finds a tape drive on your system, you can choose it as the destination. Otherwise, you must save the backup as a file. Specify the file location or select a tape name in the **Backup media or file name** box.

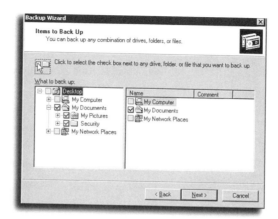

FIGURE 12.12
The Backup Wizard gives you the option to back up only files in the My Documents folder, as shown here.

After you enter these details, you see a summary dialog box like the one in Figure 12.13. If the options shown here are acceptable, click **Finish** to begin the backup.

FIGURE 12.13
Check the settings carefully, especially the output location, before clicking Finish.

For a full backup, the default settings are usually acceptable. In some cases, however, you may want to specify additional options. In that case, click the **Advanced** button to continue the wizard. The straightforward options let you verify the backup, label the backup set with a descriptive name, and schedule the backup to run automatically at a later time. Most importantly, you can specify the exact type of backup, using settings from Table 12.1.

Table 12.1 Choosing a backup type

Backup Type	What It Does
Normal	Copies all selected files and clears the Archive attribute, which tells Windows the file has been backed up. Use this option for the first backup you do in a set; later, when you create new files or change existing ones, Windows sets the Archive bit to indicate that the new or changed files have not been backed up.
Copy	Copies all selected files without clearing the Archive attribute. Most users never need to select this option.
Incremental	Backs up only files whose Archive bit is set, and then clears the Archive bit for those files. This option is ideal after you've performed a backup using the Normal option. An incremental backup in the same location saves only the files that have been added or changed since the original backup.
Differential	Like an incremental backup, except that it doesn't clear the Archive bit. Most users never need to select this option.
Daily	Backs up all files in selected locations that are marked as created or modified the day you perform the backup. Does not reset the Archive bit.

Keep backups organized!

Using a normal backup followed by regular incremental backups is an excellent way to keep data safe, but it imposes an organizational challenge on you. To restore a file from an incremental backup, you must have access to the normal backup and all incremental backups. Label the backups well so that you don't have to stumble around in the event of a disaster.

Tape trauma

The Windows 2000 Removable Storage Manager feature was designed to help large organizations manage multi-tape devices designed to do massive backup jobs. For a user with a simple tape drive, the process of preparing backup tapes can be more complicated than it needs to be in Windows 2000. If you plan to use this feature, read this section carefully—and be prepared for a long, steep learning curve!

Preparing Backup Tapes

A new feature in Windows 2000 is nearly guaranteed to make life miserable (at least at first) for anyone who uses a tape drive for system backups. Before you can use a backup tape with Windows 2000's Backup program, Windows has to *prepare* the tape. This procedure verifies that the tape is compatible with the backup program and writes an electronic label on the tape. Next, you have to move the tape into a *media pool* that is available to the backup program. The Removable Storage Manager utility uses the following four media pools:

- **Free**. As the name implies, these tapes are available for use at any time.
- **Import**. This pool typically contains tapes that you originally prepared using the backup programs in previous Windows versions. Windows 2000's Backup program can read and write data on most such tapes.
- **Unrecognized**. Before you can use a tape from this pool, you must prepare it and move it to the Free or Backup pools.

- **Backup**. The first time you back up data to a tape, the
  Removable Storage Manager moves it to this pool.

If you insert a tape into the tape drive and then attempt to perform a
backup, the Backup program will automatically use that tape if
possible. For tapes that contain data prepared by the backup program
in a previous Windows version, you see the dialog box shown in
Figure 12.14. From the Action box, choose the option to move the
tape to the Free or Backup media pools—in either case, you'll be
able to use that tape for your next backup.

FIGURE 12.14
If you've used a backup
tape in a previous
Windows version, the
Windows 2000 backup
program will recognize it
and offer these options.

If the tape drive is empty or if the tape is new, you see the dialog box
shown in Figure 12.15. Before you can use a new tape, you must
prepare it. The Windows 2000 Backup program will usually handle
these details automatically. If you are preparing a large number of
new tapes, however, you can do this procedure manually.

FIGURE 12.15
If you see this dialog box
after inserting a tape into
the tape drive, you need
to open the Removable
Storage Manager and
prepare the tape for use
with the backup
program.

Preparing backup tapes

1. Log on as a member of the Administrators or Backup Operators
   group.

2. Open Control Panel, double-click the Administrative Tools icon,
   and open the Computer Management console.

SEE ALSO

➤ *For more details on how the Microsoft Management Console works, see "Creating Custom Management Consoles," p. 446.*

3. In the tree pane at left, click the Removable Storage icon (if necessary, expand the Storage section of the tree).

4. Expand the Physical Locations icon, expand the entry for the tape drive you want to use, and select the Media icon, as shown in Figure 12.16.

FIGURE 12.16
You use the Removable Storage Manager to prepare a new tape before using it with Windows 2000's Backup program.

5. If the right pane is empty, right-click anywhere in that pane and choose **Refresh** from the shortcut menu. Then select the icon that represents the current tape.

6. Right-click the tape icon and choose **Prepare** from the shortcut menu.

7. If you have more new tapes to prepare, right-click the tape icon and choose **Eject**. After removing the tape, insert a new tape and repeat steps 5 and 6.

Restoring Files from a Backup Set

Use the Restore Wizard to recover data from a backup set. You can restore a single file, a group of files, or an entire set. From the Welcome tab, choose the **Restore Wizard** option and follow the prompts. Specify the location of the file or tape that holds the files you want to restore, and then check the drives, folders, or files in that backup set that you want to restore. Like its Backup counterpart, the Restore Wizard stops halfway through to let you accept default settings. You see the summary dialog box shown in Figure 12.17.

FIGURE 12.17
To restore an entire backup set to a newly formatted drive, use these options.

The default settings are fine if you're trying to recover an entire drive, but what if you accidentally deleted a few valuable files? In that case, select the files you want to restore and click the **Advanced** button on the summary dialog box. In the Where to Restore step, choose **Alternate location** or **Single folder** and enter the location where you want to restore the files.

Recovering from Disaster

No roller coaster in the world can compete with the sinking feeling you get when you turn on your computer and…nothing happens. If you hear grinding and screeching noises coming from the general vicinity of your hard disk, or if smoke starts pouring out of the back of the PC's case, you can bet that it's a hardware problem. But if the system won't start, there's an excellent chance you can perform a minor repair and be back in business before you know it.

Careful with replacements

The Restore Wizard includes a slew of options that let you choose when to replace files in a folder on your hard drive with files in the backup set that have the same name and location. Be extremely careful when choosing this option, because you can inadvertently replace newer files with out-of-date copies. For crucial files, I recommend that you restore to another location and compare the contents of the two folders carefully.

If Your System Hangs at Startup...

...or boot from the CD

Most recent-model PCs can boot directly from a CD. If you have the Windows 2000 CD handy, slide it into the CD-ROM drive and restart the computer. (You may need to set an option on your computer's BIOS Setup menu to enable booting from CD—watch the messages at startup to see which keys to push to begin this process.) If the Windows 2000 Setup program appears on the screen, you can set aside the floppy disks and proceed directly.

Each time you turn on your PC, your computer checks to see that all its internal parts are in working order. If everything checks out OK, it hands over control to Windows 2000. What happens if someone fumbles the handoff? You stare at a blank screen.

Typically, when Windows 2000 refuses to boot up, the problem is damage to one of a handful of system files that control the startup. Although the lack of any activity may be unnerving, the cure is often surprisingly easy: Start the Windows 2000 Setup program and use its built-in Repair option.

Repairing Windows startup files

1. Find the four Setup disks. Place Setup Disk 1 in the system's A: drive and restart the system.

2. Follow the onscreen instructions, swapping disks when prompted, to load the basic setup files for Windows 2000.

3. At the main Welcome to Setup screen, look for the option to repair an existing Windows 2000 installation and press **R** as instructed.

4. At the Repair Options menu, press **R** to run the emergency repair process.

5. At the next menu screen, press **M** to see a list of available repair options and select the ones you want to try, or press **F** to do a fast repair, which uses all available options.

6. If you have a current Emergency Repair Disk, supply it when prompted; otherwise, press **L** to have the repair program look for the Windows 2000 boot files.

7. Select the partition on which your Windows system files are installed (for most users, this menu displays only one choice) and begin the repair. A series of progress bars provide status messages during the repair process.

8. When the repair process completes, your system reboots. If all went well, it should start again as normal. If you continue to have problems, restart and choose the option to recover from a damaged disk.

What about the console?

The other repair option is the *Recovery Console,* essentially a command prompt from which you can run a limited number of utilities. The console is strictly for experts who know how to work at the command line and are comfortable with commands. If that describes you, feel free to investigate the Recovery Console. You must log in using the Administrator's password. Type **HELP** at the prompt to see a list of available commands. Type **HELP** *commandname* (substituting the name of a command from the previous list) to see instructions on the purpose and syntax of that command.

You'll find the option to create an Emergency Repair Disk (ERD) on the Welcome screen of the Backup utility. Open the **Programs** menu, the **Accessories** group, and then the **System Tools** group to start backup. The ERD is not bootable, and it doesn't contain any of your program or data files. Used in conjunction with the four Setup disks, it provides configuration information that can help the system recover more quickly.

If You See a Blue Screen...

If your system is capable of booting, Windows 2000 presents the Startup menu and lets you choose the operating system you want to start. After you choose Windows 2000 from this menu, you should see a line of white squares, which scrolls from left to right as Windows loads drivers for hardware devices. In some cases, however, the row of dots disappears abruptly, to be replaced by a bright blue screen filled with rows of...well, basically, gobbledygook.

The blue screen is the way Windows announces a serious and unrecoverable memory conflict. Blue-screen errors are almost always caused by hardware drivers; often, the top few lines of text help identify the offending driver.

If you recently added a new device or updated a driver, the newcomer is almost certainly the offender. You may be able to find an updated driver that will install the device properly, but first you need to uninstall the driver that's causing the problem.

Shut down your system and remove the hardware component that's causing the problem, if possible. Then restart your system and press **F8** when you see the Startup menu. From the next menu, select **Use Last Known Good Configuration**. This option restores your *Registry* to the state it was in before you installed the crashing code.

If Windows Doesn't Start...

If you get past the Startup menu and you see the row of white squares, but you never get to the graphical logon screen, you may be able to repair the damage by booting in safe mode.

Create your emergency kit

If you don't have a repair kit handy, now might be a good time to make one. You must have the Windows 2000 CD to create the four setup disks; you may create the disks from any computer running any version of Windows. Have four blank disks ready, and then pop the CD into the drive. Click the **Start** button, open the **Run** dialog box, and type `<d>:\bootdisk\ makeboot`. Press **Enter** and follow the prompts to create the disks.

Beware the BSOD

Windows veterans have a colorful name and even an acronym for the screen that appears when a driver causes an unrecoverable error. The *Blue Screen of Death*, or BSOD, is common enough that one enterprising developer with a macabre sense of humor even developed a BSOD screen saver, which replaces the image on the screen with a fake BSOD after a period of inactivity.

New for 2000

Windows 95 and 98 have always had the capability to boot into safe mode to repair problems. Windows NT 4.0, the predecessor of Windows 2000, did not offer this capability.

In safe mode, Windows 2000 uses plain-vanilla system options—VGA monitor at 640×480 resolution, a basic mouse driver, no network connections, and only those device drivers absolutely required to start Windows. If a new device driver or piece of software caused problems with your system, booting into safe mode may allow you to zap the troublemaker.

To boot into safe mode, press **F8** when you see the Startup menu. Table 12.2 describes the menu options that appear when you press this startup key.

Troubleshooting 101

The log file can be a tremendously useful tool for tracking down trouble when your system hangs at startup. Enable boot logging and try to start Windows. When the system hangs, restart and use the Safe Mode with Command Prompt option without boot logging. The last line of the log file typically identifies the driver or service causing the problem. If you can disable that component in safe mode, you may solve the problem.

Table 12.2   Safe mode boot options

Option	What It Does
Safe Mode	Starts Windows 2000 using only essential system files and device drivers, without any networking. If you cannot start up in safe mode, try to use the Emergency Repair Disk to repair your system. If that doesn't work, you may have a damaged hard disk.
Safe Mode with Networking	Same as safe mode, with the addition of network features. Use this option only if you must connect to another computer to transfer files as part of the repair process.
Safe Mode with Command Prompt	Same as safe mode, except that the system starts at a command prompt rather than at the Windows desktop.
Enable Boot Logging	Creates a log file that lists all drivers and services that the operating system attempts to load at startup. To view the log file after startup, look for Nbtlog.txt, a text file located in the Windows folder (typically C:\Winnt).
Enable VGA Mode	Starts Windows 2000 normally, but uses the basic VGA driver instead of your regular video driver. Use this option if you recently installed a new video driver and you're now experiencing startup problems. If you start up successfully, change to a different video driver.
Last Known Good Configuration	Starts Windows 2000 normally, using configuration information that Windows saved the last time you shut down successfully. Any changes you made to your configuration since the last shutdown will be lost.

Option	What It Does
Directory Service Restore Mode	Although it's on the menu, this option does not apply to Windows 2000 Professional.
Debugging Mode	Starts Windows 2000 using the debugger to send information to another computer. This mode is useful only for experienced software developers.

SEE ALSO

➤ *If Windows starts properly but a program causes problems, see "Troubleshooting Problems with Programs," p. 98.*

➤ *If a device driver is causing problems after startup, see "Troubleshooting Hardware Problems," p. 269.*

Scheduling Common Maintenance Tasks

When you set up the Backup program to run automatically at a later time, you're actually creating a new task in the Scheduled Tasks folder. This Windows System folder lets you set up almost any program to run on a schedule that you define. It's most useful with disk-checking and antivirus utilities, and leading developers in these categories typically tap directly into the Scheduled Tasks folder to automate tasks.

The Scheduled Tasks Wizard is simple to use. To get started, double-click the **Scheduled Tasks** option in Control Panel. The wizard asks you to choose from a list of registered programs, although if the program isn't in the list, you can browse to find its executable file. Next, it asks you to choose when and how often you want the program to run. You can set programs to run automatically every time you start up, when you log in, or on a daily, weekly, or monthly basis.

One good use of the Scheduled Tasks folder is to automatically run the Disk Cleanup utility (described earlier in this chapter) at a predetermined time every week. After you walk through the steps of the wizard, Windows creates an icon for the new task and adds it to the Scheduled Tasks folder. The info pane shows some details about the selected task, as in the example in Figure 12.18.

Don't expect miracles

Scheduling a task to run automatically sounds like a great benefit, but the advantages are sometimes lost in the execution. For instance, scheduling the Disk Cleanup Wizard to run at midnight every Friday sounds like a good idea—except that when it starts, it pops up a dialog box asking you to choose a drive. When you come in on Monday morning, you'll discover that it's been sitting there patiently awaiting your input for well over 48 hours. You're better off scheduling this program to run during the day, so you can deal with it promptly. If the utility you're trying to run has any special startup options that allow it to run unattended, you may be able to work around this limitation.

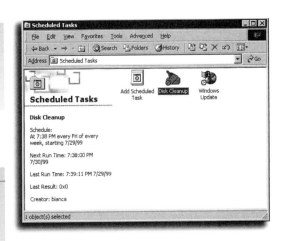

FIGURE 12.18
Click the icon for any scheduled task to see details about it.

Not for ordinary users

You must log in with an administrator's account to perform most common tasks. Although the Scheduled Task Wizard will run for any user, you must enter an account name and a password as the final step.

After you create a task, you can adjust its properties, including its schedule, by right-clicking the task icon and choosing **Properties** from the shortcut menu. Figure 12.19 shows the Settings tab of this dialog box, which lets you set advanced options for tasks. For instance, you might want to tell Windows not to run a task if you're currently working on your PC. In that case, click the **Settings** tab and choose one or both of the options in the Idle Time section.

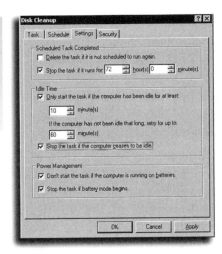

FIGURE 12.19
Right-click any task's icon to adjust its properties. These settings can be adjusted only after you've created a task.

chapter

13

Using Windows 2000 on a Notebook Computer

Special Considerations for Portable PCs

When you run Windows 2000 on a portable computer, you expect more out of your operating system. On a notebook PC, you have at least five special considerations that force you to work differently than you would when sitting in front of a conventional desktop PC:

- **Power management.** Portable computers are designed to run on batteries as well as on AC power. It's the responsibility of the operating system to help you manage the available power and keep your system from shutting down unexpectedly when your battery runs out of juice. See the following section for details on how to make the most of battery power.

- **Removable devices.** Most notebook computers include one or two *PC Card* slots for quickly adding and removing hardware such as network cards, modems, and hard drives. In addition, you can attach scanners and other external devices to your computer. The operating system needs to offer you a way to unplug these devices without causing data loss when you're ready to hit the road.

- **Docking stations.** Some high-end portable PCs include a "home base" that sits on a desktop and contains connections to an external monitor, keyboard, and mouse, as well as network adapters and additional disk drives. If Windows 2000 recognizes the *docking station*, you can move from the desktop configuration to a portable arrangement using the **Eject** command on the Start menu.

- **Keyboards and pointing devices.** To keep notebook PCs portable, hardware designers typically cut keys down in size and arrange them in odd layouts that only vaguely resemble desktop keyboards. Likewise, pointing devices on portable computers typically assume strange shapes that look nothing like a conventional mouse. Using these unconventional input devices can be a challenge on a portable PC.

PCMCIA? PC Card?

Because they're designed to be light enough to carry, portable PCs don't have room for internal expansion slots, such as the PCI slots in a desktop PC. Instead, the standard format for add-on hardware is the PC Card, a device roughly the size of a credit card, which is designed to pop in and out with ease. In some cases, you may see references to *PCMCIA* slots and devices—short for Personal Computer Memory Card International Association. The older, tongue-twisting acronym means the same thing as PC Card.

- **File management.** How do you keep track of files when you have a desktop computer and a portable PC? How do you work with files that are stored on your office network after you've disconnected? Windows 2000 allows you to *synchronize* files in multiple locations using a fiendishly complicated interface, which I explain later in this chapter.

Making Batteries Last Longer

On most PCs—desktop or notebook—Windows 2000 keeps track of whether you're actively using your computer. On a desktop PC, power management is a low priority. But when Windows detects that you've pulled the plug on your portable PC and are using a battery as your main source of power, it switches by default into a more aggressive power-saving stance.

SEE ALSO

➤ *For more details about how to set up power management features in Windows 2000, see "Changing Power Options," p. 51.*

As part of the setup process, Windows automatically detects the presence of a battery and tries to determine how much energy remains in that power source. After a few minutes pass without any keyboard or mouse activity, Windows shuts down the monitor to save power. After a few more minutes, it turns off the power to local hard drives. Eventually, if it appears that you're no longer using the computer, Windows switches into suspend mode, in which all systems are using as little power as possible. For the maximum in power savings, you can tell Windows to hibernate—that is, to save the contents of memory to a file on the hard disk and shut down completely.

Keeping Track of Power Usage

On a notebook computer, Windows displays a small icon in the right side of the taskbar (often called the tray) to indicate whether you're currently running on AC power or batteries. Figure 13.1 shows the icons for AC power (left) and batteries (right).

Try these keyboard tricks

Because of the odd arrangement of buttons and keys on notebook computers, simple tasks such as right-clicking can be difficult. The following keyboard shortcuts are useful ways to keep your fingers from being twisted into pretzels on your portable PC:

Shift+F10 Same as right-click.

Ctrl+F4 Close current window.

Alt+F4 Close current program.

Alt+Tab Switch to next open window.

F10 Activate menu for current window (use left and right arrow keys to move among menu choices, up and down arrow to choose menu options).

Ctrl+Esc Display Start menu.

Always save first

Be certain you save all data files before hibernating. It's possible (although unlikely) that something could go wrong when restarting; don't risk losing irreplaceable work.

When you're running on batteries, let the mouse pointer hover over the tray icon to see what percentage of battery life is left. For a more informative display, double-click the tray icon to see the power meter shown in Figure 13.2. If your notebook includes more than one battery, you can see individual statistics for each battery in this dialog box.

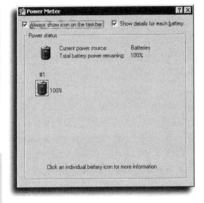

Controlling How Your PC Uses Power

Managing power usage on a portable computer is a constant balancing act. At full power, your system responds to keystrokes and mouse clicks quickly, but your battery may run out before you've finished working. Using the most aggressive power conservation settings, your battery may last for hours, but you may have to wait for the system to wake up if you pause for even a few minutes. Depending on the precise circumstances, you may choose to tip the balance in favor of performance or power saving. For instance, if your battery normally lasts for two or more hours and you plan to work for an hour on the train to work, you can safely tell Windows to run at full speed. On the other hand, if you plan to take notes for a few minutes each hour at an all-day meeting, you will want Windows to conserve as much power as possible so that you can stretch your two hours of battery life over an eight-hour period.

To take complete control of your system's power management settings, open **Control Panel** and double-click the **Power Options** icon. Click the **Power Schemes** tab (see Figure 13.3) to choose one of six built-in collections of power settings, called *power schemes*, each designed for a specific scenario. Or create your own scheme and save it for reuse at any time.

FIGURE 13.3
Windows includes six built-in power schemes that balance power savings against performance. If you can't find one you like, create your own scheme and save it.

- **Home/Office Desk.** Assumes that you have ready access to power. Under this setting, if you switch to battery operation, your computer eventually stands by and then hibernates.

- **Portable/Laptop.** Manages power more aggressively than the previous option.

- **Presentation.** Especially useful if you're using a notebook to show PowerPoint slides to an audience. The monitor stays on at all times.

- **Always On.** Despite the name, this power scheme will eventually switch into power-saving mode, but it attempts to run as long as possible first.

- **Minimal Power Management.** Use this setting if you plan to work continuously under battery power and you're not concerned about running out of juice.

- **Max Battery.** Use this setting if you want your battery to last as long as possible. Be prepared to wait while the system comes out of standby or hibernation.

Are your settings different?

Notebook computers are like snowflakes—no two are exactly alike. Your computer hardware and Windows work together to manage power, and in some cases the hardware won't offer the same options you see here. Check with your computer manufacturer to see if an upgraded BIOS will enable additional power-management features.

If none of the built-in power schemes matches your needs, create your own.

Creating a custom power scheme

1. Open the **Power Options** dialog box and click the **Power Schemes** tab.

2. Adjust the settings for all available power options to suit your preferences.

3. Click the **Save As** button and enter a name for your new power scheme into the Save Scheme dialog box. Choose a descriptive name that's different from the built-in schemes.

4. Click **Apply** to save the scheme. Repeat steps 2 and 3 to create new schemes, or click **OK** to close the Power Options dialog box.

The fastest way to switch between power schemes is with the help of the battery icon in the right side of the taskbar. Click this icon once to pop up a list showing all available power schemes—including built-in schemes as well as those you've defined. Select any scheme from this list to apply it immediately, without having to go through dialog boxes.

Hibernating for Maximum Power Saving

If you plan to stop using your computer for a brief period of time, switching into Standby mode is an effective power-saving technique. If you plan to step away from your PC for several hours, *hibernation* is a much better way to ensure you can get back to work quickly. When you start back up, Windows loads much more quickly because it can skip the process of loading hardware drivers and checking your personal settings. If it normally takes two or three minutes to start your computer, you'll probably find that it takes less than a minute to resume from hibernation. And because the system restores all the programs and files that were previously open, you can pick up precisely where you left off, which is another time-saver.

If the Hibernate option is not available on the Shut Down menu, you may need to enable this feature. Open the **Power Options** dialog box, click the **Hibernation** tab (see Figure 13.4), and check the **Enable hibernate support** box. Note that because Windows copies all the data in RAM to a file on your hard drive, you must have at least as much free disk space as you have memory in your system.

Change the defaults, if you want

The predefined power settings are nothing more than Microsoft's best guess at how you might want to use your notebook. If you don't like these settings, change them! For instance, if you want Always On to mean exactly that, select this scheme and change each power setting to **Never**. Then click the **Save As** button and save your changes using the **Always On** name.

FIGURE 13.4
Check this box to enable hibernation on your portable or desktop computer.

Standing By or Hibernating Manually

In some cases, you may not want to wait for the Windows timers to automatically switch your system into power-saving Standby or Hibernate modes. You can manually switch from normal operation in either of two ways:

- Click the **Start** button, choose **Shut Down**, and select **Stand by** or **Hibernate** from the Shut Down Windows dialog box. To return to normal operation, push the power button on your computer.

- If your machine supports the *Advanced Configuration and Power Interface (ACPI)* standard, you can click the **Advanced** tab of the Power Options dialog box to redefine the way the power button and computer lid work. In Figure 13.5, I've told Windows that I want it to switch to Standby mode when I press the Power button, and it should hibernate when I close the lid when the computer is running.

If you're concerned about security, by all means enable password protection for when your computer resumes from standby or hibernation. On the **Advanced** tab of the Power Options dialog box, check the **Prompt for password when computer goes off standby** box and click **OK**. With this setting enabled, you'll have to enter your password (but not your username) when you resume from standby.

Be sure to save

If you redefine your power button so that it puts your computer into Standby mode, remember to save your work before you press that button! If you forget that you're in Standby mode, your computer will run out of battery power after several hours and may shut down completely. If you haven't saved your work, you could lose data when that happens. Saving your work is a good habit, but it's especially important when you depend on batteries.

301

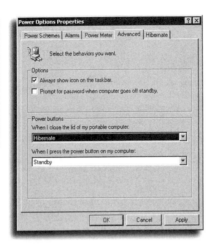

FIGURE 13.5
If your computer supports ACPI, you can redefine the power button and the computer lid as quick power-saving aids.

Working with PC Cards

Versatile add-ons

Although network adapters and modems are the most common PC Card types, they're not the only uses for this expansion route. If you have a digital camera, you can transfer images from its flash memory to a notebook PC with a PC Card adapter. Some enterprising manufacturers have put hard drives into the PC Card format. And if you search hard enough, you can find TV tuners, video conferencing kits, and even printers that connect using this slot.

Some portable computers have modems and network adapters built-in. For those that don't, the most common expansion route is to add a PC Card that contains either or both functions.

To add a new PC Card device to your system, just insert it into an empty slot (most notebook computers have two PC Card slots). Windows should detect the new device and attempt to load a driver. If this is the first time you've used this particular device, you may have to supply the driver files before the card will work. If you previously installed the driver, Windows loads it automatically without any extra effort on your part.

SEE ALSO

➤ *For more details about installing and configuring hardware and drivers, see "Using the Wizard to Add or Remove Hardware," p. 258.*

To remove a PC Card, don't just pop it out of the slot. In the case of a network adapter or a hard drive, that can cause serious problems if you have open files that depend on the suddenly missing device. Instead, double-click the **Unplug or Eject Hardware** icon in the notification area at the right of the taskbar. In the Unplug or Eject Hardware dialog box, select the device and click the **Stop** button. In Figure 13.6, for example, I've selected a combination device that includes a modem and a network adapter.

FIGURE 13.6
Be sure to give Windows fair warning before removing a PC Card device.

A one-click shortcut

If you routinely insert and remove a particular PC Card device, try this simple shortcut. Instead of opening the dialog box, click the **Unplug or Eject Hardware** icon in the taskbar to display a pop-up list of devices; select the one you want to stop using and wait until Windows tells you it's okay to remove it.

By using this option, you make certain that Windows can prompt you to save and close any open files, thus preventing data loss.

If you forget to stop a PC Card device before removing it, Windows will admonish you with the dialog box shown in Figure 13.7. For some types of devices, it's perfectly okay to remove the card without stopping it first; however, it's a good practice to heed the advice from Windows whenever possible.

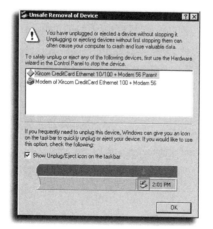

FIGURE 13.7
If you remove a PC Card without first stopping it, you can expect to get a scolding from Windows.

SEE ALSO

➤ *For details on how to work with other removable devices, see "Using the Wizard to Add or Remove Hardware," p. 258.*

Keeping Files Organized

The point of a portable PC is to make you mobile. Unfortunately, when you hit the road, you lose the capability to access files stored on network servers. Windows 2000 offers a feature called Offline Files, which lets you synchronize copies of files on your portable computer with those on the network. By carefully setting up and managing Offline Files, you can continue to work with files even when the network is not available; later, when you return to the office and reconnect to the network, Windows 2000 automatically synchronizes the local and network copies of the file to ensure that you're working with the most recent version.

Set up carefully!

Working with Offline Files is a fiendishly complicated process. Be sure you follow the instructions outlined in this chapter carefully, and experiment with some sample files and folders before you rely on this feature for any important work. The last thing you want is to be on the road, far from your network, without access to the files you need to get your job done.

Synchronizing Network Files

To work with Offline Folders, you must go through the following steps, in order:

1. Enable the Offline Folders feature and make sure you have enough free disk space to keep copies of all the files you want to make available offline. To check your current settings and adjust them if necessary, double-click the **Folder Options** icon in Control Panel and click the **Offline Files** tab (see Figure 13.8).

FIGURE 13.8
If you plan to use Offline Files, be sure this box is checked and that you've reserved enough disk space to hold all your files.

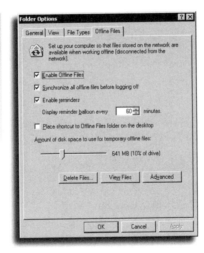

2. Open a shared network drive or folder and select the files or folders you want to make available offline.

SEE ALSO

➤ *For instructions on how to browse and open network files, see "Opening and Editing Shared Files," p. 340.*

3. Right-click and choose **Make Available Offline** from the short-cut menu. The first time you do this, the Offline Files Wizard (see Figure 13.9) appears. Set initial synchronization options here.

Check your settings

If you used the default options when setting up Windows 2000, Offline Files support is on, and Windows automatically reserves 10% of available disk space on the same drive that contains your Windows 2000 program files. To be certain you've reserved the correct amount of space, you need to monitor the contents of the Offline Files folder carefully, at least initially.

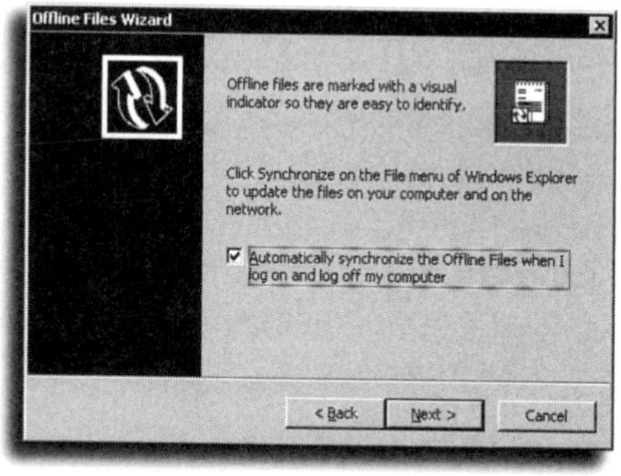

FIGURE 13.9
This wizard appears the first time you make a file or folder available offline. To change settings later, use the Folder Options dialog box.

4. Click **Finish** to synchronize the selected files or folders. When the Synchronizing dialog box disappears, that means Windows has copied the files from the network to your local computer and you're ready to go.

5. When you're ready to disconnect from the network, tell Windows to compare the files in the shared network location with the copies stored on your portable PC and make sure that the two copies of each file are identical. You can configure Windows so that this synchronization step occurs automatically when you log on or log off, or you can specify that you want to synchronize files manually.

Change settings anytime

If you're not sure what each option in the Offline Files Wizard is for, don't worry about it. The wizard sets three general options in one convenient place. To change any of these three settings later, open the **Folder Options** dialog box, click the **Offline Files** tab, and check or uncheck the boxes that control synchronization, reminders, and the Offline Files shortcut on the desktop.

6. Disconnect your computer from the network and begin working offline. When you open a file or folder stored on the network, Windows opens the local copy instead and allows you to work with it. You can browse for files using the My Network Places folder or shortcuts you've created; only files and folders you've made available for offline use will be visible in Explorer windows when you work offline.

If you no longer need offline access to a file or folder, right-click its icon and choose again to remove the check mark. Windows immediately removes any local copies of the selected files from your computer.

Organizing Files for Offline Use

Which files should you select for offline use? That depends on your work needs.

If you want to work with a small number of files and you're not likely to create new ones, select each individual file from its shared network location and check the **Make Available Offline** option. Suppose you're about to leave on a trip and you just want to make sure you can work with two important files—a PowerPoint presentation and a budget worksheet. The individual files option is best for you.

On the other hand, your requirements are different if you're about to leave on an extended trip and you want to continue to work on all your current files and create new ones. In that case, right-click the icon for a shared network folder or folders and check the **Make Available Offline** option. When you synchronize files, Windows copies all the files in that folder to your portable computer. On the road, you can edit existing files and add new ones; when you return to the office and reconnect to the network, Windows automatically copies your changes to the shared network folder.

To sync or not to sync?

If you travel frequently and it's crucial that you always have access to the most recent files and folders, be sure to set up automatic synchronization so that you don't inadvertently forget to copy changed files to your portable computer before a trip. On the other hand, if you travel only once a month, you might prefer to avoid waiting for synchronization to complete each time you log on or off. In that case, turn off the option to synchronize automatically.

No menu option

The Make Available Offline menu choice appears only on shared network drives, not on local drives. If the network computer is running any version of Windows, you should be able to make it available for offline use; however, you cannot use this option with files on a Novell NetWare server. If this option isn't available for a network drive, make sure Offline Folders is enabled on your computer and that the shared folder is on a Windows machine.

When and How Should You Synchronize?

When it's time to synchronize files you've marked for offline use, you have two primary options:

- **Automatic or manual?** Using Synchronization Manager, you can control when Windows updates the local copy of a shared file: at logon and logoff, in the background when your computer is idle, or only when you choose this option manually.

- **Full or quick?** Doing a full synchronization each time you log off makes sure you always have the most current version of all files. If you turn this option off, Windows only checks to make sure you have a full copy of each file at logoff, without matching up versions.

For full control over synchronization schedules, open the **Start** menu, choose **Programs,** and then click **Accessories.** Click **Synchronize** to open the Synchronization Manager (see Figure 13.10).

Rules for offline shortcuts

When you create shortcuts to shared network files, the **Make Available Offline** option may or may not be available. If the shortcut points to an individual file, Windows allows you to mark the file for offline use; if the shortcut points to a folder, however, this option is not available. Make the original folder available offline and the shortcut will observe its settings.

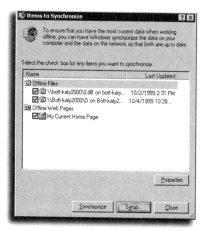

FIGURE 13.10
Settings in this dialog box let you control exactly when and how to synchronize offline files.

To synchronize all files manually, check the boxes to the left of each item in the Offline Files list and click the **Synchronize** button. To set automatic synchronization options, use these techniques:

- **Automatically, every time you log on or off.** By default, Windows always synchronizes offline files at logon. To change this setting, open the **Synchronization Manager** and click the

S̲etup button. On the **Logon/Logoff** tab of the Synchronization Settings dialog box (see Figure 13.11), check or uncheck boxes as appropriate.

FIGURE 13.11
Normally, Windows 2000 synchronizes files automatically at logon and logoff. Use this dialog box to make the process completely manual.

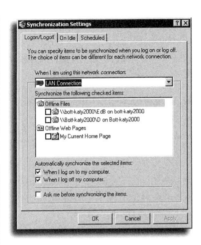

Keep offline files manageable

If you've specified a large number of files and folders to be available offline, it can take a long time to synchronize, causing frustrating delays at logon and logoff. If you want Windows to prompt you before it launches this process, check the **Ask me before synchronizing the items** box in the Synchronization Settings dialog box. With this option on, you can skip the synchronization to speed up logon and logoff when you're in a hurry.

■ **Automatically, whenever you're not using your computer.** If you leave your computer on all day as you work, you can let Windows do synchronization in the background. That way, when you log off, most of the file-copying work has already been done and you can disconnect quickly. Click the **On Idle** tab of the Synchronization Settings dialog box and choose the files or folders you want to synchronize in the background. For control over exactly when and how to synchronize during idle time, click the **Advanced** button and use the Idle Settings dialog box (see Figure 13.12).

FIGURE 13.12
Use these options if you want Windows to do file synchronization in the background whenever you're not using your computer.

- **At specific times.** Click the **Scheduled** tab of the Synchronization Settings dialog box and define specific times when you want to synchronize Offline Files—at lunchtime, for instance, or every morning at 8:00, or every Friday at 5:00 p.m.

In each of these cases, you can also specify separate settings for different types of network connections. For instance, you may want to synchronize all files in the background every hour when you're in the office on a LAN connection, but if you're dialing in to the network by modem, you can keep synchronization time to a minimum by removing all automatic synchronization options and choosing only specific files you want to update.

Working Offline

What happens when you go offline and come back online?

When you pull the plug on the network connection, Windows should notice the change almost immediately and switch you into Offline mode. When this happens, an Offline Files icon appears in the notification area (the tray at the right of the taskbar), and Windows displays a balloon like the one shown in Figure 13.13 to alert you that the network is no longer available.

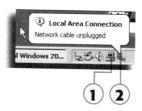

When you begin working offline, you continue to use shared network folders the same as you would online. You can double-click shared folders and display their contents in folder windows the same as if you were on the network. The contents of the Explorer window are slightly different when you're working offline, however, as Figure 13.14 demonstrates.

> **Synchronize at logon**
>
> I strongly recommend that you leave the default setting that tells Windows to synchronize offline files every time you log on to your network. If you change this option, you risk working with outdated copies of files.

FIGURE 13.13
This cartoon balloon alerts you that you no longer have access to network files.

① Offline Files indicator

② Network status icon

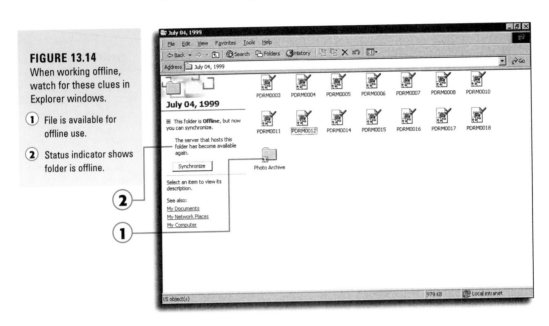

FIGURE 13.14
When working offline, watch for these clues in Explorer windows.

(**1**) File is available for offline use.

(**2**) Status indicator shows folder is offline.

When changes collide

What happens if you change a file while working offline, and someone else changes the copy on the shared network folder? When you reconnect and synchronize files, Windows lets you save your version of the file, keep the newer version on the network, or save both versions using slightly different names. This last option is your best bet if you're not certain which version is more up-to-date and you want to be certain that you don't inadvertently erase someone's work. (Afterward, you can go through the different versions manually and reconcile the changes.)

- Each offline file and folder has a double-arrow icon in its lower-left corner.
- If Web view is enabled, the info pane at the left side of the folder window tells you that the current file or folder is offline and a Synchronize button enables you to update files immediately.
- Only files and folders that you have marked for offline use will be visible when you're working offline.

To see all the network files you've made available for offline use, open the Offline Files folder. If the Offline Files shortcut is visible on the desktop, double-click it. If this shortcut isn't visible, open the **Accessories** folder on the **Programs** menu, click **Synchronize**, and click the **Properties** button. Figure 13.15 shows a sampling of what you're likely to see.

To change synchronization settings for an individual file or folder, right-click its entry in the Offline Files folder. In general, however, it's easier and less confusing to work with the original network path for the file.

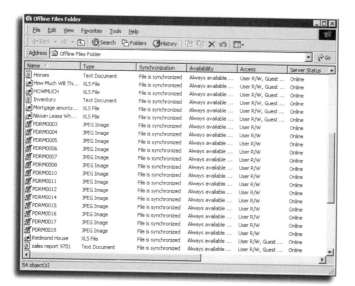

What about the Briefcase?

Windows 2000 still includes the Briefcase utility—a clunky, slow, and buggy way to share files using a direct cable connection or floppy disks. Just as in Windows 95, the Briefcase is a nightmare to configure and use. I strongly recommend that you avoid it in Windows 2000—if you need to share files between PCs, use a network connection instead.

part

IV

IN THE OFFICE

Working with a Network

Setting Up a Simple Network

You don't have to be a Fortune 500 company to benefit from a local area network. In fact, if you have two computers at your home or small office, you can reap powerful benefits from connecting them—and you don't need an advanced technical degree to make it all work.

In this section, I'll explain everything you need to do to connect two or more computers running Windows 2000 Professional.

Making the Connection

Before you can have a network, you have to create a physical connection between the computers you want on the network. Typically, this means a *network adapter* in each computer. On a desktop machine, the network adapter is usually installed in an internal *PCI slot*. Portable computers most often depend on *PC Cards* for add-on network support. An increasing number of computers, desktop and notebook, have *ethernet* hardware built in, and network adapters that plug into *USB ports* are also available, although they're typically slower than internal PCI or PC Card adapters.

SEE ALSO

➤ For details on PC Cards, see "Working with PC Cards," p. 302.

Before you even think about purchasing a network card of any format for use in a Windows 2000 computer, make sure that the card's manufacturer offers drivers that are compatible with Windows 2000. Drivers for Windows 95/98 or Windows NT 4.0 will not work. When in doubt, check Microsoft's Hardware Compatibility List and the manufacturer's Web site.

SEE ALSO

➤ For details on how to use the Hardware Compatibility List, see "Checking Compatibility," p. 254.

No servers, please

In this section, I assume you have two or more computers running Windows 2000, along with one or two Windows 98 or Windows 95 machines. This type of setup is often called a peer-to-peer network. If your network includes even a single computer running Windows 2000 Server, however, the rules change dramatically; in that case, I recommend that you find a book that covers the Server edition before proceeding any further—try *Special Edition Using Windows 2000 Server*, by Roger Jennings, also published by Que.

Ethernet or Fast Ethernet?

The overwhelming standard for network adapters is a venerable technology called Ethernet, which transmits data at a maximum speed of 10Mb per second. A newer networking standard allows data to move an order of magnitude faster, at 100Mb per second. Not surprisingly, this standard is called Fast Ethernet. Can you mix and match the two types of hardware? Maybe. Check the specs on the faster card; if it says it can work at 10/100Mb per second, it can adapt to the slower pace of an ethernet network.

If you've performed other hardware upgrades, you should have no trouble installing a network adapter. On the other hand, if the thought of popping the cover off your PC makes you break into a cold sweat, call in a professional and have the job done right—it shouldn't take more than 10 minutes per PC.

After installing adapters in each computer you intend to use on the network, you need to connect them with cables. For a direct connection between two computers, find a well-stocked computer store and get a *crossover cable*; a regular network patch cable will not work. If you have more than two PCs, get a *network hub* and connect each PC to the hub (and thus to all other PCs) using simple patch cables. On an Ethernet network, the piece at each end of the cable is called an RJ-45 connector.

Installing Networking Software

Hardware installed? Cables connected? Then you're ready to restart your computer. When you do, Windows 2000 automatically installs the following networking components. (If the network adapter is installed correctly when you set up Windows 2000, you should be prompted to set up your network as part of the initial system configuration.)

- **Adapter driver.** If Windows 2000 includes a driver for your adapter, it installs it automatically. If not, it asks you to supply the correct driver, either from a floppy disk or a downloaded file.

SEE ALSO

➤ *To learn how to configure networking as part of Windows Setup, see "Choosing a Network Configuration," p. 40.*

➤ *For more details on how to install drivers, see "Using the Wizard to Add or Remove Hardware," p. 258.*

Look ma, no cables

Are you tempted by the prospect of a wireless network? Several options enable you to use radio or infrared transmitters instead of cables, although these are usually pricey and slower than physical connections. For home use, where running a long cable between the upstairs bedroom and the downstairs den is impractical, look for network solutions that use existing electrical or phone wiring to carry network signals. Just be sure the hardware is compatible with Windows 2000. Check the Hardware Compatibility List (`www.microsoft.com/hcl`) for a complete list of supported products.

- **Client software.** This crucial component acts as the traffic cop for data that goes across the network cable. The default client software is called Client for Microsoft Networks and can communicate with any version of Windows.

- **Services.** Although you can choose from a number of network services, the only one installed with every new network connection is called File and Printer Sharing for Microsoft Networks. As the name implies, this software makes it possible for you to share drives, folders, and printers with other network users.

- **Protocols.** In simplified terms, a *protocol* is the language that a network connection speaks. For your network to work properly, each computer on the network must have the same protocol installed and configured correctly. In Windows 2000, the default protocol is *TCP/IP*.

To verify that you have a local area network connection and view its current settings, click the **Start** button, choose **Settings**, and click the **Network and Dial-up Connections** option. When you do, you should see a Local Area Connection icon. Double-click it to see a Local Area Connection Status dialog box, like the one shown in Figure 14.1.

TCP/IP preferred

Older versions of Windows used a hodgepodge of different protocols. The original version of Windows 95, for example, installed NetBEUI, IPX/SPX, and TCP/IP, making configuration a troublesome mess. In Windows 98 and Windows 2000, TCP/IP is the default protocol, and every aspect of the operating system has been optimized for TCP/IP. Not coincidentally, this also happens to be the universal protocol of the Internet. Unless you have a compelling reason to do otherwise, I strongly recommend that you stick with TCP/IP exclusively.

FIGURE 14.1
If you have a working network connection, you can check its status here.

To view the current settings for your local area connection, click the **Properties** button. The Local Area Connection Properties dialog box (see Figure 14.2) lists the name of the adapter in the upper box; in the lower box, each installed component has its own entry, with a check box to the left that lets you enable or disable that component.

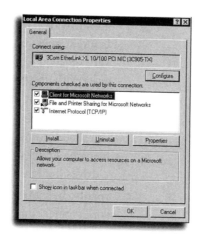

FIGURE 14.2
Your network adapter
may be different, but the
networking components
in the bottom of this dialog box are absolutely
standard.

- To view or change settings for any installed component, select its entry in the list and click the **Properties** button.

- To add a protocol, a service, or a client, click the **Install** button, choose a category, and click the **Add** button.

- To temporarily disable a protocol, a service, or a client, clear the check box to the left of its entry in the list.

- To permanently remove a network component, select the item and click the **Uninstall** button.

Configuring Network Settings

Entering the right TCP/IP settings for your network connection can be devilishly tricky or ridiculously simple. If all the computers you're connecting are running Windows 2000 Professional, it will almost certainly be the latter. By default, Windows configures your TCP/IP protocol to set all its addresses automatically. If you inspect the Properties dialog box for the Internet Protocol (TCP/IP) portion of your network connection, you see a dialog box like the one shown in Figure 14.3. With the default settings, Windows tries to set IP addresses without any input from you. You may have to assign IP addresses, DNS server addresses, or both.

Adjust adapter settings with care

If you've logged on with administrative rights, you can click the **Configure** button just below the adapter name to display hardware-specific options for your network card. In general, Windows does an excellent job of getting these settings right. I recommend that you leave these settings alone unless specifically requested to adjust them by a technical support professional.

Limited options

Some network components offer few or no adjustable settings. For instance, if you select the File and Printer Sharing for Microsoft Networks service, the **Properties** button is grayed out. Similarly, selecting the Client for Microsoft Networks option gives you only a single esoteric option that should not need adjusting except under rare circumstances.

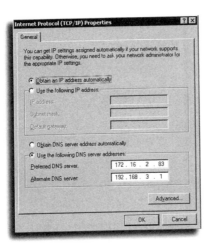

FIGURE 14.3
By default, Windows sets Internet Protocol (TCP/IP) addresses automatically. In some cases, you need to configure options manually, as I've done here.

Private IP addresses

For Web servers and other machines designed for access over the Internet, IP addresses must be registered with an official naming agency, such as Network Solutions. On a private network, however, you can freely use any of several ranges of addresses that have been officially designated for this purpose. Any IP address in the range 192.168.xxx.yyy, for instance, can safely be used on a private network without fear of interfering with other machines on the Internet.

Every TCP/IP configuration includes the following four components:

- **IP address.** This number is the primary identifier that Windows uses to move *packets* of information around the network. An IP address consists of four numbers separated by dots, with each number in the range 0 to 255; for example, 198.137.240.92 is the address of the White House Web site, www.whitehouse.gov. Each IP address on your network must be unique. If you try to configure a machine with an IP address that's already in use on the network, Windows will display an error message.

- **Subnet mask.** Windows uses this setting to determine which computers are on the same network. A subnet mask consists of four numbers, just like an IP address, with the number 255 and 0 indicating which numbers are common and which are unique, respectively. The subnet mask 255.255.255.0, for example, means that all machines on the network use the same numbers in the first three positions, with unique numbers in the fourth position. Thus, 192.168.3.12 is on the same network as 192.168.3.199; but 192.168.2.1 is on a different network and can't communicate directly with either of those machines.

- **DNS server(s).** On the Internet, specialized servers manage the Domain Name System (DNS). This lookup service is crucial to the smooth operation of the Internet. For example, when you type a name such as www.microsoft.com into a Web browser, a

DNS server finds the corresponding IP address and adds that information to outgoing packets so that they get to the correct destination.

The exact details of your IP configuration depend on your network configuration. Windows first checks to see whether you've entered a specific IP address and subnet mask. If so, it uses these settings unless the address is in conflict with another machine on the network.

If you've told Windows to assign an IP address automatically, it uses one of the following three techniques:

- If it finds a *Dynamic Host Control Protocol (DHCP) server* on your network or at your Internet service provider, that server assigns your computer an IP address, subnet mask, and other settings automatically. The exact address varies, depending on the configuration of the DHCP server.

- If your network includes a Windows 2000 machine that is running Internet Connection Sharing, it provides an IP address, subnet mask, and DNS settings to all other machines on the network. These addresses will be in the range 192.168.0.*xxx*, with each machine on the network getting a unique number in the final position and a subnet mask of 255.255.255.0.

- If you simply connect two or more Windows 2000 Professional machines with a crossover cable or a hub, Windows automatically assigns each one an address in the range 169.254.0.1 through 169.254.255.254, with a subnet mask of 255.255.0.0. If your machine includes any Windows 98 machines, they will also use these network settings; however, you will have to configure IP addresses manually on any network machines running Windows 95.

How can you tell which IP address your machine is using? The easiest way is to open a command prompt window and run the IPCONFIG /ALL command. As Figure 14.4 shows, this command gives you details of all the network connections on your computer, including dial-up connections and network adapters.

Get the DNS servers right

If your Web browser suddenly loses the capability to find addresses on the Internet, the most likely culprit is a faulty DNS configuration. Check the DNS servers carefully. If they appear to be configured correctly, call your ISP and ask if they're having DNS troubles. If the network develops troubles suddenly, without you having made any hardware changes, don't assume the problem is at your end.

Baffled by IP addresses?

Two excellent Help topics can help you make sense of automatic IP addressing. Open the **Help** window, click the **Index** tab, and enter **Automatic addressing, configuring** as the term to look for. Look for "Internet Connection Sharing, overview" to read details about how this feature works.

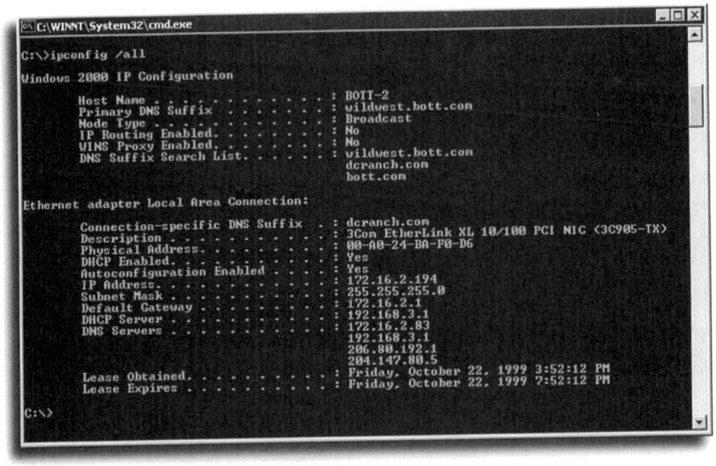

FIGURE 14.4
Open a command prompt window and use the IPCONFIG command to find out details about your TCP/IP configuration.

Identifying Your Computer

The last crucial part of your network configuration is the name that Windows uses for your computer and your workgroup or domain. The computer name is the primary way that other network users find shared resources. On a machine without a Windows 2000 or Windows NT server, the workgroup name helps group machines on your network into a common location in the My Network Places folder.

To enter or change your computer's name and workgroup, use the Network Identification Wizard. Curiously, this wizard isn't available from the Network and Dial-up Connections folder. Instead, you have to open **Control Panel**, double-click the **System** icon, and click the **Network Identification** tab. Figure 14.5 shows a typical display from this dialog box. Click the **Network ID** button to run the Network Identification Wizard and change your machine's name or the name of the workgroup you belong to.

SEE ALSO
➤ *For more details on how to enter your computer and workgroup or domain names, see "Choosing a Network Configuration," p. 40.*

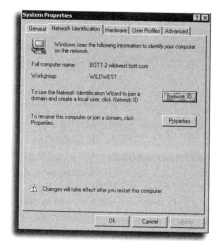

FIGURE 14.5
This confusing dialog box gives you two buttons that do almost the same thing. I recommend that you use the wizard, which is easier and offers a few user-friendly options.

Testing Your Connection

Is your network working properly? The best way to check is to open the My Network Places folder and browse for other machines on your network. If you don't see any icons there, open a command prompt window and use the **PING** command to send a stream of four packets of information to another computer on the network. If your computer is at IP address 192.168.0.10 and another is at 192.168.0.20, issue the command **PING 192.168.0.20** and see what happens. If you get a reply, your TCP/IP connection is working properly; if you see four Request Timed Out messages, you need to check your IP configuration.

Windows 2000 includes a network troubleshooter that can help you track down other problems as well. Open a Help window and search for **troubleshooters**; then scroll through the list until you find the Networking topic (see Figure 14.6). This useful tool walks you through all the steps required to fix common networking problems.

Play the name game with care

Don't arbitrarily change your computer's name unless you're certain of the consequences. If other users have created shortcuts to shared files or folders on your computer, their shortcuts will no longer work after the name change. And if you're a part of a Windows domain, you could lose the capability to access the network completely.

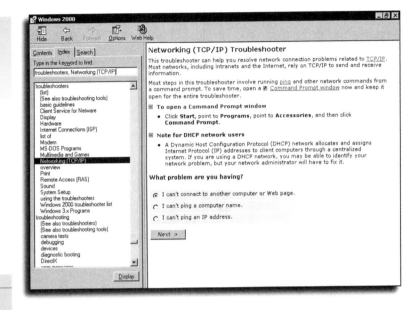

FIGURE 14.6
Use this troubleshooter to diagnose and fix TCP/IP problems.

Trouble with NetWare?

If you're having trouble connecting with a NetWare server, use the troubleshooter devoted specifically to this topic. Windows 2000 does a good job of connecting to NetWare servers, but the details can be confusing.

Missing some options?

If you're connected to a corporate network and some of the options described here are unavailable, your network administrator may have used Microsoft's Internet Explorer Administration Kit to set up your browser from a central location. In that case, many options described here will be grayed out and inaccessible. See your network administrator if you need to change one of these settings.

Creating a Direct Internet Connection

When you run the Internet Connection Wizard, one option lets you connect through your local area network. If you select this option on a properly configured corporate network, Internet access should be automatic. If you encounter problems, the most likely reason is that a corporate security policy won't allow it.

To minimize the risk of unwanted intrusions, most corporate networks include a *firewall*—a secure gateway made up of one or more computers that prevent outsiders from connecting directly with machines inside the network, while allowing legitimate users to access resources on the Internet. *Proxy servers* are crucial components of most corporate firewalls. When a client computer inside the firewall requests a Web page from the Internet, for example, the proxy server intercepts the request and handles the transaction.

Internet Explorer 5.0 can directly detect settings from some proxy servers, literally configuring itself in the process. If your network includes a proxy server and you encounter problems when you try to access a Web page, pull down the **Tools** menu, choose **Internet Options**, and click the **LAN Settings** button to display the Local Area Network (LAN) Settings dialog box (see Figure 14.7).

FIGURE 14.7
Check the top box to configure your proxy server automatically; fill in the bottom boxes if your proxy server doesn't support automatic configuration.

Setting Up a Personal Web Server

Even on a small network, a Web server can be incredibly useful. Without Web authoring skills, you can convert basic documents into HTML format and publish them so that co-workers can access information from their Web browsers. If you have extensive Web experience, you can turn a simple personal Web server into a full-fledged corporate *intranet*, using it as a central repository of documents and data for your entire organization.

Windows 2000 Professional includes a full-featured copy of Microsoft's award-winning Web server software, Internet Information Services 5.0. The only difference between this software and the version that runs many high-powered Web sites is a limitation on the number of simultaneous connections—with Windows 2000 Professional, only 10 users can access the Web server at a time.

The most noteworthy difference between a site on the World Wide Web and one on a corporate network is the address. To access your personal Web server over the network, other users type the Web address using the syntax http://server_name. Thus, if your computer is named Mktg-2, co-workers can access your Web site by browsing to http://Mktg-2.

Personal Server?

You may see occasional references to Personal Web Server in the Help files for Windows 2000's Web server. Don't be fooled—this is really Internet Information Services 5.0. If you want to learn the intricacies of Web administration, this is as good a place as any to start, and any book on IIS will be perfectly relevant to this program.

Administrators only

Don't even think of installing and configuring the Web server components unless you're logged on as a member of the Administrators group. If you see an error message when you attempt to add the service, exit the Add/Remove Programs option and log off; then log back on as Administrator and try again.

Installing and Configuring Internet Information Services

The default setup options for Windows 2000 do not include IIS. If you want to run a Web server, you first need to install the software. Open **Control Panel**, double-click the **Add/Remove Programs** icon, and click the **Add/Remove Windows Components** option.

In the first portion of the Windows Components Wizard (see Figure 14.8), check the **Internet Information Services (IIS)** box.

FIGURE 14.8
Before you can publish pages on your own Web server, you must install the server software using this wizard.

IIS actually consists of a number of component pieces, including an FTP server, an SMTP server (to handle email-related tasks), documentation, and management tools. By default, all these components are installed. If you prefer not to install the FTP and SMTP servers, click the **Details** button to display the list of components (see Figure 14.9), and then clear the check box to the left of each item.

Managing your Web site

Although theoretically you can create and publish pages with a simple text editor, you'll find life much easier if you invest in a high-powered Web authoring package. I highly recommend Microsoft's award-winning FrontPage, which is available on its own or as part of Office 2000, Premium Edition. Don't expect much from the wimpy FrontPage Express, which is good for rudimentary Web pages but has no Web management tools at all.

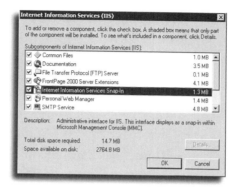

FIGURE 14.9
If you don't plan to use an FTP server, why install it? Clear the check mark from the box to the left of any component to omit it from the installation.

Managing Your Web Server

After you install the Web server software, check to make sure that everything is running correctly. Start with the Personal Web Manager, a simple tool that lets you start and stop the Web server and adjust its basic settings. The IIS Setup program installs an icon for Personal Web Manager in the Administrative Tools group within Control Panel. Double-click this icon to launch the utility, shown in Figure 14.10.

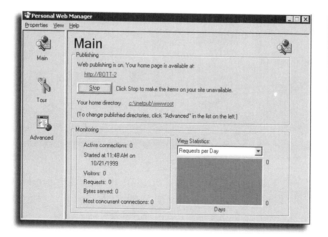

FIGURE 14.10
Want to turn off your Web server temporarily? Click the button at the top of this dialog box.

Clicking any of the three icons at the left of the Personal Web Manager window gives you a different set of tools:

- **Main.** Click the **Stop** button to temporarily disable the Web server; it changes to a Start button that lets you run the server again when you're ready. This window also shows statistics about your server, such as the number of users and the amount of data they're retrieved.

- **Tour.** A quick and informative tutorial that introduces the main features of IIS (it takes only a few minutes to run through the entire tour).

- **Advanced.** These tools (see Figure 14.11) enable you to adjust the properties of the directories in your Web site. You can also define the name of the page that the Web server displays by default when a browser doesn't specify a filename.

<table>
<tr><td>

Web services start automatically

By default, Windows 2000 Professional configures Internet Information Services to run automatically at startup. If you stop the service and then restart your computer, the Web server restarts without any warning to you. To configure the service so that it starts only when you specifically enable it, use the Services icon in Control Panel's Administrative Tools group.

</td></tr>
</table>

FIGURE 14.11
Use these options to create virtual directories, which you can use to quickly share files on your hard disk through a Web browser.

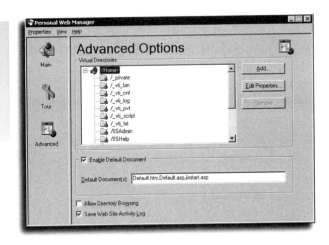

Using the Advanced options here, for example, you can create *virtual directories* that make it possible for you to share files with any co-worker who has a Web browser.

Sharing files in a Web browser

1. Open the **Personal Web Manager** and click the **Advanced** icon.

2. Click the **Add** button to open the Add Directory dialog box.

3. Use the **<u>Browse</u>** button to fill in the **<u>Directory</u>** box with the name of the folder you want to share.

4. In the **<u>Alias</u>** box, enter the name you want to use for this folder on your Web server; this name does not have to be the same as the directory you specified in step 3. The alias becomes part of the Web address for the virtual folder, in the syntax `http://server_name/alias_name`.

5. Click **OK** to create the virtual directory.

6. Create an HTML document that explains the purpose of the shared folder; be sure to include hyperlinks to files in that folder in your document, and then save it in the shared folder using any of the names in the **<u>Default Document(s)</u>** box—`Default.htm`, for example.

7. Close the Personal Web Manager utility.

Now, when anyone on your network wants to view shared files, all they have to do is enter the Web address of the virtual folder. Suppose your machine is named `Mktg-2` and you've shared a folder full of project files using the alias `Projects`. Anyone on your network who enters the URL `http://Mktg-2/Projects` will see the default introductory page you created, complete with clickable hyperlinks to the files you want them to see.

Advanced Configuration Options

It can take months or even years to explore and master all the options in IIS 5.0. In this section, I won't even try to explain those options in detail; instead, I'll introduce some of the tools you can use to configure more advanced options, and you can take it from there.

Internet Services Manager (see Figure 14.12) is a snap-in for the Microsoft Management Console. Use it to start and stop all the services included with IIS, including the FTP and SMTP servers. You can find its icon in the Administrative Tools group within Control Panel.

Need Web tools?

The software you need to create a great Web page may be right under your nose. Any reasonably up-to-date word processor, for example, including recent versions of Microsoft Word, lets you save a document as a Web page; Word 2000 does a better job than Word 97, although the latter will do in a pinch. Publisher 2000 also makes good-looking Web pages. And if none of these tools are available, you can always install FrontPage Express from the Windows 2000 CD.

Don't mess with those folders

When IIS creates a Web site, it fills it with all sorts of oddly named folders. Avoid the temptation to rename, delete, or edit the contents of any of these folders unless you're certain you understand the consequences. In particular, the folders that begin with _vti_ are essential for the smooth operation of FrontPage.

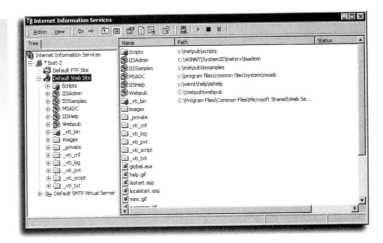

FIGURE 14.12
Toolbar buttons in this service manager let you start, stop, and pause all the IIS services.

Want to explore all the properties for a Web site you've created? Right-click the Web site's name in the Internet Services Manager window, and then choose **Properties**. Figure 14.13 shows the many options available in this multitabbed dialog box.

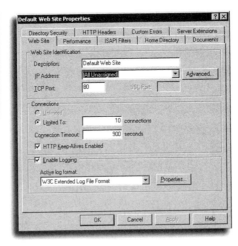

FIGURE 14.13
What's that Web site? Give it a better name by replacing the Default Web Site text with a more descriptive label.

Finally, if you're concerned about security on your mini-Web site, be sure to run the Permissions Wizard to make sure all security settings are correct. Right-click any empty space in the Internet Services Manager and choose **All Tasks**; then click **Permissions Wizard** on the cascading menu. The wizard offers a series of options, written in plain English, that let you reset security for all folders on your Web site so that only Administrators can add, change, or delete files, but it allows users to read files without hassle. Figure 14.14 shows the final step of the wizard, which summarizes the changes it's about to make.

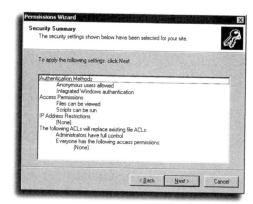

FIGURE 14.14
Be sure to run the Permissions Wizard to keep your Web pages safe from tampering.

How do you publish pages?

After you've created a Web site, you can publish pages to it by using the Web Folders feature in the My Network Places folder. From any Explorer window or a Save As dialog box, enter the URL of the server (including a folder name if necessary). You can drag files directly into the Web Folder, or save files from programs such as those found in Office 2000, the same as you would save them on a local or a network hard drive.

chapter 15

Sharing Files, Folders, and Other Resources

Sharing Folders and Drives

If your Windows 2000 computer is connected to a network, you can *share* one or more folders—or an entire drive, for that matter—with other network users. To share folders and drives, you must be logged on as a member of the Administrators or Power Users group.

By setting *permissions* on a shared folder or drive, you control which users can access files in that location and which are locked out. Don't confuse share permissions with file and folder permissions you set on an NTFS drive. Share permissions apply only across the network, whereas file and folder permissions apply to users on the local machine as well. In fact, by combining share permissions with file permissions, you can give one group of users the ability to view the contents of a shared folder and still allow only a small group of users to open and edit specific files within that folder.

When you share a folder, the setting is persistent—that is, it remains in force, regardless of which user is currently logged on. In fact, shares remain active even when no user is logged on, allowing you to treat your Windows 2000 Professional computer as if it were a server. When you leave the office, log off, but leave your PC turned on. Your computer is perfectly secure—no one can log on to it without a user account and password, but anyone who has access to shared folders can still open and edit them from across the network.

Sharing a folder helps you maintain control of a group of files while allowing others to work with those files. For instance, if you and several co-workers are preparing this year's annual report, you might create a folder on your machine to hold all the files that will make up the report. By sharing the file and giving members of your workgroup access to the shared folder, you can enlist their help on key portions of the project.

Sharing a folder

1. Open any Explorer window, right-click a folder icon, and chose **Sharing** from the shortcut menu. (You can also share an entire drive by starting with a drive icon in the My Computer window.)
2. On the **Sharing** tab of the Properties dialog box (see Figure 15.1), click the **Share this folder** option.

One PC at a time

You can share folders, drives, and printers only on your own machine, and then only if you have proper rights. If you have the right to access shared files on another computer, you can't turn around and share those files with other users—only the administrator of that machine can do so.

Keep it simple and safe

When you're sharing files over a home or a small office network, try to keep files organized so that you share only the folders you really need to share. Giving other people access to an entire drive is generally a bad idea; instead, consider creating a Data or Projects folder, with subfolders to contain files for each project or workgroup. By sharing each of those subfolders and carefully setting permissions for each one, you can make sure that co-workers have access only to files they need.

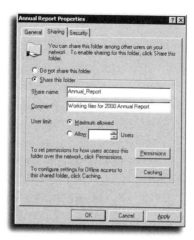

FIGURE 15.1
By default, Windows uses the name of the folder as the name of the share. Go ahead and change the share name—the folder name doesn't change.

3. In the **Share Name** box, enter the name you want other users to see when they browse share icons on your computer. The default share name is the name of the folder or (in the case of a drive) the drive letter. Add an optional description of the shared folder's contents in the **Comment** field; users will see this text when they browse the list of shares from other networked computers.

4. By default, all users who can connect to your machine can access the shared folder or drive. Click the **Permissions** button to define who can access the shared folder. (See the following section for more details.)

5. If the files in the shared folder are extremely large and your computer is short on memory, adjust the **User Limit** options to restrict the number of users who can simultaneously access the shared drive or folder. In Windows 2000 Professional, the limit is 10 simultaneous connections, regardless of the number you type here. In most cases, you should leave this setting alone.

6. Click **OK** to close the Properties dialog box and apply the changes to the folder or drive. When you view the shared folder or drive in an Explorer window, notice that a hand now appears below its icon, indicating that sharing is on.

Use comments to clarify

On a busy workgroup where many users share folders and drives, comments can make life easier on your co-workers. Use a short (14 characters or fewer) share name and add comments to help explain what types of files users will find in the shared folder.

335

You can create more than one share for a single folder or drive. This technique allows you to define different access permissions for different tasks. For instance, you might allow one group of users to read but not change files in a folder when they use the share named `Annual_Report`; you could create a second share called `AR_Changes$` and adjust the permissions so that users can add, change, or delete files in the same folder. The dollar sign at the end of the share name means that the share is hidden; it doesn't show up when other users browse through the network, and the only way to access it is to enter the name directly.

After you create a share for a folder or a drive, a **New Share** button appears at the bottom of the Sharing tab of its Properties dialog box. Click that button to open the New Share dialog box (see Figure 15.2).

Use comments to clarify

On a busy workgroup where many users share folders and drives, comments can make life easier on your co-workers. Use a short (14 characters or fewer) share name and add comments to help explain what types of files users will find in the shared folder.

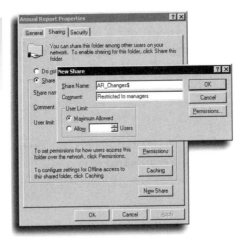

FIGURE 15.2
Use this simpler dialog box to create a second share for a folder.

Although this dialog box is considerably smaller than the previous one, it allows you to adjust almost all the same settings. Give the share a name and an optional comment, if you want. Adjust permissions, and then click **OK** to save the new share.

Restricting Access to Shared Folders or Drives

By default, when you share a folder, any user who can log on to your computer from the network has access to files in that folder. When you look at the default permissions for the share, you see that the Everyone group has been assigned all rights to that folder.

If the files in the shared folder are public documents that you want to distribute widely, leave the default permissions alone. For confidential information, however, you will usually want to modify these permissions. Click the **Permissions** button on the Sharing tab to open the Permissions dialog box (see Figure 15.3); then click the **Add** button and adjust the access permissions for each user or group. Click **OK** to continue.

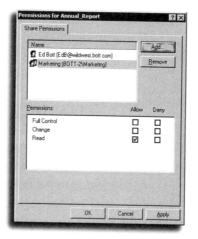

FIGURE 15.3
Members of the Marketing group can read files in this shared folder, but they can't change them. Using permissions like this helps avoid accidentally overwriting important files.

You can set only three levels of permission for a shared drive or folder:

- **Full Control.** As the name implies, this permission allows a network user to add, change, or delete files in the shared folder. Use this permission for folders that contain shared files for an entire workgroup, and be aware that if a network user inadvertently deletes a file, it's gone for good.

- **Change.** Allows users to add, open, and edit files, as well as to create and delete subfolders. Without the Read permission, this setting is nearly useless. With the Read permission, it's equal to Full Control.

- **Read.** Users can browse the list of files and open them for editing, but they can't add new files, delete existing files, or make any changes to files.

Hide that share

Normally, any user who can see your computer's icon in the My Network Places folder can browse a list of all shared folders. When you create a share name that ends in a dollar sign, however, the share is hidden. The only way for someone to access files in a hidden share is with a shortcut or by typing the exact name of the server and share into the Run box or the Address bar of an Explorer window.

Check the **Allow** or **Deny** box for each user or group you add to the list. Most of the time, you should work with the **Allow** box; the **Deny** box is used only when you want to make certain that a particular user or group doesn't have Change rights, even though they normally would have those rights as members of a different group. This sort of hair-splitting over rights is usually only found in very large networks.

Finally, be sure you think carefully about the way share permissions interact with file and folder permissions on an NTFS drive. In particular, remember that giving Full Control to a group of users allows them to delete files and subfolders, *even if they don't have the right to open those files because of NTFS permissions you've set!*

SEE ALSO

➤ *For a full explanation of your choices in disk formats, see "Choosing the Right File System," p. 240.*

Removing a Folder or a Drive from Shared Use

You might want to share a folder while you and some co-workers are collaborating on a project. After the project is over, you might want to stop sharing that folder. To do so, use either of the following techniques:

- Delete, rename, or move the shared folder. When you do, Windows will warn you that you're about to remove the folder from shared use. Click **OK** when prompted, and your files are now exclusively for local access.

- Right-click the shared folder or drive icon, choose **Sharing**, and click the **Do not share this folder** option. When you close the Properties dialog box, Windows removes the folder from shared use.

If you're a member of the Administrators group on your local computer, you can see and manage all shared folders from a central location in the Computer Management console. To open this utility, right-click the **My Computer** icon and choose **Manager** from the shortcut menu, or use the **Computer Management** icon in the

What about FAT32?

On a shared FAT32 drive, only the share permissions control access to files. Because FAT32 drives don't include security settings, all files in a shared folder are automatically available to anyone who can access that folder. If you have sensitive information to share, be sure that you only do so on a well-protected NTFS drive.

Administrative Tools group in Control Panel. As you can see in Figure 15.4, this view shows all shares on all disks—including hidden shares—on the current computer.

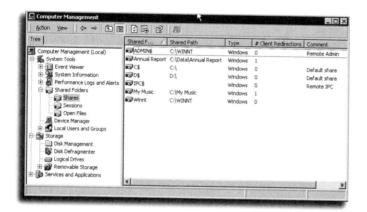

FIGURE 15.4
Right-click any shared drive or folder in this list to adjust its permissions.

The Shared Folders *snap-in* gives you a view of every shared drive and folder on your computer, including a few you might not have known you had. By default, Windows 2000 creates hidden *administrative shares* that allow anyone in the Administrators or Backup Operators group to connect to the root directory of a drive. These shares appear in the Shared Folders snap-in as A$, C$, D$, and so on. Other administrative shares include IPC$ and ADMIN$, which are used by the system for remote communication and administration.

These administrative shares are hidden from anyone who is casually browsing over the network, as you can tell by the dollar sign at the end of each name. But anyone who knows the username and password of an account in the Administrators group on your computer can access them from across the network. That poses a potential security problem, especially if your Administrator password is blank or easy to guess. In that case, anyone who can see your computer across the network can log on using your Administrator account and look at the entire contents of any drive on your hard disk.

If you're concerned about security and your computer is connected to a network, I strongly recommend that you follow these guidelines:

- Use a strong, secure password for the Administrator account on your computer. Make sure it's impossible to guess, and never, ever use a blank password.

> **Administrative shares are permanent**
>
> Administrative shares can't be permanently deleted, no matter how hard you try. If you succeed in deleting one temporarily, Windows will re-create it the next time you start the computer.

SEE ALSO

➤ *To learn how to make the most of passwords, see "Creating and Managing Passwords," p. 75.*

- Change the password on your Administrator account regularly, especially after an employee or co-worker who previously had administrative rights leaves.

- If you don't intend to share files and folders with other network users, uninstall File and Printer Sharing from your Local Area Connection. (You'll find this icon in the Network and Dial-Up Connections folder.)

- To prevent all network access to your computer, you can stop the Server service. This is a particularly radical step; don't do it unless you're certain that you don't want any outside contact with your computer (you can still access shared resources on other computers, even with this service turned off).

SEE ALSO

➤ *For instructions on how to configure Windows services, see "Managing Windows Services," p. 444.*

Opening and Editing Shared Files

The easiest (although not always the fastest) way to open or manage files stored on another computer on your network is to browse through the My Network Places folder. To open this system folder, double-click its icon on the desktop or find it in the left tree pane of any Explorer window. After you first set up Windows 2000, this folder is sparsely populated with only two or three icons. When you've worked over the network for a while, however, the folder begins to fill with icons for shared folders, such as those shown in Figure 15.5.

Double-click any icon in this folder to connect to the shared location, where you can browse files as though they were on a local drive. If the share is in another domain or workgroup, you may be required to enter a username and password before the other machine will display the folder's contents. Figure 15.6 shows this additional dialog box.

Domain administrators have master keys

If your computer is part of a domain, any member of the Domain Administrators group is automatically a member of the Administrators group on your computer as well. As a result, any Domain Administrator on your network has the equivalent of a master key to all your files. If that makes you nervous, open the Local Users and Groups utility and remove that group from the local Administrators group.

Or enter it directly

If you know the exact name of a shared folder or drive, enter it in the Run dialog box or in the Address bar of an Explorer window. Be sure to use the UNC syntax:

`\\computer_name\share_name`.

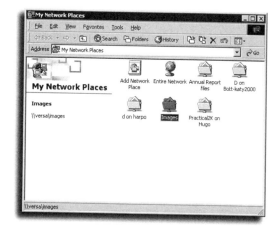

FIGURE 15.5
Every time you open a shared network drive or folder, Windows adds an icon in the My Network Places folder.

FIGURE 15.6
You may have to enter an authorized username and password before you can access some network resources.

Browsing for Shared Resources

How do you find shared resources on your network? Open the My Network Places folder and look for a shortcut to the shared folder. If one doesn't exist, try any of these techniques:

- Double-click the **Computers Near Me** icon. This icon is available only if your network is configured as a Windows workgroup rather than as a domain. It shows all other computers that share the same workgroup name as yours. Double-click the icon for an individual computer to browse through its shared resources.

- If you know the name of the computer that contains the shared resource, search for it. Double-click the **Entire Network** icon and choose the **Search for computers** link. Enter the name you're looking for in the **Computer Name** box and click **Search Now**.

Domain name required?

If your network includes at least one Windows 2000 domain, you may need to enter the domain name as part of your username when accessing shared resources. This is particularly true when you've logged on to a local computer instead of the domain. In that case, your rights and permissions are all based on the local user account database, which the domain doesn't recognize. In the User Name field, enter your username in this format:
domain_name\ user_name.

- Browse all available computers on the network. Double-click the **Entire Network** icon and choose the **entire contents** link. Double-click the **Microsoft Windows Network** icon to see a folder filled with all other computers and domains on your network.

When you double-click a computer's icon, you display a list of all shared resources available on that computer, including drives, folders, and printers. When you find the one you want to work with, double-click its icon to open an Explorer window.

SEE ALSO

➤ For a refresher course on how Explorer works, see "Browsing Files with Windows Explorer," p. 110.

Saving Shortcuts to Network Places

Browsing for shared resources can be a tedious, trial-by-error process, especially on large networks. Instead of double-clicking until you find the shared folder you're looking for, use shortcuts to go straight there. You can exchange network shortcuts with other users or use a wizard to create them yourself.

To create a network shortcut from scratch, double-click the **Add Network Place** icon in the My Network Places folder and use the wizard shown in Figure 15.7.

Quick search

If you prefer the keyboard, try this handy shortcut. Open the **My Network Places** folder and press **F3**. That opens the search pane with the **Computer Name** box highlighted, ready for you to begin your search.

Browse from within a program, too

Remember that the common Open and Save As dialog boxes in Windows programs are actually scaled-down versions of Explorer. When you use a program's dialog boxes to browse for files, use the My Network Places icon to search for shared files on other computers.

FIGURE 15.7
Use this wizard to create a shortcut to a shared network resource.

The wizard lets you create four distinct types of network shortcuts. In any case, you can browse to the location you want to use or enter its name directly:

- **Shared computer.** Use the syntax *Computer_name*. Shows all the shares available on a given computer.
- **Shared drive or folder.** Opens an Explorer window and displays the contents of the specified drive or folder. Use the syntax *Computer_name**share_name*.
- **Web folder (HTTP server).** Allows you to save files directly on a Web server so that they can be opened in a browser window. Use the syntax *http://server_name*.
- **FTP server.** Lets you browse for files and folders on a server running the industry-standard File Transfer Protocol (FTP). Use the syntax *ftp://server_name*.

By default, shortcuts in the My Network Places folder use a convoluted name that includes the share name and the computer name. If you create a shortcut to \\Harpo\Software, for instance, the shortcut uses the default name Software on Harpo. If you create the shortcut with the Add Network Place Wizard, the final step lets you enter a more descriptive name. After creating a shortcut, you can change its name to one that's shorter or more descriptive; click the label beneath the shortcut icon and rename it just as you would any shortcut.

Mapping Drive Letters

Windows 2000 lets you assign a drive letter to a shared network resource—a computer, a drive, or a folder. This technique, called *mapping* a drive letter, lets you treat the shared resource as if it were a local drive. On my network, for example, all downloaded programs are available for installation from a shared folder called Software on a network server named Harpo. It's tedious to type \\harpo\software every time I want to install a new utility or update a program, though, so I've mapped this location to the drive letter S:. That drive letter appears in the My Computer window and in Browse dialog boxes for programs. Now, when I want to see what software is available, all I need to do is open the S: drive and begin browsing.

Automatic shortcuts

When you access a shared resource for the first time, Windows automatically creates a shortcut in the My Network Places folder. You can copy any of these shortcuts and place them on the Start menu, in a folder, or in an email message. To copy the shortcut to the desktop, right-click and choose **Send To**; then click the **Desktop (create shortcut)** option.

Mapping can be a lifesaver

Some older 16-bit Windows programs don't recognize UNC names at all, which makes it difficult to open or save files. My favorite image-editing software, a 16-bit program originally written before Windows 95, falls into this category. To open or edit a file from this program, I have to map a drive letter to the network folder and fool the program into thinking that it's working with a local hard drive. If this happens with a program you use, look for a **Network** button in the Browse dialog box—that feature is always available to create a permanent or a temporary drive mapping.

Mapping a network location to a drive letter

1. From any Explorer window, pull down the **T**ools menu and choose **Map Network Drive**. The Map Network Drive Wizard appears (see Figure 15.8).

FIGURE 15.8
Use this wizard to assign a letter to a shared network drive or folder. Windows programs treat the mapped drive as if it were just another local hard drive.

You can't choose A:, B:, or C:

Windows won't allow you to map a network location to the reserved letters **A:** and **B:** (which are for floppy drives only) or **C:** (your main hard drive). In addition, if you have hard drives, CD-ROMs, or other drives currently assigned to drive letters, those letters won't appear in the list of choices for mapping.

2. In the **Drive** box, select an available drive letter. You can choose any letter that appears on the list, although I recommend that you pick a letter that reminds you of what the mapped drive contains: P: for Projects, S: for Software, and so on.

3. In the **Fo**lder box, enter the name of the shared resource. You can type the name directly, using UNC syntax (*servername**sharename*) or click the **Browse** button to locate the drive or folder by pointing and clicking.

4. If you want the drive mapping to be permanent, check the **Reconnect at logon** box. Clear this box if you need the drive mapping only for the current session and you don't expect to reuse it.

5. If the shared resource requires a different username and password than the account you used to log on for the current session, click the **different user name** hyperlink and enter this information. Later, when you access the mapped drive, Windows supplies these credentials automatically for you.

6. Click **Finish** to complete the drive mapping. A new Explorer window opens, showing the contents of the shared folder.

To disconnect a mapped drive, use either of the following techniques:

- Open the My Computer window, right-click the icon for the mapped drive, and choose **Disconnect** from the shortcut menu.

- Open an Explorer window, pull down the **Tools** menu, and choose **Disconnect Network Drive**. Windows displays a list of all currently mapped drives, like the one shown in Figure 15.9. Select an entry from the list and click **OK** to remove the association between the drive letter and the share.

To assign a mapped drive to a different drive letter, first disconnect the drive and then remap it to a new drive letter using the wizard.

Skip one step

If you've browsed through My Network Places to a shared computer, drive, or folder, you can right-click the icon for that share and choose **Map Network Drive** from the shortcut menu. This step starts the Map Network Drive Wizard with the location filled in automatically. Choose a drive letter, set any additional options, and click **Finish**.

FIGURE 15.9
All currently mapped drives show up in this window, along with open network connections. Select any entry and click **OK** to stop using the mapped drive letter.

Sharing Printers

On small networks, sharing a local printer attached to your computer is an excellent way to keep down the total cost of your network. If you and your assistant or a nearby co-worker both have easy access to the same printer, why should each of you have a separate one? The economic argument is particularly compelling for expensive hardware—color printers, for example, and high-speed laser printers that can do sophisticated paper-handling chores such as printing two-sided jobs or producing booklets.

During the Setup process for a new printer, you can choose whether to share it. If you say no during the initial setup and change your mind later, here's how to share your printer.

Stay away from spaces

When giving a printer a share name, I strongly recommend that you use a name that contains no spaces. Share names that contain spaces can cause problems over a network, particularly when someone tries to access the share using a machine with an older version of Windows.

Sharing a printer

1. Open the Printers folder.

2. Right-click the icon for the printer you want to share and choose **Sharing**.

3. On the **Sharing** tab of the printer's Properties dialog box (see Figure 15.10), click the **Shared as** option and give the share a name. This is the name other users will see when they browse on the network. By default, Windows suggests an eight-character share name, without spaces, derived from the name you gave the printer.

FIGURE 15.10

When sharing a printer, use a short, descriptive name without spaces.

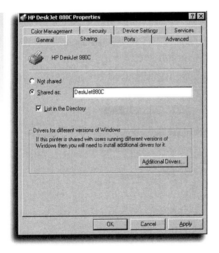

4. If you're connected to a Windows domain, you can check the **List in the Directory** box to allow other network users to find your computer by searching for it in the Active Directory. This check box is not visible if you're on a simple workgroup. Leave this box unchecked if you want to share only with one or two co-workers.

5. If other users who will share the computer are using different versions of Windows, click the **Additional Drivers** button to install drivers for them. Figure 15.11 shows the most common use of this feature—to allow other users with Windows 95 or 98 running on an Intel-compatible machine to use your printer.

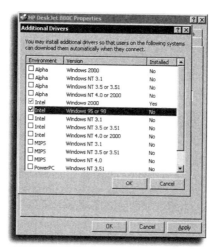

FIGURE 15.11
Use this dialog box to make sure drivers are available for network users running older versions of Windows.

6. Click the **Permissions** tab to specify which users and groups can work with the shared printer. As you can see in Figure 15.12, these permissions are similar to those for a shared file or folder.

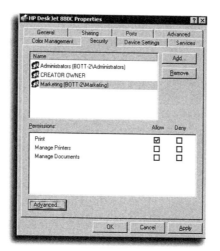

FIGURE 15.12
Do you have a color printer that uses a small fortune in supplies for each printed page? Use permissions to restrict access to it.

Hide printers, too

Just as with shared files and folders, you can hide a shared printer by placing a dollar sign ($) on the end of the share name. Anyone who knows your computer name and the name of the shared printer will be able to connect to it, but no one will be able to see it by browsing the network.

7. Click **OK** to save your changes. The hand icon under the printer icon indicates that you've successfully shared the printer.

Sharing an Internet Connection

Do you have one Internet connection and two or more computers? If every computer on the network needs Internet access, your costs can quickly soar out of reach if you have to add a phone line or cable connection for each one. Windows 2000 Professional offers a low-cost alternative called Internet Connection Sharing. As the name implies, this feature lets you set up Internet access on a single computer, and then allow other computers to access the Internet through that computer.

Internet Connection Sharing is designed for use on small networks—typically those with two or three computers. It works great at home or in a small office, but it is not appropriate for networks of more than five computers. In particular, it's incompatible with any network that contains Windows 2000 *domain servers, DNS servers,* or *DHCP controllers.*

The instructions I outline in this section make the following assumptions about your network setup:

- You're a member of the Administrators group. You must have administrative rights on a computer to enable Internet Connection Sharing.

- You do not have any Windows 2000 servers on your network. If your network includes even a single server, check with the server's administrator before attempting to install ICS.

- One and only one computer on the network is connected to the Internet. For the purpose of these instructions, I'll refer to this as the *gateway computer.* It will handle all the work of assigning addresses and connection settings to the rest of the machines on the network.

- The gateway computer must have two network connections—one that connects the computer to the Internet, the other connecting it to the rest of the machines on the network. The Internet connection can be a regular dial-up modem, a cable modem, or a second network card attached to a DSL interface.

Read instructions carefully!

Internet Connection Sharing is deceptively simple to set up. As long as you allow Windows to manage the allocation of all network resources, you'll have no problem. If you try to customize your network setup, however, by specifying static IP addresses, DNS servers, or other settings, you'll almost certainly cause ICS to break—and you may cause the entire network to lose the capability to access the Internet. When in doubt, read the online Help files carefully.

Sharing an Internet Connection

1. Set up Internet access on the gateway machine and verify that it works correctly.

2. Log on to the computer that will act as the Internet gateway for the rest of the network. Click the **Start** button, choose **Settings**, and open the **Network and Dial-Up Connections** folder.

3. Right-click the icon that represents the connection between the gateway computer and the Internet, and then choose **Properties**. Click the **Sharing** tab to display the dialog box shown in Figure 15.13.

4. Check the box labeled **Enable Internet Connection Sharing for this connection**.

5. If you want the gateway computer to connect to the Internet automatically when other computers access a Web page or send and receive email, check the **Enable on-demand dialing** box.

> **High-speed connections work best**
>
> Although ICS works tolerably well with dial-up connections, it is most effective with high-speed connections such as cable modems and DSL lines. If your only Internet access is over a dial-up line, be prepared to pay a performance penalty when two or more users try to share the same connection simultaneously. On a 56K connection, the effect is to cut apparent download and upload speeds in half when both users are actively browsing the Web or downloading files.

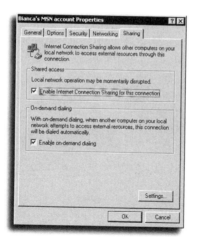

FIGURE 15.13
Setting up Internet Connection Sharing is deceptively simple. Log on as Administrator, check the top box shown here, and you're ready to go.

6. Click **OK** to save your changes and close the Properties dialog box.

7. On each network computer that will access the Internet across the network, configure the local network connection to automatically get an IP address and DNS server addresses.

Installing ICS makes the following changes to your network:

To dial or not to dial?

If you pay for Internet access by the minute, you may want to exercise tight control over when your network is connected. In that case, clear the **Enable on-demand dialing** box. You can connect to the Internet when you want to; if the connection is inactive, other computers will get an error message when they try to access the Internet.

- On the gateway machine, the network adapter that's connected to the other local computers uses the private IP address 192.168.0.1.

- The Internet Connection Sharing service is installed and started on the gateway machine.

- The gateway machine allocates IP addresses to other computers automatically, using the addresses 192.168.0.2, 192.168.0.3, and so on.

- On all other computers, the default gateway handles DNS chores and routes IP addresses.

By default, any other computer on the network can browse the Web and check email using standard POP3 and SMTP servers. If you want to use other Internet-based programs, including streaming media players and multiplayer games, you may need to configure special settings. Contact the developer of the software in question and ask it to supply the port settings you need to enter (be sure to specify that you're using ICS in Windows 2000). Then right-click the shared connection and choose **Properties**. Click the **Sharing** tab, click the **Settings** button, and enter the information the developer supplied.

part

V

EXPLORING THE INTERNET

Connecting to the Internet

Connecting to the Internet Over a Phone Line

There are two obvious prerequisites to any dial-up connection: You need a modem (or another type of connecting device, such as an ISDN adapter), and you need a phone line. If you've already connected a modem to your PC and plugged a phone line into it, double-click the Internet Explorer icon to launch the Internet Connection Wizard (see Figure 16.1). If you haven't set up your modem previously, the Internet Connection Wizard includes a series of steps that automatically installs the correct drivers and configures your modem.

SEE ALSO

➤ *For instructions on how to set up and configure a modem, see "Installing and Configuring Common Upgrades," p. 261.*

FIGURE 16.1
Use the middle option in this wizard to configure your computer for dial-up Internet access.

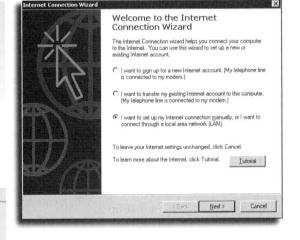

Rerun the wizard anytime

To run the Internet Connection Wizard again, double-click the Internet Options icon in Control Panel, click the Connections tab, and click the **Setup** button. Use this option if you want to use the wizard to set up a new dial-up connection icon, for example.

For experienced users, the Internet Connection Wizard may feel like a nuisance. Whenever you log on to a user account for the first time, you must repeat this process. (After you complete this initial setup routine, double-clicking the Internet Explorer icon opens a browser window, as it should.) It doesn't have to be more than a minor nuisance, however, after you learn the secrets of running through the following three options:

- Use the top option to sign up for a new account with an Internet service provider in your area. When you choose this option, the

Internet Connection Wizard connects with a referral server to generate a list of Internet service providers in your area. Choose any of the entries in this list (see Figure 16.2 for an example) to sign up for a new account and automatically configure your system for access through that account.

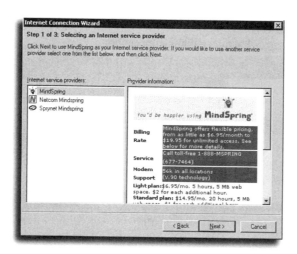

FIGURE 16.2
The Internet referral server generates a short list of available Internet service providers available in your location.

- Choose the middle option if you already have a dial-up Internet account and you want Windows to automatically configure it for access through Windows 2000. Although this option sounds convenient, don't be fooled—it works only with ISPs that are listed on Microsoft's Internet Referral Service. If your ISP hasn't paid its fees to Microsoft, you'll have to set up your connection manually.

- Use the third option if you already have a dial-up Internet account and you want to set it up manually. Assuming you have all required information from your ISP—including *TCP/IP* settings, account name, and password—the process need not be complex. This option also lets you set up your system for Internet access through a network.

Do your own research

The Internet Connection Wizard offers a quick, hassle-free way to change Internet service providers or set up a new account, but this list is by no means complete. The choices you receive from the referral server are typically skewed in favor of national ISPs that have paid Microsoft a fee for the listing. You may get a better price and service from a local provider or from a national ISP that isn't available through Microsoft. Check around before you make a long-term commitment.

SEE ALSO

➤ *For instructions on how to connect to the Internet over a corporate network, see "Creating a Direct Internet Connection," p. 324.*

➤ *To learn how to share a single Internet connection among several computers, see "Sharing an Internet Connection," p. 348.*

Creating a Dial-Up Internet Connection

Although experienced users may be tempted to dismiss the Internet Connection Wizard as a tool for beginners, it's actually a useful tool for setting up and managing Internet connections. When you use the wizard to configure a dial-up connection manually, you go through three steps, with several advanced options available at each step:

Creating a dial-up connection

1. Enter the phone number you use to connect to your ISP. Are you setting up on a desktop machine from which you will always dial the same local or long-distance number? If so, clear the check mark from the **Use area code and dialing rules** box (as shown in Figure 16.3) and enter the entire number exactly the way you want it dialed, with or without area code and prefix, in the **Telephone number** box.

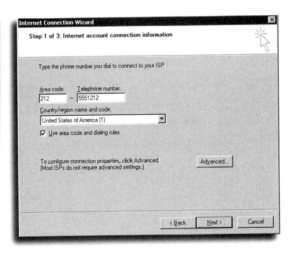

FIGURE 16.3
To dial a local number, with or without area code or prefix, uncheck the box and enter the number exactly the way you want it dialed.

2. Enter your username and password. Note that this information will usually be different from your Windows 2000 logon information.

3. Give the connection a descriptive name, such as `Mindspring Phoenix`, and follow the wizard's prompts to finish setting it up.

Of course, that simple three-step process can actually turn into many more steps if you choose advanced options. For instance:

- If you have more than one modem or other connection device set up, Windows 2000 will ask you to specify which one you want to use. If you have no modem set up, the Add New Hardware Wizard runs.

- The default settings assume you're making a standard *Point-to-Point Protocol (PPP)* connection and that your Internet service provider automatically assigns you an IP address and DNS settings each time you dial up. If your ISP requires that you enter static numbers for any of these settings, click the **Advanced** button in step 1.

- After completing the three preceding steps, the wizard offers to help you set up an email account in Outlook Express. You can do so at this point or skip this step and do it later.

SEE ALSO

➤ *For full instructions on how to set up Outlook Express, see "Setting Up an Email Account," p. 412.*

Using a Dial-Up Connection

After you complete the wizard, Windows saves your settings in a connection file within the Network and Dial-Up Connections folder. If you logged on as Administrator, the connection icons you create are available for all users; if you log on using an ordinary user account, connection icons are visible only in your account. To open this system folder from the Start menu, click **Start** and choose **Settings**, **Network and Dial-Up Connections**. You can establish a connection to the Internet using any of these three methods:

- Open the Network and Dial-Up Connections folder and use that icon to manually connect to the Internet. This option takes an extra step, but it lets you decide exactly when and how you connect to the Internet.

- Set up Internet Explorer to automatically open a dial-up connection whenever you attempt to access a Web page. By default, Windows 2000 asks you to click **OK** in a confirmation dialog

---

10 digits? No problem...

Does your phone company require that you dial 10 digits to access some local numbers? For notebook computers or for desktop configurations where you routinely dial different access numbers, you can define dialing rules by editing your *location*. Open Control Panel's Phone And Modem Options dialog box to adjust settings for your default location, and Windows can automatically use these rules to dial any number correctly.

Faster is better

For some users, dial-up connections are the only practical option for Internet access. However, if you have access to high-speed Internet alternatives, such as *cable modems* or *digital subscriber line* (DSL) connections, I strongly recommend that you choose the high-speed option. The faster speeds make it possible to take full advantage of the Internet's capabilities to find and organize information and to view rich multimedia content, and best of all, you don't have to go through the hassle of making a connection—typical high-speed connections are always on and ready for you.

---

box before actually dialing, making this your best choice if you have only one phone line that you share for voice and data calls.

- By adjusting advanced settings in the Network and Dial-Up Connections folder, you can make a hands-free connection that doesn't require confirmation from you whenever you attempt to access any Internet resource. This option is best if you have a dedicated data line and you want Windows to automatically connect to the Internet on demand, without asking your permission.

Making a Manual Connection

If you want to choose exactly when and how you connect to the Internet, make a manual connection.

Making a manual Internet connection

1. Open the Network and Dial-Up Connections folder and double-click the icon for the connection you want to create. A dialog box like the one shown in Figure 16.4 appears.

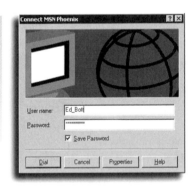

FIGURE 16.4
To temporarily change the phone number, location, and other settings for your Internet connection, click the **Properties** button.

2. Check your username and enter a password if necessary. To store the password for reuse, check the **Save Password** box.

3. To check the phone number and other settings, click the **Properties** button and go to the **General** tab (see Figure 16.5). If necessary, enter the correct number in the **Phone** number box. If the format (area code, prefix, and so on) is incorrect, edit the number to include the required prefixes, or check the **Use dialing rules** box and click the **Rules** button to change the dialing preferences. Click **OK** to apply your changes (any changes you make here are saved with the connection icon).

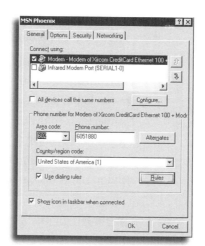

4. Click the **Dial** button. Windows opens a modem connection and attempts to dial the number. You see a series of status messages as the connection proceeds.

After you successfully complete the connection, you should see an informational dialog box like the one in Figure 16.6. At the same time, a Dial-Up Connection status icon appears in the notification area to the right of the taskbar.

Should you save your password?

If other people have access to your computer and you store your Internet password with the Dial-Up Connection icon, anyone can connect to the Internet and pretend to be you. To prevent that possibility, leave the **Save Password** box blank and enter this value manually each time you connect.

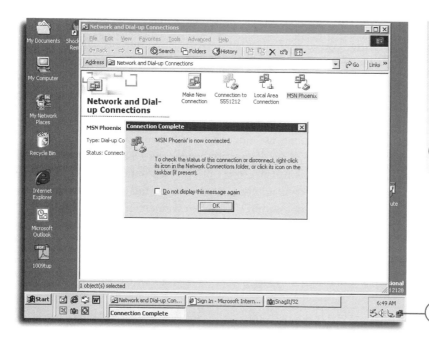

FIGURE 16.6
If you prefer not to see this dialog box after every completed connection, check the option just above the **OK** button.

① Connection status icon

Fast access to dial-up icons

You needn't open the Network and Dial-Up Connections folder every time you want to make or break a connection. Open that folder once and drag the connection icon to the Start menu or the desktop to create a shortcut. Use this icon and its right-click menus to connect and disconnect from the Net anytime.

When you've finished working with your Internet connection, you have three options for closing it:

- Right-click the icon in the notification area and choose **Disconnect** from the shortcut menu.
- Right-click the connection icon in the Network and Dial-Up Connections folder and choose **Disconnect**. This technique is useful if the taskbar icon is not visible.
- Double-click the icon in the notification area to open the connection status dialog box, and then click the **Disconnect** button.

Configuring Windows 2000 to Dial Automatically

As in previous versions, Internet Explorer 5 includes the capability to automatically establish an Internet connection whenever you attempt to access a Web page or check mail using Outlook Express. You can set up Windows to pause for confirmation from you (handy if you want to prevent your computer from trying to dial when you're on the phone already) or to dial automatically.

Many roads to Internet options

As with many Windows 2000 features, you can take your choice of several ways to open the Internet Options dialog box. Use the Internet Options icon in Control Panel, or pull down the **Tools** menu in an Internet Explorer window, or right-click the Internet Explorer icon on the desktop and choose **Properties**. Each of these three techniques has exactly the same effect—use whichever one is more convenient for you.

To set up automatic dialing on a system that uses only dial-up Internet access, open the Internet Options dialog box and click the **Connections** tab (see Figure 16.7). Choose the **Always dial my default connection** option and click **OK**.

After you've configured automatic dialing options, click **OK** to close the Internet Options dialog box. Then open Internet Explorer and try to access a Web page. If you don't have an open Internet connection, you'll see a Dial-up Connection dialog box like the one shown in Figure 16.8.

If you sometimes use a network for Internet access and at other times use a dial-up connection, check the **Dial whenever a network connection is not present** option. This option is especially useful when you carry a notebook that accesses the Internet from a network at the office but requires a modem connection on the road. If Windows sees that your network is available, it won't try to dial out.

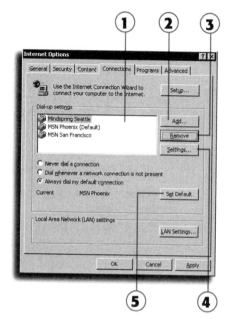

FIGURE 16.7
Use the **Connections** tab to set up automatic dialing and to manage multiple dial-up connections.

① Choose a connection icon from this list.

② The **Add** button does not let you create a new dial-up connection; use the Internet Connection Wizard instead.

③ Use this button to remove a connection icon.

④ Click **Settings** to edit the phone number, username, password, etc. for the selected connection.

⑤ Select any connection icon and click here to make that icon the new default.

FIGURE 16.8
By default, Windows asks for your permission before trying to make a dial-up connection.

Windows 2000 gives you a wide and potentially confusing array of automatic dialing options. If you can sort out the alternatives, however, you can fine-tune settings so that your modem works exactly the way you want it to. After double-clicking the connection icon, you can set any of the following options:

- Use the drop-down **Connect to** list to choose a different connection.

- Change the information in the **User name** and **Password** boxes before connecting, if you want to use a different account. These changes apply only to the current session and are not saved with the connection icon.

- Check the **Save Password** box to store your password so that you don't have to enter it every time you connect. Remove the check from this box if you're concerned about system security.

- If you see the Connection Manager dialog box but you're not ready to connect, click the **Work Offline** button.

SEE ALSO

➤ *To learn what you can and can't do when working offline, see "Browsing the Web Without an Active Internet Connection," p. 380.*

- To permanently change settings for the current connection (including the username and password) click the **Settings** button.

- Check the **Connect automatically** box if you want Windows to dial without any further prompts.

If you dial automatically, you may want Windows to automatically hang up as well, so that your phone line is free for other uses. (If you pay by the minute for calls or Internet access, this capability is especially important.) To adjust the amount of time Windows waits before hanging up, open the Internet Options dialog box, click the **Connections** tab, and select the connection from the list. Click the **Settings** button, and then click the **Advanced** button. The Advanced Dial-Up dialog box appears, as shown in Figure 16.9.

- The **Disconnect if idle for *nn* minutes** option automatically closes your dial-up connection if you don't use your Web browser, email program, or any other Internet application for the specified time. The default value is 20 minutes; choose a value between 3 and 59 minutes to fine-tune this feature.

Undoing Autodial

The **Connect automatically** option can drive you crazy, especially if you change your mind. Although it's not documented anywhere, there is a way to undo this setting. Open the Network and Dial-Up Connections folder, right-click the connection icon you want to change, and choose **Create Copy** from the shortcut menu. Give it a name slightly different from the original icon and delete the original. Now open the Internet Options dialog box, click the **Connections** tab, and set the newly created connection as the default. The next time you dial, you must enter your username and password, but the autodial option will be disabled.

362

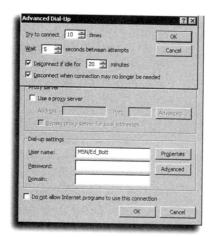

- Check the **Disconnect when connection may no longer be needed** box to have Windows automatically hang up as soon as you close all programs that may require it. With this option set, Windows will offer to hang up as soon as you close your Web browser and email program rather than waiting for the interval set by the idle timer.

If you're working with a Web page or composing an email message when the idle timer expires, Windows doesn't abruptly close the connection. Instead, you see an Auto Disconnect warning dialog box like the one shown in Figure 16.10. You have 30 seconds to respond before your connection to the Internet goes away.

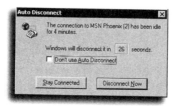

The Auto Disconnect dialog box gives you these options:

- Click the **Disconnect Now** button to close the connection immediately.

- Click the **Stay Connected** button to reset the timer and continue working with Internet Explorer.

- Check the **Don't Use Auto Disconnect** box to disable this feature until you reset it.

Creating a "Hands-Free" Internet Connection

Online indefinitely?

Even if you configure Windows to disconnect automatically, you may discover that your system sometimes refuses to hang up on its own. The culprit is usually a Web page that automatically reloads every few minutes; portal-style home pages such as Excite (www.excite.com) work this way, as do sites that play music or deliver video via RealPlayer or the Windows Media Player. Don't expect Windows to disconnect automatically if you leave one of these pages open and then walk away from your computer.

If you prefer not to dial automatically when you open Internet Explorer or Outlook Express, open the Internet Options dialog box, click the **Connections** tab, and choose the **Never dial a connection** option. With this setting enabled, you will be able to view Web pages or exchange email only when you connect to the Internet manually using a connection icon from the Network and Dial-Up Connections folder.

This option is especially useful if you prefer a non–Microsoft browser, such as Netscape Navigator, or a non-Microsoft email program. In either case, you need to handle the details of connecting to the Internet before you can use your Internet program, and the settings in the Internet Options dialog box will have no effect.

If you configure your system carefully, you can make the dial-up process work with one click.

Creating a one-click Internet connection

1. Click the Start button, choose **Settings**, and select **Network and Dial-Up Connections**.

2. Double-click the connection icon you want to automate. Enter the correct username and password and check the **Save Password** box.

3. Click the **Dial** button. Verify that the connection works properly, and then disconnect.

4. In the Network and Dial-Up Connections folder, right-click the connection icon and choose **Properties** from the shortcut menu.

5. Click the **Options** tab to display the dialog box shown in Figure 16.11.

6. Clear all the check boxes in the Dialing options section at the top of the dialog box. Adjust redial and **Idle time before hanging up** options as required, and then click **OK**.

7. Drag the connection icon from the Network and Dial-Up Connections folder onto the desktop, the Start menu, or the Quick Launch bar—wherever it's most accessible for you.

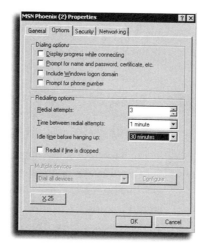

FIGURE 16.11
Clear all four check
boxes at the top of the
dialog box to make a
one-click dial-up
Internet connection icon.

The shortcut you created requires only one click (well, OK…two if you put the shortcut on the desktop) to make a connection to the Internet. After you successfully connect, you can use any Internet program, even if it's not from Microsoft.

Working with High-Speed Connections

Telephone companies are no longer the only sources of access to the Internet. Regardless of where you live, you have an increasing number of high-speed alternatives to traditional dial-up access that use different types of wires—and in some cases, no wires at all.

Many phone companies now offer systems that use digital subscriber line (DSL) technology to provide Internet access at speeds in excess of 1MB per second, while allowing you to use the same line for voice calls. Some cable TV companies now offer Internet access over the same cable you use to receive television signals. In rural areas, you can sign up for Internet access over a satellite dish.

Depending on the system configuration, these solutions can deliver data at speeds of up to 10MB per second, roughly on a par with local area network performance. In most cases, Windows 2000 treats these cutting-edge technologies as if they were network adapters. If you plan to use any of these services, be sure to ask the provider for a

Confusing redial options

Don't be confused by the different redial options. The connection icon in the Network and Dial-Up Connections folder offers one set, and the Advanced Dial-up dialog box offers another set intended for use with Internet Explorer's autodialer. Both sets of options control what happens when you get a busy signal, but only the first one lets you tell Windows to redial automatically if you're disconnected during a session.

Compatibility is key

Don't dodge the question of compatibility. Windows 95 and 98 are still the standards for most software products today, especially those intended for home and small office use. Some vendors refuse to support Windows 2000, even if the software and hardware are capable of working with the service. A few direct questions up front can save headaches later on.

guarantee that the hardware and any required software are compatible with Windows 2000. Get detailed installation instructions, too—or better yet, ask the service provider to do the configuration for you.

Monitoring and Troubleshooting Dial-Up Connections

If your modem is configured correctly and the phone cord is plugged in, your dial-up connection should just work. If you can't connect, try turning the modem off and back on to reset it. Check the modem configuration to be sure you have the correct driver files loaded, and make sure the cord runs from the correct outlet on the modem to the phone jack on the wall. If you can hear dialing sounds through the modem's speaker but you can't make a connection, the problem is almost certainly a hardware problem at your ISP's end.

After you successfully connect to the Internet, you can check the status of your connections in various ways. If the connection icon is visible in the notification area at the right of the taskbar, double-click it to display a status dialog box like the one shown in Figure 16.12. The statistics shown here tell you how long this connection has been open, the speed of the connection, and the total number of bytes you've received and sent.

FIGURE 16.12
Connect to a complex Web page and check this status window to see how well your connection is transferring data.

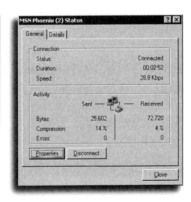

If the taskbar icon is not visible, right-click the connection icon (or a shortcut to that icon) and choose **Status** from the shortcut menu.

Watching the status counter as it displays the number of bytes sent and received can help you see at a glance whether your Internet connection is working properly. If you suspect your Internet connection is no longer working properly, try loading a complex Web page and watch the status display. If it shows no bytes received, your best bet is to hang up and try to reconnect.

Status at a glance

To see status information at a glance without opening a dialog box, aim your mouse pointer at the connection icon in the notification area. After a few seconds, a ScreenTip will appear showing the name of the connection, the speed, and the number of bytes sent and received.

chapter

17

Using Internet Explorer

Browsing the Web

U-R-L or URL?

To retrieve pages stored on a Web server—on the Internet or on a corporate intranet—you must specify a *Uniform Resource Locator*, or *URL*. Experts generally agree that you can pronounce this acronym whichever way you prefer, as a word that sounds like *earl* or as the letters U-R-L.

Unlike Windows 95, Windows 2000 includes Internet Explorer 5 as a standard component, not as an option. You can't leave it out when you set up Windows 2000, nor can you uninstall it—and for good reason. The same software code that runs the browser lets you manage files stored on your own PC and on the network, and it serves as the viewer for information in the Help files as well.

To open Internet Explorer and go directly to your home page, use the Internet Explorer icon on the desktop or on the Quick Launch bar. If you've used Internet Explorer 4.0 or later, you should recognize most of the basic elements in the browser window. If you've used Netscape browsers (Navigator or Communicator) exclusively in the past, some elements of the IE5 interface will be brand new. Most of the Web-browsing capabilities of IE5 will be familiar, but the tools for managing bookmarks (called Favorites in Internet Explorer jargon) and browsing the history list will be very different. Figure 17.1 includes an overview of the browser window.

Opening a blank page

To display a blank page in your Web browser, type **about:blank** into the Address bar.

Which slash is which?

Don't confuse the forward slashes used in Web addresses with the back-slashes used to refer to local and network files. Suppose you have a server called Groucho on your net-work. If you enter
groucho in the Address bar, you'll see a list of all the shared resources available on that server, while //groucho jumps to the default HTML page on the Web server with that name—
http://groucho/
default.htm, for example.

Before you can open a Web page, you have to specify its location—usually by clicking a shortcut or a hyperlink that points to the file, or by entering its full name and path in the Address bar. To open HTML documents stored on a network file server rather than on a Web server, use the familiar *[drive]:\filename* or
servername\sharename\filename syntax.

To open a Web page, you can type its URL into the Address bar or into the Run box on the Start menu. You can click a hyperlink on a Web page or double-click an Internet shortcut on the desktop, in a folder, in the Favorites list, on the Links bar, or in a mail message. To return to a page you've viewed previously, use the drop-down list on the Address bar, click the **Back** or **Forward** button, or use the History Explorer bar.

FIGURE 17.1
Internet Explorer 4 users
will notice the customiz-
able toolbars and more
flexible Explorer bars in
the Windows 2000 ver-
sion of Internet Explorer 5.

1 Customize the size, text
labels, and selection of
buttons on the stan-
dard toolbar.

2 The URL for the current
page appears in the
Address bar; enter
another address to
move to a new page.

3 Check this status bar
for useful information
about the current page,
especially as it loads.

4 Point to any underlined
hyperlink or graphic to
see a ScreenTip that
identifies it.

5 You can hide the Quick
Links bar or move it to
another location at the
top of the browser win-
dow.

6 Use the Go button
instead of pressing
Enter after pasting text
into the Address bar.

7 Explorer bars (Search,
Favorites, History, and
Folders) occupy this
space.

Time-Saving Navigation Shortcuts

Click in the Address bar and type a full URL if you insist, but a
faster, easier way often exists. You can usually save at least a few keystrokes if you know the following shortcuts:

- You don't need to start with a prefix when you enter an Internet
  address. Internet Explorer automatically adds the `http://` prefix
  for most addresses; if the address begins with `ftp`, it adds the
  `ftp://` prefix instead.

- To view the default page on a Web server on your company's
  intranet, enter its name.

- To jump to a page whose address begins with www and ends with .com, click in the Address bar, enter the middle part of the address, and press **Ctrl+Enter**.

- If you enter a single word that doesn't match the name of a local Web server, Internet Explorer opens the AutoSearch pane and jumps to the page that most closely matches the keyword you entered.

SEE ALSO

➤ *For details about how AutoSearch works and how you can customize it, see "Using the Address Bar for Quick Web Searches," p. 384.*

Stopping and Reloading a Web Page

Just as on a crowded highway, traffic on the Internet can sometimes keep a page from loading properly in your browser window. This is especially true when the server you're trying to reach is in heavy demand or is running on a slow connection. If you're tired of waiting for a page to appear and you don't want to wait for Internet Explorer to display an error message, click the **Stop** button 🔘 (or press **Esc**) to immediately stop the download.

The Refresh button 🔄, on the other hand, reloads the current page with the most up-to-date version. This button is especially valuable when you're working with pages that change regularly, such as weather information, traffic maps, or stock quotes. Click the **Refresh** button to check the online Web page against the version in the Internet Explorer cache and reload the Web page if it's newer than the cached version. This step is also useful if a download fails in mid-page and some parts of the page fail to load.

Working with Internet Shortcuts

Just as you use shortcuts to organize documents stored on your own hard disk or on the network, you can use *Internet shortcuts* to keep track of Web pages you visit regularly. Suppose you're browsing the Web and you come across a page that contains an interesting news story. To save it as a shortcut on the desktop, pull down the **File** menu, choose **Send**, and click **Shortcut to Desktop**. After the

Bypass the cache

If Internet Explorer refuses to fetch the latest version of a Web page, try holding down the Ctrl key as you click the Refresh button; this step forces Internet Explorer to retrieve the latest version of the page, regardless of what's in the cache. If you prefer to use the keyboard, press the **F5** key to Refresh, or **Ctrl+F5** to force the browser to load the most recent page.

Missing a picture?

You don't have to refresh the entire page if a small portion of the page fails to load. A red X or a broken image icon means that a linked file failed to load, often because Internet Explorer timed out. To refresh only the missing portion of the page, right-click the red **X** and choose **Show Picture** from the shortcut menu.

shortcut is on your desktop, you can rename it, modify its properties, move it to another folder, or send it in an email message to a friend or co-worker.

SEE ALSO

➤ *For an overview of file and folder shortcuts, see "Using Shortcuts," p. 146.*

Internet shortcuts resemble those that refer to local or network files. Instead of pointing to a target file, however, Internet shortcuts point to a URL—usually the address of a Web page. When you right-click an Internet shortcut and choose **P**roperties, you see a Web Document tab that includes settings like those shown in Figure 17.2.

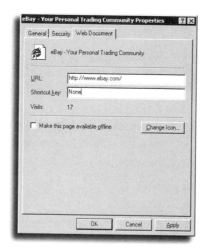

FIGURE 17.2
The target for an Internet shortcut is a Web page address rather than a file on your computer or network.

Home, James?

As with ordinary shortcuts, you can assign a keyboard shortcut to an Internet site. I use this trick to keep my home page one keystroke away, and so can you. Create a shortcut to your home page (your Favorites folder is a good place to stash it), and then right-click the shortcut and choose **Properties**. Click in the **Shortcut key** box and press an easy-to-remember key combination, such as Ctrl+Alt+Home (for home page). Click **OK** to save your changes. Now, to open your Web browser or jump to your home page at any time, press that combination of keys.

Working with Multiple Browser Windows

You can open two or more Internet Explorer windows at a time. In fact, I strongly recommend that you get in the habit of working with multiple browser windows; it can save you a surprising amount of time and mouse clicks. When I'm searching for information on the Web, for example, I follow dozens of hyperlinks, many of which are dead ends. If I click one of these links and discover that it's not what I was looking for, I have to click the **Back** button and wait for the original page to reload before I can follow the next link. If, on the other hand, I open the link in a new window, I can close it or minimize it and return immediately to the previous window.

To open a new browser window, use either of these techniques:

Throw those windows open

In theory, there is no limit to the number of separate browser windows you can open simultaneously; in practice, your available memory and your ability to keep track of all those windows should keep you from opening more than 15 or 20 windows. If you're doing research, I recommend that you open as many windows as you need and can comfortably monitor, and close a window only when you no longer need it.

- Before clicking the hyperlink, pull down the **File** menu and choose **New**, **Window**, or use the keyboard shortcut **Ctrl+N**. In either case, you end up with a new copy of the existing browser window. Click the hyperlink to jump to the new page without disturbing the original window.

- Or, right-click the hyperlink and choose **Open in New Window** from the shortcut menu. The original window remains undisturbed, and a new window opens containing the link you right-clicked.

Completing Web Addresses Automatically

As you wander around the Web, Internet Explorer keeps a record of every page you've visited. When you start to type a new URL into the Address bar, Internet Explorer's *AutoComplete* feature attempts to finish the entry for you, using the first address it finds in the History list that matches the characters you've typed. You can see the results in Figure 17.3. Note that the characters you type appear in the Address bar itself, whereas the suggested completions appear in a drop-down list.

FIGURE 17.3
Internet Explorer's AutoComplete feature tries to guess which Web page you want, using the characters you've already typed.

If any of the suggested completions match the page you want to open, use the down arrow or the mouse to select that entry, and then press **Enter** or click the **Go** button. If not, keep typing and Internet Explorer will revise its suggestion based on each new character you type; or ignore AutoComplete suggestions altogether and continue typing the address.

If you find AutoComplete more confusing than helpful, turn the feature off.

Disabling AutoComplete

1. Pull down the **Tools** menu and choose **Internet Options**.

2. Click the **Content** tab.

3. In the Personal Information section, click the **AutoComplete** button.

4. In the AutoComplete Settings dialog box (Figure 17.4), clear the **Web addresses** check box in the **Use AutoComplete for** section.

5. Click **OK** to close the AutoComplete Settings dialog box and then click **OK** to close the Internet Options dialog box and save your changes.

Entering Passwords and Other Information Automatically

A significant number of Web sites require you to log on with a username and password before you can access content on that site. In some cases, the logon requirement is designed to capture your name for marketing and customization purposes. In other cases, however, the password protects sensitive data. If your bank or brokerage allows Internet access, for instance, you typically have to enter an account name or number and a password before you can see your balance, buy stocks, or transfer funds.

Internet Explorer 5 includes a variant of the AutoComplete feature that can memorize and automatically fill in usernames, passwords, and other fill-in-the-blanks information. Although it sounds convenient, think carefully about the pros and cons before you take advantage of this feature:

- On the plus side, it's undeniably convenient. Each time you visit a Web site that requires you to enter a username and password,

Using AutoComplete the smart way

AutoComplete can be confusing, especially if you've visited dozens of pages that begin with the same domain name, such as `www.microsoft.com`. After AutoComplete makes its first suggestion, use the down arrow to cycle through every entry in your History list that begins with that name. When you reach the right address, press **Enter** or click the **Go** button to load the page.

you can blast through the page with just a few keystrokes and a mouse click or two.

- On the minus side, anyone who has access to your computer can access any password-protected site, including those filled with personal details such as your bank balance. Of course, if your machine is in a locked office and you never leave your desk without locking your computer, you might decide that the risk is low. But before you use this feature, be sure you've considered the possibility that a stranger could access a password-protected page.

If you're concerned about security (and you should be), I recommend that you check the configuration of this feature carefully. To do so, pull down the **Tools** menu, choose **Internet Options**, and click the **Content** tab. Click the **AutoComplete** button to open the AutoComplete Settings dialog box, shown previously in Figure 17.4.

- The safest, most secure strategy is to completely disable the password-saving capability of Windows. To do so, clear the **User name and passwords on forms** box.

- If you've already saved some passwords and want to start over with a clean slate, click the **Clear Passwords** button. This option completely flushes the cache of saved passwords.

- Do you also want to save other types of information you commonly enter in a form you use often, such as your address or zip code? If so, check the **Forms** box. This option is off by default.

- To automatically save all passwords without being prompted each time, clear the **Prompt me to save passwords** box. (I do not recommend that you leave this box unchecked unless you're absolutely certain of the consequences.)

To allow Internet Explorer to save only selected passwords on pages where you believe the risk is low, use this strategy: Open the page that contains the password you want to save, and then open the AutoComplete Settings dialog box. Check the **User name and passwords on forms** box and close the dialog box. Fill in the password and save it. Now return to the AutoComplete Settings dialog box and disable the capability to save future passwords. This technique guarantees that you never accidentally save a sensitive password, yet

Too many passwords?

My Favorites list includes at least 30 sites that require passwords, including the New York Times, the Wall Street Journal, several online shopping sites, and three banks. I've devised a strategy for dealing with these sites based on the sensitivity of the data on each one. For most garden-variety Web sites, I use an easy-to-remember "throwaway" password. I don't care if someone can guess it, because it's not protecting anything I consider personal or sensitive. For sites that require payment but that don't store my personal information, I use a different password—one that's less easy for a stranger to guess. Finally, for truly sensitive Web sites, such as banks, I use a different password for each one, and I make sure it's impossible to guess. And I never, ever reuse my local login password on a Web site.

it still allows you to have the convenience of memorized passwords on low-security Web sites.

The first time you view a Web page that contains spaces for a username and password, Internet Explorer waits for you to enter the requested data and press **Enter**. When you do, you see the dialog box shown in Figure 17.5.

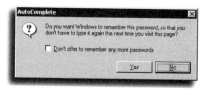

FIGURE 17.5
Answer carefully! If you click **No** here, you will never have another chance to save your password for this page.

Internet Explorer saves the password that is associated with each username you enter. Thus, if you access a page where you have a choice of logging on with several usernames, you will be prompted to save a password for each one.

When you open a Web page that contains a saved username/password combination, tab to the box that contains the username and enter the first character of the name. As soon as you enter that character, you see a drop-down list that contains all saved usernames that begin with that character. Use the down-arrow key to select the saved username, and then press **Tab** to copy the saved name to the form and move to the password field. Internet Explorer automatically fills in the password, displaying a row of asterisks instead of the actual text. Click the button to log on.

What happens if you change your password after saving it? What if you mistype your username? You can't view and edit the list of saved passwords directly, but in either of these cases you can delete or edit the saved username/password combination indirectly, by returning to the page where you normally enter the information.

To delete a saved username/password combination, open the Web page that contains the logon form, type the first character of the username, and use the down arrow to select the saved name. Now press the **Delete** key. You see the dialog box shown in Figure 17.6. Click **Yes** to delete the entry, and then enter the correct name and password.

One chance only!

The first time you encounter a Web page with a password, Windows asks you if you want to save the password. If you click the **No** button, you will never again see the prompt for that page. The only way to save a password for that page in the future is to clear your entire password list (from the AutoComplete Settings dialog box) and open the page again.

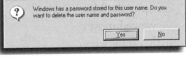

FIGURE 17.6
You can delete any saved username and password combination by selecting the name and pressing the **Delete** key.

To change a saved password, select the username as described previously, and then press **Tab** to move to the password field. Select the entire row of asterisks, press **Delete** to clear it, and enter the new password. When you click the logon button, you should see the dialog box shown in Figure 17.7. Click **Yes** to change the saved password for that username.

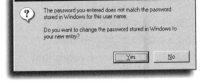

FIGURE 17.7
Have you changed your password? Enter the new password and let Windows save the change to your password cache.

Finding Sites You've Visited Recently

After opening a Web page by clicking a hyperlink or entering a Web address, you can use the **Back** and **Forward** buttons to return to a page you previously viewed in that window. But how do you return to a Web page you viewed in a different browser window, whether it was five minutes ago or last week? That's the job of the *History folder*.

You won't read this elsewhere

The instructions I've outlined here are not documented anywhere in the Windows 2000 Help system, nor will you read them in most other Windows 2000 books, which gloss over the nuances of the password AutoComplete feature.

Internet Explorer keeps a list of the URL for every Web page you load, regardless of how you load it. This History list is extremely useful when you want to return to a page you visited recently but can't remember its exact address. Each user who logs in gets a private History folder in his or her user profile.

Click the **History** button 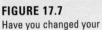 to open an Explorer bar like the one in Figure 17.8. Like other Explorer bars, the History bar snaps into position along the left edge of the browser window.

In previous versions of Internet Explorer, you could view the History list only by date. That's the default view in Internet Explorer 5 as well, but in this version, you can also choose different sort orders. Click the **View** button and then choose **By Site**, for example, to group all the history items by the top-level domain name of the Web page in question—microsoft.com, for example. **By <u>M</u>ost Visited** arranges the list so that the pages you've viewed most often are at the top. **By <u>O</u>rder Visited Today** is especially useful when you remember viewing a site very recently but it doesn't appear when you click the **Back** button.

FIGURE 17.8
Every time you view a Web page, Windows makes an entry in this History list. You can sort or search to find a page you viewed previously.

When you click an Internet shortcut in the History list, Internet Explorer loads the page in the browser window at the right. If you're currently connected to the Internet, you should see the most recent version of the page. If you're working offline, you'll see the saved copy from the browser's cache. (See the following section for a discussion of how to work offline.)

The most frustrating Internet searches are those in which you know you saw a page that contained information about a given topic, but you can't remember the site name, when you last viewed it, or what the page title was. If you can't remember any of those details, but you can recall a word or phrase that was in the page, open the History pane and click the **<u>S</u>earch** button at the top of the pane. Enter the text you can remember in the **<u>S</u>earch for** box, and click the **Search Now** button. The results appear in the History pane, as shown in Figure 17.9.

Can't decipher the titles?

The titles of pages in the History list can be inscrutable, especially when the list turns up "pages" that are actually part of a larger page made up of multiple frames. If you can't find the page you're looking for when you search through the list of titles, try using the Search window instead.

FIGURE 17.9
If you're certain you saw a Web page recently but you can't remember anything except a word or phrase on it, use the **Search** button in the History pane to track it down.

Clear your tracks

You can delete entries from the history list by right-clicking any entry in the list and choosing **Delete**. This can be useful if you find the list too long and confusing, or if you don't want to leave a record that you visited a certain Web site. You can zap an individual page shortcut or all items in a group, such as those from a particular site or date.

By default, the History folder keeps a record of all pages you've viewed in the previous 20 days. To change the size of the History list, pull down the **View** menu and choose **Internet Options.** Click the **General** tab and use the spinner control to select a number between 0 and 999. Choosing 0 clears the History list every day, although you can still recall any page you visited earlier in the same day. Choosing a high number like 999 tells Internet Explorer you never want it to discard items from the History list.

Browsing the Web Without an Active Internet Connection

Can you view Web pages when you're not connected to the Internet? The answer, surprisingly, is yes—but only if you've already viewed the page and it's currently in your browser's *cache*. When you use the History Explorer bar, you can pull down the **File** menu, choose **Work Offline**, and then view any files stored in the cache, even if you're sitting in an airplane seat with no way to connect to the Internet.

When you work with Internet Explorer offline, a network icon with a red X appears at the right side of the status bar along the bottom of the browser window. When that indicator is visible, you can browse pages in the History cache the same as if you were working with a live Internet connection. When you point to a link that is not cached locally, a circle with a slash across it appears next to the mouse pointer, and you see the dialog box shown in Figure 17.10. Before you can view the selected page, you must open an Internet connection.

FIGURE 17.10
If you see this dialog box, the page you attempted to access is no longer in your browser's cache and can't be viewed offline.

Click the **Connect** button to go back online; click the **Stay Offline** if you want to continue to work offline. When you have a slow connection, working offline can be a tremendous productivity booster; instead of waiting as Internet Explorer checks to see whether any updates to a page exist, you can load the saved version from your hard disk in a fraction of the time. Of course, when you work offline you always run the risk that you'll end up working with outdated data.

Saving Links to Your Favorite Web Sites

After you use a Web browser for even a few weeks, you start to find yourself returning to the same sites again and again. As in previous versions, Internet Explorer lets you save shortcuts to these Web sites in a system folder appropriately called Favorites. You can manage the contents of the *Favorites folder* the same as you can any other folder—by opening an Explorer-style window and creating subfolders to organize shortcuts by category.

You can view your current collection of saved Web sites from the pull-down **Favorites** menu. An easier way to see and use this list, however, is to open the Favorites Explorer bar; click the **Favorites** button to open this frame, which appears along the left side of the main browser window. As you can see in Figure 17.11, this view shows all the shortcuts and folders in your Favorites list, with the current page in the window to the right.

In Windows 2000, the Favorites folder is saved as part of your *user profile*. Each user with a profile on the computer gets a personal Favorites folder. The contents of the Favorites list appear in the

What happened to that page?

Internet Explorer's cache doesn't always work the way you might expect. Sometimes, relatively recent pages disappear for no reason, whereas older pages stick around seemingly forever. If you absolutely want to make sure that pages on a particular site are available offline, create a shortcut for that page and choose the **Make available offline** option, described in "Browsing the Web Without an Active Internet Connection," Chapter 18, "Customizing Internet Explorer."

order in which you create them, both on the pull-down Favorites menu and in the Explorer bar. To reorder items in the list, drag any entry to a new position.

FIGURE 17.11
Click any folder icon to see its contents in the Favorites Explorer bar. Drag icons up or down to move them to a new folder or to reorder them in the list.

Netscape users, take note

Netscape browsers save pointers to favorite Web sites in a *bookmark* list. If you had a copy of Netscape Navigator installed when you upgraded to Windows 2000, all your Netscape bookmarks are available in the Favorites folder. If you plan to use both browsers, see the section at the end of this chapter for hints on how to keep bookmarks and Favorites in sync.

To add the current page to the Favorites list, use either of the following techniques:

- Pull down the **Favorites** menu and choose **Add to Favorites**. This opens the Add Favorite dialog box (see Figure 17.12). Click the **Create in** button to choose an existing folder; click the **New Folder** button if you want to create a new subfolder and store the shortcut there. Edit the text in the **Name** box, if necessary, and click **OK**.

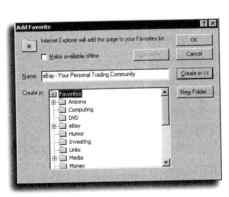

FIGURE 17.12
If you don't specify a folder, Internet Explorer adds your new shortcut to the bottom of the Favorites list.

- If the Explorer bar is visible, drag the small page icon from the far left side of the Address bar and drop it into the Favorites Explorer bar. To add the new shortcut to a folder, let the mouse pointer rest over that folder's icon for a few seconds until it opens. When you use this technique, the name of the shortcut is the same as the title of the current page.

After you add 10 or 20 items to the Favorites folder, the list can become too long to work with comfortably. When you reach that point, use subfolders to help organize the Favorites list. You can create an unlimited number of subfolders in the Favorites folder, including new folders within subfolders.

With the Favorites Explorer bar open, you can easily move, copy, delete, or rename one item at a time: select an icon, right-click, and use the appropriate shortcut menu choice. You can also right-click any shortcut or folder icon and use the **Create New Folder** menu choice to add a new folder icon at the bottom of the list; after creating the new folder, give it a descriptive name and move it where you want it to appear in the list.

If you don't like working with the Explorer bar, pull down the **Favorites** menu and choose **Organize Favorites**; that opens the dialog box shown in Figure 17.13, which provides a different interface for creating, managing, and organizing the contents of the Favorites folder. You can drag items directly (one at a time only, unfortunately) in the list at the right or use the buttons on the left to copy and delete items.

> **Anything goes**
>
> Although the Favorites folder is most useful with Internet shortcuts, you can move or copy any file there, including documents, text files, and shortcuts to documents or programs. Clicking the icon for an Office 2000 file (a Word document or an Excel worksheet, for example) in the Favorites bar will usually open the document in the browser window.

> **What's in a name?**
>
> The default name for a new Internet shortcut in the Favorites bar is the same as the page title. In some cases, that name can be long and unnecessarily detailed; renaming a page can make it easier to find in the list. Instead of "Front Page-Interactive Wall Street Journal," for example, you might prefer the simpler "WSJ."

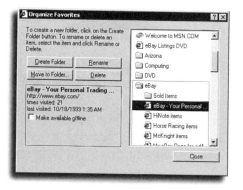

FIGURE 17.13
Use these buttons to rename or delete shortcuts in the Favorites folder. The window at the bottom left provides detailed information about a shortcut.

There's only one way to work with multiple Internet shortcuts simultaneously in the Favorites folder: open any Explorer window and type `%userprofile%\favorites` into the Address bar. (Be sure to include the percent signs.) You can't change the order of shortcuts in an Explorer window, but you can add or delete items wholesale here.

Secrets of Successful Web Searches

Looking for a specific piece of information on the World Wide Web? Good luck. With hundreds of millions of pages on the Web, finding the exact fact you're looking for can seem like an impossible dream. Still, you can increase the odds of successfully tracking down a stray piece of information by using Internet Explorer's built-in search tools.

Using the Address Bar for Quick Web Searches

For simple searches—in which you're trying to find information on a well-known company, product, or personality, for instance—all you have to do is type a word or phrase, complete with spaces, directly into the Address bar.

The *AutoSearch* feature first tries to match the word or phrase you entered to a matching entry in the RealNames database. This is an industry-standard collection that tries to guess what you're *really* looking for and then whisks you to that site. In addition, the AutoSearch pane shows other sites that are likely to be close matches to the word or phrase you typed.

Using the Search Assistant to Find Web Pages

For more complex searches, or if AutoSearch doesn't produce the results you were hoping for, Internet Explorer offers direct access to several popular search engines through the Search Assistant. When you click the **Search** button, an Explorer bar like the one shown in Figure 17.14 appears. Enter your search text and click the **Search** button ; after a brief delay, you see the results in the Search pane.

What is the *Search Assistant*? Microsoft would like you to believe it's a sophisticated utility that carefully analyzes your input and returns exactly the right results. Actually, it's nothing more than an Explorer bar that sends your search term to a randomly selected search engine from its list of approved sites. When you click the **Search** button, the Search pane opens along the left side of the browser window. Look just below the box where you enter search text to see which search engine will be used.

To try the next search engine in the list, click the **Next** button. If those results are also less than satisfactory, keep clicking the **Next** button to cycle through all available search engines.

Customizing the Search Assistant

If you prefer one search engine over others, you can tell Internet Explorer to take you to that site instead of the default selection each time you use AutoSearch or the Search Assistant.

To customize Search Assistant settings, click the **Search** button and then click **Customize** in the toolbar at the top of the Search pane. In the Customize Search Settings dialog box (see Figure 17.15), run through all available options.

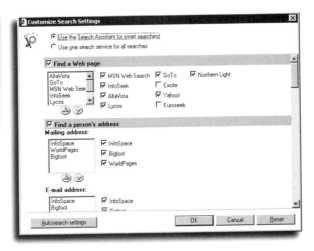

FIGURE 17.15
If you prefer a particular search engine, set up Internet Explorer to use that search engine instead of others.

Reset the defaults

If you experiment with custom search settings and decide that you prefer the default options, it's easy to set things back the way they started. Open the Customize Search Settings dialog box and click the **Reset** button.

When the **Use the Search Assistant for smart searching** box is checked, you can choose any of several Web sites to handle each type of search: for Web pages, people, businesses, and so on. In the **Find a Web page** section, for instance, clear check boxes to remove search engines from the list of available choices and use the up and down arrows to reorder items in the list. Clear the check mark next to a category if you don't want to see that category in the Search pane.

What if you want to use only one search engine? In that case, check the **Use one search service for all searches** box. When you do, note that the list of choices in the Customize Search Settings dialog box (see Figure 17.16) changes to display only a list of search engines. Choose one and click **OK** to save the changes.

FIGURE 17.16
Pick a search engine, any search engine. Whichever one you select from this list is the one that you'll use at all times in the Search pane.

To adjust AutoSearch settings—the way Internet Explorer responds when you type a word or phrase into the Address bar—open the Customize Search Settings dialog box and click the **Autosearch settings** button. In the Customize Autosearch Settings dialog box (see Figure 17.17), you can choose a default search engine to use for Address bar searches, and you can specify whether you want the search results to appear in the Search pane or in the main window.

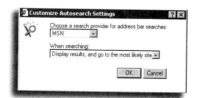

FIGURE 17.17
You can choose your favorite search engine for use with Address bar searches, although some options aren't available with all search engines.

Playing Audio, Video, and Other Multimedia Files

With the help of add-in programs and plug-ins, you can access audio and video content through your browser. Two highly regarded add-ins for Internet Explorer are RealNetworks' RealPlayer and Microsoft's Windows Media Player. Both programs enable your browser to receive live audio and video broadcasts over the Internet. Both are free (Windows Media Player is installed with the version of Internet Explorer 5 in Windows 2000, and you can download RealPlayer from www.real.com); upgrades to a more powerful version of RealPlayer are available for a price.

One of the most entertaining uses of Windows Media Player is to listen to radio broadcasts over the Internet. To use this feature, open Internet Explorer, pull down the **View** menu, choose **Toolbars**, and click **Radio**. In this configuration, Windows Media Player is an embedded control that lives within the browser window rather than in its own window. As you can see in Figure 17.18, the Radio toolbar includes the following elements:

- A Stop button, which turns to a Play button if you stop playing the current station
- A sliding volume control

Plug-ins install themselves

Literally dozens of plug-ins are available for Windows 2000 and Internet Explorer 5. Fortunately, most of them install themselves when needed. If you encounter a Web page that includes content that requires a plug-in, you should see a dialog box informing you of that fact. You may have to go through a brief setup process to get things working properly.

- A speaker button you can click to mute the sound temporarily—handy if the phone rings while you're listening to a radio station
- A drop-down Radio Stations menu, which includes links to a Web-based program guide; you can also save shortcuts to your favorite radio stations here

FIGURE 17.18
A huge number of radio stations from around the world now make their signals available over the Internet. Use the Radio toolbar to listen in.

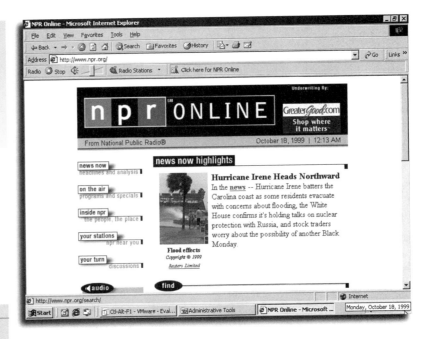

Send from the menu
If you see a Web page that you think a friend or co-worker might enjoy, try sending them a link or the entire page via email. With the page visible in your browser window, pull down the **File** menu, choose **Send**, and select either **Link by E-mail** or **Page by E-mail**. The former sends a shortcut; the latter sends a copy of the page itself so that the recipient can view the HTML page directly in the mail message.

Saving, Sharing, and Printing Web Pages

How do you capture a Web page for posterity, or share it with someone else? The simplest way to share a Web page is to send a shortcut as an attachment to an email message. As long as the recipient has access to a browser and an Internet connection, he or she can open the page by double-clicking the shortcut

Saving a Web Page As a File

Only the simplest Web pages consist of a single text document. More often, the page you see in the browser window actually consists of at least one (and often several) HTML documents and several linked images. In previous versions of Internet Explorer, there was no way to save all the elements on the entire page in one smooth operation. In Internet Explorer 5, you can choose four formats in which to save a Web page. In every case, pull down the **File** menu and choose **Save As**. Then, from the **Save as type** list, choose one of the following options:

- **Web page, complete**. This saves the main page using the name you enter in the **File name** box. All linked files, such as graphics, are saved in a folder that has the same name as the main page, with files tacked onto the end of the name. Thus, if you save a page called Annual Report, all the linked graphics and other support files go into a folder called Annual Report_files.

- **Web archive, single file**. This option saves the file and all linked files in a single file with the MHT extension. The advantage is that you don't have to worry about managing a folder full of linked files; the disadvantage is that anyone viewing the file must do so with Internet Explorer 5.

- **Web page, HTML only**. This option saves only the HTML source code from the original page, with links to any graphics and other supporting files. Anyone who tries to open the saved file must be able to access the linked files, or the page won't load properly. This format has the advantage of being small and compact; it's most useful when you want to preserve the text, and the graphics on the page aren't of great concern.

- **Text file**. Saves the text from the page, but strips out all graphics, hyperlinks, and HTML formatting. Use this option for pages that have very little formatting, where your goal is to preserve only the words.

Saving Pictures and Other Page Elements

To save a graphical image from a Web page, right-click the picture and choose **Save Picture As** from the shortcut menu. Right-click any hyperlink and use the **Save Target As** menu choice to save the linked page without opening it first.

SEE ALSO
➤ *For more details on how to use Web graphics and other items on the desktop, see "Taming the Active Desktop," p. 182.*

Smart moves

If you save a Web page in the complete format and then move or copy it, Windows is smart enough to recognize that it also needs its supporting files. When you move the HTML file, the supporting files move as well.

Editing a Web page

The Edit button on the Internet Explorer toolbar lets you open an HTML page in a program in which you can modify the text and formatting of the page. The default editor is Notepad, but if you've installed FrontPage Express, any version of Microsoft FrontPage, or Microsoft Word 2000, you can use one of these programs instead.

Instant wallpaper

With the help of a handy Internet Explorer shortcut, you can turn any Web graphic into wallpaper for your desktop. When you find an image you'd like to install on the desktop, right-click and choose **Set As Wallpaper**.

Printing Web Pages

And, of course, you can share any Web page with other people by printing it. Successfully transferring a Web page to paper usually requires only that you click the **Print** button, although complex page designs require some preparation for best results.

To print a full Web page that doesn't include *frames*, click the **Print** button 🖨 on the standard toolbar. This action sends the current page to the printer without displaying any additional dialog boxes. Internet Explorer scales the page to fit on the standard paper size for the default printer. The entire Web document will print, complete with graphics, even if only a portion of the page is visible in the browser window.

By default, Internet Explorer ignores background images and colors when printing. That behavior is by design because these decorations usually make text harder to read on a black-and-white printout. If you're using a color printer, however, you may want to include the backgrounds. To add background images or colors to printed pages, pull down the **Tools** menu, choose **Internet Options**, click the **Advanced** tab, and check the **Print background colors and images** box. Don't forget to reset this option after you finish printing your color pages.

For more complex pages, especially those that include frames, pull down the **File** menu and choose **Print** (or press **Ctrl+P**). That opens the Print dialog box, shown in Figure 17.19. Using the settings here, you can specify exactly how you want to arrange the page on paper.

Paper-guzzling option

An option at the bottom of the Print dialog box lets you print all linked documents along with the current page. Avoid this option unless you're sure you know what it will do. If the page you've selected includes links to 30 pages of moderate length, using this option can gobble up a hundred sheets of paper with a single click.

FIGURE 17.19
Watch the preview pane at the left of the Print Frames box to see how a frame-based page will appear when printed.

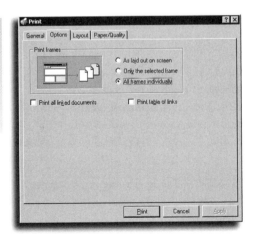

chapter 18

Customizing Internet Explorer

Keeping Your Data Safe

Every time you connect to a Web site or an email server on the Internet, you send packets of data out into an insecure world. You have no control over which route your data takes, and you run the risk that a complete stranger can intercept it. Likewise, when you click a *hyperlink* on a Web page, you risk launching a *script* or downloading a program that could have dire consequences to your computer and data.

Should you be paranoid when browsing the Web or sending and receiving email? No, but a healthy respect for the hazards of the Internet is always in order. Whenever you connect your computer to the Internet, you should be alert for hazards that can compromise your security.

In fact, Internet Explorer includes dozens of security features designed to protect you from inadvertently running unsafe programs or scripts. Although you can apply each of those options to individual Web sites, Internet Explorer starts with a more workable approach—grouping all Web sites into *security zones*, each with its own security settings.

Making Your Web Browser More Secure

When you first install Windows 2000, all sites are divided into two security zones: *local intranet* sites (those on your own computer or inside your company's network) and *Internet sites*. In addition, you can designate specific Web sites as *trusted* or *restricted*, giving them greater or less access to machines inside your network.

To work with the security settings for each of these four groups, pull down the **Tools** menu, choose **Internet Options**, and click the **Security** tab. Figure 18.1 shows this dialog box in action—note that by default, the Internet zone uses the Medium security level.

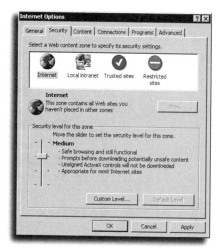

FIGURE 18.1
By default, sites in the
Internet zone use
Medium security set-
tings. Do not choose the
Low security option for
this zone!

Internet Explorer allows you to choose one of five built-in security
levels for each zone, or you can select a Custom option that lets you
pick and choose security settings for a zone. The following list
explains what you can expect from each group of security settings:

- **High.** Extremely restrictive. You can't download *ActiveX controls*
  and many *Java* programs, and Internet Explorer will not accept
  cookies; you're also prohibited from downloading files, and
  you'll see a dialog box before logging on to a secure site. Choose
  this option if you work in an extremely sensitive environment
  and you're willing to sacrifice most advanced Web features to be
  certain you're safe.

- **Medium.** This is the default level for the Internet zone. With
  these settings in effect, you can download files and run signed
  ActiveX controls (Internet Explorer will ask for your permission
  before downloading any potentially dangerous files). Most Java
  programs will work well, and all forms of scripting are permitted. These options should work well for most general-
  purpose Web use.

- **Medium-low.** Uses most of the same settings as the Medium
  level, with fewer prompts. An appropriate choice for the local
  intranet zone, but acceptable for the Internet zone only if you
  are extremely careful in your Web-browsing habits.

Turn off scripting, too

Curiously, the High security
level doesn't block scripts
from running—and scripts
can represent one of the
most common security
threats on the Internet. If
you are determined to
browse with the absolute
highest level of security,
click the **Custom Level**
button and choose **High**
from the **Reset** to box;
then scroll through the
Settings box, find the
Active scripting option,
and click **Disable**. If you
choose this option, be prepared to click through error
messages, because many
pages simply won't work.

- **Low.** The default setting for the local intranet zone. With these settings in place, you can run all ActiveX controls and Java programs, including those that are unsigned. Do not assign this security level to the Internet zone—you open your computer and data to potentially dangerous content.

- **Custom.** Allows you to select security settings individually. Start by choosing one of the built-in security levels, and then adjust individual settings to make it more or less restrictive. This is an excellent way to tighten security if you're concerned about specific types of content, such as ActiveX controls.

As you move between Web sites, the system checks to see what zone the current address belongs to and then applies the security settings that belong to that zone. (Watch the status bar at the bottom of the browser window to see which zone you're currently in.) If you open a Web page on a server inside your corporate intranet, for example, where the security level is Low, you can freely download files and work with ActiveX controls or Java applets. When you switch to a page on the Internet, however, security settings may prevent you from downloading files or using ActiveX programs.

The most serious security risk of all crops up when you use your browser to download and run files. Double-clicking a program file always runs the obvious risk of introducing a virus onto your system, but even document files can be dangerous. Any Microsoft Office file, for example—including Word documents and Excel workbooks—can include *macros* that are as powerful as any standalone program.

When you attempt to download a file, you see the dialog box shown in Figure 18.2. I strongly recommend that you save a downloaded file to a safe location and check it with up-to-date antivirus software before running it.

To completely prevent all file downloads, select the built-in High security level for the Internet zone, or define custom security settings and change the setting for File Downloads to **Disable**. With this setting in place, you'll see a dialog box like the one shown in Figure 18.3 whenever you attempt to download a file from a Web page.

> **Settings are per user**
>
> Internet Explorer security settings are separate for each user. If you tweak your security settings carefully but allow other people to log on to your machine, they could introduce a virus or a dangerous program because they're not subject to the same restrictions. To set Internet Explorer security for all users, you must use the Internet Explorer Administration Kit. Read all about it at http://www.microsoft.com/windows/ieak.

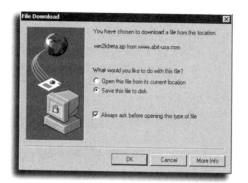

FIGURE 18.2
Don't run that file! Save it and scan it with up-to-date antivirus software before going any further.

FIGURE 18.3
If you're concerned about viruses, you can disable all file downloads; if you try to retrieve a program or document through the Web, you see this dialog box instead.

Using Secure Web Connections

On the Internet, packets of information hop from server to server without any control on the part of the sender. At least in theory, anyone with the technical knowledge can "listen in" as you communicate with a distant Web server. Normally, that doesn't matter—if you're downloading today's sports scores from ESPN.com, you don't care whether anyone reads the pages as they go by.

But what happens if you fill in a form that includes private information, such as a credit card number? What if you ask your online stockbroker to send you the current holdings from your account? Clearly, you don't want this Web data sent "in the clear," as plain text that anyone can read. For sensitive transactions like these, you want the information to be *encrypted* so that only you and the trusted site at the other end of the connection can read it.

To safely send confidential information over the Internet, you have to first establish a *secure connection*, using a standard security protocol called *Secure Sockets Layer* (SSL). (All banks and brokers offer this option, as do most e-commerce sites.) The URL for a secure connection uses a different prefix (https://). When you click the link for a secure connection, Internet Explorer first checks the data received from the Web server to see if it includes details about a security

Is that site secure?

Internet Explorer provides at least two sure indicators when you've made a secure connection: you'll see a warning dialog box each time you begin or end a secure connection; you also see a padlock icon in the status bar at the bottom of the browser window. (You can disable the confirmation dialog box by clearing a check box.)

certificate from a known Certification Authority (CA). It then connects with the CA to verify that the certificate is valid. To check the certificate's details, load the secure page, pull down the **File** menu and choose **Properties**. The resulting dialog box tells you whether you've made an SSL connection—click the **Certificates** button to see more details about the security certificate, as shown in Figure 18.4.

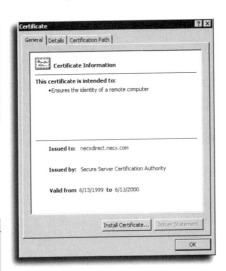

After Internet Explorer has verified the certificate, it scrambles every bit of data sent from each end of the secure connection and unscrambles it at the receiving end. Only your computer and the secure server have the digital keys required to decode the encrypted packets. Because of the extra processing time on either end, loading HTML pages over a secure connection takes longer.

Although the built-in encryption capabilities of Internet Explorer 5 are strong enough to protect your data from casual snoops, the default encryption routines are too weak to be safe, according to many U.S.-based banks and brokers. The effectiveness of the encryption routine is directly based on the length of the digital key. Because of United States Government export restrictions, the encryption software in many copies of Windows 2000 uses a 56-bit digital key; residents of the United States or Canada can upgrade to a more powerful version of the encryption software, which uses a 128-bit key that is nearly impossible to crack.

Which version of the encryption software do you have installed? To check, open an Internet Explorer window, pull down the **Help** menu, and choose **About**. As you can see in Figure 18.5, this dialog box shows which version of the encryption software is currently installed.

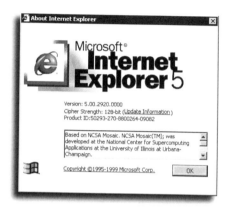

FIGURE 18.5
After you upgrade Internet Explorer with the 128-bit security code, commercial transactions are considerably safer.

To upgrade your encryption software from the default 56-bit version, click the **Update** link in this dialog box and follow the instructions to download and install the Windows 2000 High Encryption Pack. (Note that you must be connected to the Internet, and you must be logged on with administrative rights to complete this process.)

SEE ALSO

➤ *To learn more about ways to keep your computer secure, see "Security Considerations," p. 19.*

Controlling Cookies

When you open a Web page in Internet Explorer, some servers give you more than you asked for—without your knowledge, they record information about you and your actions in a hidden file called a *cookie*.

Cookies make it possible for a Web server to keep track of your preferences. There are dozens of legitimate uses for cookies: at online shopping sites, a cookie keeps track of items as you add them to your shopping basket. At some Web sites (the *New York Times* and *Wall Street Journal*, for instance) cookies store your username and password so that you can log in automatically. If you've customized a

Location check

On some computers, you may be unable to update your encryption software. This generally happens when Microsoft's servers can't verify that your machine is physically located within the United States or Canada. In that case, your best bet is to download the 128-bit security components from another computer. Copy the downloaded files to a floppy disk or to a location that is accessible through your network, and then run the installation program from the floppy disk or the network.

home page at Yahoo!, Excite, MSN, or another *portal*, a cookie stores your identity so that the server can retrieve your custom page.

Should you be concerned about cookies? The privacy risks are minimal, thanks to strict security controls built in to your Web browser that limit what the server can and cannot do with cookies. Some privacy advocates paint a dark picture of cookies, but the truth is far more benign. Here, for example, are the definitive answers to some myths you may have heard about cookies:

- Cookies can only track information you specifically enter—by filling in a form, for example. They can't "steal" your username, password, or email address and send it without your knowledge.

- Details in a cookie can be retrieved only by the server that saved that cookie in the first place. If you enter your name in an online form at one site, no other site can get that information without asking you for it.

- You cannot get a virus from a cookie.

- You can view the contents of any cookie on your system and delete a cookie if you want to.

To see all the cookies that Internet Explorer has saved on your computer, pull down the **Tools** menu, choose **Internet Options**, and click the **General** tab. Under Temporary Internet Files, click the **Settings** button, and in the Settings dialog box click the **View Files** button. In the resulting list of cached files, all your cookie files should appear at the beginning of the list. To remove one or more cookies, right-click and choose **Delete** from the shortcut menu.

Don't like the idea of sharing information with Web sites? You can disable cookies completely, or you can set Internet Explorer so that it asks your permission before saving a cookie. Unlike previous versions of Internet Explorer, Internet Explorer 5 lets you exercise separate control over persistent cookies (those that are permanently saved on your hard disk) and temporary cookies that last only as long as you keep the current browser window open. To control your cookie collection, follow these steps:

1. Pull down the **Tools** menu, choose **Internet Options**, and click the **Security** tab.

2. Select the Internet zone from the group of four icons at the top of the dialog box, and then click the **Custom Level** button.

Don't give away personal details

Some sites insist that you give them a name or other details before they allow you to proceed. At an online store where you plan to make a purchase using a secure server, go ahead and use your real name. But if the site demanding your personal information has no legitimate reason to ask for it, why should you hand it over? If you're uncomfortable entering your real information, try John (or Jane) Doe, from 123 Main Street, Anytown, NY.

Peek into the cookie jar

An obscure Internet Explorer feature comes in handy in two ways. Pull down the **File** menu and choose **Import and Export**. This opens the Import/Export Wizard, which you can use to save and restore your list of favorite Web sites. Follow the wizard's prompts to export your Favorites and cookies to text files. Open the `Cookies.txt` file and you can see exactly what's buried in each cookie. If you see something you don't like, delete that cookie.

3. In the Security Settings dialog box, scroll through the **Settings** list until you locate the Cookies section (see Figure 18.6).

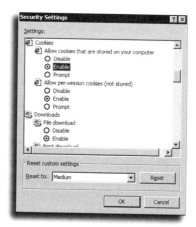

FIGURE 18.6
To control how and when you share personal information with Web sites using hidden "cookie" files, change these default options.

Prepare to be annoyed

If you disable Internet Explorer's capability to save cookies, some Web sites simply won't work. If you ask it to prompt you every time it sets a cookie, you'll be barraged with dialog boxes. A good compromise is to click **Enable** for the **Allow per-session cookies (not stored)** option but choose **Prompt** for the **Allow cookies that are stored on your computer** option.

4. For each type of cookie, choose the option you prefer: **Enable** (the default), **Disable** (which prevents Internet Explorer 5 from setting any cookies), or **Prompt** (which displays a dialog box that allows you to accept or reject each cookie request).

5. Click **OK** to save the new settings.

If you configure Internet Explorer to prompt you before accepting a cookie, be prepared to deal with dialog boxes such as the one shown in Figure 18.7. (Click the **More Info** button to see exactly what's in that cookie.) Many times you can click **No** without adversely affecting the operation of the Web site in question.

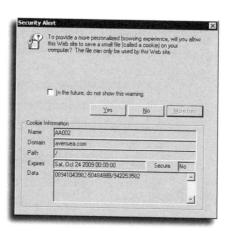

FIGURE 18.7
Configure Internet Explorer to warn you before it accepts a cookie; the **More Info** button lets you see the contents of the proposed cookie file.

Handling ActiveX Programs Safely

By far the most controversial feature of Internet Explorer is its support for *ActiveX controls*—small programs that run in the browser window and enable you to display content that ordinary HTML can't handle. With the help of an ActiveX control, a Web page can display cascading menus, stock calculators, and charts, and it can even display live streaming video.

The same thing that makes ActiveX controls powerful also makes them potentially dangerous. Unlike most programs, which require that you download and save a file before running it, ActiveX controls download and installs automatically when needed. Depending on your security settings, Internet Explorer may refuse to install ActiveX add-ins, or you may have to click a confirming dialog box.

Commercial publishers and Web site developers use digital *certificates* to sign ActiveX controls so that you can be certain that the program comes from a safe source. When you open a Web page that includes a signed ActiveX control, you see a Security Warning dialog box like the one shown in Figure 18.8.

What makes ActiveX dangerous?
ActiveX programs offer a direct connection between your Web browser and files on your hard disk. In theory, an ActiveX program can tamper with data stored on your hard drive without your knowledge. In practice, this is highly unlikely, especially if you're vigilant with ActiveX controls you download and run. Signed ActiveX controls pose a very low security risk for the average Internet user.

FIGURE 18.8
Click the links in this dialog box to learn more about an ActiveX add-in before installing it.

Click **Yes** to allow the program to install itself on your computer, or click **No** if you don't want the program to install.

If you set the Internet zone to the High security level, or if you set up custom security levels with tight controls over ActiveX security, Internet Explorer will download the prohibited control but refuse to install it. Instead, you will see an error message like the one shown in Figure 18.9.

FIGURE 18.9
You see this dialog box
anytime you encounter
an unsigned ActiveX
control. If you've
enabled the High secu-
rity level, all ActiveX
add-ins are disabled.

Using Java Applets Safely

Java applets are browser add-ins that download and run each time
you access a particular Web page. The security settings for Java
applets prohibit them from interacting with your local hard disk and
or shared network drives, and you can't install them permanently, as
you can ActiveX controls. When you've finished with the applet, it
disappears from memory, and the next time you access the page you
have to repeat the download.

Like ActiveX controls, Java applets make it possible for you to view
types of data that you normally can't see in a browser window with
HTML code. Unlike ActiveX add-ins, however, Java applets run in a
virtual machine within your browser, with strict security rules to
define what they can and can't do.

Internet Explorer's Security Settings dialog box lets you control how
Java programs interact with your browser. You can assign ready-
made Low, Medium, or High options to Java applets, for example. In
general, the default security settings are perfectly safe for Java programs.

Setting Scripting Options

Internet Explorer allows Web designers to add *scripts* to pages, using
two well-known Web languages, *JavaScript* and *VBScript*. With the
help of scripts, a designer can create pages that calculate expressions,
ask questions (and record your answers), check data that you enter in
forms, link to other programs, and respond when you click buttons.

If you make it a practice to keep Windows and your browser updated
with the most recent security patches, the security risks posed by
scripts are slight. If you don't want to allow scripts to run at all, open
the Security Settings dialog box (described earlier in this chapter)
and disable the **Active scripting** option.

Do you trust Microsoft?

The most popular source of
ActiveX programs is (sur-
prise!) Microsoft. If you
don't want to be prompted
every time you encounter a
Microsoft ActiveX program,
check the **Always trust
content from Microsoft
Corporation** box at the
bottom of the Security
Warning dialog box. In fact,
you can use this option
with any publisher—if
you're confident that a publisher produces safe, high-
quality software, you can
bypass a few dialog boxes.

How do they do that?

Curious about how a Web
page is put together? You
can get a pretty good idea
by viewing the source code
for the page, which typi-
cally includes the scripts
that make the page and
any buttons and other controls work. Pull down the
View menu and choose
Source to see the HTML
code, complete with
scripting.

401

Using Ratings to Block X-Rated Content

Not every site on the Internet is worth visiting. Some, in fact, are downright offensive. That can represent a problem at home, where children run the risk of accidentally stumbling across Web sites devoted to pornography, violence, and other inappropriate content. It's also potentially a problem at the office, where offensive or inappropriate content can expose you or your business to legal liability in the form of sexual harassment suits.

Internet Explorer includes a feature called the Content Advisor, which uses a rating system (much like the one used in the United States with movies) to restrict the types of content that can be displayed within your browser window. By default the Content Advisor is off; you have to enable it before you can use it. Even then, you may find that it allows you and other users to see objectionable sites.

Using the Content Advisor

1. Pull down the **Tools** menu, choose **Internet Options**, and click the **Content** tab.
2. Click the **Enable** button in the Content Advisor section.
3. In the Content Advisor window (see Figure 18.10), use the slider controls to define acceptable levels of sex, violence, language, and nudity. These ratings will be matched against ratings on the Web pages themselves.

Better options

The chief advantage of the Content Advisor is that it's free with Internet Explorer. However, it works so poorly that it's hard to recommend. Third-party software does a much better job of keeping the uglier side of the Internet at bay. Try Net Nanny (http://www.netnanny.com) as a solution for home use; for businesses, most firewall programs offer features that can help restrict access to specific sites and keep a log of all sites that users visit.

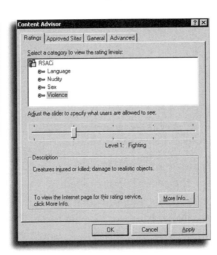

FIGURE 18.10
Use the Content Advisor's ratings system to restrict access to Web sites that contain unacceptable content.

4. Enter a supervisor's password when prompted. Don't forget this password—you must supply it to change or disable Content Advisor later.

5. Click the **Approved Sites** tab to enter the names of sites that you want to allow users to view. Despite the misleading name, you can also enter sites that you want to prevent users from browsing, regardless of their rating.

6. If you want to allow users to view unrated sites, click the **General** tab and check the <u>U</u>sers can see sites that have no rating box.

7. Click **OK** to save your changes. Exit and restart Internet Explorer to make the changes effective.

Surprisingly, many adult-oriented sites (that is, those that focus on sex, gambling, and other controversial topics) adhere to the rating system. An increasing number of mainstream business sites have added the necessary HTML tags to their sites as well. Unfortunately, many popular business and commercial sites don't use these ratings; as a result, you'll almost certainly want to set the option to allow users to view unrated sites.

When you encounter a page that contains content not allowed by the Content Advisor, you see a dialog box like the one shown in Figure 18.11. Click **Cancel** to go back to the previous page, or enter the supervisor's password and select one of the options in the bottom of the dialog box to allow the specific page (or the entire Web site) to be viewed.

FIGRE 18.11
When Content Advisor is enabled, you see this dialog box all too frequently.

Changing Your Start Page

Netscape takeover?

When you install Netscape Communicator version 4.6 or later using the default options, it takes over your home and search pages, even in Internet Explorer! To reset the default home and search pages, open the Internet Options dialog box, click the **Programs** tab, and click the **Reset Web Settings** button.

Every time you start Internet Explorer, it loads the page you designate as your *home page*. The default home page is Microsoft's MSN.com, but you can designate any Web page as your home page. Some people prefer a Web portal, such as Yahoo or Excite; if your company has a well-developed intranet, on the other hand, you may prefer to set a local page to load automatically at startup.

To reset your home page, first load the page you want to use. Then pull down the **Tools** menu, choose **Internet Options** and click the **General** tab. Click **Use Current** to set the current page as your home page. If you have a particularly slow dial-up connection, you might want to use a blank page as your home page because it loads instantly, with or without an active Web connection. Click the **Use Blank** to set this option.

Changing Fonts, Colors, and Other Browser Options

Help!

If your eyes are over 40, you may have trouble making out the tiny text in Help windows. Because Help screens actually use Internet Explorer as their viewer, you can tweak some settings to make things a little easier to read. From Internet Explorer, pull down the **View** menu, choose **Text Size**, and choose **Larger** instead of the default **Medium**. This setting makes Help text much easier to read, although it also changes the look of Web pages, unfortunately.

On most commercial Web sites, the designer of a Web page specified the size, position, color, font, and other attributes that control the appearance of each page. You can change the appearance of some elements on Web pages, but only when they use standard *HTML tags*. You can specify fonts and colors you prefer when viewing basic Web pages, for example.

The primary benefit of adjustments in the appearance of Web pages is for people who have physical disabilities that make it difficult to read the screen. To adjust any of these settings, pull down the **Tools** menu, choose **Internet Options**, and then click the **General** tab.

To change colors on standard Web pages, click the **Colors** button. As you can see in Figure 18.12, the Colors dialog box gives you only a few options. By default, Internet Explorer uses the standard Windows colors for text and backgrounds on basic Web pages; with the Standard Windows settings (defined using Control Panel's Display option), that means black text on a white page.

SEE ALSO

➤ *For help adjusting colors in Windows, see "Changing Fonts and Colors Used Throughout Windows," p. 174.*

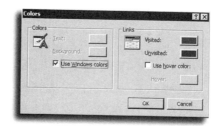

FIGURE 18.12
You can adjust the colors Internet Explorer uses for hyperlinks, but that's about all.

To adjust the default fonts used on standard Web pages, click the **Fonts** button. As Figure 18.13 shows, you can select from a limited assortment of fonts for use on Web pages and in text files displayed in a browser window. This is not the place, however, to change the size that Internet Explorer uses for basic Web pages. For that task, pull down the **View** menu and choose from any of the options in the **Text Size** menu.

Try a new hover color

Of all the color settings in Internet Explorer, the **Use hover** color option is the most interesting. If you have trouble picking out a hyperlink when the mouse passes over it, change this color to bright red. You'll never miss another link.

FIGURE 18.13
The alternate fonts you choose here apply only to the most basic Web pages.

Changing all Web pages

When you change default fonts and colors for Internet Explorer, your changes don't apply to heavily designed pages with specified fonts and sizes. To make these pages use your fonts, click the **Accessibility** button on the General tab of the Internet Options dialog box and check the appropriate boxes to tell the browser to ignore colors, font styles, and font sizes specified in the page design. This is a radical change, however, and on some pages the result is literally unreadable.

Customizing Toolbars and the Browser Window

Sometimes, parts of the browser window get in the way of data, especially when your display is running at a low resolution (800×600 or less). By hiding, rearranging, and reconfiguring these parts of the Internet Explorer interface, you can make more space available for data in the browser window.

The simplest way to grab a little extra space is to hide the toolbars and status bar. To hide the status bar, pull down the **View** menu and uncheck **Status Bar**; to eliminate one or more of the built-in toolbars, pull down the **View** menu and clear the check marks to the left of **Standard Buttons**, **Address Bar**, **Links**, or **Radio**.

You can rearrange any of the toolbars, placing them side by side or one on top of the other. To move a toolbar, click the raised handle at the left, and then drag the toolbar to its new position. Drag the same handle from right to left to adjust the width of the toolbar.

You can also change the size and labels on toolbar buttons. Larger buttons are easier to read, small ones leave more room for data in the browser window, and labels just take up space. To change the look of the built-in toolbars, pull down the **View** menu, choose **Toolbars**, and click the **Customize** option. In the Customize Toolbar dialog box (see Figure 18.14), use the **Text options** list to choose a treatment for labels; the **Icon Options** list lets you choose large or small icons.

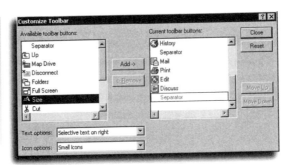

The menu is a toolbar

In Internet Explorer 5, the menu bar is actually just another toolbar. As a result, you can position any toolbar to the right of the menu bar to save a little space.

FIGURE 18.14
Use this dialog box to change the size, shape, and arrangement of icons on the Standard toolbar of Internet Explorer 5.

Unlike previous versions of Internet Explorer, you can also rearrange the buttons that appear on the Standard toolbar. Use the **Add** and **Remove** buttons, for instance, to move buttons from the **Available toolbar buttons** list at left to the **Current toolbar buttons** list at right.

Want to get rid of all toolbars temporarily? Pull down the **View** menu and choose **Full Screen** (or press the keyboard shortcut, **F11**). This view hides the title bar, pull-down menus, and the Address bar. The Standard toolbar shrinks to its smallest setting, and even the minimize and close buttons in the upper-right corner adjust their size and position. To switch back to normal view, press **Esc** or click the **Full Screen** button again.

The toolbar that just won't die

Give the Links toolbar the starring role in a horror film, because it will not die, no matter how hard you try to get rid of it. If you delete the Links bar, Windows will re-create it the next time you start up. To put it out of sight, clear out its icons and uncheck its entry in the Toolbars list.

Of all Internet Explorer's toolbars, the least understood is the Links bar. The idea is to give you one-click access to the handful of sites you visit most frequently—like a super-selective version of the Favorites folder. When the Links toolbar is visible, its shortcuts are never more than a click away, and you can arrange them for fast, convenient access.

To show or hide the Links bar, right-click the menu bar or any visible toolbar and click **Links**. (If the Links bar is visible but is tucked all the way to the right of the Address bar, double-click the Links text to expand it to full width. Or, drag it to a new position below the Address bar if you want it to be always visible.)

When you first start Internet Explorer, there are only three shortcuts on the Links bar, including one that points to a tutorial page on how to customize the Links toolbar. Drag any shortcut onto the Links bar (from the Address bar or the Favorites folder, for example) to add it as a button; then drag buttons from left to right to rearrange them. To delete a button from this toolbar, right-click its icon and choose **Delete** from the shortcut menu.

> **Rename those links**
>
> The width of each button on the Links toolbar is defined by its label. The shorter the name, the more links you can see at one time. By default, each new shortcut you add to the Links bar uses the page title as its label. After adding a link, I routinely right-click, choose **Rename**, and replace the label text with a short, clearly identifiable label.

Using the Cache to Speed Up Web Access

What's the best way to improve the speed at which pages pop into your browser window? Make sure the browser's *cache* is correctly configured. Each time you retrieve a new Web page, Internet Explorer downloads every element and stores a copy of each one in a cache directory on your hard disk. The next time you load that page, the browser first checks the cache; if it finds a copy of the page, it loads the entire document from your hard drive, dramatically increasing performance.

When the cache fills up, Internet Explorer throws out old files in the cache to make room for new ones. To increase the likelihood that you'll be able to load a cached copy of a page instead of having to wait for it to reload from the Internet, adjust the size of the cache. Pull down the **Tools** menu, choose **Internet Options**, and click the **General** tab (see Figure 18.15) to find all the controls you need to fine-tune the Web cache.

FIGURE 18.15
By increasing the size of the browser cache, you can make Internet Explorer load Web pages faster.

Get up-to-date

In the case of Web pages that update frequently, such as news headlines or stock quotes, you'll want to make sure you're always seeing the most recent version. To force Internet Explorer to load a fresh copy of the current Web page without checking the cache, hold down the **Ctrl** key as you click the **Refresh** button.

- The options at the top of the Settings dialog box allow you to control how often Internet Explorer checks the date and time stamped on the Web page against the date on the cached page. Choosing the **Never** option improves performance dramatically, but it greatly increases the risk you'll see an out-of-date page.

- To make the cache larger or smaller, move the slider labeled **Amount of disk space to use.**

- Click the **View Files** button to see all the files in the cache. You can delete them individually from this window or return to the Internet Options dialog box and click the **Delete Files** button to completely empty the cache.

chapter

19

Managing Email with Outlook Express

Should You Use Outlook Express?   ●

Setting Up Outlook Express   ●

Sending and Receiving Mail   ●

Reading Messages in
Outlook Express   ●

Managing Mail with Folders, Rules,
and Views   ●

Composing New Messages   ●

Organizing the Address Book   ●

Backing Up and Restoring Your
Messages and Address Book   ●

Should You Use Outlook Express?

Outlook Express is the free email client included with Windows 2000 and Internet Explorer 5. Unlike Outlook 2000, the full-featured email and contact-management program that comes with Office 2000, Outlook Express does a limited number of things reasonably well.

If your email requirements are relatively undemanding, you should find Outlook Express more than adequate. In fact, because it does such a good job with Internet-standard email and includes a surprisingly powerful message rules feature, even demanding email users may choose to use it.

If you currently use another email program, should you switch to Outlook Express?

- If you use nothing but standard Internet mail accounts, you can safely switch to Outlook Express, although you don't need to do so. Windows 2000 will work perfectly well with other email client software.

- Do you use Web-based email accounts? Outlook Express can retrieve email from Microsoft Hotmail servers, but not from other Web-based email systems.

- If your corporate email works through a *Microsoft Exchange* server, you must use an Exchange-compatible client program (such as Microsoft Outlook 2000), not Outlook Express.

Figure 19.1 illustrates the basic elements of the Outlook Express interface, which I'll touch on throughout this chapter.

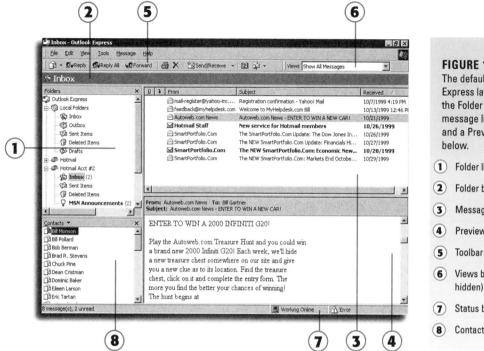

FIGURE 19.1
The default Outlook
Express layout includes
the Folder list at left, the
message list at top right,
and a Preview Pane
below.

① Folder list

② Folder bar

③ Message list

④ Preview Pane

⑤ Toolbar

⑥ Views bar (normally
    hidden)

⑦ Status bar

⑧ Contacts list

Setting Up Outlook Express

Before you can send and receive email with Outlook Express, you
must supply some basic configuration information—mail-server
names, your email address, and the username and password, for
starters.

If you're upgrading to Windows 2000 on a computer that includes
an existing email program, Outlook Express offers to import messages and addresses the first time you run the program. If Outlook
Express doesn't detect your installed mail program, you can still copy
your existing email messages, addresses, and settings; use the **Import**
choice on the **File** menu (you may need to run the import utility as
many as three times to grab messages, addresses, and mail settings).
As the dialog box shown in Figure 19.2 demonstrates, Outlook
Express can import data from an impressive array of programs,
including the widely used Eudora and Netscape programs, as well as
other Microsoft email programs.

No news

Outlook Express also
serves as a reader for
newsgroups—public
forums, available over the
Internet, devoted to the
discussion of a staggering
variety of topics. Most
people never use this feature, but if you want to
learn more about how
newsgroups work and how
Outlook Express can help
you work with them, you
should refer to an Outlook-
specific reference, such as
Gordon Padwick's *Special
Edition Using Microsoft
Outlook 2000*, published
by Que.

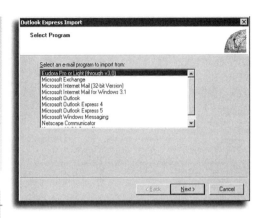

FIGURE 19.2
When switching to Outlook Express, use this wizard three times— once to import messages, once to copy over contact information, and finally to import mail settings.

Your old data is still there

When you import messages or addresses from another program, the original data remains intact. You can continue to use your previous email program; however, any messages you download into that program will not be available in Outlook Express. Likewise, any changes you make in either program's address book will not appear in the other's.

By any other name…

Most people enter their real name in this box, but you don't have to—you can enter any name you choose in this field. If you have multiple email accounts, you may want to add a company affiliation or other information as part of your display name so that mail recipients can identify your messages. If you're trying to remain anonymous, enter a pseudonym here—there's no technical or legal reason to enter your real name.

Setting Up an Email Account

When you first run Internet Explorer on a fresh copy of Windows 2000, the Internet Connection Wizard offers to set up Outlook Express. If you skip this step, the Internet Connection Wizard runs automatically the first time you try to use Outlook Express. Why is the wizard so persistent? Because setting up your main email account is a crucial first step before you can use Outlook Express, and the wizard is the only tool you can use to set up an account.

If you've used the Escape key to bypass the new account wizard, you can always start it manually. Pull down the **Tools** menu and choose **Accounts**. Then, in the Internet Accounts dialog box, click the **Add** button and choose **Mail** from the cascading menu. The Internet Connection Wizard asks you to fill in the following four blocks of information:

- **Your Name.** This is the display name that recipients see in the From box for messages you send.

- **Your Email Address.** Enter your email address. When recipients reply to messages you send, this is the address their mail software will use, unless you specify a different address in the Reply to field, as described in the next section.

- **Server Names.** In this step of the wizard (see Figure 19.3), choose the server type (typically *POP3*) and enter the names of the servers that handle incoming and outgoing mail for your account. If you're setting up an existing Hotmail account, choose the HTTP option and the wizard will automatically fill in the other fields in this step.

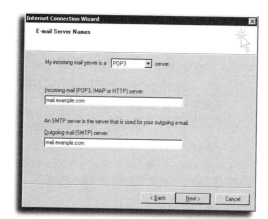

FIGURE 19.3
Enter names for the servers that handle your incoming and outgoing mail. In many cases, one name identifies both servers.

One server or two?

To make life simpler for users, many Internet service providers use the same name for incoming and outgoing mail servers. You must fill in an address for each server, even if the name is identical.

- **Logon Information.** In the Internet Mail Logon step (see Figure 19.4), fill in the Account Name and Password boxes. This combination is not necessarily the same as the username and password you use to log on to your computer. Do not check the Secure Password Authentication option unless you are setting up an email account on The Microsoft Network (msn.com).

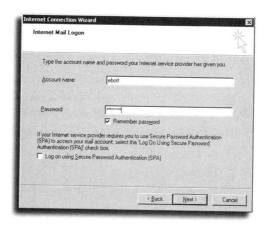

FIGURE 19.4
Leave this password box blank if you want to keep other users from accessing your mail. Outlook Express will ask for your password each time you connect to the server.

Click **Finish** to close the wizard and save your changes. If you need to specify any further settings for the account, follow the instructions in the next section to configure other settings manually.

Working with Multiple Mail Accounts

Outlook Express lets you use more than one mail account—in fact, there's no theoretical limit to the number of accounts you can create and use. Many people have separate personal and business email accounts, for example. After setting up the first mail account, you can configure additional mail accounts by pulling down the **Tools** menu and choosing **Accounts**. In the Account dialog box (see Figure 19.5), click the **Add** button, choose **Mail**, and run through the relevant portions of the Internet Connection Wizard again.

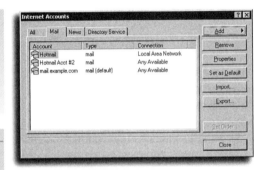

FIGURE 19.5
Click the **Mail** tab to see which of several mail accounts is set up as the default.

The first mail account you create becomes the default account—the server that Outlook Express uses when sending messages. To choose a different mail account as your default, select the account in the Accounts dialog box and click the **Set as Default** button.

Customizing Your Mail Accounts

To change the settings for a mail account after you've set it up using the Internet Connection Wizard, pull down the **Tools** menu, choose **Accounts**, and click the **Mail** tab. Select the entry you want to change and click the **Properties** button.

- Click the **General** tab (see Figure 19.6) to change the friendly name of an account—the name that appears in the Accounts list and on the menus you use to send and receive mail. By default, Outlook Express uses the name of the mail server as the account name. Instead of referring to `mail.example.com`, I prefer to see an account listed as `Ed's personal mail`.

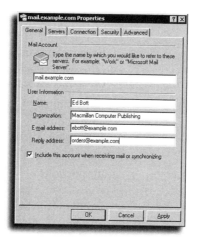

FIGURE 19.6
Edit the Reply Address field if you want to receive replies at an address other than the one from which you send messages.

- Also on the **General** tab, you can change the reply address for an account. This can be useful if you send a message using your corporate mail account but prefer to receive replies via your personal Internet mail account. In that case, enter the personal address into the Reply address box; when recipients reply to your message, their mail software should automatically insert the address you specified.

- To change your username or password, click the **Servers** tab (see Figure 19.7) and fill in the appropriate field.

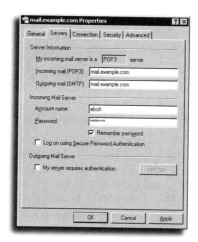

FIGURE 19.7
If you change the password for your email account, click here to change the saved setting in Outlook Express.

■ Click the **Advanced** tab to see a variety of advanced server settings. In general, I recommend that you avoid changing the server configuration unless specifically instructed to do so by the server's administrator.

Configuring Your Internet Connection

For each Outlook Express account, you can specify how you prefer to connect to the Internet—over a network or via a particular dial-up connection. By default, Outlook Express uses the same connection settings as those you specify for Internet Explorer. If your computer is permanently connected to a network with Internet access, you can set all your accounts for LAN access and be done with it. But if you use a dial-up Internet connection, especially from a portable computer, you should pay close attention to these settings.

SEE ALSO

➤ *For details on configuring dial-up settings with Internet Explorer, see "Creating a Dial-Up Internet Connection," p. 356.*

If you use dial-up connections, I recommend that you adjust connection properties immediately after you create a new account. From the **Tools** menu, choose **Accounts**, select the account name, and click **Properties**. Click the **Connection** tab to display the dialog box shown in Figure 19.8.

Location, location, location

If you dial in to one server and try to send mail through a server at another ISP, you will almost certainly receive an error message. Most ISPs today won't send your mail unless you make a connection to their network with your username and password. That security setting keeps unauthorized users from hijacking the server to send *spam*. If you must use that outgoing server, be sure to dial in to that ISP. If you connect to another ISP, you can still receive mail from any POP3 server, but you must choose the authorized server for all outgoing messages.

FIGURE 19.8
With this configuration, Outlook Express automatically dials a specific Internet connection whenever you send and receive mail from that account.

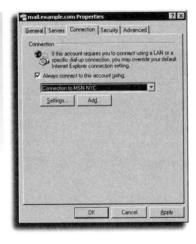

By default, each account dials up using the systemwide settings in Internet Explorer. Check the **Always connect to this account using** box on the Connection tab to tell Outlook Express you always want to use a specific dial-up connection for that account.

Sending and Receiving Mail

The process of sending and receiving email is completely under your control. Mail servers don't just seek out your computer and begin transferring messages automatically. Instead, you have to send a request to the server to send and receive messages. You can configure Outlook Express to send the "get my mail" request at regular intervals, or you can click a button to send and receive messages when you're connected and ready.

Delivering the Mail Manually

To check for mail immediately, click the **Send/Receive** button on the standard toolbar. This button automatically connects with every mail account you've set up. Of course, you may not want to check every account, every time. For instance, I've set up a Hotmail account to receive messages from several mailing lists I belong to, and I only want to check this account once a week or so. To avoid having to connect to the Hotmail server every time I check my work mail, I removed that account from the list of servers to be checked automatically.

Setting a mail account for manual access only

1. Pull down the **Tools** menu, choose **Accounts**, click the **Mail** tab, and select the account from the list.

2. Click the **Properties** button to display the account's dialog box.

3. Click the **General** tab and uncheck the **Include this account when receiving mail or synchronizing** box. This setting tells Outlook Express you do not want to automatically check for messages when you click the **Send/Receive** button.

4. Click **OK** to make the change effective, and then close the Accounts dialog box.

> **Check whenever you want**
>
> You can manually send and receive mail even if you've configured Outlook Express to check for messages at regular intervals. If you've set Outlook Express to check your email once every two hours, for instance, but you know a co-worker just sent you a new message, click the **Send/Receive** button. You'll get any messages that are currently waiting for you, and Outlook Express will continue to check on its normal schedule.

If you have set up multiple mail accounts, you can connect with a single account manually, regardless of the connection settings for that account. Pull down Outlook Express's **Tools** menu and choose **Send and Receive**. Look at the bottom of the cascading menu for the list of mail accounts you've set up. Choose any item from this list to exchange messages with that server.

Collecting Mail Automatically

If you have a full-time Internet connection, you don't have to remember to click the **Send/Receive** button to get your messages. Instead, set up Outlook Express to automatically check for new messages and send outgoing mail at regular intervals. By default, Outlook Express does this every 30 minutes. You can adjust this setting so you check for mail more or less frequently.

Retrieving email automatically

1. Pull down the **Tools** menu, choose **Options**, and click the **General** tab (see Figure 19.9).

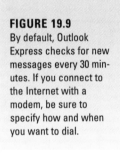

FIGURE 19.9
By default, Outlook Express checks for new messages every 30 minutes. If you connect to the Internet with a modem, be sure to specify how and when you want to dial.

2. Be sure that the **Check for New Messages Every** *x* **Minute(s)** box is checked.

3. Use the spinner control to adjust how often Outlook Express sends and receives mail. This number must be in the range of 1 (every minute) to 480 (every 480 minutes, or 8 hours).

4. If you use a dial-up Internet connection, choose one of the two **Connect** options under **If My Computer Is Not Connected at This Time**.

5. Click **OK** to make the change effective.

Regardless of how you check your email, Outlook Express provides two notices when you've received new mail. A letter icon appears among the icons at the right of the taskbar, and the program plays a sound. To turn off either notification, pull down the <u>T</u>ools menu, choose **Options**, click the **General** tab, and remove the check mark for that option.

SEE ALSO

➤ *To learn more about adjusting sounds associated with Windows 2000 events, see "Setting Sound and Multimedia Options," p. 49.*

Checking the Mail from Another Location

An obscure option buried deep in the Options dialog box lets you handle a common problem that arises when you want to check your email from a location other than the one you normally use.

Suppose you normally check email from your office PC, and you want that machine to have a complete record of all the messages you receive. If you check your email from your home computer, Outlook Express will delete the messages from the server and you'll end up with messages in two locations and no way to bring them together.

The solution? Change the account settings on your home PC so that it lets you read messages without deleting them from the mail server. Later, when you return to the office and check your email, Outlook Express will download all the messages, including the ones you read earlier at home. You must set this option for each account you check from home.

Pull down the <u>T</u>ools menu, choose **Accounts**, select the account, and click the **Properties** button. Click the **Advanced** tab, and then check the **Leave a Copy of Messages on Server** option, as shown in Figure 19.10.

> **How often is too often?**
> Some people swear that checking your email too often drags your productivity down because you're so busy reading messages and composing replies that you can't concentrate on your real work. They wouldn't last a day at the company I work for, where email is preferred to all other forms of communication. I check my messages every 10 minutes. If you and your co-workers don't require this sort of constant communication, but you still want to get urgent messages on a fairly timely basis, I recommend that you set Outlook Express to check your mail every 120 minutes, or 2 hours.

> **"You've got mail!"**
> You don't have to settle for a generic beep or ding when new mail arrives. To assign a different sound, open **Control Panel**, double-click the **Sounds and Multimedia** option, and assign a different .wav file to the New Mail Notification event.

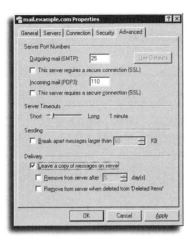

FIGURE 19.10
When you check your mail from a location other than your main computer, configure the account to leave messages on the server so that you can retrieve them later.

Do you want to avoid downloading unimportant messages when you return to the office? On the Advanced tab of the properties dialog box for the mail account, check the **Remove from server when deleted from Deleted Items** option. Don't let the confusing wording fool you: with this option checked, you can download messages from the server and delete the messages you don't want to preserve in your permanent email collection back at the office. To send the delete instructions to the mail server, be sure to empty the Deleted Items folder and then click the Send/Receive button again.

Reading Messages in Outlook Express

Block that click

I find the start page a nuisance that keeps me from getting straight to my messages. If you want to go directly to your messages list each time you start Outlook Express, wait until the start page appears again, and then check **When Outlook Express starts, go directly to my Inbox**.

To start Outlook Express, use its icon in the Quick Launch bar, on the Programs menu, or on Internet Explorer's standard toolbar. Normally, Outlook's Web-style start page (see Figure 19.11) is the first stop. Click the **Read Mail** hyperlink to display the messages list.

All new messages come into the Inbox. When you display the contents of the Inbox, you should see a screen like the one shown in Figure 19.12.

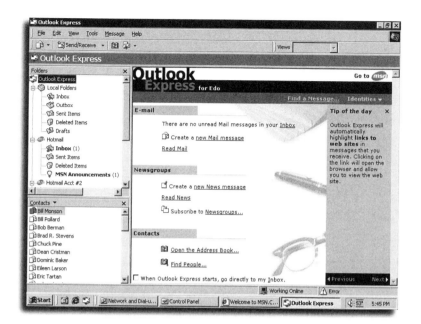

FIGURE 19.11
From this start page, you can jump to your Inbox, find a message, or search for address information.

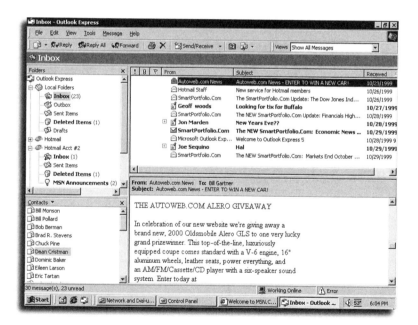

FIGURE 19.12
Use this view to quickly scan through all the messages in your Inbox and other folders. Messages you haven't read yet appear in bold.

The Folder list includes the default mail folders, any additional folders you've created, icons for any Hotmail accounts you've created, and icons for any news servers and newsgroups to which you've subscribed. Click any folder icon to display its contents in the message list at right, with each message in its own row. Unread messages are in bold. Below the message list is a Preview Pane that shows the contents of the currently selected message.

Changing the Layout

To alter the basic look of Outlook Express, open the **View** menu and choose **Layout**. The Window Layout Properties dialog box (see Figure 19.13) lets you show or hide eight parts of the Outlook Express screen, including the folder bar, the Folder list, and the Preview Pane. (The message list is always visible; there's no way to make it disappear.)

You can clear out some elements of the Outlook Express interface without opening this dialog box. If you don't want the Contacts folder taking up space, for instance, you can clear it off the screen by clicking the **X** in the upper-right corner. To restore the Contacts folder, however, you must use the dialog box.

If you use Outlook 2000 on one computer and Outlook Express on another, you can make the interfaces more closely resemble one another by replacing the Folder list with the Outlook Bar.

Sort by any column heading

To sort the contents of the message list, click any column heading. To add or remove columns and change the order of those that are displayed, pull down the **View** menu and choose **Columns**. Click the border between two column headings and drag to adjust column widths.

One-click shortcuts

If you want to make it easy to show or hide certain parts of the Outlook Express interface, try adding toolbar buttons for the pieces you're interested in. Pull down the **View** menu, choose **Layout**, and click the **Customize Toolbar** button. You can add buttons that show and hide the Preview Pane, the Contacts list, and the Folder list, for example.

FIGURE 19.13
Use these options to change the arrangement of the Outlook Express interface.

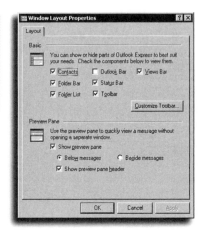

Using the Preview Pane

The fastest way to read all the messages in your Inbox is in the Preview Pane. When this pane is visible, Outlook Express displays the contents of the currently selected message here, without requiring that you open the message. Several options in the Window Layout Properties dialog box allow you to change the appearance of this pane.

To change the size of the Preview Pane, point to the bar between the message list and the Preview Pane. When the mouse pointer turns to a double-headed arrow, click and drag.

Each entry in the message list appears first in bold to indicate you haven't read it yet. If you allow the message to appear in the Preview Pane for more than a few seconds, Outlook Express assumes you've read it and clears the bold formatting. If you're a speed-reader and flash through messages in the Preview Pane quickly, you may find that messages you've read remain marked as unread. That's because the default setting waits until the message has been in the Preview Pane for 5 seconds before clearing the bold formatting. To fix this behavior, pull down the **Tools** menu and choose **Options**. On the **Read** tab, find the Mark Message Read After Displaying for *n* Seconds box and use the spinner to change the value to one or two seconds instead.

Opening Individual Messages

Double-click any item in the message list to open it in its own window, as shown in Figure 19.14.

Unlike the Preview Pane, which forces you to view the message contents in a small window, you can maximize a message window to see as much of its contents as possible. In fact, you can manage messages and navigate through the entire message list from a single message window.

- To print or delete the current message, click the respective buttons on the message window toolbar.

- To move to the next or the previous message in the list, click the up or down arrow on the toolbar.

One-touch viewing

Use the spacebar for the absolute fastest viewing of messages in the Preview Pane. If the current message is larger than what will fit in the Preview Pane, pressing the spacebar scrolls through the message. Keep pressing the spacebar to read more of the message. When you reach the end, pressing the spacebar goes to the next message in the list. By tapping the spacebar repeatedly, you can work through even a crowded Inbox without having to touch the mouse or any other keys.

Clear the list as you read

Want to see only new messages? If you speed through the message list using the Preview Pane, filter the message list first so that it shows only those messages you haven't yet read. Start with the **View** menu and choose **Current View**, then **Unread Messages**. Press the spacebar to move to the first unread message and begin reading. Keep clicking the spacebar until you've worked your way through every unread message. Switch to another view to see messages you've already read.

- To move to the next unread message in the list, skipping over any messages you've previously read, press **Ctrl+U**.

- Tired of scrolling through long messages? Pull down the **View** menu, choose **Text Size**, and select **Smaller** instead of the default Medium size. (Or make the text larger if you're having trouble focusing.)

- To move or copy a message to a folder, pull down the **File** menu and choose **Move To Folder** or **Copy to Folder**.

FIGURE 19.14
When reading messages in a window, use the up and down arrows to avoid having to return to the message list.

Button, button...
If you use folders to keep your messages organized, customize the single-message window for easier access to folders. Open a message in its own window, pull down the **View** menu, choose **Toolbar**, and click **Customize**. Select the **Move To** and **Copy To** buttons from the pane on the left and click the **Add** button to move them onto the standard toolbar. Click **Close** to save your changes.

Managing Mail with Folders, Rules, and Views

Even a casual Outlook Express user can quickly amass a collection of hundreds of messages. Email fanatics can easily end up with thousands, even tens of thousands of messages on hand. How do you get a handle on all those megabytes of mail? Start by using the same tools you use for files: organize related messages into folders. Then set up *message rules* that tell Outlook Express to process messages automatically as they arrive—deleting junk mail and moving other messages into folders by project or category. Finally, use custom *views* to filter the list of messages so that you can focus on the ones you need to work with right now.

Organizing Messages with Folders

By default, Outlook Express includes five top-level local folders, designed to let you manage mail on standard Internet servers. You cannot delete these basic mail folders, which perform the following crucial functions:

- Outlook Express places all incoming messages into the **Inbox** folder; as I explain in the following section, you can use rules to move messages from the Inbox into other folders automatically, as soon as they arrive.

- After you compose a new message and click the **Send** button, Outlook Express saves it in the **Outbox** folder until the next time you connect to your mail server.

- Every time you successfully send a message, Outlook Express saves a copy in the **Sent Items** folder.

- When you delete a message, Outlook Express moves it to the **Deleted Items** folder, which works much like the Recycle Bin handles files. If you discover that you inadvertently deleted a crucial message, you can often recover it from this folder.

- In some cases, you may begin composing a message but get interrupted before you can finish it. When that happens, choose **Save** from the **File** menu (or use the **Ctrl+S** shortcut). Outlook Express saves the partial message in the **Drafts** folder. Double-click this message item when you're ready to resume working.

You can add an unlimited number of folders and subfolders to Outlook Express.

Creating a new folder

1. If the Folders list is not visible, pull down the **View** menu and choose **Layout**; then check the **Folder list** box and click **OK**.

2. Select the folder in which you want to create the new subfolder. To create a new top-level folder at the same level as the Inbox and other local folders, click the Outlook Express icon at the top of the Folders list.

3. Right-click the icon you selected and choose **New Folder** from the shortcut menu.

Hotmail is different

Hotmail accounts work a bit differently from local folders. They don't include a Drafts or Outbox folder; when you compose new messages, those are saved in your local folders until you're ready to send them. Hotmail accounts include a Microsoft Announcements folder, which (naturally) contains official announcements from Microsoft and can't be deleted. Also, you can't empty the Deleted Items folder from a Hotmail account within Outlook Express; you must go to the Hotmail Web site to perform that chore.

Emptying the trash

Normally, Outlook Express lets the Deleted Items folder grow to fill up as much room as you have spare room on your hard disk. If you'd prefer to keep this folder from getting too large, open the Options dialog box, click the **General** tab, and check the **Empty messages from the Deleted Items folder on exit** box.

4. In the Create Folder dialog box (see Figure 19.15), enter a name for the folder. If you made a mistake when selecting the location in step 2, use the tree-style folder list in this dialog box to change the location in which the new folder will be created.

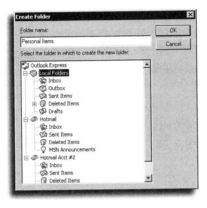

FIGURE 19.15
Use the **Create Folder** dialog box to create a folder or subfolder in any location.

5. Click **OK** to create the new folder.

To move messages between folders, drag the message icons from the message list and drop them onto the folder icon in the Folders list. To copy messages to a folder but leave the original file intact, hold down the **Ctrl** key as you drag.

If you use folders extensively, you may find it easier to select one or more messages first, and then use right-click shortcut menus to move and copy them. Using the shortcut menus is especially effective when you want to create a new folder on-the-fly.

Defining Rules for Processing Mail

If you work in an organization that is firmly committed to email, you may receive dozens or even hundreds of messages every day. (Imagine how many messages Bill Gates must receive, even if you filter out the threats and complaints from random crazies.) Managing that raging torrent of messages can be a full-time job—which is unfortunate if you already have a full-time job. Why not enlist Outlook Express to do at least part of the work of sorting your mail? The secret is to define rules for Outlook Express to follow when you receive new mail.

Managing folders

To move a folder and all the messages it contains to a new location, open the Folders list and drag the folder icon. Use the right-click shortcut menus to delete or rename a folder. When you delete a folder, you actually move it and its contents to the Deleted Items folder. Naturally, you can't move, rename, or delete the default local folders.

To define rules that automate mail processing, pull down the **Tools** menu, choose **Message Rules**, and select **Mail** from the cascading menu. If this is the first time you've used this feature, you'll jump straight to the New Mail Rule dialog box shown in Figure 19.16.

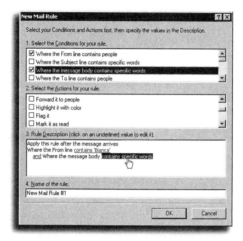

FIGURE 19.16
To create a message rule, first define one or more condition, and then select an action to be performed when a new message meets that condition.

Each rule consists of a set of criteria and a matching action. Whenever a message arrives in your Inbox, Outlook Express compares it with the conditions defined in your entire collection of mail-handling rules; when it finds a match, it performs the action defined for that rule. To create a new rule, make selections and fill in the blanks in the following four numbered areas of the New Mail Rule dialog box.

1. **Select the Conditions for your rule.** Check the box or boxes that correspond to the *conditions* you want to use for the rule. Don't worry about the details—you'll get to those shortly. For now, choose from conditions such as the following:

   - Search for text in any part of the address or in the subject line.

   - Look for messages that come through a specific mail account.

   - Check the size of each incoming message or check for the presence of an attachment (handy if you're using a slow Internet connection and you want to avoid having to download large attachments).

Mix and match

It's OK to select multiple conditions for a rule. In fact, multiple conditions make for especially powerful rules. You might want to check all incoming mails from your boss, for instance, and highlight them in bright red if they're addressed to you personally. If, on the other hand, your name is in the cc (courtesy copy) list, you could color the message a soothing blue or green.

Delete with care

Before using the Delete action, it's always a good idea to test a rule carefully for several days or weeks with an action such as moving messages to a folder. You may discover that the condition you defined accidentally snags messages you really want to read. After you're certain the message rule works properly, switch the action to Delete.

And? Or? Not?

Click the **Options** button to reverse a condition— where the message does not contain the text you entered, for example— or to specify that you want the condition to match all the words you typed rather than any of those conditions.

- Apply the rule to all incoming messages (useful as the last rule in the list, for handling messages that don't meet any other conditions).

2. **Select the <u>A</u>ctions for your rule.** Check the boxes that define, in general terms, what you want Outlook Express to do when it encounters a message that meets the preceding condition. For instance:

   - Move or copy the message to another folder, or delete it without reading.

   - Forward it to another recipient. If the message is from your boss and it's addressed to a particular mailing list, for example, you might want to forward it automatically to a co-worker who's helping with a project.

   - Reply automatically with a saved message; this action is useful when you're away from the office for a few days.

   - Leave the message on the server.

   - Delete the message from the server (useful when you know a message contains a large attachment that you don't want to download).

3. **Rule <u>D</u>escription.** As you check conditions and actions in steps 1 and 2, Outlook Express fills in the description here. When you see an underlined box, you need to supply additional details, such as the text to search for or the folder to which you want messages moved. Figure 19.17, for example, shows the dialog box you use to enter search text.

4. **<u>N</u>ame of the rule.** By default, each new rule gets a generic name; replace this with descriptive text that helps you understand what the rule actually does, and then click **OK** to save the rule.

Note that rules are applied in the order in which they appear in your list. If two or more conditions apply to the same message, Outlook Express may apply only the first rule. This type of conflict between rules can produce effects you didn't anticipate. Suppose you normally want to send messages that contain the words "for sale" to a Junk Mail folder. You'll be extremely embarrassed if this causes you to miss a message from your boss that reads: "I've just learned that our division is for sale. I need your help with the financials today!"

If you discover a conflict in rules, or if you need to edit a rule after creating it, pull down the **Tools** menu, choose **Message Rules**, and click **Mail**. Then use the Message Rules dialog box (see Figure 19.18) to modify existing rules, as needed.

FIGURE 19.17
Click an underlined item and supply more details for the rule description.

FIGURE 19.18
Make sure your most important message rules are at the top of the list.

Get rid of junk mail
One of the most effective uses of message rules is to delete items if the subject contains key junk-mail phrases ("make money fast," for example) or if the message was sent by someone from whom you don't want to receive mail (this feature is often called a "bozo filter").

The following is a sampling of some of the things you can do with the help of this dialog box:

- To adjust the order in which Outlook Express applies rules, select a rule from the list and click the **Move Up** or **Move Down** button.
- To delete a rule, select it and click **Remove**.
- To temporarily disable a rule without eliminating it, clear the check box to the left of its entry in the list.

Copy for a quick start

To create a new rule based on the settings in another rule, select the existing rule, click the **Copy** button, and then edit the new rule. This technique is particularly effective when you've defined multiple conditions for a rule, and you need to change the details of only one condition to create your new rule.

Spring cleaning

Message rules usually apply to incoming messages, but you can use them instead to clean up a cluttered mail folder. Suppose you want to clean up your Sent Items folder. Create a rule that deletes any message with an attachment. Leave the rule unchecked so that it does not work on incoming messages. Then open the list of rules, select the **Clean Up Attachments** rule, click the **Apply Now** button, and use the **Browse** button to pick your Sent Items folder in the Apply Mail Rules Now dialog box. When you click **OK**, Outlook Express processes all the messages in that folder and any subfolders and applies the action you specified to any messages with attachments.

- To change the conditions or actions associated with any rule, select its entry in the list and click the **Modify** button.

Composing New Messages

Outlook Express gives you many ways to compose a new message:

- Click the **New Message** button on the standard toolbar.
- Press **Ctrl+N**.
- Open a message you received and click the **Reply**, **Reply All**, or **Forward** button.
- Double-click any name in the Contacts list to open a new message window and fill in the email address associated with that record.
- Open an Explorer window, select any file or files, right-click, and choose **Send To Mail Recipient**; this action creates a blank mail message with the selected files as *attachments*.

In every case, you need to fill in some crucial details (in addition to the message text, of course) before you can actually send the message.

Filling in Message Fields

Naturally, you need to supply an email address if you expect Outlook Express to deliver your message to its destination. To accomplish this task, use any of the following techniques:

- Click the **To** button to open the Contacts list and choose from all the names in your Windows Address Book.
- Begin entering a name that appears in your Address Book. Outlook Express fills in the correct email address automatically if it recognizes a unique name from your address book. As Figure 19.19 shows, the AutoComplete portion of the name appears in blue. Continue typing to find the next matching name. If the name isn't immediately recognizable, you see a dialog box that asks you to select the correct name.

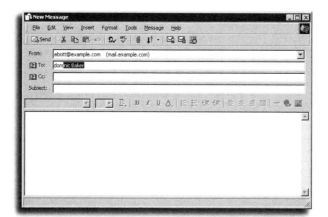

FIGURE 19.19
If you enter a name that's in your Address Book, Outlook Express fills in the complete address automatically.

- Enter a legal email address in the format *username@domain*. Outlook Express will try to deliver the message to the username you specify, even if that name is not listed in your Address Book.

After filling in the address fields, enter a Subject for your message. What makes a good subject? The text you enter here should be clear, concise, and above all, descriptive. "Meeting agenda" is much better than "Things to think about," for example. And "Dinner Saturday?" is a better subject line than "Hello!" Remember that the recipient of your message will see only the subject line in his or her Inbox; help convince them that the message is worth reading!

Finally, press the **Tab** key to move to the message body and begin entering the text of your message.

Two or more names

You can enter more than one email address in each of the three fields in a new message. Use commas or semicolons to separate multiple entries in address fields.

Choosing a Message Format

Each time you compose a message using Outlook Express, you must choose one of two message formats:

- Plain text, as the name implies, includes only letters and numbers, with absolutely no fonts, colors, pictures, or other fancy formatting.

- HTML, on the other hand, uses the same language as Web pages, allowing you to add colors and rich text formatting to each message.

If you're certain that most of your messages will go to people using Outlook Express (or other mail programs that can correctly decipher HTML messages), feel free to use HTML. Its rich text formatting can make your messages livelier and more readable. With HTML formatting, your messages look and behave like Web pages; you can specify fonts and their sizes, change text colors, use paragraph styles, and control text alignment. You can add background colors and graphics, bulleted and numbered lists, and hypertext links to other Web pages.

Sophisticated formatting is a wasted effort, however, if your correspondents use email software that can't interpret HTML. Instead, they see a plain text version of your message, along with a file attachment that they can open in a Web browser.

Unless you're certain that the overwhelming majority of your email recipients can handle HTML attachments, I recommend that you switch the default settings so that you send plain text mail messages.

Pull down the **Tools** menu, choose **Options**, and click the **Send** tab. You see the dialog box shown in Figure 19.20. In the Mail Sending Format box, select **Plain Text** as the default format for mail messages.

When is HTML OK?

If the people you correspond with most use Netscape mail products or recent versions of Eudora, they can send and receive HTML-formatted mail just fine. You may notice minor differences in the look of messages sent between Netscape and Microsoft mail programs, but the majority of formatting and all text should come across fine. If, however, you correspond with people who use Lotus Notes, avoid HTML like the plague.

FIGURE 19.20
Change these default settings or all your mail messages will go out in HTML format, even to people who can read only plain text.

Organizing the Address Book

Outlook Express saves email addresses using a separate program called the Windows Address Book. Each contact record includes fields that enable you to track additional details about a person, including home and business addresses and phone numbers. The Windows Address Book also lets you create group records so that you can send email to several individuals by entering an *alias* (Marketing Dept., for instance) instead of a lengthy list of addresses.

To create a new record from scratch in Outlook Express, pull down the **File** menu, and then click **New** and **Contact**. Fill in details about the new contact, starting on the **Personal** tab. As Figure 19.21 shows, you can enter more than one email address for a contact. In that case, choose one address and click the **Set as Default** button to tell Outlook Express you normally want to use that email address when you create a new message based on this record.

Address Book from anywhere

Although the Windows Address Book appears to be integrated into Outlook Express, it's actually a separate program. If you use the Address Book outside of Outlook Express, you may want to create a shortcut to this program (enter **Wab.exe** as the name of the executable file that runs the program) and place it on the Start menu or the Windows desktop.

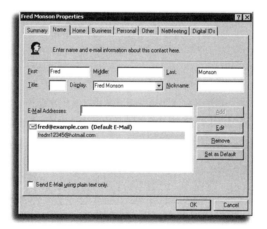

FIGURE 19.21
You can enter multiple email addresses in a contact record—personal and business addresses, for example.

A mailing group (also known as an *alias* or *distribution list*) lets you send messages to multiple people without having to enter each name in the message. When you enter the name of a mailing group into the address box of a message, Outlook Express substitutes the names that make up that group before sending the message.

Groups within groups

A mailing group doesn't have to contain names of people only; it can also contain names of other groups. Use this feature when you have a lot of turnover within a group and you want to avoid having to update multiple groups. For instance, you might create separate mailing groups for each department in your company: Accounting, Sales, Marketing, and so on. Then create an All Employees list consisting of those three department lists. When a new employee joins the company, you have to add the new person's name only to the department list; the master list will automatically be updated.

Creating a mailing group

1. Click the **Address Book** button to open the Address Book program.

2. Click the **New Group** button.

3. Enter a name for the mailing group in the Group Name box. Although a group name can legally be up to 255 characters long, I suggest you keep the name to 15 characters or fewer. The name may contain spaces and special characters.

4. Click the **Select Members** button. A dialog box containing names from your Address Book appears.

5. Click a name in the list and then click the **Select** button to add that person's entry to the list. Continue adding names individually, or hold down the **Ctrl** key to select more than one name at a time.

6. When you've finished adding names to the group, click **OK**.

7. Add notes about this group in the field at the bottom of the Group Properties dialog box, if you want, and then click **OK** to save the new group.

The easiest way to create new Contact records in your Windows Address Book is to copy the address from a message you receive. Open the message in its own window and right-click any name in the From, To, or CC fields; from the shortcut menu, choose **Add to Address Book.**

Backing Up and Restoring Your Messages and Address Book

How important is your collection of email messages and your address book? Priceless? Absolutely. So you'd think Windows 2000 would make it easy to back up and restore these crucial files, right?

Wrong. Outlook Express contains absolutely no easy way to back up your mail. In fact, the program goes out of its way to hide your messages so that you can't find them when you need to perform a backup. Outlook Express stores data in a hidden folder within a hidden folder. And even if you can figure out how to back up that data, there's no documented technique for restoring it.

At least once a month, I receive a panic-stricken message from someone who's lost all email, begging for the key to bring it all back. I usually can't help that person. Fortunately, I can help you, with the following procedure that can help you keep your email safe and sound.

Backing up Outlook Express

1. Open the **My Documents** folder (or any other folder that's easy to find and whose contents you regularly back up).

2. In the folder you just opened, create a new folder called `My Outlook Express Messages` (or another, equally descriptive name).

3. Open Outlook Express, pull down the **Tools** menu, and choose **Options**. Click the **Maintenance** tab of the Options dialog box, and then click the **Store Folder** button.

4. The Store Location dialog box appears, listing the current location of your mail files. Click the **Change** button to display the Browse for Folder dialog box.

5. Select the folder you created in step 3 from the dialog box and click **OK**.

6. Click **OK** in the Store Location dialog box. Click **OK** when you see the warning that you must shut down and restart Outlook Express to make the change effective.

7. Log off your Windows 2000 account and log back on again. Restart Outlook Express and note the dialog box that informs you it's copying the message files to a new location.

8. Pull down the **File** menu, choose **Export**, and select **Address Book**. Follow the wizard's instructions to back up your entire address book to a text file, and save it in the folder you created in step 2.

9. Close Outlook Express and perform a complete backup of the folder you created in step 2. Your data is now safely backed up and can be restored in the event of a disaster.

Back up now!

It's easy to turn the page and say that a data disaster will never happen to you. Unfortunately, no one is immune from trouble. It takes only a few minutes to set up your system so that your email files get backed up with the rest of your data. Do it today while you're thinking about it.

What's that long number?

Amazingly, Outlook Express stores your mail by default in a hidden folder that contains an incredibly long number. That number is your Security ID, or SID— a unique code that identifies your user account to Windows 2000. Don't even think of trying to type this address into a dialog box; instead, create a new folder with an easy-to-remember name, as described in this section.

Follow these instructions exactly!

The warning dialog box here says that you need to restart Outlook Express to make the change effective. That's wrong! Actually, you need to log off your user account in Windows 2000 and then log on again for this procedure to work properly.

If you need to restore your messages later, on this machine or on another one, start with an empty set of message files. Follow the preceding instructions to move those files to the folder specified in step 2. After you log on again, restart Outlook Express and make sure the empty files are moved. Then close Outlook Express and copy your backed-up files over the files you just moved. When you start up Outlook Express again, all your messages will be there waiting for you. Use the **Import** choice on the **File** menu to restore your Address Book, and you're in business again.

part

VI

APPENDIXES

Managing a Windows 2000 Computer

Setting Startup Options •

Managing Security Settings •

Managing Windows Services •

Creating Custom Management Consoles •

Adding and Removing
Windows Components •

Installing Patches and Updates •

Working with the Windows Registry •

Setting Startup Options

Do you have more than one operating system installed on your computer? If so, you can specify how long the menu of operating system choices remains visible when you power up your computer. You can also designate one operating system as the default operating system that starts up automatically if you don't make a choice in the allotted time.

SEE ALSO

➤ *To learn the dos and don'ts of multiple operating systems, see "Keeping Your Old Operating System," p. 32.*

To adjust either or both settings, open the **System** option in Control Panel, move to the **Advanced** tab, and click the **Startup and Recovery** button. Figure A.1 shows typical settings you might see in this dialog box.

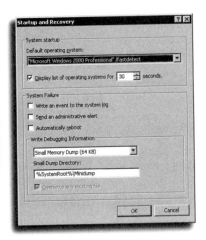

FIGURE A.1
To speed up logon time on a system that includes multiple operating systems, change the menu display time from the default of 30 seconds to a more reasonable 5 seconds.

By default, Windows starts up with the version of Windows you installed most recently. Choose from the drop-down **Default operating system** list to change to another operating system.

This dialog box also lets you set options that control what happens when Windows 2000 crashes with a blue screen. Normally, on the rare occasions when this occurs, you simply restart your system and get back to work. However, if you're having repeated problems with this type of error, a technical support specialist (at Microsoft or at your company) may ask you to adjust settings in the System Failure section so that you can capture debugging information in a file. I recommend that you leave these boxes unchecked unless someone specifically asks you to save the debugging information.

SEE ALSO

➤ *For step-by-step instructions on troubleshooting Windows startup problems, see "Recovering from Disaster," p. 289.*

Managing Security Settings

On any system running Windows 2000, your first line of defense from unwanted access to your files is the *user account database* and the permissions that are set on *NTFS*-formatted drives. To keep a computer secure, be sure you require that users log on with a username and password, and that you restrict access to specific files and folders using the Permissions tab. Beyond those crucial first steps, you can also restrict access to various features and capabilities of the operating system by using the Local Security Policy utility (see Figure A.2).

No startup menu?

If you install a single copy of Windows 2000 on your computer, Windows ignores the menu display time setting and skips past the menu completely, automatically loading Windows 2000 for you. To choose from other startup options, press **F8** when you see the Starting Windows 2000 bar running along the bottom of the display.

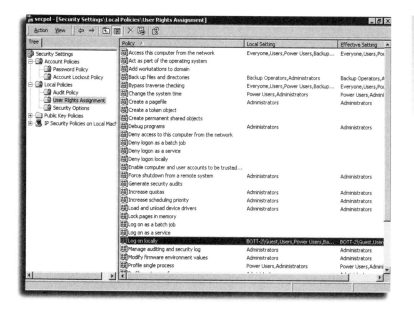

FIGURE A.2
To restrict what users can do on a computer, use the Local Security Policy utility.

Security settings available in this window appear in the following four groups:

- **Account Policies.** These settings define the rules users must follow when creating and managing passwords. For instance, by default all users must change their passwords every six weeks (42 days). This section also determines how many incorrect passwords users can enter before they're locked out of the computer.

- **Local Policies.** The 80+ options in this group define policies ranging from the highly technical to the extremely practical. Go through the User Rights Assignment subgroup to fine-tune what users can and can't do on the system—for example, you might allow only Administrators and Power Users to shut down the system.

- **Public Key Policies.** Contains specialized tools required for use with encrypted files. Most Windows 2000 Professional users will never use this feature.

- **IP Security Policies on Local Machine.** Contains advanced tools that enable you to control the flow of network traffic that uses the TCP/IP protocol.

Changing a Local Security Policy

1. Open the **Administrative Tools** group in Control Panel, select the **Local Security Policy** icon, right-click, and choose **Run as** from the shortcut menu. Enter the username and password of a member that belongs to the Administrators group and click **OK**. The Local Security Policy console opens.

2. In the tree pane at left, select the group of settings you want to work with.

3. In the right pane, double-click the entry for the permission you want to adjust. A Local Security Policy Setting dialog box like the one shown in Figure A.3 opens.

4. To remove a user or group from the setting, clear the check box to the right of its name.

5. To add a user or a group to the policy, click the **Add** button. In the Select Users or Groups dialog box (see Figure A.4), select the users or groups from the list at the top and click **Add** to move them to the bottom. Click **OK** to save your changes.

Domain settings always win

If you're a member of a Windows 2000 domain, you need to be aware of the interplay between domain and local security settings. If the network administrator sets up group policies for computers and user accounts within the domain, these policies will always override settings you make locally. Therefore, if you decide that it's fine for anyone in the Users group to reset the system clock, but the network administrator doesn't want them to have that right, the network policy will apply.

Don't mess with IP security

Although the IP Security Policies category appears in this dialog box with the other types of policies, this section is intended for use only by networking experts. The default settings are more than adequate for most users. Do not adjust the settings in this category unless you understand the full consequences of your actions. Randomly tinkering with settings here will not make you and your network safer; in fact, you could end up with a network that no longer works at all!

FIGURE A.3
Double-click any security setting to see which groups and users currently are assigned to that policy.

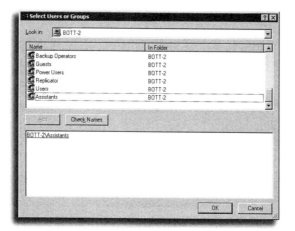

FIGURE A.4
Use this list to add users and groups to a system policy. The drop-down list at the top lets you choose users from the local computer (as shown in this example) or from a domain.

6. Repeat steps 3 through 5 for any other rights you want to adjust.

7. Close the Local Security Policy console to record your changes. Note that individual policies may not take effect until users log off and log back on.

After adjusting any security policy, I recommend that you do two things right away:

- Open the Local Security Policy console again to be certain the value in the Effective Setting column matches the one in the Local Setting column. If the settings are different, the problem may be a domain-based policy that is in conflict with the local policy.

■ Test the new policy carefully. If your objective is to allow some users to perform a certain action but not allow others to do so, log on using both types of accounts and make sure the policy is actually working.

Managing Windows Services

Administrators only

Although you do not need to be an Administrator to view the list of services, you must log on with administrative rights to adjust a service's properties.

Windows 2000 *services* are programs that run independent of a user account, usually to make essential system functions possible. Each time you start your computer, an assortment of services start up, and they remain running even when you log off, as long as the computer is turned on. The routines that allow computers to communicate over the network are services, as are the functions that allow users to print or fax. Windows 2000 includes a huge collection of its own services; in addition, third-party programs such as virus scanners and disk defragmenters may add their own.

To see a list of all services currently available on a Windows 2000 system, open the **Administrative Tools** group in Control Panel and double-click the **Services** icon. From this list (see Figure A.5), you can start, stop, pause, and configure any service.

FIGURE A.5
Services like these run independently of the currently logged-on user. This window lets you start, stop, and configure services.

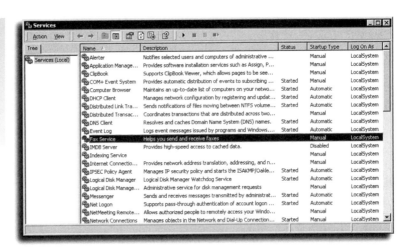

The columns in the Services window tell you at a glance whether a service is currently running.

In general, you should allow Windows to manage services directly. At times, however, you may want to adjust the properties of a service directly. For example, if you rarely use a service, you may want to run it only when required. That way, you can avoid using system RAM unless you need to. If a service is causing problems with other programs, you may want to temporarily disable it for troubleshooting purposes. VCR-style buttons at the right side of the toolbar in the Services window let you start, stop, pause, and restart the selected service.

If you start or stop a service, Windows follows your wishes until the next time you restart the computer. As part of the boot process, Windows checks the startup settings for each service and acts according to the following instructions:

- **Automatic.** The service starts automatically. Services that are required to identify computers on the network typically use this setting.

- **Manual.** The service is disabled until a user or a program requests access to it. When you open the Disk Management console to view information about disk drives, for example, Windows starts the Logical Disk Manager Administrative service.

- **Disabled.** The service will not run unless you specifically start it using the Services console.

To change the startup settings and configuration details for any service, double-click its entry in the Services list. Figure A.6, for example, shows settings for the Fax Service. If you want the Fax Service to be unavailable on a given computer, change its entry in the **Startup type** list to **Disabled**.

Finding Services

If you are comfortable using the Computer Management console, you can manage services from this location. Look for the Services entry in the Services and Applications group; this item displays the same list as the Services icon in Control Panel's Administrative Tools group.

FIGURE A.6
Change the entry in the **Startup type** box to control what Windows does with a service when you restart the computer.

Creating Custom Management Consoles

Manage multiple computers

The prebuilt MMC collections are intended primarily for use with the computer you're currently working with. But you can also use management tools across the network—to diagnose hardware problems or set up shared folders on a co-worker's computer, for instance. If other people depend on you to manage their PCs, custom consoles can be a true time-saver.

Windows 2000 is packed with management tools. Unlike previous Windows versions, however, the utilities in Windows 2000 share a common interface called the *Microsoft Management Console (MMC)*. The MMC is a blank palette, with a tree pane on the left and a contents pane on the right. Windows includes an assortment of ready-made management consoles, the most noteworthy of which is the Computer Management utility. But you can also build your own, making it easier to assemble all your favorite management utilities in one place.

Each MMC management tool add-in is called a *snap-in*. To build your own management console, open an empty MMC window and fill it with the snap-ins you want to use.

Building a custom management console

1. Click the **Start** button, choose **Run**, type MMC into the Run dialog box, and click **OK**. An empty management console window opens, like the one shown in Figure A.7.

2. Pull down the **Console** menu and choose **Add/Remove Snap-In**.

3. Click the **Add** button to open the Add Standalone Snap-in dialog box (see Figure A.8).

446

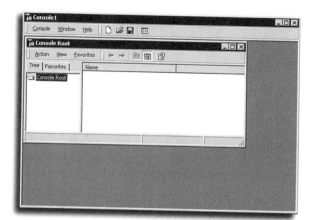

FIGURE A.7
To create a custom console, start with a blank MMC window like this one.

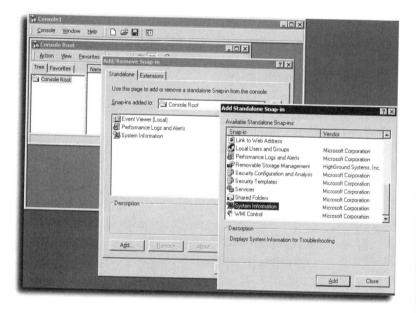

FIGURE A.8
Use the keyboard shortcut **Ctrl+M** to open this dialog box and add any available snap-in to your custom console.

Organize snap-ins in folders

Use the **New Folder** option in the Add Standalone Snap-in dialog box to add a folder to your custom console. (You can rename the folder later.) Organizing snap-ins into folders lets you keep a console from becoming cluttered. See the Computer Management console for a good illustration of how folders can organize similar snap-ins.

4. Select an entry from the list and click the **Add** button to add it to the current console.

5. Repeat steps 3 and 4 to add more snap-ins to your console. If the snap-in you've chosen will work with other networked computers, Windows displays the dialog box shown in Figure A.9. Choose whether you want the snap-in to work with the current computer or display information from a remote computer.

447

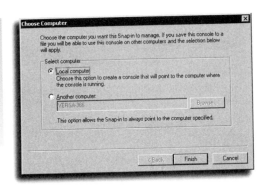

FIGURE A.9
Choose the **Another computer** option to build a console that lets you manage a computer by remote control from across the network.

6. After adding all snap-ins, pull down the **Console** menu and choose **Options**. In the Options dialog box (see Figure A.10), give the console a descriptive name; this will appear in the title bar for your console.

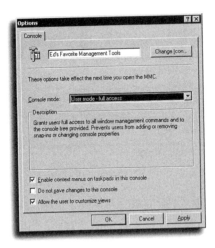

FIGURE A.10
Give your new console a descriptive name and set other options to prevent users from making changes to your care-fully customized console.

7. In the **Console mode** drop-down list, change from **Author mode** to **User mode** to simplify the interface. Choose other options if you want, and click **OK** to save your changes.

8. Pull down the **Console** menu and choose **Save**. Give the console file a name and save it in a convenient location.

By saving custom consoles as separate files, you can share them with other users or open them from any location on the network. The effect is to simplify management tasks and make everyday administration simpler.

Figure A.11 shows a custom console I created that lets me view essential information about three different network computers, regardless of which computer I'm logged on to. Note that I used folders to organize each set of tools by computer. I also specified that each snap-in should display information about a specific computer.

FIGURE A.11
Custom consoles can help you manage an entire network without leaving your office.

Adding and Removing Windows Components

Unlike previous Windows versions, Windows 2000 adds virtually every option as part of the default setup. The roster of optional components includes a handful of relatively obscure add-ins, which are necessary only in special circumstances, and Internet Information Server, a Web server that lets you turn your computer into a Web site for other network users.

To access these optional Windows components, open the Add/Remove Programs option in Control Panel and click the Add/Remove Windows Components icon. Figure A.12 shows the options available from this window. Follow the wizard's prompts to add any of these options.

Limitations of custom consoles

Working with MMC snap-ins across the network is convenient, but it has some limitations. For instance, you can use the Device Manager to view settings for hardware on another networked computer, but you can't update drivers or change resource settings for a remote computer. Still, being able to view another computer without having to leave your desk can be a tremendous time-saver.

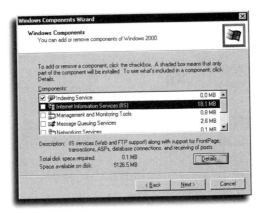

FIGURE A.12
Want to add any of these extras to Windows 2000? Use the Add/Remove Programs utility.

Installing Patches and Updates

Is Windows 2000 bug-free? Hardly. Every version of Windows ever made has eventually needed an assortment of patches and updates to make it run more smoothly. As I write this, Windows 2000 is brand new, but I can confidently predict that you will want to add any of the following items to your Windows 2000 installation:

- **Service packs**. These are large collections of bug fixes that typically come out every three to six months. Service packs are typically well tested, and most users should install the latest service pack to bring their copy of Windows up–to-date.

- **Option packs**. As the name implies, these updates add new features but are not required to fix problems. Some new software may require an option pack to run properly.

- **Hotfixes.** These are small patches that fix a specific problem, usually a serious one that can cause data loss or affect security. Over time, Microsoft will release dozens of hotfixes for Windows 2000; all hotfixes are eventually rolled up into service packs.

How do you find these updates? Your best source of information by far is the Windows Update Web site (see Figure A.13). Click the **Windows Update** shortcut at the top of the **Start** menu to go to this Web site; then follow its instructions.

Read the notes first!

Don't just assume that you should install every new hotfix that appears on Microsoft's Web site. Many such fixes are aimed at problems that occur only with specific hardware or software configurations. If your system configuration doesn't include the specific piece of hardware or software for which the update was designed, skip the hotfix.

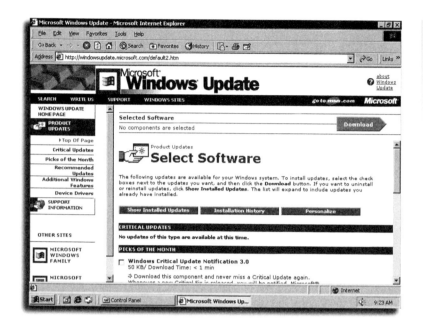

FIGURE A.13
Visit Windows Update
frequently to keep your
copy of Windows 2000
up to date.

Working with the Windows Registry

Windows 2000 stores every detail of your system's configuration in the *Windows registry*. When you start your system, Windows reads the registry to set up hardware and software according to the settings and preferences you've previously defined. Then, every time you install a new device driver, set up a new program, or configure an application such as Microsoft Office, Windows writes the new information into this enormous database.

Web sites and magazine articles are full of tips and tricks that require you to edit the registry to make some type of system configuration change. Many of these tips are of dubious value to begin with; worse, they run the risk of fouling up your system configuration so thoroughly that you can't even start up again. However, you will occasionally encounter circumstances in which the only solution to a thorny problem involves using the *Registry Editor* tool to change a setting directly. Typically, Microsoft publishes registry changes as part of articles in the Knowledge Base when those are the only way to work around a known bug in Windows.

Handle the registry with care

Every Windows expert I know, inside and outside of Microsoft, is unanimous on one subject: The registry is not a place for tinkering. Open the Registry Editor only when you have no alternative, and then be extremely careful. Changes you make here can have dire consequences, including serious data loss, if you make a mistake.

451

SEE ALSO
➤ *For an explanation of how Microsoft's Knowledge Base works, see "Searching the Microsoft Knowledge Base," p. 61.*

When should you edit the Windows registry? I follow these principles strictly, and I suggest you do the same:

- If you can solve a problem without using the Registry Editor, you should do so. Even if the solution takes dozens of steps through complex dialog boxes, it is almost always better to manipulate the registry through Windows utilities than it is to do so directly.

- Open the Registry Editor only when you are certain you know the consequences of what you're doing. If you're not sure which key holds the information you want to change, do some more reading first.

- When using the Registry Editor, always log on using an account in the Administrators group.

- Always create an Emergency Repair Disk before using the Registry Editor to make a significant change. If your change has catastrophic consequences, you can use the ERD to restore your previous configuration.

SEE ALSO
➤ *For full details on how to back up your system configuration with an Emergency Repair Disk, see "Preparing for Disaster," p. 272.*

After you've made a backup of your system configuration, open the Registry Editor by clicking the Start button, choosing **Run**, and entering **Regedit** in the Run box. The Registry Editor (see Figure A.14) closely resembles the Windows Explorer tool, with a tree pane on the left and a details pane on the right.

The registry is organized into *keys* and *subkeys*, each of which contain *values* that store details for your system configuration. At its highest level, the registry is divided into six *root keys*, each of which sits one level below the My Computer icon in the Registry Editor. Each of the root keys begins with the cryptic string HKEY (short for "hardware key").

Regedit or Regedt32?

Like previous versions of Windows NT, Windows 2000 includes two utilities for use when you need to edit the registry. Regedit.exe is easier to use, and it follows the standards of other modern Windows applications. The alternative, Regedt32.exe, is much more difficult to use, and its design betrays its roots, which go back to the earliest versions of Windows NT, before the Windows 95 interface appeared. Why is it there at all? Regedt32.exe, despite its flaws, includes two advanced features: the capability to edit security settings for individual registry keys, and the capability to create several esoteric data types. Under normal circumstances, you will never need to use this advanced tool.

FIGURE A.14
Double-click your way through the Registry Editor's tree display on the left to find a specific key. Add and edit keys and registry values in the right pane.

① Six root keys sit one level beneath the My Computer icon

② Keys and subkeys are organized in a strict hierarchy

③ Values contain the data used to configure system settings

By double-clicking through the hierarchy of the registry, you can work your way to the setting you want to read or change. For instance, to see most Windows settings, double-click the following keys: HKEY_LOCAL_MACHINE, SOFTWARE, Microsoft, Windows, and CurrentVersion. Click the plus sign to the left of any item to see the choices available under that branch of the tree.

Values assigned to a given key appear in the right pane when you select that key. To edit a registry value, double-click the value name in the right pane. This opens the editing window shown in Figure A.15. In the bottom half of the dialog box, enter or edit the data as needed, and click **OK**. As soon as you close the editing window, your change is effective.

On rare occasions, you may find it necessary to create a new subkey. To do so, select the key under which you want to create the subkey. Then right-click in the right pane and choose **N**ew, **K**ey from the

Edit someone else's registry

Although I concentrate in this section on the details of editing the registry of the machine you're currently using, you can also use Registry Editor to examine and edit the registry on another machine across the network. If you have administrative rights on the other machine, pull down the **Registry** menu and choose **Connect Network Registry**. After connecting with the other machine, you can edit configuration details as if you were sitting in front of that computer.

453

shortcut menu (see Figure A.16). To create a new value for the key that's currently selected in the left pane, you need to know which data type to use for that key—choose **String Value**, **Binary Value**, or **DWORD value** from the shortcut menu.

FIGURE A.15
To edit a registry value, use the text box in the bottom of this window.

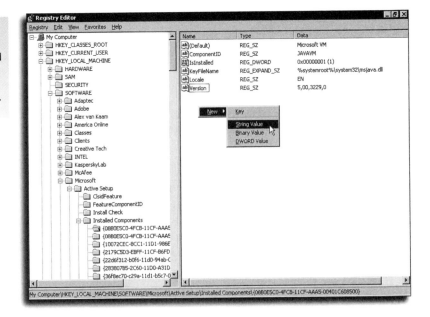

FIG. A.16
No guessing! If you need to create a new value, check the instructions for the correct data type.

Appendix

B

Using the Command Line

When Should You Use the Command Prompt?

Did you begin working with computers before the advent of Windows 95? If so, you probably remember the dreaded c:\ prompt—the so-called *command line interface (CLI)*, which requires you to enter commands one at a time to perform simple tasks such as starting a program, reading the list of files in a directory, copying files to another drive, and so on.

In Windows 2000, you can accomplish virtually every common task from the graphical user interface. However, the operating system also includes a CLI, which you can use any time you want to. A Command Prompt window is especially well-suited for people who are comfortable working with a command prompt for file-management tasks. For some advanced file-management tasks, in fact, it's required:

- To see the short names that Windows 2000 automatically generates when you create a long filename, you must use the Windows 2000 command interpreter. These short names are not visible in any Explorer window.

SEE ALSO
➤ *To learn about the way Windows automatically creates short filenames, see "The Long and Short of Filenames," p. 159.*

- From a Command Prompt window, it's easy to copy a directory listing and paste it into a text file. There is no way to do this from an Explorer window.

- Although you can change the Read-only and Hidden file attributes in an Explorer window, you must use the command line to set or change the System attribute for a file.

SEE ALSO
➤ *To learn how file attributes work, see "Working with Hidden and System Files," p. 161.*

- Do you want to rename a group of files all at one time? This can be done only from a Command Prompt window.

- Windows 2000 includes several command-line utilities that are invaluable when you're troubleshooting an Internet connection. Likewise, several network configuration tasks can be accomplished only at the command line.

One-click command line?

Ordinarily, opening a Command Prompt window takes four clicks as you burrow down through the Start menu. If you use the command line often, make your life easier by putting a Command Prompt shortcut on the Quick Launch bar, where you can open it with one click. Use the right mouse button to drag the Command Prompt shortcut from the Accessories menu and drop it on an empty spot on the Quick Launch bar.

The Windows 2000 command interpreter may look just like the familiar MS-DOS prompt, but it is not. As I'll demonstrate later in this chapter, many MS-DOS commands don't work in Windows 2000 (usually for good reason), and Windows 2000 includes an assortment of new commands that accomplish tasks you can't do in MS-DOS.

Opening a Command Prompt Window

To open a Command Prompt window, you need to run the Windows 2000 command interpreter program, Cmd.exe. Click the **Command Prompt** shortcut in the **Accessories** group on the **Programs** menu, or type **CMD** into the Run box to open a window like the one shown in Figure B.1.

To execute a command, type the command name, followed by any necessary *arguments*, *parameters*, or *switches*, and press **Enter**. The command interpreter responds differently, depending on what you type:

- **The name of a Windows program.** The program opens, using the permissions of the account with which you started the Command Prompt window.

- **The name of a document, including its extension.** Windows opens or switches to the program associated with that *file type* and loads the document.

CMD **versus** COMMAND

In Windows 95 or 98, you can open an MS-DOS Prompt window by typing COMMAND into the Run box. Don't use this technique in Windows 2000, though. COMMAND opens the MS-DOS command processor, which is used strictly to run old MS-DOS programs. Be sure to use CMD when you want to open the Windows 2000 command interpreter.

FIGURE B.1
It looks like the familiar MS-DOS C: prompt, but the Windows 2000 Command Prompt window lets you do much more.

- **The command start, followed by the name and full path of a drive or folder.** Opens an Explorer window and displays the contents of the drive or folder.
- **Any built-in command, such as DIR.** Runs the specified command and returns the result to the current window.

Anything you enter at the command line is fully editable. Use the left and right arrow keys to move back and forth along a line and change what you've typed. By default, when you move the cursor along the line and type another character, the command interpreter inserts the character at the current position. If you want to replace the character under the cursor, press the **Insert** key. This key lets you toggle back and forth between Insert and Overtype modes.

Repeating a Previous Command

Unlike its MS-DOS counterpart, the Windows 2000 command interpreter automatically keeps a running list of all commands you enter while a Command Prompt window is open. You can recall any previous command, edit it if necessary, and press **Enter** to execute the command. If you want to change the attributes of a handful of files in a folder, for example, you can issue the command once and then recall that command and edit it for the second and subsequent files.

By default, the command interpreter remembers the last 50 unique commands you used in a session (skip to the end of this chapter for instructions on how to increase the size of the buffer, if needed). To recall a command from the buffer, use any of the following techniques:

- Press the up and down arrows to scroll back and forth through the list of saved commands.
- Press the right arrow key repeatedly to issue the previous command, one character at a time. This option is useful when you want to reuse the beginning of a complex command and change the name of the file or folder used as the argument.
- Press **F3** to repeat the entire previous command.
- Press **F2** to copy the previous command to the current command line, up to a specified character, which you enter in a pop-up box.

Run as Administrator

If you plan to use the Command Prompt window to perform administrative tasks, be sure to start the Cmd.exe program using your Administrator account. Instead of clicking the Command Prompt shortcut in the Accessories menu, hold down the **Shift** key and right-click that shortcut; then choose **Run as**. This option lets you enter a different username (Administrator, typically) and password. Any commands you enter into the Command Prompt window use the permissions of that user account.

Keep that window open

When you close a Command Prompt window, Windows removes all information it has stored about that window, including commands you've issued and the output from previous commands. To keep this information handy so that you can reuse it, get into the habit of leaving the Command Prompt window open. The command interpreter takes up very little memory, and having it running will save you a few mouse clicks the next time you want to use it.

- Press **F4** to delete the previous command up to a specified character, which you enter in a pop-up box. This is useful when you want to skip the first portion of a long command. (If you leave blank space at the beginning of a command line, the command interpreter ignores it.)

- Press **F7** to pop up a scrolling list of all the commands you've issued since opening the current Command Prompt window, as shown in the example in Figure B.2. Use the up and down arrows to scroll through the list. After highlighting any command in the list, press **Enter** to run the command immediately, or use the left or right arrow keys to enter it on the command line where you can edit it.

- Press **Esc** to completely clear the contents of the command line so that you can start over.

> **Like DOSKEY, only better**
>
> If you've ever used the old MS-DOS utility **DOSKEY**, you already know how to work with the command buffer in Windows 2000. This version is better overall, however, because it can keep track of more commands than the DOS version can.

FIGURE B.2
Press **F7** to scroll through a list of commands you've used previously.

Selecting and Copying Information in a Command Prompt Window

Cutting and pasting from a Command Prompt window takes some practice, and the procedures aren't always intuitive. You *can* use the Windows Clipboard with a Command Prompt window, however, and the results can be invaluable; if you want to create a list of all the files in a folder, for example, this is the best way to do it.

> **Funky function keys**
>
> The function-key shortcuts for Command Prompt windows are nearly impossible to remember. Frankly, the only one worth memorizing is F7, which lets you see the entire command buffer in a single window. Use the arrow keys for the rest.

Find text in a window

Need to find a specific word or filename in a long listing of information? Surprisingly, the Command Prompt window has its own Find utility built in—although it's not easy to find. Right-click the title bar and choose **Edit** from the shortcut menu; then select **Find**. Enter the text you want to search for and click **OK**. Other options let you search up or down from the current position in the window. Windows selects whatever text you find; press **Ctrl+C** to copy it to the Clipboard.

Selecting text in a Command Prompt window uses techniques that are generally different from those you use in a Windows program. Unlike a typical program window, the Command Prompt window doesn't understand the concept of wrapping lines. Instead, you select rectangles of text on the screen:

- Click at any point and begin dragging in any direction to begin selecting all the text underneath the cursor. If you want just a list of filenames, for example, start with the first character of the first name in the list and extend the selection down and to the right.

- If the selection extends into a portion of the history window that has scrolled out of the window, your selection scrolls the window automatically. This lets you select more text than you can see in the current window.

- To select a single word, point to the text and double-click.

How can you tell when you've made a selection in a Command Prompt window? Figure B.3 illustrates two clues you can look for. First, notice that the word Select appears at the beginning of the title bar; second, the selection itself appears in the reverse colors of the rest of the window (blue type on a white background, for example).

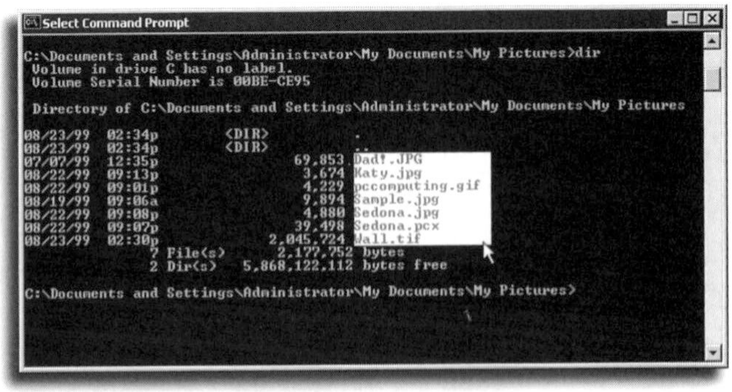

FIGURE B.3
Look at the title bar and the Command Prompt window itself to see when you've successfully selected text.

Press **Ctrl+C** to copy the selection to the Windows Clipboard so that you can paste it into any other program. After copying a file listing to the Clipboard, for example, open a text editor such as Notepad and press **Ctrl+V** to paste the listing into a document you can edit or save.

You can also use a cool and undocumented technique called QuickEdit to copy and paste information within the Command Prompt window itself. Suppose you've used the **DIR /AD** command to produce a list of all the subdirectories within a directory, and now you want to list the contents of each subdirectory in turn.

Start by dragging the mouse pointer to select the subdirectory name. Right-click to copy the name to the Clipboard. Now type the beginning of the new command at the command line—in this case **DIR**, followed by a space. Right-click to paste the contents of the Clipboard at the end of the command line.

Repeat this process—right-click to copy and then right-click to paste—with each of the other subdirectories in the list.

Using Wildcards at the Command Line

When you issue a command that works on a file or a directory, you can specify which drive, directory, or file you want to use as the *argument* for that command. Just as in MS-DOS and in previous versions of Windows, you can use wildcard characters to define a group of objects based on their name or location.

- Use the * character to fill in for any character or characters. For instance, **DIR *.doc** tells the Windows 2000 command interpreter to list all the files in the current directory that have the extension DOC. Likewise, **COPY ltr*.* C:\Backups** finds all files in the current directory that begin with LTR and copies them to the Backups directory on the C: drive.

- Use the ? wildcard to fill in for a single character. **DIR ltr???.***, for example, lists all files that begin with LTR and have exactly six characters in addition to the extension.

Getting Help at the Command Line

If you're not certain which commands are available, ask for help. At the command line, type **Help** and press **Enter** to see a full list of available commands. To see additional details on any of the commands in that list, type the command name followed by **/?**. Figure B.4, for example, shows the syntax for the IPCONFIG command, which you can use to see all the TCP/IP settings for a computer.

Filenames are words, too

If a filename does not include spaces, you can select it by pointing to it in the Command Prompt window and double-clicking. The Windows 2000 command interpreter considers the entire filename, including its extension, to be a single word. This technique does not work with long filenames that include spaces.

461

FIGURE B.4
Use the / ? switch after
a command to get a
quick summary of
options available with
that command.

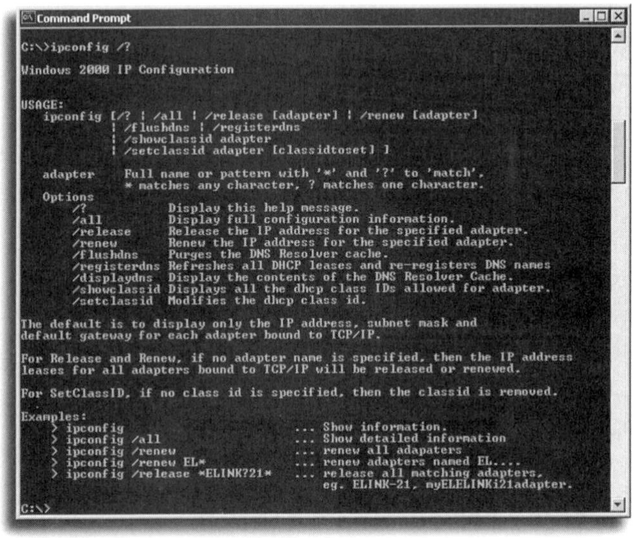

Note that the help in Figure B.4 is extremely detailed, and it goes on for more than 25 lines. In an MS-DOS prompt window, which is limited to 25 lines, you would have to use the MORE command to pause between screens; in Windows 2000, you can drag the bottom border of the window to make more room, or you can use the scrollbar at the right side of the window to look back through all the Help text.

Useful Commands

Every Windows 2000 command has its own characteristic syntax—the precise order in which you must issue the command to get back the results you're looking for.

To list every Windows 2000 command with all its arguments, parameters, and switches would take up a book larger than this one. The Windows 2000 Help files include detailed definitions of the syntax for each command, and in many cases the Help file also includes useful examples. In this section, I list only those commands that are most useful, with examples of how you can get valuable information from each one.

Setting the Current Directory

When you enter a command that requires a drive or directory as an argument, you can usually leave that argument off; in that case, Windows assumes you meant to use the current drive or directory. That can save you lots of keystrokes when using a command such as COPY or XCOPY, for example. To change the current drive, type the drive letter followed by a colon, and press **Enter**. To change to a different directory on the current drive, use the CD command.

You can use the CD command repeatedly to march through a group of folders one at a time. Or you can use an entire path as the argument of the CD command to jump through several directory levels all at once. One of my favorite command-line shortcuts uses the CD command:

```
CD %userprofile%\My Documents
```

When you use the *environment variable* (the part between percent signs), Windows automatically substitutes the drive and path of the directory that holds your personal profile. This shortcut switches instantly to your personal My Documents folder so that you can work with saved data files.

SEE ALSO
➤ *For more details on how to use and customize the My Documents folder, see "How Windows Organizes Your Files," p. 106.*

To switch to the parent directory of the current directory, use the shortcut **CD** ..—a single dot means the current directory; two dots means the parent directory.

Viewing Directory Listings

The single most popular (and useful) command in a Windows 2000 Command Prompt session must be DIR (short for Directory). This command dates back to the days before MS-DOS, and the Windows 2000 version of this command works much like its DOS counterpart.

The basics of the DIR command are pretty simple. Enter the command by itself to list the contents of the current directory, in alphabetical order. Add an argument to list files in another folder or on another drive; use wildcards to restrict the listing to only those files that match specified criteria.

Use the short version

Believe it or not, the actual Change Directory command is CHDIR, but no one ever uses that long version. Use the two-letter CD version instead; it does the same thing, with less typing required.

Use the online Help

Want to see every imaginable switch for the DIR command? Just type **DIR /?** at the command line.

Case doesn't count

The Command Prompt window doesn't distinguish between upper and lowercase letters. If you see a switch such as /S, you can safely enter it with or without pressing the **Shift** key, and the Windows 2000 command interpreter will process it correctly.

Save your favorite settings

Do you prefer to see all DIR listings using specific settings? Instead of typing the same switches every time you use the DIR command, preset them in the DIRCMD environment variable. To specify that you always want to see short filenames and four-digit years, for example, set this variable to /X /4. Open **Control Panel**, double-click the **System** option, and click the **Advanced** tab. In the **User variables for *username*** section, click the **New** button. Enter **DIRCMD** as the Variable Name and /X /4 as the Variable Value. Save your changes, and Windows will apply them automatically the next time you open a Command Prompt window.

Finally, use *switches* to control the amount and type of data displayed for each entry in the directory listing, as well as to control the order of items in the listing. The following switches represent the most useful DIR options:

- **/S**. Displays files in the specified directory and all subdirectories; use this when you want to list all similar files in a single list, regardless of subdirectory. To find all the DOC files in your Projects folder, for instance, use the command DIR c:\ projects*.doc /S.

- **/L**. Uses lowercase letters in the listing.

- **/X**. In addition to the long filename, lists the short filenames that Windows generates automatically when you create a long filename. If no short name is present (because the long filename is already a legal short name), the DIR command displays a blank entry in the space where the short name would go.

- **/O**. Lists files in sorted order; this switch must include at least one of the following letters: N (by name, in alphabetical order); E (by extension, in alphabetical order); S (by size, smallest files first); D (by date/time, oldest files first); G (group directories first). Use the minus sign (-) before any letter to reverse its sort order, and combine two or more letters to sort a complex listing using several criteria. For example, DIR /S /X /OGD-S displays a listing of all files in all folders and subfolders in the current directory, sorted by date, with the largest files in each group listed first; it also includes long and short filenames.

- **/4**. Displays four-digit years. This switch is especially useful when your directory listing includes files from the 20th and 21st centuries.

Managing Files and Folders

Six commands are especially useful for basic and advanced file-management tasks in a Command Prompt window.

- COPY. In general, it's easier to use an Explorer window and the Search Assistant for basic file-management tasks. The command-line version does one particularly useful trick the graphical version can't, however. When you want to combine two or more text files into a single file (a process called *concatenation*), you can use the COPY command with the following syntax:

```
COPY filename1 + filename2 + ... newfilename
```

Specify as many files as you want in the first half of the command, separating them with plus signs, or use wildcards:

```
COPY *.txt newfilename
```

- **DEL (ERASE).** This is another task that is usually easier from an Explorer window. The command-line version is an easy way to delete a group of files using wildcards. For example, if you have a program that creates temporary files with the extension TMP, you can erase all such files in a given folder using the command **DEL *.tmp /S.**

- **MKDIR (MD).** Makes a new subdirectory in the current directory.

- **MOVE.** Works like COPY, except that it deletes the original version of the files after creating copies in the new location. Note that you must use the MOVE command to rename a directory.

- **RENAME (REN).** Possibly the most useful file-management command, day in and day out. Use wildcards with this command to change the name or extension of a whole group of files at one time—something you can't do in a graphical Explorer window. For instance, you can change the extension of all Web page files in a given directory using a command such as this: **REN *.html *.htm.**

- **XCOPY.** An extremely powerful command for copying groups of files and directories. See the online Help file for full details on its many switches. Use this command with the /T (tree) switch to copy an entire directory structure from one location to another, without copying files. Use the /H switch to copy Hidden and System files as well.

Changing File Attributes

Use the ATTRIB command when you want to view or change attributes for a group of files. This command works with four attributes: Read-only (R), Hidden (H), System (S), and Archive (A).

> **No typos tolerated here**
>
> For DOS veterans and swift typists, the command line represents a fast way to work. But the command line presents one huge disadvantage: unlike Explorer windows, where you point and click to select files, you must type file and folder names exactly as they appear in the file system. If you type a name incorrectly, Windows won't find the file you're looking for. And if you type a command name or switch incorrectly, you'll get an irritating error message instead of the results you're looking for.

SEE ALSO

➤ For an explanation of what each file attribute does, see "Working with Hidden and System Files," p. 161.

- If you enter the command with no switches, it shows you the attributes of all files in the current folder or in the drive and folder you specify.

- To turn an attribute on for a file or a group of files, use a plus sign with the first letter of the attribute. Use **ATTRIB +R *.doc**, for example, to turn on the Read-only attribute for all DOC files in the current directory.

- To turn an attribute off for a file or a group of files, use a minus sign with the first letter of the attribute. To remove the Hidden and Read-only attributes for all files in a directory, enter the command **ATTRIB -R - H *.***.

- Use the **/S** switch at the end of the command to apply your changes to files in all subdirectories of the specified directory.

- Normally, the ATTRIB command works only on files. To tell the Windows 2000 command interpreter that you want to set or view attributes for directories, too, use the **/D** switch.

You can also combine attribute information with the DIR command, using the **/A** switch. For instance, to see a listing of only hidden files and folders, use the command **DIR /AH**.

Managing Disks and Drives

Windows 2000 includes three commands that let you work with disks at the command line:

- **FORMAT.** Use this command to format floppy disks. (Although you can use the command line for hard drive partitions as well, I recommend that you use the Disk Management utility for that task instead.) With the **/Q** (quick) and **/U** (unconditional) switches, this command is the fastest way to erase a floppy disk in drive A:

```
FORMAT a: /Q/U
```

SEE ALSO

➤ For details on how to prepare a new hard disk, see "Setting Up a Hard Disk," p. 232.

➤ To learn how to use floppy disks, see "Working with Floppy Disks," p. 247.

XCOPY is a true power tool

If you're comfortable managing files at the command line, you should learn how to use all of XCOPY's switches. Suppose you have a complex directory structure that you've created to help organize all the files in a project, with dozens of subfolders and special file permissions on each one. You're about to start a new project and you want to use the same basic directory structure. To "clone" the directory structure from the old location to the new one, use the command XCOPY project1 project2 /T /E /O (substituting the correct folder names, of course).

List all directories

Want to see a list of just the subdirectories in the current directory? Use the command DIR /AD, which lists only directories. DIR %userprofile% /ADHS shows all the hidden and system directories in your personal profile.

- **CHKDSK.** Has the same effect as using the graphical disk-checking tools, without the informative dialog boxes. Be sure to specify the **/F** switch if you want Windows to fix any errors it finds.

SEE ALSO

➤ *For an overview of Windows 2000's built-in disk-checking tools, see "Checking Disks for Errors," p. 275.*

- **CONVERT.** Allows you to convert a FAT or FAT32 disk to the NTFS file system. This is a one-time conversion, and it can be done only from the command line.

Working with Networks

One command, NET, performs an enormous number of tasks in the Command Prompt window, from gathering information about network users and settings to starting and stopping services. By itself, the NET command does nothing; however, when you add a helper command to it, you can accomplish nearly any network-related task.

The following is a small sampling of NET commands that can be useful on any network, large or small:

- Find out which users are members of the various local groups on the current computer. Use the following command to see the full membership list of the Administrators group; substitute Users or "Power Users" (with the quotation marks) to see the members of those groups.

  NET LOCALGROUP Administrators

- To send a message to another computer or user on the network, try the NET SEND command. If you specify a computer name, the message pops up in front of whoever is logged on to that computer; enter a username if you want the message to go to a specific person, regardless of where he or she is logged on. Suppose you're about to take a printer offline so that you can make some repairs. Broadcast a message to anyone who normally uses that printer so they know not to use it for a while. The syntax is simple: NET SEND *username message*. Use this command to send a message to a user named Bianca, for example, as shown in Figure B.5:

  NET SEND Bianca Printer going off-line in 10 minutes!

Which slash is which?

Don't confuse backslashes and forward slashes. Typically, you use the backslash character (\) to separate directory and subdirectory names in a path, as in C:\Program Files\Acrobat. Use a forward slash (/) to indicate a switch that modifies a command, such as /T or /AD. Although Explorer windows can often interpret what you mean when you enter the wrong type of slash, the Windows 2000 command interpreter is ruthlessly literal and will respond with an error message if you mix slashes.

Try the Help system

Want to see a list of all the extra commands you can use to modify NET? Type **NET /?** and press **Enter**. To see details about any of the commands in this list, enter **NET HELP** *commandname* or **NET** *commandname* **/HELP**.

467

FIGURE B.5
Use the NET SEND command to pop up a message like this on another Windows 2000 computer on your network.

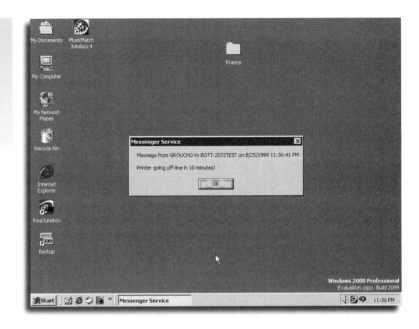

Send with discretion

Using the NET SEND command may sound like fun, but it can be extremely annoying to other users. Reserve this tool for occasions when you genuinely need to get a message out to other people about a potential problem on the network. Don't use it as a substitute for email—any number of chat or "instant message" programs are much better for that sort of task.

- Do you have a computer that consistently loses track of time? Use the **NET TIME** command to synchronize it with another network computer whose clock is known to be accurate. If your administrator has designated a particular machine as the time server, use the command **NET TIME \\computername**; if the administrator has set up the entire domain to control time settings, you can use the command **NET TIME /DOMAIN:domain** (substituting the name of the domain as the final argument).

SEE ALSO

➤ *For an overview of commands you can use to solve Internet problems, see "Monitoring and Troubleshooting Dial-Up Connections," p. 366.*

Unsupported MS-DOS Commands

How is the Windows 2000 command interpreter different from the command processor found in MS-DOS and older Windows versions? A number of familiar commands from those older operating systems are no longer available. In general, this is true for any of three reasons:

- Windows 2000 no longer needs the function provided by a given command; this is especially true of memory-management features.

- Windows 2000 doesn't support the feature, usually because it requires direct access to hardware drivers.

- Windows 2000 has a different technique to accomplish the same goal.

Table B.1 lists some of the MS-DOS commands that are no longer supported in Windows 2000.

Table B.1   Obsolete MS-DOS Commands

MS-DOS Command	Comment
Emm386, Memmaker, Smartdrv	Windows 2000 handles all memory management and disk caching directly.
Mscdex	Windows 2000 handles CD-ROM access with its own drivers.
Dblspace, Drvspace	These drive-compression techniques are not supported; to compress files and folders, set the compression attribute on an NTFS partition.
Scandisk	The ScanDisk utility will not run under Windows 2000; use the built-in disk-checking utility or the CHKDSK program instead.
Msav	Windows 2000 does not include an antivirus program.
Undelete, Unformat	These disk utilities will not work under Windows 2000.
Sys	Windows 2000 will not create a single bootable disk; you must use the four setup disks or the Windows 2000 CD to repair a damaged system.
Menucolor, Menudefault, Menuitem, Submenu, Choice, Include	All these commands are used to set up different configurations of the MS-DOS environment at startup; Windows 2000 does not support this feature.
Defrag	You must use the graphical version of the disk defragmentation utility; no command-line version is available.
Deltree	This command is not available; to delete a directory that contains subdirectories, use the RD command with the /S switch.
Backup, Restore, Msbackup	These older backup programs have been replaced by the Ntbackup program.
Fdisk	Use the Disk Management tool to set up a hard disk and manage partitions and volumes

See Help for a full list

If you are having trouble with a command that worked in MS-DOS, check the Help files to see whether the command is supported in Windows 2000. Search for the topic "What's New or Different from MS-DOS."

Check this list carefully!

If you upgraded to Windows 2000 on a computer that had a previous version of Windows or MS-DOS installed, many of the commands listed here may still be on your hard drive. However, if you try to use them under Windows 2000, you will receive an error message.

469

Customizing a Command Prompt Window

If you use the Command Prompt window regularly, take advantage of several customization features to make yourself more productive. These range from cosmetic changes, such as the color and font that Windows uses to display information in a Command Prompt window, to changes in the way the command history and screen buffers work.

To make changes that will apply every time you run the default Command Prompt shortcut, right-click its icon in the Accessories group and choose **Properties**. Figure B.6 shows the settings available on the Options tab.

FIGURE B.6
Use these options to change the general look and feel of the Command Prompt window.

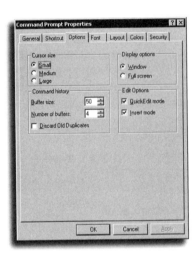

The following sections are available in this dialog box:

- **Cursor size.** If you have trouble seeing the cursor, increase its size here.

- **Command history.** By default, Windows 2000 keeps track of the last 50 commands you used in each of four Command Prompt windows. For most people, this is plenty; if you need more space in the command buffer, increase this number.

- **Display options.** Allows you to choose between a window and a full-screen mode. In general, I recommend that you avoid full-screen mode because it makes it difficult to see other running programs.

- **Edit options.** If you don't want to use QuickEdit (which I described earlier in this chapter), clear its check box here. Likewise, you can uncheck the **Insert mode** box if you always want your typing to replace the characters on the current command line when you're editing.

After setting the options the way you like them, click the **Font** tab (see Figure B.7). This option allows you to choose the size of the characters used in the Command Prompt window; it also allows you to specify which font you want to use.

Experiment with the different settings until you find a font that's clear and readable. Your choice of fonts will be extremely limited. Even if you have hundreds of fonts installed on your computer, only a handful will be available for use in this window. If you choose a TrueType font, you can set its size; the size settings for raster fonts include the width and height of each character, in pixels.

Switch on-the-fly

If you prefer to use the Command Prompt window in full-screen mode occasionally, don't set its default size to full screen. Instead, use the shortcut **Alt+Enter** to toggle back and forth between a full MS-DOS–style screen and a window. You can switch back to the Windows desktop anytime by pressing **Alt+Tab**.

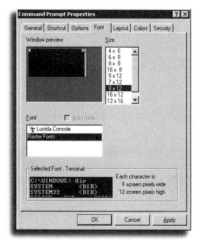

FIGURE B.7
If your computer uses a language other than U.S. English, you may need to choose a TrueType font here.

Next stop is the Layout tab (see Figure B.8). By default, the Command Prompt window wraps lines of text when they reach 80 characters in width, and it keeps a screen buffer of 300 lines. You can increase the screen buffer dramatically, to as many as 9,999 lines. You can also change the width to any number you like (although it's a bad idea to make the width less than 80 lines).

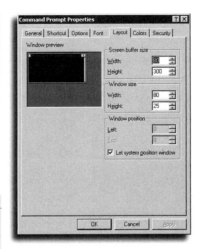

FIGURE B.8
Adjust the size of the screen buffer here so that you can scroll back further.

Block that buffer

A buffer that's too large can use up a significant chunk of memory for no good reason. If you find yourself scrolling through the Command Prompt window regularly, try increasing it to 1,000 lines first, and see if that does the trick. Increase the number further, in 1,000-line increments, until you're satisfied with the results.

The Window size options are tricky. You can't set the width of the window to be wider than the width of the screen buffer—if you try to do so, Windows automatically adjusts the other setting for you. Also, you can adjust the height and position of the window anytime, simply by dragging it into position.

Finally, click the **Colors** tab (see Figure B.9) if you want to adjust the text and background colors used in the Command Prompt window. Most of the options in this section are self-explanatory. Just make sure you choose colors that contrast well.

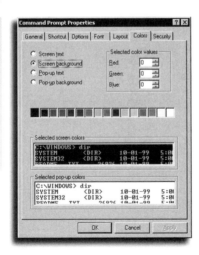

FIGURE B.9
Adjusting the colors used in the Command Prompt window can make it easier to work with. Dark text on a light background, for example, is more soothing on the eyes.

GLOSSARY

.bmp   See bitmap image.

.gif   See GIF image.

.jpg   See JPEG image.

ACPI   See Advanced Configuration and Power Interface.

Active Desktop   A feature that allows users to place Web-style objects and graphics on the Windows desktop.

Active Directory   The central catalog of users, computers, printers, and other network resources on a Windows 2000 domain. By storing information in the Active Directory, network administrators can manage resources from a central location, and users can access those resources from any network computer with a single logon.

ActiveX control, ActiveX program   Add-in programs, commonly used with Internet Explorer, which allow a Web page to display data or perform functions not available with HTML.

administrative rights   Special permissions that allow administrators to perform system and network configuration tasks not available to ordinary user accounts.

administrative share   A hidden *share* that allows administrators to access a resource, such as a drive or a printer. Administrative shares are created automatically when Windows 2000 starts and cannot be removed. All administrative shares include a dollar sign ($) as the final character.

Administrator   A built-in *user account* that has the right to perform general setup and configuration tasks not permitted for ordinary user accounts.

Adobe Type 1 font   Font format originally developed for use with printers that use the PostScript language. Windows 2000 can use Type 1 fonts without conversion or third-party font-management utilities. See also *OpenType font, TrueType font*.

Advanced Configuration and Power Interface (ACPI)   A computer industry standard that defines power-management capabilities for desktop and portable PCs.

alias   See *distribution list*.

argument   A word or phrase that follows a command and further defines how that command works when executed.

assigned programs   On a Windows 2000 network, programs that an administrator defines as mandatory for network users. Assigned programs are automatically installed at startup and cannot be removed by the user.

association   The link between a *file type* and the program that runs automatically when a user double-clicks an icon of that file type. Text files, for example, are associated by default with the Notepad program; double-clicking a text file's icon opens that file in Notepad.

attachment   A file that is included with an email message.

attribute   Information stored with a file's directory listing that indicates whether the file is read-only, hidden, ready for archiving (backing up), compressed, or encrypted.

AutoComplete   Internet Explorer feature that automatically offers to fill in a long URL after you enter the first few characters of that URL.

AutoSearch   Internet Explorer feature that automatically sends text entered in the Address bar to one or more search engines if the text does not specify a proper *URL*.

basic disk   A physical disk that contains primary partitions, extended partitions, and/or logical drives. Basic disks are compatible with older versions of Windows and MS-DOS. See also *dynamic disk*.

BIOS   Basic Input/Output System. The software stored in a chip on your computer; it runs at startup, before you load an operating system such as Windows.

bitmap image   Standard graphic file format used for Windows wallpaper, among others. Because they are much larger than other graphic file formats, bitmap images are rarely used in Web pages. See also *JPEG image*, *GIF image*.

Blue Screen of Death   The most fatal of all fatal Windows 2000 errors. When a bad hardware driver or other problem crashes Windows, it kills all running programs and dumps a screen full of technical gobbledygook in white characters on a blue screen—hence the name.

bookmark   Netscape Navigator's term for a saved Internet shortcut; the Internet Explorer equivalent to the bookmark list is the Favorites folder.

cable modem   A high-speed Internet access system that sends and receives information to a computer using the same cable that carries television signals.

cache   Internet Explorer feature that stores a copy of Web pages you've previously accessed, permitting you to browse some Web pages without being connected to the Internet.

cascading menu   A submenu that "flies out," usually to the right, when you select a menu item that requires additional choices. The Programs menu, for example, cascades out from the Start menu.

certificate   A digital signature that allows you to verify the identity of a Web site or a remote connection and exchange sensitive information in an encrypted format that cannot be read by any third party.

cluster   Individual segment of a disk that is allocated to hold a portion of a file. Large files may be divided into many clusters scattered over a disk, resulting in *fragmentation*. See also *file system*.

color depth   The number of separate colors that Windows can display on the screen; color depth is defined using Control Panel's Display option and is restricted by the display adapter. See also *high color, true color*.

color matrix   Grid found in several Control Panel options that allows users to select a specific color by dragging a pointer.

command line interface   A text-based interface similar to the MS-DOS operating system, in which the user enters commands one at a time.

comment   Explanatory note included with a shortcut file; comments appear in a pop-up window when you let the mouse pointer hover over the shortcut icon.

common dialog box   The Open and Save As dialog boxes used in all Windows programs; because these are stripped-down versions of the Windows Explorer, users can perform rudimentary file-management tasks (creating folders, for example) when opening and saving files.

condition   In a *message rule*, the test that Outlook Express applies to an incoming message before taking the action defined in the rule.

console   A program window that contains one or more management tools that allow you to configure system or network settings.

context-sensitive help   Online documentation that is tailored to the current task.

cookie   Webspeak for a file that stores information about a Web site, allowing you to customize the display of information on a site. Cookies are often used for shopping carts in online commerce sites, for example.

475

crossover cable   A specially wired network cable that allows you to connect the Ethernet adapters in two computers directly, without using a hub.

desktop   The background area of the screen that is visible when no programs are open. By default, Windows 2000 installs a handful of icons, including My Computer and My Network Places, on the desktop.

desktop theme   A collection of colors, mouse pointers, screen savers, and other personalized settings saved as a group. Windows 2000 supports themes created in Windows 95 and 98.

device driver   See *driver*.

DHCP controller, DHCP server Computers that run the *Dynamic Host Configuration Protocol*, which automatically assigns *IP addresses* to other computers on a network.

dialing rules   Instructions that tell Windows which prefixes and area codes to use when dialing a number—for dial-up Internet access, for example. See also *location*.

Digital Subscriber Line   A high-speed Internet access system that transmits and receives data over the unused portion of a conventional telephone line while still allowing voice communications.

directory   Basic organizational unit in MS-DOS and older Windows versions; in Windows 2000, more commonly called *folder*.

disk   Physical device for storing data. See also *drive*.

disk compression   The capability to store more data than would normally fit on a disk by temporarily removing duplicate information. In Windows 2000, compression is allowed only on *NTFS volumes*.

disk format   See *file system*.

distribution list   In Outlook Express, a single address that includes two or more email addresses. See *alias*.

DNS server   A computer that runs the Domain Name System, which translates Internet host names to *IP addresses*.

docking station   Expansion unit that allows a portable computer to function as a desktop computer, typically containing a power connection, expansion slots, and connections to external hardware such as a monitor, keyboard, mouse, and printer.

domain   A group of networked computers that share a common directory. Windows 2000 uses domains to enforce security at a central level. On the Internet, domains are defined by top-level names, such as microsoft.com and whitehouse.gov.

domain controller, domain server A Windows 2000 or Window NT server that manages access to a network and shared resources.

drive Formatted storage area on a hard disk; in Windows 2000, a single hard disk can contain multiple drives.

drive letter Convention used to identify drives on MS-DOS and Windows computers. The letters A and B are reserved for floppy drives, and C is typically the boot drive.

driver Software that enables communication between Windows and a hardware device.

DSL See *Digital Subscriber Line*.

dynamic disk A physical disk format created by the Disk Management utility that contains dynamic volumes rather than partitions or logical drives. Dynamic disks offer advanced features, such as the capability to combine multiple physical disks using a single drive letter, but they cannot be accessed by MS-DOS or earlier Windows versions. See also *volume*, *partition*.

Dynamic Host Control Protocol A network service that allows a server to automatically assign *IP addresses* from a pool of available numbers to individual computers on the network. See also *DHCP controller*.

ethernet The standard interface for connecting personal computers in a local area network.

executable file A file that runs a program when double-clicked or entered at the command line; executable files typically include the .exe extension.

Explorer view Two-pane configuration in Windows Explorer that includes a tree-style list of drives and folders on the left, with the contents of the selected drive or folder in the right pane.

extend To increase available storage on a dynamic disk volume by using additional free space on a different *volume* on the same disk or on a different *dynamic disk*.

extended partition A portion of a *basic disk* that contains *logical drives*. Only one extended partition can be created on a disk. See also *partition*.

FAT File Allocation Table. The basic file system used by older versions of MS-DOS and Windows. See also *NTFS*.

FAT32 A more efficient version of the *FAT* file system used by Windows 95 OSR2, Windows 98, and Windows 2000. This file system includes no security features. See also *NTFS*.

Favorites folder A system folder that contains shortcuts to Internet sites and other remote locations. See also *bookmark*.

file extension   The portion of a file name that follows the final period in that name and is used to define the *file type*; most file extensions are three letters in length.

file system   The organizational structure used for storing, naming, and retrieving files on a drive. See *NTFS, FAT, FAT32*.

file type   The description that identifies the *association* between a file and the program used to open or edit that file. File types are associated with a *file extension*. For instance, a file with the .txt extension is of the Text Document type and opens by default using Notepad.

file/folder permissions   On an *NTFS volume*, the security settings that define which users can view, open, change, or delete that file.

firewall   A computer that sits between a corporate network and the Internet and prevents unauthorized users from accessing information on computers within the network.

firmware   Software contained in a chip on a hardware device (such as a SCSI adapter). In some cases, a firmware upgrade is required before you can install Windows 2000.

folder   Basic unit of organization in Windows 2000, analogous to a *directory* in MS-DOS.

Folders pane   In Windows Explorer, the left pane that displays the tree structure of drives and folders. Clicking an icon in this pane displays its contents in the contents pane to the right.

font   A graphic design that defines the appearance, size, spacing, and other attributes of numbers, symbols, and characters on the screen and in printed output. See also *TrueType font, Adobe Type 1 font*.

fragmentation   Describes the state of a file when pieces of the file are scattered over different areas of a disk. By regularly *defragmenting* files, you can improve overall performance.

frame   Individual pane that contains part of the data that makes up a Web page. By using multiple frames, a Web page designer can make navigating on a complex Web site easier.

gateway computer   On a network, the computer through which other computers access the Internet.

GIF image   Graphics Interchange Format. A standard format for saving image files for use on the Internet.

group account   A collection of *user accounts* that share common rights and permissions; group accounts simplify management by allowing administrators to define a user's rights by assigning the user account to an existing group.

group policy   Systemwide settings that define security and customization options for groups of users. For example, an administrator can create a policy that prevents any network user from changing a desktop color or installing unauthorized programs.

Hardware Compatibility List
Microsoft's official list of hardware devices tested and certified to work with Windows 2000; available on the Web at www.microsoft.com/hcl.

Help topic   In Windows 2000's online documentation, a single Web-style page that covers a single task or feature.

hertz   One cycle per second. In the case of a monitor, used to measure the refresh rate; a higher refresh rate means less flicker.

hibernate   To save the entire contents of memory to a disk file and then shut down the computer. When you restart the computer after hibernating, Windows 2000 restores the system state exactly, including all running programs.

hierarchy   The arrangement and order of objects used throughout Windows; for instance, My Computer is at the top of a hierarchy that contains *drives*, which in turn contain folders and subfolders and sub-subfolders.

high color   Setting that lets you view onscreen images using 16 bits per pixel (up to 65,536 unique colors), if your display adapter supports it. See also *true color*.

History folder   Internet Explorer's storage area for browsing previously viewed Web pages.

home page   The Web page that appears when you open Internet Explorer; by default, this is set to Microsoft's msn.com, but you can change the home page to any location.

hotfix   A patch issued by Microsoft to repair a specific, usually serious, bug in Windows 2000. See also *service pack*.

HTML tag   Markers that define the beginning and end of formatting in a Web page that uses Hypertext Markup Language (HTML).

HTML template   In Windows Explorer, a set of Web-style instructions that define how to display a folder's contents.

hyperlink   Clickable link (in a Web page of a Help topic, for example) that leads to another related page or topic.

IMAP   Internet Message Access Protocol. A standard that allows users of Outlook Express and other email clients to access messages from a remote mail server.

479

incremental backup   A backup set that includes only files created or changed since the last regular backup.

Industry Standard Architecture (ISA) slot   Mostly obsolete standard for internal hardware devices. Newer desktop computers typically include no more than one or two ISA slots for compatibility with old hardware.

inherit   To derive *permissions* from membership in a group; in the case of shared folders, inherited permissions derive from a higher-level folder.

insertion point   The location where text appears when typed, typically indicated by a thick, flashing vertical line.

Internet Protocol   A standard used for communication between computers across the Internet; the IP in *TCP/IP*.

Internet shortcut   Icon that contains information about a Web page or other Internet site. Items in the Favorites folder, for example, are Internet shortcuts.

intranet   Corporate network that allows users to share data using the same types of servers and browsers used on the Internet, with access restricted to authorized users.

IP address   A numeric identifier that allows computers on a TCP/IP network to communicate with one another. Each address consists of four numbers between 0 and 255, separated by periods—for example, 192.168.1.101. Windows 2000 allows you to specify a fixed IP address for a given machine or dynamically assign the address using a *DHCP server*.

Java applet   A program written using the Java language and designed to run in a browser window. See also *virtual machine*.

JavaScript   One of two popular scripting languages that allow Web page designers to create pages that perform certain tasks automatically. See also *VBScript*.

JPEG image   Common graphic file format used on the Internet and named after the Joint Photographic Experts Group, which developed the standard. See also *GIF image*, *bitmap image*.

jump button   In Windows Help, a clickable link that opens the utility referred to in a Help topic, such as Control Panel option.

key   Entry in the *Windows Registry*; keys store *values*, which Windows uses to save user and machine settings.

keyword   In Windows Help, the alphabetical list of terms that lets you search for a specific topic.

legacy device   Generally older hardware that is no longer manufactured but is still supported in Windows 2000.

list control   The portion of an Explorer window that contains the list of files and folders in the current location.

local intranet site   One of several Internet Explorer *security zones.* Specifying that a site is in this zone allows you to relax security standards because files on your intranet are unlikely to contain viruses or other undesirable or dangerous content.

local user profile   Collection of user-specific settings that Windows 2000 creates automatically when a new user logs on. See also *user profile, roaming user profile, mandatory user profile.*

location   Country code, area code, and dialing requirements used when Windows 2000 makes a dial-up connection—to the Internet, for example.

logical drive   Formatted storage area within an *extended partition* on a *basic disk.* Each logical drive typically gets its own drive letter.

logical volume   See *logical drive.*

macro   Small programs created using built-in programming languages in Microsoft Office and other Windows applications. Macros allow you to automate program functions, but they can also be used to carry destructive viruses.

mandatory user profile   Collection of user settings created by a network administrator and loaded automatically when a user logs on to a Windows 2000 *domain.* As the name implies, settings in a mandatory profile typically cannot be changed by the user. See also *user profile, local user profile, roaming user profile.*

map   To assign a drive letter to a shared network folder.

media pool   A collection of backup tapes or other removable media managed by Windows 2000.

message rule   Outlook Express feature that automatically moves, deletes, or performs other actions to an incoming message, based on its content.

Microsoft Exchange   Microsoft's popular corporate email program. If your company uses Exchange on the server, you cannot use Outlook Express as your email client.

Microsoft Knowledge Base   Huge, searchable source of information about bugs and updates to Microsoft software, including Windows 2000. Access the Knowledge Base on the World Wide Web by going to `http://support.microsoft.com` and following the links.

481

Microsoft Management Console (MMC) Customizable program window that contains one or more management tools used to configure system or network settings. All the items in Control Panel's Administrative Tools group, for example, use the MMC. See also *snap-in*.

motherboard Main circuit board in a personal computer, typically containing the CPU chip, memory, and expansion slots.

navigation pane Left pane in a Help window, containing lists of *keywords* or a tree-style view of topics. When you select an item from the navigation pane, Help displays the selected topic in the right pane.

network adapter Hardware device that connects two or more computers and allows them to communicate information and share data. See also *ethernet*.

network hub Connection point on a network that links together network adapters from multiple machines.

notification area The region at the right of the taskbar, which contains small icons that display information and menus for running programs. Sometimes referred to as the *system tray*.

Novell NetWare Popular operating system used in corporate networks. Windows 2000 Professional can communicate with NetWare servers with no additional software.

NTFS The Windows NT File System, a format for storing information on a hard disk that allows you to restrict access to specific user and group accounts. See also *file system*, *FAT*, *FAT32*.

NTFS volume Drive formatted using the NTFS file system.

Offline Files Windows 2000 feature that allows users to automatically create copies of network files on their local computers. This feature is especially useful on notebook computers because it allows the user to work with network data when the network is unavailable. See also *synchronize*.

offline printing Windows 2000 feature that allows you to print a file to a printer that is not currently available—for instance, because your notebook computer is not connected to the network. Windows stores the request and automatically prints the page or pages when it detects that the printer is again available.

OpenType font Outline fonts that can be scaled and rotated so that they look the same in all sizes, on the screen and on printers. OpenType is an extension of *TrueType font* technology. See also *font*; *Adobe Type 1 font*.

option pack   Microsoft's term for a comprehensive Windows update designed to add new features; contrast with *service packs*, which are intended to fix bugs.

outline font   Representations of letters, numbers, and special characters stored as basic outlines in Windows 2000. Outline fonts can be scaled to a variety of sizes and shapes on the screen and on printed pages. See also *TrueType font, OpenType font, Adobe Type 1 font*.

packet   On a *TCP/IP* network, the basic unit of data transmission; each packet contains the *IP address* of the sending and receiving computers, along with instructions on how to assemble the collection of packets at the receiving end.

parallel port   On a typical PC, the connector used for sending data to a printer. See also *Universal Serial Bus*.

parameter   Information that follows a command typed in a Command Prompt window. For instance, parameters to the COPY command tell Windows which files to copy and the name of the destination drive and folder. See also *switch*.

partition   A division of a *basic disk* that appears to Windows as if it were a separate disk. See also *primary partition, extended partition, logical drive, dynamic disk, volume*.

patch   Small software update usually designed to fix a specific bug in Windows or a Windows program.

path   The MS-DOS–style designation that identifies the location of a file or folder, usually including the drive, directory, and any subdirectories.

pattern   Small arrangement of pixels used to customize the Windows desktop.

PC Card   Credit card-sized hardware device, such as a network adapter or a modem, that can be plugged into a slot on a portable computer and removed easily. See also *PCMCIA*.

PCI slot   Popular standard for adding internal hardware devices to a computer; acronym stands for Peripheral Component Interconnect. See also *legacy device, ISA slot*.

PCMCIA   Personal Computer Memory Card International Association. The organization that devised the *PC Card* standard. This acronym is sometimes used to refer to PC Card slots.

peer-to-peer network   Common term for a local area network that does not include a dedicated server.

permission   A rule that defines which users can gain access to a file, folder, printer, or other resource. Permissions can be assigned to *group accounts* or *user accounts*.

Personal Web Server   Add-in program that enables Windows 2000 Professional users to create a Web site on their computer and allow up to 10 network users at a time to access it.

Personalized Menus
Windows 2000 feature that "hides" entries on the Start menu and Internet Explorer's Favorites menu that the user has not clicked recently.

pixel   Short for picture element, the smallest element used to display letters, numbers, and graphics on a monitor. See also *resolution, color depth*.

Plug and Play   Hardware specification that enables a computer to automatically detect and configure a device. Windows 2000 fully supports the Plug and Play standard.

Point-to-Point Protocol   An Internet standard that defines communication between computers when you make a dial-up connection to the Internet.

policy   Windows 2000 feature that allows an administrator to define settings automatically for users and computers. Also known as group policy or system policy.

POP3   Post Office Protocol, Version 3. An Internet standard that defines how email client software such as Outlook Express retrieves messages from a server. See also *SMTP*.

port   An outlet, usually found on the back of a computer, into which you plug a printer, a modem, or other external hardware devices. See also *parallel port*.

portal   A Web page designed to serve as the home page for Internet users. Yahoo, Excite, and msn.com are common portals.

PostScript printer   A printer such as the Apple LaserWriter that uses the PostScript page-description language to produce output. Commonly found in graphic-arts departments but less common in mainstream businesses.

power scheme   Saved settings that define how and when a computer shuts down system resources to conserve power.

PPP   See *Point-to-Point Protocol*.

prepare (a tape)   A feature in the Removable Storage Manager that lets you write information to a new backup tape and add it to a media pool so that you can use it with Windows 2000's Backup program.

primary partition   Subdivision of a *basic disk* used to store data. You can create up to four primary partitions on a basic disk, or three primary partitions and one *extended partition*. See also *dynamic disk*.

print queue   The list of jobs that have been sent for printing but have not yet moved into the printer's memory.

print server   A computer that includes connections to one or more shared network printers and manages the *print queues* for those printers.

printer font   Fonts intended for use with a printer; to see documents onscreen as they will appear on printed pages, you must install matching screen fonts.

program shortcut   Saved instructions that launch a program when double-clicked. Program shortcuts are commonly found on the Start menu, on the Quick Launch bar, and on the Windows desktop.

protocol   A set of rules that define how two or more computers share information over a network.

proxy server   A gateway computer that handles Internet access for computers on a network. Proxy servers can improve performance and security by not allowing outside computers to directly access computers within a network.

published programs   On a Windows 2000 network, programs that an administrator defines as available but not required for network users. These programs are installed automatically when a user double-clicks an icon whose file type is associated with that program. See also *assigned programs.*

raster font   A font that is stored as a bitmap and that can be displayed only in specific sizes. Windows 2000 includes a handful of raster fonts for compatibility with older programs, but it uses *OpenType fonts* for most tasks.

Recovery Console   Special startup option that allows you to repair a damaged Windows 2000 installation. You can start the Recovery Console from the Windows 2000 Setup disks.

refresh   To update information, such as the listing of files in an Explorer window.

refresh rate   How often Windows updates the video display to prevent flicker. The default setting of 60Hz is annoying for most users; flicker-free monitors support a refresh rate of 70Hz or better. See also *Hertz.*

registered file type   Windows setting that defines which program opens a given file when you double-click its icon. See also *association, file extension.*

Registry Editor   A Windows utility that allows users to view and change *values* stored in *keys* within the *Windows Registry.*

resolution   The number of horizontal and vertical *pixels* that define the screen area settings for the current monitor. The higher the number of pixels, the more information you can display on your screen.

485

restricted site Internet Explorer *security zone* used to identify potentially dangerous locations on the Internet. When viewing sites in this group, Internet features such as *ActiveX* are disabled for safety reasons.

Restricted User Built-in group account; users assigned to this group can run programs installed by an administrator but are prevented from installing software or performing all but the most basic tasks. See also *Standard User.*

roaming user profile Collection of user-specific settings stored on a server in a Windows 2000 domain. By using a roaming profile, a user can see the same desktop settings and installed programs even when logging on to different machines. See also *user profile, mandatory user profile.*

root folder The first folder in any drive, typically identified by a slash. c:\, for example, represents the path of the root folder of the C: drive.

root key In the Windows Registry, one of six top-level keys that store essential system-configuration information.

ScreenTip Explanatory label that pops up when you allow the mouse pointer to hover over an object, such as an icon or a *taskbar button.*

script Computer programming code, often contained in a Web page, which allows that page to perform specialized functions not normally available in a browser window. See also *JavaScript, VBScript.*

SCSI Small Computer Systems Interface. A standard for high-performance connections between hardware devices (such as hard disks and scanners) and a computer.

Search Assistant Internet Explorer feature that automatically sends information you type into the Address bar to one or more search engines for processing.

secure connection In a browser window, a link to a Web page that uses digital certificates and encryption to verify the identity of a Web site and scramble data so that only authorized users can read it. The *URL* of a secure connection typically begins with *https://*.

Secure Sockets Layer Internet standard that allows users to encrypt data transmitted and received using a Web browser.

security zone Internet Explorer feature that allows a user or administrator to define different security settings for different Web locations.

service A program that runs on a Windows computer even when no user is currently logged on. The Internet Information Service, for example, allows you to publish Web pages on a Windows 2000 computer.

service pack   A collection of Windows updates issued by Microsoft to repair known bugs. See also *hotfix, option pack*.

share   *Verb:* to make a resource (such as a file, folder, or printer) available for other users on a network. *Noun:* the name used to identify a shared network resource.

shortcut   A saved link to another item (such as a program, a file, a folder, or a Web page) on your computer, on a network, or on the Internet.

shortcut keys   Combination of keys that you assign to a shortcut for quick access; custom shortcut keys always consist of Ctrl+Alt in addition to a key you choose.

signature   A unique identifier on each hard disk, which Windows 2000 reads at startup.

simple volume   Data storage that consists of space from a single *dynamic disk*. You can *extend* a simple volume using additional space on the same disk; if you extend a simple volume to another disk, it becomes a *spanned volume*. See also *basic disk, volume*.

single-folder view   In Windows Explorer, the view that shows only the contents of a folder, without displaying the *Folders list*. See also *Explorer view*.

sizing handle   The vertical line at the left of toolbars in Explorer windows and on the Windows desktop; click this handle to move or resize the toolbar.

SMTP   Simple Mail Transfer Protocol, an Internet standard for storing and forwarding email on servers. See also *POP3*.

snap-in   Administrative tool available for use in the *Microsoft Management Console*.

sound scheme   Saved collection of sounds associated with system events, such as startup, shutdown, and error messages.

spam   Unsolicited commercial email, usually sent anonymously and often containing solicitations for pornography or products of dubious value.

spanned volume   Disk storage that consists of space on more than one physical disk. You can create spanned volumes only on *dynamic disks*. See also *extend, volume*.

spool   Disk file that contains documents waiting to go to a printer. Sending print jobs to a spool lets users get back to work more quickly, even if the printer is still warming up.

Standard User   Built-in group account; users assigned to this group can install and run most programs but are prevented from performing administrative tasks. See also *Restricted User*.

487

standby Power-management option that sends a computer into a "sleep" state, where it uses a minimal amount of power but can return to full operation quickly. See also *hibernate*.

streaming media Technology that allows a Web server to send a continuous flow of audio or video data, allowing a client machine to play back the performance without downloading the entire file first; Windows 2000 includes Windows Media Player, which can handle some types of streaming media.

striped volume A data storage arrangement that stores files on two or more physical disks, with data divided evenly among disks in the set. You can create striped volumes only on *dynamic disks*. See also *volume*.

subkey See *key*.

subnet mask A TCP/IP setting that defines which group of IP *addresses* belong on the same network.

switch Additional information that follows a command and modifies the action of that command; for example, following the DIR command with the /P switch causes Windows to display a directory listing one screen at a time, pausing between each screen. To see available switches for any command, open a Command Prompt window and type the command followed by the /? switch.

synchronize To copy changes between network files and local copies that are used when the network is unavailable; this feature allows users of portable computers to continue working with network files even when they leave the office. See also *Offline Files*.

system event Program actions, such as error messages and startup or shutdown, that can be associated with sounds.

system folder Locations in an Explorer window that don't correspond to physical locations on a drive, such as My Computer or My Network Places.

system tray See *notification area*.

system variable Keywords used in shortcuts and commands to identify specific information or file locations regardless of how the computer is configured. For instance, the system variable %systemroot% always refers to the folder that contains the Windows 2000 system files. This is typically C:\Winnt, but using this variable will open the correct folder even if it is on another drive.

target The location—such as a drive, a folder, or a Web page—referred to by a shortcut.

TCP/IP Transmission Control Protocol/Internet Protocol. The standard that defines how different computers communicate with one another over the Internet.

tile   To arrange windows side-by-side or one over the other on the screen so that you can see the contents of each one.

title bar   The horizontal bar at the top of a program window that contains the title of the program and/or its data file. In Windows Explorer, the title bar displays the name of the selected drive or folder.

topic pane   The part of the Windows Help interface that displays the contents of the selected *topic*.

tray   See *notification area*.

troubleshooter   Built-in Windows Help tool that helps you identify and solve common hardware, software, and system configuration problems.

true color   Setting that lets you view onscreen images using 24 bits per pixel to display more than 16 million unique colors, if your display adapter supports it. See also *high color*.

TrueType font   A *font* that is stored as an outline and can be sized (or scaled) to any height and appears the same on the printed page as on the screen.

trusted site   One of Internet Explorer's *security zones*; this one allows you to set more relaxed standards than you would on a site in the *Internet zone*.

Uniform Resource Locator (URL)   The unique address that identifies a file (such as a Web page or an FTP server) on the Internet or a corporate intranet.

Universal Serial Bus   A standard connection that allows you to add external hardware devices, such as a scanner, a keyboard, or a handheld computer, to a PC. USB devices fully support the *Plug and Play* standard.

upgrade package   Updated software that fixes incompatibilities between older programs and Windows 2000.

URL   See *Uniform Resource Locator*.

USB   See *Universal Serial Bus*.

user account   A record that defines a user on a Windows 2000 computer or domain. Saved settings include the username, password, and any rights and *permissions* the user has, either individually or by virtue of membership in a *group account*. See also *Active Directory, domain controller*.

user account databases   The collection of information for all user accounts authorized to log on to a computer or to access shared resources on that computer.

user profile   The collection of user-specific settings that Windows 2000 loads when a user logs on, including available programs, desktop customizations, network connections, and installed printers.

value In the *Windows registry*, a piece of data that defines a *key*. A value entry has three parts: name, data type, and the value itself.

VBScript One of two standard scripting languages used to automate Web pages. See also *JavaScript*.

vector font A scalable font used mostly in plotters that produce line drawings such as blueprints.

view In Outlook Express, saved collections of settings that let you quickly sort and filter a group of messages.

virtual directory Shared storage locations that other users can access via a Web browser rather than in Windows Explorer.

virtual machine The portion of system memory in which a Java program runs; for the sake of security, the virtual machine is unable to access local resources such as disk drives.

volume On a *dynamic disk*, a formatted region that appears as a separate drive, usually with its own drive letter. See also *partition*.

wallpaper The background pattern that appears on the *desktop* of a Windows computer.

Web Folders A location in the My Network Places folder that allows you to open and save files on a Web server the same as you would on a local or network drive.

Windows Registry The Windows database that contains information about a computer's configuration, including user profiles, hardware settings, and preferences for installed programs. The registry is organized in a tree-style hierarchy made up of keys, subkeys, and values.

workgroup A group of users on a network that does not include a Windows 2000 or Windows NT *domain controller*.

WYSIWYG What You See Is What You Get. Refers to output that appears identical on the screen and in printed copy.

INDEX

495

The IT site
you asked for...

InformIT is a complete online library delivering
information, technology, reference, training, news,
and opinion to IT professionals, students,
and corporate users.

Find IT Solutions Here!

www.informit.com